First World War
and Army of Occupation
War Diary
France, Belgium and Germany

61 DIVISION
Divisional Troops
Royal Army Medical Corps
2/1 South Midland Field Ambulance
1 September 1915 - 31 July 1919

WO95/3051/1

The Naval & Military Press Ltd
www.nmarchive.com
Published in association with The National Archives

Published by

The Naval & Military Press Ltd

Unit 10 Ridgewood Industrial Park,

Uckfield, East Sussex,

TN22 5QE England

Tel: +44 (0) 1825 749494

www.naval-military-press.com

www.nmarchive.com

This diary has been reprinted in facsimile from the original. Any imperfections are inevitably reproduced and the quality may fall short of modern type and cartographic standards.

© **Crown Copyright**
Images reproduced by permission of The National Archives, London, England, 2015.

Contents

Document type	Place/Title	Date From	Date To
Heading	2/1 South Midland Field Ambulance RAMC (T. Ford)		
Heading	61st Division 2-1st 5th Midland Fld Amb. 1915 Sep 1919 Jly		
Heading	War Diary 2/1st Field Ambulance R.A.M.C.T. 61st (S. Mid) Div From September 1st 1915 To September 30th 1915		
War Diary	Epping	01/09/1915	05/09/1915
War Diary	Epping & Chelmsford	06/09/1915	06/09/1915
War Diary	Chelmsford	07/09/1915	30/11/1915
Heading	War Diary 2/1st. South Midland Field Ambulance. 1-30 January 1916.		
War Diary	Oaklands Chelmsford.	01/01/1916	31/01/1916
Miscellaneous	Appendix 1 Field Manoeuvres.4th January 1916.	04/01/1916	04/01/1916
Miscellaneous	Appendix 2 Field Manoeuvres.12th January 1916.	12/01/1916	12/01/1916
Miscellaneous	Appendix 3 Field Manoeuvres.18th January 1916.	18/01/1918	18/01/1918
Miscellaneous	Appendix 4 Field Manoeuvres.21st January 1916.	21/01/1918	21/01/1918
Miscellaneous	Appendix 5 Field Manoeuvres.25th January 1916.	25/01/1918	25/01/1918
Miscellaneous	Appendix 6 Field Manoeuvres.26th January 1916.	26/01/1918	26/01/1918
Heading	2/1st. South Midland Field Ambulance. 1st May 1916. 31st May 1916.		
War Diary	No.I. Camp Perham Down	01/05/1916	08/05/1916
War Diary	No.I. Camp Perham Down & Hurstbourne Priors	08/05/1916	08/05/1916
War Diary	Hazeldown Farm. Longstock.	09/05/1916	09/05/1916
War Diary	Moxton Oakouts & No. I. Camp. Perham Down.	10/05/1916	10/05/1916
War Diary	No. I. Camp. Perham Down.	10/05/1916	22/05/1916
War Diary	Havre	23/05/1916	25/05/1916
War Diary	Le Vertbois Ferme	26/05/1916	31/05/1916
Heading	2/IST. South midland Field Ambulance War Diary. May 1916		
Miscellaneous	Special Orders By Major George Mackie.R.A.M.C. (T).	01/05/1916	01/05/1916
Heading	2/IST. South midland Field Ambulance War Diary. May 1916		
Miscellaneous	Special Orders By Major George Mackie. R.A.M.C. (T).	05/05/1916	05/05/1916
Heading	2/IST. South Midland Field Ambulance War Diary		
Miscellaneous	Narrative of Divisional field Operations	10/05/1916	10/05/1916
Heading	2/IST. South midland Field Ambulance War Diary		
Miscellaneous	Report on Divisional Route March	19/05/1916	19/05/1916
Heading	2/IST. South MIdland Field Ambulance War Diary		
Miscellaneous	Narrative of The embarkation etc of The 2/IST. South Midland Field Ambulance R.A.M.C. (T).		
Heading	2/1st S.M. Field Ambulance June 1916		
Heading	War Diary Of 2/1st Field Ambulance (South Midland) FA 61st Division. June 1916		
War Diary	Le Bertbois K.26.a.5.8.	01/06/1916	09/06/1916
War Diary	La Gorgue. L.34.b.6.2.	10/06/1916	30/06/1916
Miscellaneous	2/1st Field Ambulance. 61st. Division.	10/06/1916	10/06/1916
Heading	2/1st S.M. Field Ambulance July 1916		
Heading	War Diary Of 2/1st South Midland Field Ambulance 61st. Division. July 1916.		

War Diary	La Gorgue. L.34.b.6.2.	01/07/1916	30/07/1916
War Diary	La Gorgue. L.34.b.6.2. and K.29.d.1.9. Merville	31/07/1916	31/07/1916
Heading	2/IST Field Ambulance 61st. Division War Diary July 1916		
Miscellaneous	Advanced Dressing Station Laventie		
Miscellaneous	Medical Arrangements		
Miscellaneous	Special Orders for The Ist Field Ambulance During Active Operations		
Miscellaneous	Headquarters Staff.		
Heading	IST Field Ambulance 61st. Division War Diary July 1916		
Miscellaneous	IST Field Ambulance 61st Division		
Heading	IST Field Ambulance 61st Division War Diary July 1916		
Miscellaneous	Copies Of Casualty Wires		
Miscellaneous	IST Field Ambulance 61st Division War Diary July 1916		
Miscellaneous	Copies of Messages Received After Active Operations	20/07/1916	20/07/1916
Heading	War Diary For The Month of 2/1 So. Midland F.A. August 1916		
War Diary	K 29.d.1.9. Merville.	01/08/1916	31/08/1916
Miscellaneous	War Diary Ist Field Amb 61st Divn		
Miscellaneous	IST Field Ambulance 61st Division		
Heading	War Diary September 1916.		
War Diary	K.29.d.1.9. K.34.d.8.8.	01/09/1916	30/09/1916
Heading	2/1st S.M Field Ambulance Oct 1916		
War Diary	K.29.d.1.9. K.34.d.8.8.	01/10/1916	27/10/1916
War Diary	P.29.b.6.4.	28/10/1916	31/10/1916
Heading	2/1st S.M. Field Ambulance Nov 1916		
Heading	War Diary. Of The 2/1st. South Midland Field Ambulance. R.A.M.C. (T). December 1916.		
War Diary	Robecq	01/11/1916	01/11/1916
War Diary	Robecq Raimbert	02/11/1916	02/11/1916
War Diary	Raimbert Rocourt.	03/11/1916	03/11/1916
War Diary	Rocourt Tinquettes	04/11/1916	04/11/1916
War Diary	Tincquette Roziere	05/11/1916	05/11/1916
War Diary	Roziere Neuvillette	06/11/1916	06/11/1916
War Diary	Neuvilette	07/11/1916	16/11/1916
War Diary	Neuvillette Bonneville	16/11/1916	16/11/1916
War Diary	Bonneville Vadencourt	17/11/1916	17/11/1916
War Diary	Vadencourt	18/11/1916	18/11/1916
War Diary	Vadencourt Albert	19/11/1916	19/11/1916
War Diary	Albert	20/11/1916	26/11/1916
War Diary	Albert Aveluy Post	27/11/1916	27/11/1916
War Diary	Aveluy Post	28/11/1916	30/11/1916
Heading	War Diary 2/1st South Midland Field Ambulance		
Miscellaneous	184th. Infantry Brigade Order	31/10/1916	31/10/1916
Heading	2/1st. South Midland Field Ambulance.		
Operation(al) Order(s)	184th. Infantry Brigade Order No. 45.	02/11/1916	02/11/1916
Heading	War Diary 2/1st South Midland Field Ambulance		
Miscellaneous	184th Infantry Brigade Order	03/11/1916	03/11/1916
Heading	War Diary 2/1st South Midland Field Ambulance		
Operation(al) Order(s)	184th. Infantry Brigade Order No. 47.	04/11/1916	04/11/1916
Heading	War Diary 2/1st South Midland Field Ambulance		
Operation(al) Order(s)	184th. Infantry Brigade Order No. 48.	05/11/1916	05/11/1916

Heading	War Diary. 2/1st. South Midland Field Ambulance.R.A.M.C. (T). December 1916.		
War Diary	Aveluy Post	01/12/1916	31/12/1916
Heading	War Diary 2/1st South Midland Field Ambulance R.A.M.C. (T)		
Miscellaneous			
War Diary	Aveluy Post	01/01/1917	15/01/1917
War Diary	Val-De-Maison	15/01/1917	17/01/1917
War Diary	Vacquerie Hanchy	18/01/1917	19/01/1917
War Diary	Gueschart	19/01/1917	31/01/1917
Heading	War Diary Of The 2/1st. South Midland Field Ambulance. R.A.M.C. (T).		
Heading	War Diary Of The 2/1st. South Midland Field Ambulance.		
Operation(al) Order(s)	61st. Division R.A.M.C. Order. No. I208.	13/07/1917	13/07/1917
Operation(al) Order(s)	182nd. Infantry Brigade Order No. 71.	13/01/1917	13/01/1917
Operation(al) Order(s)	182nd. Infantry Brigade Order No. 72.	14/01/1917	14/01/1917
Operation(al) Order(s)	182nd Infantry Brigade Order No. 73.	16/01/1917	16/01/1917
Heading	War Diary Of The 2/1st South MIdland Field Ambulance		
Heading	War Diary. February 1917. February. 2/1st South Midland Field Ambulance.		
War Diary	Gueschart	01/02/1917	05/02/1917
War Diary	Vauchelles-Les-Quesnoy	05/02/1917	15/02/1917
War Diary	Marcelcave	15/02/1917	27/02/1917
War Diary	Guillacourt	27/02/1917	28/02/1917
Heading	War Diary Of The 2/1st South MIdland Field Ambulance. R.A.M.C. (T)		
Operation(al) Order(s)	182nd. Infantry Brigade Order No. 74.	03/02/1917	03/02/1917
Heading	War Diary Of The 2/1st South Midland Field Ambulance.		
War Diary	Guillacourt.	01/03/1917	22/03/1917
War Diary	Tour Carre	22/03/1917	28/03/1917
War Diary	Bethancourt	28/03/1917	31/03/1917
Heading	War Diary Of The 2/1st South Midland Field Ambulance. For The Month of April 1917.		
War Diary	Bethencourt	01/04/1917	30/04/1917
Heading	War Diary Of The 2/1st South Midland Field Ambulance. For The Month of May 1917.		
War Diary	Bethencourt	01/05/1917	13/05/1917
War Diary	Mesnil-St-Nicaise	13/05/1917	15/05/1917
War Diary	Rivery	15/05/1917	17/05/1917
War Diary	La Vicogne	17/05/1917	21/05/1917
War Diary	Hem. Douliens.	21/05/1917	23/05/1917
War Diary	Barly	23/05/1917	24/05/1917
War Diary	Duisans.	24/05/1917	31/05/1917
Heading	2/IST South Midland Field Ambulance War Diary 1917		
Operation(al) Order(s)	184th. Infantry Brigade Order. No. 95.		
Heading	War Diary Of The 2/1st South MIdland Field Ambulance		
Operation(al) Order(s)	184th. Infantry Brigade Order No. 96.	14/05/1917	14/05/1917
Heading	War Diary Of The 2/1st South MIdland Field Ambulance		
Miscellaneous	184 Infantry Brigade No. Q.I69.	13/05/1917	13/05/1917
Heading	War Diary Of The 2/1st South MIdland Field Ambulance		

Operation(al) Order(s)	184th. Infantry Brigade Order No. 97.	16/05/1917	16/05/1917
Heading	War Diary Of The 2/1st South MIdland Field Ambulance		
Operation(al) Order(s)	184 Infantry Brigade Order No. 98	20/05/1917	20/05/1917
Heading	War Diary Of The 2/1st South MIdland Field Ambulance		
Operation(al) Order(s)	184 Infantry Brigade Order No. 99.	22/05/1917	22/05/1917
Operation(al) Order(s)	184th. Infantry Brigade Order No. 100	23/05/1917	23/05/1917
Heading	War Diary Of The 2/1st South MIdland Field Ambulance		
Heading	War Diary of 2/1st South Midland Field Ambulance From 1st June 1917-30th June 1917 Volume 3		
War Diary	Duisans Tilloy	01/06/1917	01/06/1917
War Diary	Tilloy	01/06/1917	10/06/1917
War Diary	Berneville	10/06/1917	10/06/1917
War Diary	Tilloy	10/06/1917	10/06/1917
War Diary	Berneville	10/06/1917	23/06/1917
War Diary	Rougefay	23/06/1917	27/06/1917
War Diary	Frohen Le Grand	27/06/1917	30/06/1917
Miscellaneous	Appendix 1	08/06/1917	08/06/1917
Miscellaneous	Appendix 2 D.M. 208.	30/06/1917	30/06/1917
Miscellaneous	Appendix 3 2/1st Field Ambulance. Entrainment Orders.	21/06/1917	21/06/1917
Miscellaneous	Appendix 4 Administrative Addendum To 184 Brigade Warning Order G.160, 20.617.	21/06/1917	21/06/1917
Miscellaneous	Appendix 5 61st Division. R.A.M.C. Order No 33.	21/06/1917	21/06/1917
Miscellaneous	Appendix 6 A.D.M.D. 955/4/17, 26.6.17.	30/06/1917	30/06/1917
Miscellaneous	Appendix 7 A.D.M.D. 955/4/17, 26.6.17.	26/06/1917	26/06/1917
Heading	2/1st South Midland F.A.		
Heading	War Diary of The 2/1st South Midland Field Ambulance, 61st Division. From 1st July, 1917 To 31st July, 1917.		
Miscellaneous	Summary Of Medical War Diaries Of 2/1st S.M.F.A. 61st Div. 8th Corps, 5th Army. From 26.7.17.		
War Diary	Frohen Le Grand	01/07/1917	26/07/1917
War Diary	Broxeele	27/07/1917	31/07/1917
Miscellaneous	A Form Messages And Signals		
Miscellaneous	Tactical Exercise		
Heading	War Diary Of The 2/1st South Midland Field Ambulance 61st Division		
Miscellaneous	Summary Of Medical War Diaries Of 2/1st S.M.F.A. 61st Div. 8th Corps, 5th Army. From 26.7.17		
War Diary	Broxeele	14/08/1917	15/08/1917
War Diary	Watou	15/08/1917	16/08/1917
War Diary	Sheet 28. G.11.a.4.6.	16/08/1917	19/08/1917
War Diary	H.8.a.9.9.	20/08/1917	22/08/1917
War Diary	Broxeele	01/08/1917	13/08/1917
War Diary	H,8.a.9.9.	22/08/1917	31/08/1917
Heading	War Diary 2/1st South Midland Field Ambulance. 61st Division From 1st September, 1917-30th September, 1917		
Miscellaneous	2/1st S.M.F.A. 61st Div.		
War Diary	H.8.a.9.9.	01/09/1917	15/09/1917
War Diary	Trappist Farm	15/09/1917	16/09/1917
War Diary	Wormhoudt	17/09/1917	19/09/1917
War Diary	Duisans L. Central	20/09/1917	24/09/1917

War Diary	St Nicholas. G.16.c.5.9.	25/09/1917	30/09/1917
Heading	War Diary. 2/1st South Midland Field Ambulance. 61st Division. From 1.10.1917 To 31.10.1917. Volume 3		
War Diary	St Nicolas G.16.c.5.9.	01/10/1917	31/10/1917
Heading	War Diary of 2/1st South Midland Field Ambulance From 1st November 1917 To 30th November 1917. Volume 3		
War Diary	St Nicholas G.16.c.5.9.	01/11/1917	30/11/1917
Heading	War Diaries Of Medical Units 61 Division. December 1st To December 31st 1917.		
Heading	War Diary of The 2/1st South Midland Field Ambulance 61st Division. From 1/12/1917 To 31/12/1917 Volume 12		
War Diary	Bapaume	01/12/1917	01/12/1917
War Diary	Bertincourt	02/12/1917	03/12/1917
War Diary	V.18.c.5.5.	04/12/1917	15/12/1917
War Diary	Lechelle	16/12/1917	23/12/1917
War Diary	Cappy-Sur-Somme	24/12/1917	30/12/1917
War Diary	Ruziere-Sur-Santerre	31/12/1917	31/12/1917
War Diary	War Diary of 2/1st South Midland Field Ambulance 61st Division From 1st January 1918 To 31st January 1918 Volume 4		
War Diary	Roziere	01/01/1918	06/01/1918
War Diary	Bethencourt Sur Somme C.23.d.3.3.	07/01/1918	09/01/1918
War Diary	Lanchy E.2.6.4.8.	09/01/1918	31/01/1918
Heading	War Diary of The 2/1st South Midland Field Ambulance. From 1st February, 1918 To 28th February, 1918. Vol 4		
War Diary	Lanchy W.26.d.4.5.	01/02/1918	28/02/1918
Heading	War Diary of 2/1st South Midland Field Ambulance 61st Division From 1.3.1918 To 31.3.1918 Volume 4		
War Diary	Lanchy. W.26.d.4.5.	01/03/1918	22/03/1918
War Diary	Lanchy and 'Y'	22/03/1918	22/03/1918
War Diary	'Y' and Cremery	23/03/1918	23/03/1918
War Diary	Cremery and Rouvroy	24/03/1918	24/03/1918
War Diary	Rouvroy and Beaufort	25/03/1918	25/03/1918
War Diary	Beaufort and Mailly-Raineval	26/03/1918	26/03/1918
War Diary	Mailly and Cottenchy	27/03/1918	27/03/1918
War Diary	Cottenchy and Hailles	28/03/1918	28/03/1918
War Diary	Hailles-Boves	29/03/1918	29/03/1918
War Diary	Boves	30/03/1918	31/03/1918
Heading	War Diary of The 2/1st South Midland Field Ambulance From 1st April 1918 To 30th April 1918 Volume 4.		
War Diary	Boves	01/04/1918	03/04/1918
War Diary	Avelesges	03/04/1918	10/04/1918
War Diary	Avelesges & Seux	10/04/1918	10/04/1918
War Diary	In Train	11/04/1918	11/04/1918
War Diary	St Venant & Berguette	12/04/1918	12/04/1918
War Diary	Berguette	12/04/1918	30/04/1918
Heading	War Diary of 2/1st South Midland Field Ambulance From 1st May, 1918 To 31st May, 1918 Volume 5		
War Diary	Berguette. O.16.c.7.8.	01/05/1918	31/05/1918
Heading	War Diary of 2/1st South Midland Field Ambulance.61st Division. From 1-6-18 To 30-6-18 Volume 6		

Type	Location	From	To
War Diary	Berguette	01/06/1918	17/06/1918
War Diary	Ligne	18/06/1918	18/06/1918
War Diary	G.10.b.99.	18/06/1918	21/06/1918
Miscellaneous	Amusements for Patients At X1th Corps Rest Station.		
War Diary	G.10.b.9.8	22/06/1918	29/06/1918
War Diary	Ling G.10.b.9.8	30/06/1918	30/06/1918
Heading	War Diary of 2/1st South Midland Field Ambulance From 1st July, 1918 To 31st July, 1918.		
War Diary	G.10.b.8.8.	01/07/1918	19/07/1918
War Diary	G.16.b.8.8.	20/07/1918	20/07/1918
War Diary	G.16.b.8.8. & N.10.b&d.	21/07/1918	21/07/1918
War Diary	N.10.b&d & B.3.a.3.4.	22/07/1918	22/07/1918
War Diary	B.3.a.3.4.	23/07/1918	31/07/1918
Heading	War Diary of 2/1st South Midland Field Ambulance 61st Division From 1st August, 1918 To 31st August, 1918		
War Diary	U.1.a.7.8.	01/08/1918	05/08/1918
War Diary	U.1.a.7.8. & 1.17.c.5.1.	05/08/1918	06/08/1918
War Diary	I.17.c.5.1.	07/08/1918	31/08/1918
Heading	War Diary of 2/1 S. Mid. Fld. Ambce From 1.9.18 To 30.9.18		
War Diary	L.17.c.5.1.	01/09/1918	01/09/1918
War Diary	K.8.c.2.2.	02/09/1918	02/09/1918
War Diary	K.8.c.2.2. & L.27.d. Central	03/09/1918	05/09/1918
War Diary	L.27.d. Central & L.26.c.8.7.	06/09/1918	30/09/1918
War Diary	L.26.C.8.7.	08/09/1918	30/09/1918
Heading	War Diary of 2/1 S. Midland Field Ambulance From 1.1.18 To 31.10.18 Volume 10		
War Diary	L26c.8.7.	01/10/1918	03/10/1918
War Diary	L26c.8.7. to I.22.c.9.3	04/10/1918	04/10/1918
War Diary	I 22 C.9.3.	04/10/1918	06/10/1918
War Diary	Beauval (Lensil)	06/10/1918	09/10/1918
War Diary	J6.a.	10/10/1918	11/10/1918
War Diary	L3.65.6	11/10/1918	17/10/1918
War Diary	A22b0.5	18/10/1918	19/10/1918
War Diary	U 28 b 0.7	20/10/1918	22/10/1918
War Diary	U 28 b 0.7 to U.18.d.9.9	23/10/1918	23/10/1918
War Diary	U 18 d 9.9.	24/10/1918	24/10/1918
War Diary	V11d9.2	25/10/1918	25/10/1918
War Diary	Q20a1.7	26/10/1918	31/10/1918
Heading	War Diary of 2/1st South Midland Field Ambulance 61st Division From 1-11-1918 To 30-11-1918 Volume 4.		
War Diary	Q20a1.7	01/11/1918	03/11/1918
War Diary	Haussy V.11.d.8.8.	04/11/1918	07/11/1918
War Diary	Vendegies Q20.a.1.7.	08/11/1918	13/11/1918
War Diary	Avesnes Les Aubert U.21.d.9.4.	14/11/1918	14/11/1918
War Diary	Cambrai A.17.6.3.8.	15/11/1918	22/11/1918
War Diary	A 17.6.3.8	23/11/1918	25/11/1918
War Diary	Hiermont	26/11/1918	30/11/1918
Heading	War Diary of 2/1st South Midland Field Ambulance 61st Division From 1-12-1918 To 31-12-1918		
War Diary	Hiermont	01/12/1918	06/12/1918
War Diary	Buigny L'Abbe	07/12/1918	31/12/1918
Heading	War Diary 2/1st. South Midland Field Ambulance For The Month of January 1919.		

War Diary	Buigny L'abbe	01/01/1919	31/01/1919
Heading	War Diary Of 2/1st South Midland Field Ambulance February 1919		
War Diary	Buigny l'Abbe.	01/02/1919	28/02/1919
Heading	War Diary 2/1st South Midland Field Ambulance. 61st Division. March 1919		
War Diary	Buigny L'Abbe (Somme)	01/03/1919	25/03/1919
War Diary	Le Treport	26/03/1919	31/03/1919
Heading	2/1st S. Mid F.A. April 1919		
War Diary	Le Treport	01/04/1919	29/04/1919
Heading	2/1st S. Mid. Field Amb May 1919		
War Diary	Le Treport	01/05/1919	31/05/1919
Heading	2/1 Sth Mid. F.A. June 1919		
War Diary	Le Treport	01/06/1919	30/06/1919
Heading	2/1st S.M. F.A July 1919		
War Diary	Le Treport	01/07/1919	31/07/1919

2/1st South Midland
Field Ambulance
RAMC T. Ford

61ST DIVISION

2-1ST STH MIDLAND FLD AMB.

~~MAY 1916-DEC 1918~~

1915 SEP — 1919 JLY

61ST DIVISION

Confidential.

War Diary
of

2/1st Field Ambulance R.A.M.C. 61st (S. Mid.) Div:

From:- September 1st 1915
To:-   "   30th 1915

Volume VIII

WAR DIARY
or
INTELLIGENCE SUMMARY
(Erase heading not required.)

Army Form C. 2118

Place	Date 1915	Hour	Summary of Events and Information	Remarks and references to Appendices
Epping	Sep 1	5 a.m.	Reveille	
		6 a.m.	Wagons loaded in preparation for a Field day	
		7 a.m.	Ambulances paraded 9.45 p.m. Lights out.	
		9 a.m.	The weather having cleared the Ambulances paraded and were given Company Drill. Stretcher & Wagon Drill and Recoveries. In the evening the Ambulances gave a concert in aid of the funds of the F.A.D. Hospitals. This was well attended although the weather was wet and a substantial sum was realized.	
"	2	3 p.m.	A.C.O's received a lecture from Lt. Graydon on Venereal Disease. Instructed by Col. Bull A.D.M.S. to make arrangements for Medical Board on Saturday 4th Sep.	
"	3		All operation Majors sent to A.D.M.S today as instructors. 4 men transferred to Home Service Details Colchester (one under age & three medically unfit) for foreign service. Sgt. Dix proceeded to Middlewoop for 3 weeks Cooking Training. The men temporarily released for work on Munitions. Received Field Cas Book from Veterinary Officer. Medical Board held Col Bull ADMS President.	
"	5	6.53 a	Church Parade for Divine Service on R.J.A.Rec Parade Ground. Loading of wagons commenced in preparation for move to Chelmsford.	

Army Form C. 2118

WAR DIARY
or
INTELLIGENCE SUMMARY
(Erase heading not required.)

Instructions regarding War Diaries and Intelligence Summaries are contained in F.S. Regs., Part II. and the Staff Manual respectively. Title Pages will be prepared in manuscript.

Place	Date 1915	Hour	Summary of Events and Information	Remarks and references to Appendices
Epping & Chelmsford	Sep 6	6am	Ambulance paraded with ground sheet & blankets & handed them over to Q.M's Stores. Rolling of wagons completed and the camp ground cleared up. NCOs & men left to hand over the Hospitals to the 2/2 S.M. Fd Amb, and to complete Sanitary duties. Lt. Risien Q Master and the Q.M Sergeant remained to hand over Camp equipment.	
		10.10a	The Ambulance proceeded by route march for Chelmsford. The O.C. proceeded to Oaklands Hutments Chelmsford by motor to take over equipment from the 2/2 S.M. Fd Amb.	
		4.30p	The Ambulance arrived at Oaklands Hutments, & began unloading wagons.	
Chelmsford	7	5.30am	Reveille.	
		6am	Remaining wagons unloaded	
		9am	Ambulance engaged in general fatigue duty.	
		10.15 p.m.	Lights out.	
"	8		C.O. and Lieut Horn went to Danbury to take over the Village Hall as a Fd. Ambulance Hospital from the 2/3 S.M. Fd Ambulance. This action was taken in accordance with verbal instructions given by Col. Bull, A.D.M.S. Fourteen NCOs Or & men were detailed for duty at the Hospital.	

1875 Wt. W593/826 1,000,000 4/15 J.B.C. & A. A.D.S.S./Forms/C. 2118.

WAR DIARY or INTELLIGENCE SUMMARY

Army Form C. 2118

Place	Date	Hour	Summary of Events and Information	Remarks and references to Appendices
Church of 1915	Sept 9	6.30 am	Ambulance paraded in full marching order and proceeded to Hatfield Peverell. The starting point for a Brigade Tactical exercise. The Ambulance opened a Dressing Station & sent out stretcher bearers and Ambulance wagons. The Cookers & Breakfast and Dinner rations was carried out in the field. The Ambulance returned at 5 pm	
"	10		Squad & Company Drill – Stretcher & wagon Drill – Lectures	
"	11		O.C. to Boreham House to arrange MO's to hiring. One Horse sent to Hospital as instructed by Veterinary Officer.	
"	12	9.15 am	1st and 2nd and 3rd S.M. 1st Ambulance proceeded to the Cathedral for Divine Service.	
"	13	6 am	Wagons loaded for Field day exercises.	
		9 am	Ambulance proceeded en route for Field day with Manoeuvres returns for Breakfast & dinner. Col. W.J. Selby Senior Chaplain called re arrangements for Church Parade. Col. J.C. Tyler CRE Colchester District inspected the Hut. Lt. Snaydon appointed Acting Transport Officer to the Ambulance. Observed Headquarters Sanction to go on leave from Sept 14th to 21st.	

WAR DIARY
or
INTELLIGENCE SUMMARY
(Erase heading not required.)

Army Form C. 2118

Place	Date 1915	Hour	Summary of Events and Information	Remarks and references to Appendices
Chelmsford	Sept 14		Lt. Col. Shannock having procured a Room of Abrevin Rend W/ P Wind 10th over Command of the Ambulance. Instructions received by him from the A.D.M.S. to commence Vaccinating the men of the 182nd Infantry Brigade.	
	15	9 am	The Ambulance moved out for Route March.	
		3 pm	The Ambulance were engaged in loading wagons for a Brigade Tactical Exercise Tomorrow.	
	16	6-30 am	The Ambulance proceeded to border Walter for Brigade Tactical Exercise. The unit arrived at 9.25 a.m.; Bearer sections advanced dressing stations at Thinsis Cross, A section from Platoon at Weatherden Walter School, C section on Coll at Weatherden Walter Church to act as Reserve. The Ambulance Commanders and medical officers of the 5th, 6th & 7th Battalions R.W. Reg. attended to casualties from the 6th Oh. Reg.	

Army Form C. 2118

WAR DIARY
or
INTELLIGENCE SUMMARY

(Erase heading not required.)

Instructions regarding War Diaries and Intelligence Summaries are contained in F. S. Regs., Part II. and the Staff Manual respectively. Title Pages will be prepared in manuscript.

Place	Date	Hour	Summary of Events and Information	Remarks and references to Appendices
Chelmsford	1915 Sep 17	9 am	Squad Infantry Drill, Lecture, Stretcher & Wagon Drill	
	18	9 am	Men paraded in their own huts with Kit laid out for inspection. The Huts were afterwards scrubbed out & all windows cleaned. New uniforms were issued to men rejoining them.	
	19	8·15 am	Church Parade for Divine Service at the Cathedral	
	20	7 am	The Ambulance proceeded to field even for a Field Day, Rations for the day were carried. 50 NCO & men of the 2/5 R.W. Ry were vaccinated at the field Amb. Hospital Railway. Received particulars of Brigade Tactical Exercise on Thurs Day 23rd inst.	
	21	9.p.m.	Ambulance proceeded for night operations on Galleywood Common. Lt. Col. Stannard having returned from leave of absence resumed Command of the Ambulance as from the 22nd inst.	

W. D. Hirst
Lieut Ram C
Acting O.C. 1st/3rd Amb. 61st SM Div.

Army Form C. 2118

WAR DIARY
or
INTELLIGENCE SUMMARY
(Erase heading not required.)

Instructions regarding War Diaries and Intelligence Summaries are contained in F. S. Regs., Part II. and the Staff Manual respectively. Title Pages will be prepared in manuscript.

Place	Date	Hour	Summary of Events and Information	Remarks and references to Appendices
Chelmsford	Sep 1915 22	6 am	O.C. resumed command of the Ambulance. The first party proceeded to the Corporation Baths & Men followed in due course in accordance with the arrangements made to provide for the members of the Ambulance having a hot bath once a week.	
		3 pm	Wagons were loaded in preparation for Field day tomorrow. Permission obtained from Brigade HdQrs to proceed by Springfield to the Starting Point. 12 Men of the Ambulance inoculated.	
"	23	6 am	Reveille - 7 a.m. Breakfast 8 a.m. The Ambulance paraded & proceeded to the starting point for the Brigade Tactical Exercise. C Section formed the Dressing Station and 13 & C Sections sent out Stretcher Bearers & Ambulance wagons, and got in touch with Reg. Aid Posts.	
"	24		Stretcher wagon drill. Demonstration on Medical & Surgical Panniers and practice in unpacking & packing same. 69 Men of the Ambulance were re-vaccinated. 25 " " inoculated.	
"	25		General fatigue duties by the whole of the Ambulance.	
"	26	9.10 am	Church Parade for Divine Service at the Cathedral.	

Army Form C. 2118

WAR DIARY
or
INTELLIGENCE SUMMARY
(Erase heading not required.)

Instructions regarding War Diaries and Intelligence Summaries are contained in F.S. Regs., Part II. and the Staff Manual respectively. Title Pages will be prepared in manuscript.

Place	Date	Hour	Summary of Events and Information	Remarks and references to Appendices
Chelmsford	Sep 27 1915	6.45 am	Staff Parade for the purpose of having read to them a letter from Divisional Headquarters re "Efficiency of N.C.O.s". Report received from Lieut Braydon (acting Transport Officer) that 26 men of the Transport section had failed to obey a lawful order given to them by him through Staff Sergeant Whelldon. A.P.M. consulted by telephone and Lt. Campbell D.A.P.M. arrived in the afternoon and advised with regard to the procedure to be adopted. The 26 men were placed under open arrest.	
"	28	11 am	Court of Enquiry held to investigate the case of the 26 men mentioned above. Summary of Evidence and application for D.C.M. forwarded to A.D.M.S.	
"	29		Application form & documents re case for D.C.M. were returned by A.D.M.S. and instructions received from him to prepare a separate Application form & document for each case. These were prepared. Capt. Phelps A.P.M. & Lt. Campbell D.A.P.M. called regarding the case. A letter signed by 25 men under open arrest was received concerning statement of Staff Sergeant Whelldon.	

WAR DIARY
or
INTELLIGENCE SUMMARY

(Erase heading not required.)

Army Form C. 2118

Instructions regarding War Diaries and Intelligence Summaries are contained in F.S. Regs., Part II. and the Staff Manual respectively. Title Pages will be prepared in manuscript.

Place	Date	Hour	Summary of Events and Information	Remarks and references to Appendices
Chelmsford	19/13	2.45pm	By appointment with Major Hoyten DADMS and Lt. Campbell DAPM the O.C. proceeded to Boreham Manor at 2.45pm re cases for C.C.M. and handed letter from men under arrest to the APM. After consultation it was decided to refer the question of procedure to the General Officer Commanding the Division for further instructions.	
		6.30pm	Called by telephone to report to G.O.C. at Boreham Manor immediately and went. Instructed by G.O.C. (1) to place Staff Sergeant Wheldon and Pte. Done in close arrest as N.C.O.'s Drew up a Summary of Evidence in each case and forward with application for D.C.M. and other necessary documents to A.G. & QMG tomorrow. (2) to admonish the 25 men and give orders that they be paraded for a route march on the afternoon of Saturday and Sunday Oct 2nd & 3rd and (3) inform them that all leave was stopped until further notice. O.C. received telegram from ADMS Third Army through ADMS of Division instructing him to report on Friday to G.O.C. 8th Provisional Brigade as O.C. 8th Provisional Field Ambulance.	

1875 Wt. W593/826 1,000,000 4/15 J.B.C. & A. A.D.S.S./Forms/C. 2118.

Army Form C. 2118

WAR DIARY
or
INTELLIGENCE SUMMARY
(Erase heading not required.)

Place	Date	Hour	Summary of Events and Information	Remarks and references to Appendices
Chelmsford	Sep 30 1915		Continued - Telephoned to ADMS re M. Field Ambulance being exercised from pieces at Jackers exercise tomorrow also wrote a letter to him explaining the circumstances.	

Wm Sturrock
Lt. Col. RAMC
O.C. 1st/ 3d Amb. 61st (S.M.) Div.

WAR DIARY or INTELLIGENCE SUMMARY

Army Form C. 2118

Instructions regarding War Diaries and Intelligence Summaries are contained in F.S. Regs., Part II. and the Staff Manual respectively. Title Pages will be prepared in manuscript.

(Erase heading not required.)

Place	Date	Hour	Summary of Events and Information	Remarks and references to Appendices
Chelmsford	Sep 1	6 am	Reveille	
		7 am	Physical Drill	
		8 am	Andrews paraded for Field Operations; the orders were cancelled and men proceeded to instruct recruits. The men were employed on various fatigue duties.	
		12 noon	Wire received from A.D.M.S. – O.C. to remain with unit pending further instructions.	
		2.45 pm	Telephone message from A.D.M.S. – Lt. Col. Sherrard to report at Headquarters on Ormsby Tanning Road. The Career of S.M.S. Whelan & The Draw was investigated. Lt. Sweeney of Enniskillen was accused on oath on cell accessory. Bowman prepare adequate. The O.C. admonished 25 had of the transport Section and informed them of the decision of the G.O.C. in relation & recension of N.C.O.s & men future regimental duties to cease & return & join chosen at instructions to A.D.M.S. there this morning.	
	2	6-12 am	am & S.D. & On Type Duties	
		6-30 am	Orient parade Staff & Bylaw will attend Scout Austinal round of Staff & Walker & the gnd.	
		3-15 pm	On Type Duties. Proceeded in Route rank with Lord Chapter.	

WAR DIARY
or
INTELLIGENCE SUMMARY
(Erase heading not required.)

Army Form C. 2118

Place	Date	Hour	Summary of Events and Information	Remarks and references to Appendices
Chelmsford	Oct 3 1915	7am	Reveille	
		9.40am	The Ambulance paraded for Church Parade and proceeded to St John's Church for Divine Service	
		11am	Lt. Col. Stannock addressed the troops	
		2pm	2 3 men of the Transport Section proceeded on a march under Lt. Craydon	
			Lt. Col. Stannock relinquished command of the Ambulance on leaving to take up the command of the 8th Divn. Bde. Field Amb. to 9 I. don't assumed command of the Ambulance until further notice	
	4	6.30am	Wagon loaded with necessary equipment for Field Op	
		8am	The Ambulance paraded in full marching order and proceeded to Galleywood Common for Field Operations. The Ambulance returned to camp 2.45 pm	

WAR DIARY
or
INTELLIGENCE SUMMARY

Army Form C. 2118

Place	Date	Hour	Summary of Events and Information	Remarks and references to Appendices
Chelmsford	Oct 4 1915	10 am	Received telegram from Divisional HQ re advising that a Div C.M. for the trial of Staff Sgt. Wheelan and Pte Done would be held at the Saracens Head Tavern at 11 o'clock a.m. The accused were warned and given copies of the charge sheet and evidence. All witnesses warned to attend. Document received from Deputy Judge Advocate at 11-50 a.m. Provided General Officer by Special messenger for accused and witnesses. Geographia received, meaning to accused and witnesses.	
		6.20 pm	Received message from A.D.M.S. that Major Wellwood D.A.D.M.S. 3rd Army and A.D.M.S. 61 (S.M.) Div would inspect the Ambulance at 10-30 a tomorrow. No wagons or equipment need be on parade.	
	5	8.6 am	The Ambulance was employed in fatigue duties.	
		10-15 a	O.C. Inspection	
		10-30 a	Inspection by Major Wellwood and Colonel O'Neil	
		11 a	Court Martial held at Saracens Head Hotel. Staff Sgt. Wheeler and Pte Done. Lieut Raven Prosecutor. Brig General J. the accused defendant. Col Shepard. Case S/M S/Sgt Wheeler: Lose a years service. S.A.D.S.S./Forms/C.2118. Tomorrow.

WAR DIARY
or
INTELLIGENCE SUMMARY

(Erase heading not required.)

Army Form C. 2118

Place	Date	Hour	Summary of Events and Information	Remarks and references to Appendices
Chelmsford	1915 Oct 5		Notice in The Times that Lieut W.J. Kirk has been promoted to Captain.	
		12 noon	Verbal instructions from Capt Boucher that the 1st Field Ambulance has to take the place of the 3rd Field Ambulance in Brigade Tactical Scheme on Wednesday.	
		3 pm	Night Route March cancelled all Wagons needed for Brigade Field Day Brown arrangements.	
			Special Idea received for Brigade Tactical Scheme	
		7 pm	Divisional Orders received. Cancelled Field Day tomorrow Wednesday.	
	6	7 am	Physical Drill. C Section went to The Battle after Breakfast. A Section proceeded to Chelmsford Baths. Other	
		9-12	Stretcher & bearer Drill. Open Air Drill. Demonstration of Mechanism of a rifle and the use of the Rifle as a Splint.	
		11 am	Coal Mental Reserved, Completed at 1.30 pm	
		4-15 pm	Vaccination of men B 9/7. R. Won Roy.	
		3:30 pm	Above message from Brig Gen 18th Bde. asking when Ambulance was on move had appeared. Full reports sent by special messenger.	
		3:45 pm	Phone message received giving details of inspection tomorrow B Capt Mackie would take temporary Command of The Ambulance until tomorrow.	

Army Form C. 2118

WAR DIARY
or
INTELLIGENCE SUMMARY
(Erase heading not required.)

Place	Date	Hour	Summary of Events and Information	Remarks and references to Appendices
Chbrufin	Oct 1915 7	7.30 am	Ambulance paraded & proceeded for Field Day at Guy Brown Reulgan Tindale. Ambulance was formed up in line & proceeded being seen by aircraft. A section formed Advanced Dressing Station being seen by aircraft — when the Artillery took up their B.C. section were held in reserve — when the Artillery took up their position then an A.D.S. it was renewed & went to village & then Hospital Dressing & a Dressing Station was formed at Danbury Church. A Divisional Collecting Station was formed at Danbury Church. Major Hogh DADMS inspected the Dressing Station. Senior Chaplain called with orders for Sunday's Church Parade. Captain Brockie Army taken on command 19th 1st Lieut. & acts as O.C. for this date. Captain Brockie having proceeded on leave of absence Captain Short assumes command 19th 10.50 — Ambulance until further notice.	
	8	9–12 10 a.t	Opened the Drill Shelter 4hrs Drill Demonstration on Sanmen but lecture. Pte Brown C sentenced to 7 days Detention in that he when on active service did leave his Piquet without orders from his superior officer. Reformulated & DORF called to take particulars & any Damage caused by fair wear & tear. NCO's Mem of C's 2nd Lieut vaccinated.	

Army Form C. 2118

WAR DIARY
or
INTELLIGENCE SUMMARY
(Erase heading not required.)

Instructions regarding War Diaries and Intelligence Summaries are contained in F. S. Regs., Part II. and the Staff Manual respectively. Title Pages will be prepared in manuscript.

Place	Date 1915	Hour	Summary of Events and Information	Remarks and references to Appendices
Cherisy	Oct 9	7 am	Physical Drill	
		9 am	The Ambulance to K1 Infection	
		10-12	Agreed to price - Sketches Died	
		10.30 am	Representatives from Munitions Dept called to inspect men Inspected by Maj Knyper D.A.D.M.S. 61st M.D. Training of Coad Mates recruits today and prisoners on special parade at 11:30 am. Staff Sgt Wheeler Packings & Trials of Captures Pte Dre and others 56 group detailed as reserves. 7t 288 ayo by Bty Lee Law Salisbury	
	10	7 am	Orville	
		8.15 a	The Ambulance paraded for Divine Service at the Cathedral Brandinia 1708 Staff Sgt Cuper appointed Sgt Major 1859 Cs. Jacques appointed Staff Sergeant 1769 Qr Mr Sgt Disc appointed Staff Sergeant Transport 2014 L Cpl Sitch appointed Sergeant	

WAR DIARY
or
INTELLIGENCE SUMMARY
(Erase heading not required.)

Army Form C. 2118

Place	Date	Hour	Summary of Events and Information	Remarks and references to Appendices
Chalups	Sep 10 1915		Promotions contd.	
			1292 Sgt Whittingham appointed to Field	
			2276 Pte Green H appointed Corporal	
			918 Cpl Yates appointed to Transport	
			2148 (Prov) S/Sgt Taylor appointed to Or. Rgt Sergeant	
			2043 Sgt Robinson appointed Orm. Staff Serjeant	
			2097 Cpl Berry appointed Orderly Corporal	
			2258 (Ams) Corporal Attwill appointed Corporal	
			2108 A/Cpl Anselm appointed Corporal	
			2213 Cpl Blackbee appointed Orm A/Cpl	
			1931 Pte L'Heir appointed Orm A/Cpl	
			Reductions	
			988 Sgt Bent Reduced to Rank Inefficiency	
			1829 Cpl Aldridge Reduced to Rank Inefficiency	
			2147 Cpl Roberts Reduced to L/Cpl Inefficiency	

Army Form C. 2118

WAR DIARY
or
INTELLIGENCE SUMMARY
(Erase heading not required.)

Instructions regarding War Diaries and Intelligence Summaries are contained in F. S. Regs., Part II. and the Staff Manual respectively. Title Pages will be prepared in manuscript.

Place	Date	Hour	Summary of Events and Information	Remarks and references to Appendices
Philops	Oct 11 1915	9/15 2pm	Stretcher Drill Signal Drill & Lectures. Wagon loaded — prepared for Divisional Inspection. 2068 Sgt Bryant } 2081 Sgt Griffiths } Proceeded to Home Service Unit Name T 1887 Pte A Brooke } Reach Colchester. 2253 – Pte St Breux was sentenced to undergo 168 Hours Detention. Officers Absence without leave. Gen'd 10/p Oct 6. 10/p Oct 9."	
		3/-	Capt Birkby is away unwell to 7/7 96p to 7/7 N96 repeated to 7/13? the Unit	
		12.9am	The ambulance proceeded to Longfont to form Divisional Station in connection with Divisional Inspection. On return one of them Officers W.O' St.M Sgt Sgt Cpls Rank & File 3 1 to 4 15 112 One section N th Ambulance followed the Unit to above and remained in reserve. One Section 17th Ambulance moved in Advance to Station at Abbeg Lasch – one section moved in Advance Drive to Station at Longfont One section was kept in reserve on Longfont. All were in position at 5pm. Remained in position until 5pm Oct 13/15	

Army Form C. 2118

WAR DIARY
or
INTELLIGENCE SUMMARY
(Erase heading not required.)

Instructions regarding War Diaries and Intelligence Summaries are contained in F. S. Regs., Part II. and the Staff Manual respectively. Title Pages will be prepared in manuscript.

Place	Date	Hour	Summary of Events and Information	Remarks and references to Appendices
Chulumpin	19th Oct 12		2069 Pte Keith transport section also the remainder of The Civil Hospital Chalumpo - Conveyance - Greenmen	
	13		Continued to Drummond Little Bay. The 1st Zelt Ambulance Stewart Convalescents with Capt Aid Posts Nos 2/5 2/6 2/7 R Warrior Rest The Dressing Station were inspected by Col Bell. Viz Hoyt - The Ambulance marched Home via Dudaing, arriving in Camp 9 pm.	
	14	9-3	Undulating boys — Pgms 16 Dress — Bay 67 Stretcher Drill	
		4.30p	The Orderly on fees in vacated to 16 Cond Hospital. The cee M. W. Northery ordered to report to Asst FSM Pr. Smith for conveyance to Burnpin. L/Cpl Baker transferred to Drummore for a course in Signalling	
	15	9-3	Pgms 16 Dress Stretcher stragn Drill Lecture. Continued Vaccinations. 25 men handed in Bon Numes. 708 hundred tot use. Capt Brooks assumed Command of The Ambulance from this date.	

Army Form C. 2118

WAR DIARY
or
INTELLIGENCE SUMMARY
(Erase heading not required.)

Instructions regarding War Diaries and Intelligence Summaries are contained in F. S. Regs., Part II. and the Staff Manual respectively. Title Pages will be prepared in manuscript.

Place	Date	Hour	Summary of Events and Information	Remarks and references to Appendices
Chelmsford	1915 Oct 16 Sat.	6.30 a.m.	Reveille	
		7 a.m.	Parade of all men below rank of Sergt. for hasty Medical Inspection.	
		9.30	Sick Parade	
		9 a.m.	Kit Inspection in Huts	
		12 noon	Scrubbing & Cleaning of all Huts. - Cleaning of Camp - Inspection of Huts by O.C.	
		10 a.m.	Parade of all Sergts. - before O.C. who addressed them on taking over Command of this unit.	
		11.6 a.m.	Parade of all other NCO's when O.C. in turn made them acquaintance and addressed them.	
		2 p.m.	Sanitary Hospital visited by O.C.	
		12.30 p.m.	Inspection of Stables - Harness & Transport by O.C.	

Army Form C. 2118

WAR DIARY
or
INTELLIGENCE SUMMARY
(Erase heading not required.)

Instructions regarding War Diaries and Intelligence Summaries are contained in F.S. Regs., Part II. and the Staff Manual respectively. Title Pages will be prepared in manuscript.

Place	Date	Hour	Summary of Events and Information	Remarks and references to Appendices
Chelmsford	1915 Oct 17th Sunday		Reveille	
		10 a.m.	Ambulance with Band paraded for Divine Service at Chelmsford Cathedral	
		9.15 a.m.		
		11 a.m.	Inspection of Ash Camp by O.C.	
Chelmsford	Oct 18th Monday	6.30 a.m.	Reveille	
		7–7.30	Physical Drill –	
		7.30	Sick Parade	
		9–12 noon	Stretcher Drill. Waggon drill & Lecture by O.C. Introductory & General	
		2 p.m.	Loading of Waggons in preparation for Field Manœuvres	
		3 p.m.	Bandaging. application of splints –	
			Riding & Driving drill –	
		9 p.m.	Instructions received from H.Q. Oct 15th by Bde regarding Field Operations for tomorrow –	
			Instructions that 51st Fd. Ambulance proceed to Liptree Village –	

1875 Wt. W593/826 1,000,000 4/15 J.B.C. & A. A.D.S.S./Forms/C. 2118.

WAR DIARY
or
INTELLIGENCE SUMMARY
(Erase heading not required.)

Army Form C. 2118

Instructions regarding War Diaries and Intelligence Summaries are contained in F.S. Regs., Part II. and the Staff Manual respectively. Title Pages will be prepared in manuscript.

Place	Date	Hour	Summary of Events and Information	Remarks and references to Appendices
Chelmsford	1915 Oct 19 Tues	6.30 a.m. 7.30 8.15 8.30	Reveille. Sick Parade. O.C's Parade. Ambulance proceeded by Route march to Zipsee via Boreham Heybridge Gt. Totham (1) & Gt. Totham (2). Ambulance bivouacked at Borrick Hall Farm Gt. Totham. O.C. reported his arrival to Brig. Gen. Bontenay & was visited by Col Powell A.D.M.S. & Capt Hartford Dm.S. Officer, who examined the site chosen encampt. suitable. Marching out state – Officers 2. men 105. Horses/mules 70. Ambulance wagons 3. G.S. waggons 3. Mess cart/water cart watering men recruits vaccinated performed. Details kept in camp watering Horses Cleaning – General Fatigues –	
	Oct 20 Wed	5 a.m. 6 a.m. 6.45 6.50 7.6.a. 8 a.m.	Reveille – Stables – Horses cleaning – Breakfast – O.C's Parade – A Section proceeded to Inworth-Tiptree Council schools & prepared to be ready to establish an A.D.S. if necessary. B & C Sections prepared a D.S. at Borrick Hall Farm Gt. Totham. Sick Parade O.C. reported as instructed at Inworth Station to visit Brig. Gen. Bontenay & Staff Commanding Officer of units engaged – to ascertain further developments of orders –	

WAR DIARY or INTELLIGENCE SUMMARY

(Erase heading not required.)

Army Form C. 2118

Place	Date	Hour	Summary of Events and Information	Remarks and references to Appendices
Chelmsford	1915 Oct 2 Contd	11 a.m.	Instructions received that Enemy has advanced to that our greatly our Operations had to consist of a retreat. Therefore a system was arranged to carried return details whereby No D.S. was moved to Paine's Hall at withdrawn Bishops reinforcements to Langford. The M.D.S. following with the rearguard to occupying each firing S.R. on turns evacuated by the D.S. Operations suspended 6.30 p.m. - A Section billeted for the night at Withdrew Bishops & B.C. Sections at Langford. - All stations were instructed by Col. Powell A.D.M.S. who reported himself on the scheme adopted its execution. Casualties treated - A.D.S. 4 D.S. 6. Field Staff as yesterday. - Details at Oaklands Camp have engaged in general fatigues. Arrival of 6 Officers charges commenced from Command Depot.	

WAR DIARY or INTELLIGENCE SUMMARY

Army Form C. 2118

Place	Date	Hour	Summary of Events and Information	Remarks and references to Appendices
Chelmsford	1915 Oct 21st	6 a.m.	Reveille — Instructions received during night that Operations were over —	
		7 a.m.	Breakfast — Sick Parade —	
		8.30 a.m.	Fatigues cleaned up Parade Room where men had been billeted for the night and field where wagons had been parked.	
		9 a.m.	A. Section marched from Wickham Bishops to join B and C Sections at Longford —	
		10 a.m.	A Section arrived at Longford —	
		10.30 a.m.	Ambulance moved back to Chelmsford via Witney Inch Nine & took men back for dinner — Hookham Walker — Danbury — Gt Baddow — tanned the streets p.m.	

Army Form C. 2118

WAR DIARY
or
INTELLIGENCE SUMMARY
(Erase heading not required.)

Instructions regarding War Diaries and Intelligence Summaries are contained in F. S. Regs., Part II. and the Staff Manual respectively. Title Pages will be prepared in manuscript.

Place	Date	Hour	Summary of Events and Information	Remarks and references to Appendices
Chelmsford	1915 Oct 22nd		Reveille	
		6.30	Physical drill –	
		7-7.30	Unloading wagons –	
		9-10	Sketching –	
		10-11	Thompson drill –	
		11-12	Lecture by O.C. on the 3 days field manoeuvres – each man furnished with sketch map of the area covered.	
		12-12.30	Cleaning Camp.	
		2-3.30 pm	Ceremonial marching drill with Band. Rehearsal of Church Parade –	
		3-3.30	Pay Parade –	
			25 NCO's & men proceeded on 5 days leave – O.C. visited Oakland Hospital with Cr. Bull A.D.M.S. and O.C. 3rd Fd Ambulance in order to take inventories preparatory to taking over Sanatorium of the Institution.	

1875 Wt. W593/826 1,000,000 4/15 J.B.C. & A. A.D.S.S./Forms/C. 2118.

Army Form C. 2118

WAR DIARY
or
INTELLIGENCE SUMMARY
(Erase heading not required.)

Instructions regarding War Diaries and Intelligence Summaries are contained in F.S. Regs., Part II. and the Staff Manual respectively. Title Pages will be prepared in manuscript.

Place	Date	Hour	Summary of Events and Information	Remarks and references to Appendices
Chelmsford	1915 Oct 23rd Sat	6 a.m.	Reveillé for transport section. -	
		6.30 p.m.	General Reveillé. -	
		7 a.m.	Medical Inspection all ranks in Huts - by O.C.	
		7.30	Sick Parade -	
		9-12 a.m.	Ambulance engaged in various general fatigues - Camp cleaning - Scouting of Huts - Beds - boards -	
		9.15	Kit Inspection -	
		10 a.m.	Inspection of Huts by O.C.	
		12.30	Inspection of Camp by O.C.	
			Rent - Rivers - proceeded on leave until Oct 25th -	
	Oct 24th Sunday	7 a.m.	Reveillé -	
		8.75 a.m.	Ambulance Paraded for Divine Service at Cathedral at 9 a.m. -	

Army Form C. 2118

WAR DIARY
or
INTELLIGENCE SUMMARY
(Erase heading not required.)

Instructions regarding War Diaries and Intelligence Summaries are contained in F. S. Regs., Part II. and the Staff Manual respectively. Title Pages will be prepared in manuscript.

Place	Date	Hour	Summary of Events and Information	Remarks and references to Appendices
Chelmsford	1915 Oct 25th Monday	6.30	Reveille	
		7-7.30	Physical drill -	
		7.30	Sick Parade -	
		9.15 to 11.15 a.m.	Field work under Capt. Hunt at Gallywood Common -	
		11.30	Lecture by O.C.	
		12.30		
		2 p.m.	Loading wagons in preparation for Parade manoeuvres -	
		2.30 to 4 p.m.	Bandaging application of splints - Ammunition of Oaklands Hospital taken over by O.C. 1st Field Ambulance - Hospital staff commence their duties this evening -	

WAR DIARY
or
INTELLIGENCE SUMMARY

(Erase heading not required.)

Army Form C. 2118

Place	Date	Hour	Summary of Events and Information	Remarks and references to Appendices
Chelmsford	1915 Oct 26 Tuesday	6 a.m. 7.40 a.m. 5.45 a.m.	Reveille — Brigade movements — B Section Paraded under Capt Hunt with 1 Ambulance wagon, 19 Stragger Carts and 1 motor cart and proceeded to Springfield, falling in in rear of 1st 2nd 3rd Bucks Batts. as forming a Blue Force operating Southward from the neighbourhood and region of Pleshey. This force eventually fought a rearguard action falling back towards ———— B Section fell back in rear — establishing & dismantling Advancing Stations & Dressing Stations as became necessary — they returned to Camp about 6.30 p.m. — A.&C. Sections paraded under O.C. with Ambulance transport & formed in rear of a White Force to the rearguard at Chignell Smealey. They erected a Dressing Station & detailed 40 Stretcher bearers with #1 motor ambulance in attendance to follow up a rapid advance on the village of Pleshey made by the troops of their side. This party rejoined their main body at 3 p.m. & reached home at 5 p.m. —	

WAR DIARY
or
INTELLIGENCE SUMMARY

(Erase heading not required.)

Army Form C. 2118

Instructions regarding War Diaries and Intelligence Summaries are contained in F. S. Regs., Part II. and the Staff Manual respectively. Title Pages will be prepared in manuscript.

Place	Date	Hour	Summary of Events and Information	Remarks and references to Appendices
Chelmsford	1915. Oct. 27th Wed.	6.30	Reveille	
		7–7.30	Physical Drill –	
		7.30	Sick Parade –	
		9.15	Indenting wagons –	
		9.45	Lecture by Capt. Stuart on the Preceding days manoeuvres –	
		10.45	Lecture in Pharmacy by O.C.	
		11–12	Squad drill –	
		2–3.30 pm	Finding company grounded	
		3–4 pm	Application of splints & wound dressing – Pte Gilbert, R.E. From T.A. 3 days to leave for having procured 3 Recruits for the Royal Eng. Corps –

Army Form C. 2118

WAR DIARY
or
INTELLIGENCE SUMMARY
(Erase heading not required.)

Instructions regarding War Diaries and Intelligence Summaries are contained in F.S. Regs., Part II. and the Staff Manual respectively. Title Pages will be prepared in manuscript.

Place	Date	Hour	Summary of Events and Information	Remarks and references to Appendices
Chelmsford	1915 Oct 25th	6.30 a.m.	Reveille	
		9.12 a.m.	All outdoor parades cancelled owing to Rain – Lecture by O.C. Physiology – Bandaging – treatment of wounds & fractures – discipline – military law – Kings Regulations – lectures on establishments and new establishments –	
		2.45 p.m.	Cpl Bull – visited unexpected Oaklands Hospital with O.C. A.D.M.S.	
			No 1763 Pte Dove E. returned from detention – 4 days sentence having been remitted for Good Conduct –	

WAR DIARY
or
INTELLIGENCE SUMMARY

(Erase heading not required.)

Army Form C. 2118

Instructions regarding War Diaries and Intelligence Summaries are contained in F.S. Regs., Part II. and the Staff Manual respectively. Title Pages will be prepared in manuscript.

Place	Date	Hour	Summary of Events and Information	Remarks and references to Appendices
Chilon/pol	1915 Oct 29 Fry	6.30	Reveillé	
		7-7.30	Physical Drill	
		7.30	Sick Parade –	
		9.15	Route March –	
		11.30		
		11.30 & 12.30	Lecture by O.C.	
		2-3pm	Medical & Surgical practice under Officers –	
		3pm	Pay Parade –	
		5-8pm	Bathing Parade –	
			10 men proceeded on 5 days leave –	

WAR DIARY
or
INTELLIGENCE SUMMARY
(Erase heading not required.)

Army Form C. 2118

Instructions regarding War Diaries and Intelligence Summaries are contained in F. S. Regs., Part II. and the Staff Manual respectively. Title Pages will be prepared in manuscript.

Place	Date	Hour	Summary of Events and Information	Remarks and references to Appendices
Chelmsford	1915 Oct 30th Sat.	6 a.m.	Reveille for Trumpeter Section	
		6.30 a.m.	General Reveille	
		6.30 a.m.	Medical Inspection – all ranks – in Huts	
		7 a.m.		
		7.30 a.m.	Sick Parade	
		9.15	Kit Inspection in Huts	
		10-12	General Fatigues – Cleaning of Huts & Something of Men Huts	
		12.1.30	Coy. Inspection by O.C.	
		2-5 p.m.	Bathing Parade	
			Skeleton Field Manoeuvres was carried out by the 184th Inf. Bde.	
			Ambulance was represented from 8.30 a.m. to 4 p.m. by 2 Ambulance Wagons with Drivers & Orderlies	

WAR DIARY
or
INTELLIGENCE SUMMARY

Army Form C. 2118

Place	Date	Hour	Summary of Events and Information	Remarks and references to Appendices
Chelmsford	1915 Oct 31st	7 a.m.	Reveille.	
		9.10 a.m.	Ambulance Church Parade – Service 9.50 a.m. Chelmsford Cathedral.	
		Sunday		

Oaklands,
Chelmsford.
November 4th 1915.

GEWMackie. W.S.
Surg. Capt. R.A.M.C.
O/C 1st Ft. Amb.
6, 1st (Lo. Mou.) Div

Army Form C. 2118

WAR DIARY
or
INTELLIGENCE SUMMARY
(Erase heading not required.)

Instructions regarding War Diaries and Intelligence Summaries are contained in F.S. Regs., Part II. and the Staff Manual respectively. Title Pages will be prepared in manuscript.

Place	Date	Hour	Summary of Events and Information	Remarks and references to Appendices
Chelmsford	1915 Nov. 1st		Usual Parades cancelled owing to bad weather. Indoor lectures and instruction substituted. — Coln. Oakwood Hospital definitely diagnosed as Smallpox. Opened & Isolation at Gallywood. All Patients in Hospital vaccinated and all doctors nurses & orderlies likewise. Disinfection done thoroughly and ambulance sent to Col. Bredden to the 2/1st S. mid. F.A. Bde from which unit the case had come. — Oakwood Hospital closed for reception of Patients & a general cleaning up of the whole building undertaken. —	
	Nov 2nd		All Parades resumed. — Special instruction given to all ranks in Emergency Operations & construction of temporary & improvised bivouacs & shelters.	
	Nov 3rd		Field Operations at Gallywood Common. Construction of dressing stations. Oakwood Hospital disinfection inspected by Div. Sanitary Officer.	

WAR DIARY or INTELLIGENCE SUMMARY

Army Form C. 2118

Instructions regarding War Diaries and Intelligence Summaries are contained in F.S. Regs., Part II. and the Staff Manual respectively. Title Pages will be prepared in manuscript.

(Erase heading not required.)

Place	Date	Hour	Summary of Events and Information	Remarks and references to Appendices
Chelmsford	1915. Nov. 4.		Brigade Field Manoeuvres. The Ambulance took part in a Brigade Field day with the 184th Inf. Brigade. Established dressing station at E. Hanningfield and an advanced dressing station at Stone Green. There was no Ambulance and they returned home at 5.30 p.m.	
	Nov. 5th		Parades. Lectures and Practical work as usual. Col. Powell inspected Oaklands Hospital and held a Medical Board on the Inspection Room in the Huts.	
	Nov. 5th		Evening of the men (carried regiment) as per weekly Programme. The Band gave the first of a Series of weekly Concerts in the Wesleyan Church Recreation Hall for Soldiers of the Division.	
	Nov. 9th		Outdoor Parades cancelled owing to very bad weather. Three Recruits arrived from Administrative Centre, Birmingham.	
	Nov. 10th		Parades as usual. Practised outdoor Field work. C/Sgt. Major Inspected Transport Horses & Mules. C. R. Bell, Inspected Oaklands Hospital.	

Army Form C. 2118

WAR DIARY
or
INTELLIGENCE SUMMARY
(Erase heading not required.)

Place	Date	Hour	Summary of Events and Information	Remarks and references to Appendices
Chelmsford	Nov. 13th	10.15	Special Instruction in Surgical Nursing - with demonstrations of Instruments and appliances - Paid route Galleywood Common - Inspection of Hospital by Col Ross A.D.M.S. - Major Hoyte A.D.M.S. - O.C. Sands Hospital once again in full working order - Reference past-program open for reception of Patients -	
	Nov. 14th		All Parades Continued as usual. Sewing them handicapped by the inclement weather - Reports when instruction continues Rev. C. Power. R.C. Chaplain - attaches 67th Field Ambulance for duty - Special Course of lectures on "Sanitation" commenced in addition to the ordinary routine programme of instruction - First few lectures general to the whole unit - Later ones specially to the Sanitary Squad and Special duty men -	
	Nov. 16th		Sarg. Capt G. Mackie transferred to R.A.M.C. (T.) promoted & taking temp. major in command of 1st Field Ambulance -	

WAR DIARY
or INTELLIGENCE SUMMARY

(Erase heading not required.)

Army Form C. 2118

Place	Date	Hour	Summary of Events and Information	Remarks and references to Appendices
Chelmsford	1915 Nov 17th		Training continued as usual. Oaklands Hospital inspected by Col Sir R.A.W.O (?) ADMS 3rd Army - accompanied by Col Paul ADMS 61st (SM) Division & Major Iremonger DADMS 3rd Army.	
	Nov 19th		Field Operations + Billeting Common. Fire/fly Alarm 10.25 p.m. The Ambulances turned out smartly & efficiently and carried out their duties successfully & well.	
	Nov 20th		The men spent several hours trying to establish communication between the huts with clinkers (provided by the Engineers - up till this day the Camp has received it impossible to keep the huts in G. readysomet state of cleanliness -	
	Nov 21st		The Ambulance spent 2½ hours on a Route March + to which the men drew up noted + plans of the Route/Allowed + submitted them for correction + criticism. They had on the whole done in an interesting and intelligent manner	

WAR DIARY
or
INTELLIGENCE SUMMARY
(Erase heading not required.)

Army Form C. 2118

Instructions regarding War Diaries and Intelligence Summaries are contained in F.S. Regs., Part II. and the Staff Manual respectively. Title Pages will be prepared in manuscript.

Place	Date	Hour	Summary of Events and Information	Remarks and references to Appendices
Chelmsford	1915 Mar 22nd		Special Field Operations at Galleywood Common - Instruments in full use & demonstrations given on them. Was re-construction troll rounds - Special Series of lectures & demonstrations commenced to Officers, NCO's, and men on First Clothing - Also Dis Cooking - with practical illustrations - Practices in loading & unloading Motoring Wagons by day & by night - 8 Cots arrived for distribution among the 3 Field Ambulances - Training continued as usual -	
	Mar 23rd		This being a memorable occasion by the 1st Field Ambulance under the Command of Lt. Col. Ross A.D.M.S. in the New Renovation that provided at Oaklands Hospital by the Church Army - a representative company gathered including all patients in the Hospital, all to whose to including Brigadier General the Honorable J. Notting - Lady Notting - The Mayor of Chelmsford, the Senior Chaplain and others - who formally opened the hut & the Mayor formally premised assistance to and to the comfort of the Hospital -	

Army Form C. 2118

WAR DIARY
or
INTELLIGENCE SUMMARY
(Erase heading not required.)

Instructions regarding War Diaries and Intelligence Summaries are contained in F. S. Regs., Part II. and the Staff Manual respectively. Title Pages will be prepared in manuscript.

Place	Date	Hour	Summary of Events and Information	Remarks and references to Appendices
Chelmsford	1915 Nov 26		Field Operations at hill from Common — The M.T. Ambulances taking all Grenadiers transport and Sup. personnel were head off by from dressing station at this destination — Sergt N.C.O. — man cooked his own midday meal — Emergency took was carried out and a met instructional example day was spent —	
	Nov 27		Usual Routine medical Camp Kit inspections were held — Information is that Equipment has arrived to be installed for and tested good — Usual Parades — Packing of all equipment in the waggons in preparation for a General Field Day tomorrow —	
	Nov 28		Field Operations — The Ambulances divided into 2 portions 1 under Capt Hunt to form an advanced dressing station 1 under O.C. to form a bearing station — Scheme worked approved! —	

Army Form C. 2118.

WAR DIARY
or
INTELLIGENCE SUMMARY.
(Erase heading not required.)

Instructions regarding War Diaries and Intelligence Summaries are contained in F. S. Regs., Part II. and the Staff Manual respectively. Title pages will be prepared in manuscript.

Place	Date	Hour	Summary of Events and Information	Remarks and references to Appendices
Chelmsford	1915 Mar. 30		Operation Orders for Field Operations. — The Ambulance will parade for Field Manœuvres and proceed as under:— Dress: Full marching Order accoutrements retted — 1. Personnel.- Remainder of A. Section & B. Section under O.C. will proceed to Galleywood Common to form a Dressing Station. — Transport — 3 Ambulance Waggons 2 G.S. Waggons 1 Maltese Cart 1 Water Cart. Starting Point. — Orchards Camp Time. 10 a.m. Route via Moulsham Street Supply. Every man will carry Haversack Ration and will cook his mid-day meal in his Mess Tin. — 2. Personnel C. Section (under Capt. Hart) will proceed to the vicinity of Br. Hammonfield Moul and establish an Advanced Dressing Station.	Reference to map O.S. Sheet 30

WAR DIARY
or
INTELLIGENCE SUMMARY.
(Erase heading not required.)

Army Form C. 2118.

Place	Date	Hour	Summary of Events and Information	Remarks and references to Appendices
Chelmsford	1915 Nov 30 contd		Transport 1 Contractors Wagon 1 G.S. Wagon Jm 1 Maltese Cart 1 Indian Cart Starting Point – Oaklands Camp Time 9.15 a.m. Route via Moulsham & Galleywood Road so far !— Special orders has been issued imagining that the two sections were in war of were defending Chelmsford on the S. and a stock N. Moulsham & Billericay. Special orders were also issued for the 2 Signallers who kept up communication between the two stations thus formed (a) Sanitary Squad who prepared their dustbin as to an actual operations (b) Mounted orderlies for carrying of messages —	Reference 5" map O.S. Sheet 20 —

WAR DIARY
or
INTELLIGENCE SUMMARY.
(Erase heading not required.)

Army Form C. 2118.

Place	Date	Hour	Summary of Events and Information	Remarks and references to Appendices
Oakhurst Camp	Nov 2nd 1915		d. Scouts — to send out all round & forward maps of the area covered. e. Stretcher parties f. Concealment of wagons & horses from hostile aircraft was also practiced — The operations had proceeded with perfect weather t. his Excellency in attendance returned instruction was made possible in fact. Cars were brought to the operating tent & walking surgical operations had gone through & performed with all the available apparatus brought into actual use —	

G.E. Mackie
Major. R.A.M.C. (T)
O.C. 1st Field Ambulance
61st (S. Mid.) Division.

CONFIDENTIAL.
0000000000000000000

WAR DIARY

OF

2/1ST. SOUTH MIDLAND FIELD AMBULANCE.

PERIOD:-

1 - 30 JANUARY 1916.

Army Form C. 2118

WAR DIARY
or
INTELLIGENCE SUMMARY
(Erase heading not required.)

Instructions regarding War Diaries and Intelligence Summaries are contained in F.S. Regs., Part II. and the Staff Manual respectively. Title Pages will be prepared in manuscript.

Place	Date	Hour	Summary of Events and Information	Remarks and references to Appendices
OAKLANDS. CHELMSFORD.	1916. JAN.1.		Camp and Hut Cleaning. Kit Inspection by Officer Commanding. Captain MC.LANNAHAN.R.A.M.C.(T). from 2/3rd. South Midland Field Ambulance arrived from HATFIELD PEVEREL to act as Medical Officer to OAKLANDS HOSPITAL and the SCABIES HOSPITAL. Authority. A.D.M.S. 30th. December 1915. Inoculation of 100 men of the 61st. Signal Co.,R.E's.	
OAKLANDS. CHELMSFORD.	JAN.2.		Church Parade.	
OAKLANDS. CHELMSFORD.	JAN.3.		Routine Training. Inoculation of 15 men of the 61st. Signal Co.,R.E's. do. 80 men of the 2/2st.South Midland Field Ambulance.	
OAKLANDS. CHELMSFORD.	JAN.4.		Routine Training. Sanitary Demonstration. Night Operations. Ambulance marched out at 8 p.m. Route WIDFORD and MARGARETTING ROAD. Night Training in Collection of Wounded; establishing Dressing Station; and Signalling with lamps, returning at 12 midnight. Travelling Medical Board No. 2 met at Medical Inspection Room,OAKLANDS. President. Colonel CROLY.A.M.S. Members. Colonel MONTGOMERY and Lieut. PRIDHAM R.A.M.C. From this Unit No. 1708 Actg.Sgt.Major Capers and No. 2261.Pte. STANLEY E. were examined, and were both recommended for transference to the Home Service Details, the former for Defective Vision and the latter for Varicose Veins. The Inspecting Dental Officer IIIrd. Army and the D.A.D.M.S. 61st.(S.M.)Div. visited OAKLANDS and inspected Dental Cases and estimates. Authority A.D.M.S. Letter 30th. December 1916.	Refce. ½ in. Map.O.S. Sheet 30.
OAKLANDS. CHELMSFORD.	JAN.5.		Field Operations. Captain McLannahan left OAKLANDS HOSPITAL and proceeded on Sick Leave. Major MACKIE returned from leave and assumed command of the Unit also taking over duties as Medical Officer to OAKLANDS and Scabies Hospitals, vice Capt. McLANNAHAN.	see App.1.
OAKLANDS. CHELMSFORD.	JAN.6.		Routine Training.	
OAKLANDS. CHELMSFORD.	JAN.7.		Routine Training.	

Army Form C. 2118

WAR DIARY
or
INTELLIGENCE SUMMARY
(Erase heading not required.)

Instructions regarding War Diaries and Intelligence Summaries are contained in F.S. Regs., Part II. and the Staff Manual respectively. Title Pages will be prepared in manuscript.

Place	Date	Hour	Summary of Events and Information	Remarks and references to Appendices
OAKLANDS. CHELMSFORD.	1916. Jan.8.		Medical Inspection of all Ranks. Routine Training. Hut and Camp Inspection by Officer Commanding. Vaccination of 64 men of 2/1st. Bucks Battn. do. 12 men of 61st. Signal Co., R.E's. do. 19 men of 2/4th. Battn.Royal Berks Regt. Inoculation of 49 men of 3/5th. Essex Regt. G.O.C. Major. Gen. R.B.ALLASON and the A.D.M.S. 61st. S.M.Div. visited OAKLANDS CAMP & HOSPITAL and inspected them. Case odf suspected Cerebro Spinal Meningitis reported from No. I Co.A.S.C. Special Orderly sent by train to COLCHESTER with fluid for examination which proved to be innocent. Case had meanwhile been detained at Infectious Hospital, GREAT BADDOW for observation.	Fd.M. Fd.M.
OAKLANDS. CHELMSFORD.	Jan.9.		Church Parade.	Fd.M.
OAKLANDS. CHELMSFORD.	Jan 10.		Routine Training. Road Making. The Unit began to tackle the problem of Road Making in the Transport Section of the Camp. Authority:- Special Verbal Order by the G.O.C. A.D.M.S. 61st. South Midland Division visited OAKLANDS HOSPITAL & CAMP. Inoculation of 40 men 2/4th. Battn. Royal Berks Regt.	Fd.M.
OAKLANDS. CHELMSFORD.	Jan.11.		Routine Training. Road Making. A.D.M.S. 61st. South Midland Division, and Divl. Sanitary Officer visited OAKLANDS CAMP.	Fd.M.
OAKLANDS. CHELMSFORD.	Jan.12.		Field Operations. A.D.M.S. 61st. (South Midland)Division visited OAKLANDS HOSPITAL and inspected the progress made by the Road Making party, and also inspected the books of the Unit at the Quartermasters Stores.	See App.2 Fd.M.
OAKLANDS. CHELMSFORD.	Jan.13.		Routine Training. G.O.C. 61st. South Midland Division visited OAKLANDS HOSPITAL, and inspected the progress made by the Road Making party.	Fd.M.
OAKLANDS. CHELMSFORD.	Jan.14,		Route March. Ambulance moved off at 8.45 a.m. for a Route March via WIDFORD—GALLEYWOOD—BADDOW—CHELMSFORD. visited OAKLANDS and held a Medical Board on all Chaplains attached to the 61st. South Midland Division.	Fd.M.

Army Form C. 2118

WAR DIARY
or
INTELLIGENCE SUMMARY

(Erase heading not required.)

Instructions regarding War Diaries and Intelligence Summaries are contained in F.S. Regs., Part II. and the Staff Manual respectively. Title Pages will be prepared in manuscript.

Place	Date	Hour	Summary of Events and Information	Remarks and references to Appendices
OAKLANDS. CHELMSFORD.	1916. Jan.14. (cont.)		Captain BOOME E.J. R.A.M.C.(T). on Sick Furlough from 1/1st. South Midland Field Ambulance in France, arrived at OAKLANDS. KENILWORTH and SCABIES HOSPITALS, as Medical Officer. Authority A.D.M.S. Letter No. 23/M.D.16 of the 13th. January 1916.	Fo. A. Fo. A.
OAKLANDS. CHELMSFORD.	Jan.15.		Routine Training and Road Making.	
OAKLANDS. CHELMSFORD.	Jan.16.		Church Parade. Administration of KENILWORTH HOSPITAL and the working of the Thresh Disinfector in the grounds of OAKLANDS HOSPITAL taken over by the 2/1st South Midland Field Ambulance from the 2/2nd. South Midland Field Ambulance who are arranging to leave the Camp tomorrow. A.D.M.S., 61st. South Midland Division inspected OAKLANDS HOSPITAL. 6 New G.S. Waggons mark VI arrived from CHELMSFORD GOODS STATION and brought to OAKLANDS CAMP. Authority A.D.M.S. Letter No. 79/M.D.16 of the 15th. inst. A.D.M.S. 61st. South Midland Division inspected OAKLANDS HOSPITAL. "A". "B". and "C". Complete Section Rolls Ambulance finally divided into proper Sections "A", "B" and "C". Complete Section Rolls published. "A" Section left OAKLANDS HOSPITAL, and took over all Departmental Duties and Camp Fatigues for one week. "B" Section furnished Staffs for OAKLANDS and KENILWORTH and SCABIES HOSPITALS. "C" Section formed into the Field Section for one week under Captain HIRST. Captain Boome appointed to special Standing Medical Board by A.D.M.S. 61st. South Midland Division for Medical Examination of all Officers in the 61st. South Midland Division. Captain MC.LANNAHAN reported for duty as Medical Officer to OAKLANDS. KENILWORTH and SCABIES HOSPITALS for a fortnight vice Captain BOOME occupied on Special Medical Board. (Auth. Divl. Order No/52 of the 14th. January.	Fo. A.
OAKLANDS. CHELMSFORD.	Jan.17.		2/2nd. South Midland Field Ambulance marched out of OAKLANDS CAMP for MALDON. One Hut formerly occupied by the 2/2nd. South Midland Field Ambulance taken over by the 2/1st. South Midland Field Ambulance as a Medical Inspection, Opthalmic and Dental Room. Authority A.D.M.S. 61st. South Midland Division. Representatives of the D.O.R.E. and The Officer in Charge of Barracks visited OAKLANDS CAMP.	Fo. A.
OAKLANDS. CHELMSFORD.	Jan.18.		Routine Training. "C" Section Field Operations under Captain HIRST. A.D.M.S. 61st. South Midland Division visited OAKLANDS CAMP including the Hut being prepared as Special Inspection Room for Divisional Dental Officer.	Fo. A.

Army Form C. 2118

WAR DIARY
or
INTELLIGENCE SUMMARY

(Erase heading not required.)

Instructions regarding War Diaries and Intelligence Summaries are contained in F. S. Regs., Part II. and the Staff Manual respectively. Title Pages will be prepared in manuscript.

Place	Date	Hour	Summary of Events and Information	Remarks and references to Appendices
OAKLANDS. CHELMSFORD.	1916. Jan. 18.		Lieut. LEITCH Divisional Dental Officer reported himself at OAKLANDS CAMP for Duty. authority A.D.M.S. 61st. South Midland Division and Divisional Order No. 82 of 19th. January 1916. Popular lecture by Capt. STORRS R.A.M.C. on his experiences as a Regimental M.O. in Gallipoli.	FEA.M.
OAKLANDS. CHELMSFORD.	Jan. 19.		Routine Training. Colonel LAW D.A.Q.M.G. 61st. South Midland Division and Colonel Wheeler O.C. 2/@th. Battn. Royal Berks Regt. visited and inspected OAKLANDS CAMP. O.C. proceeded to Royal Army Medical College, Millbank, London to attend special lecture by Major STARLING R.A.M.C. on "Poisonous Gases - their use in War and methods of defence against them".	FEA.M.
OAKLANDS. CHELMSFORD.	Jan. 20.		Routine Training. Road Making. Inspecting Dental Officer IIIrd. Army held a Dental Inspection at OAKLANDS CAMP. G.O.C. 61st. (South Midland) Division visited OAKLANDS HOSPITAL. Divisional Sanitary Officer inspected OAKLANDS CAMP as left by the 2/2nd. South Midland Field Ambulance, and made further arrangements for the cleaning of that part.	FEA.M.
OAKLANDS. CHELMSFORD.	Jan. 21.		Routine Training. "C" Section proceeded for Field Operations to MOUNTNESSING Trench School. Colonel SELBY Senior Chaplain 61st. South Midland Division paid a farewell visit to OAKLANDS HOSPITAL AND CAMP.	See A app. 4 FEA.M.
OAKLANDS. CHELMSFORD.	Jan. 22.		Medical Inspection of all Ranks. Hut and Camp Inspection. Assistant Director of Medical Services 61st. (South Midland)Division visited OAKLANDS and inspected Dental Inspection Room. No. I708 Acting Sgt. Major Capers and No. 2261 Pte. Stanley H. proceeded to Newcastle on Tyne, to join the 8th. Provisional Brigade Field Ambulance. Auth. Officer in Charge of Records. No. P/2071 dated 17th. January 1916.	FEA.M.
OAKLANDS. CHELMSFORD.	Jan. 23.		Church Parade. Divisional Sanitary Officer inspected OAKLANDS CAMP.	FFA.M.

1875 Wt. W593/826 1,000,000 4/15 J.B.C. & A. A.D.S.S./Forms/C. 2118.

WAR DIARY or INTELLIGENCE SUMMARY

Army Form C. 2118

Place	Date	Hour	Summary of Events and Information	Remarks and references to Appendices
OAKLANDS. CHELMSFORD.	1916. Jan.24.		"C" Section took over all Departmental and Camp Duties for a week. "A" Section prepared and cleared all equipment preparatory to taking up Field Work for one week under the Officer Commanding. Routine Training.	J.E.M.
OAKLANDS. CHELMSFORD.	Jan.25.		Road Making. "A" Section. Field Operations.	J.E.M. See app 5.
OAKLANDS. CHELMSFORD.	Jan.26.		Road Making. "A" Section. Field Operations.	J.E.M. See app 6.
OAKLANDS. CHELMSFORD.	Jan.27.		Routine Training. Road Making. Colonel Wheeler O.C. 2/4th. Battn. Royal Berks Regt. and Major Symmonds visited OAKLANDS CAMP with representatives of the Road Board and D.O.R.E. and discussed the further improvements contemplated in the Camp Area. - Special Fatigue Party of 20 men under a Sergeant reported for Road Making, from the 2/4th.Battn. Royal Berks. Regt.	J.E.M.
OAKLANDS. CHELMSFORD.	Jan.28.		Routine Training. Cleaning Waggons and Equipment. G.O.C. 61st. So. Mid. Div. (Major General R.B.ALLASON with Col. BURROWES visited and inspected OAKLANDS HOSPITAL and CAMP. A.D.M.S. and D.A.D.M.S. visited OAKLANDS.	J.E.M.
OAKLANDS. CHELMSFORD.	Jan.29.			J.E.M.
OAKLANDS. CHELMSFORD.	Jan.30.		Routine Training. Inspection of Equipment. Road Making.	J.E.M.
OAKLANDS. CHELMSFORD.	Jan.30.		Church Parade. Road Making.	J.E.M.
OAKLANDS. CHELMSFORD.	Jan.31.		Routine Training. Written Examination for all Ranks. Road Making.	J.E.M.

J.E.Mackie.
MAJOR R.A.M.C.
OFFICER COMMANDING
2/1st SOUTH MID. FIELD AMBULANCE.

1 Feb. 1916.

APPENDIX. 1.

—o—o—o—o—o—o—o—

Field Manoeuvres. 4th January 1916.

—o—o—o—o—o—o—o—

2/1st. South Midland Field Ambulance.

Oaklands,

Chelmsford.

Reference ½ inch Map.   Sheet 30.

MARCHING ORDERS. TUESDAY. JANUARY 4TH. 1916.

The Ambulance will parade in full Marching Order. Overcoats rolled and worn.

STARTING POINT. OAKLANDS.

TIME.   9 a.m.

ROUTE. By main road CHELMSFORD-INGATESTONE.

SUPPLY. Cooks will carry all Rations for the day.

DRESSING STATION. Cross Roads E. of G in FRYERNING.(C. SECTION.)

REGIMENTAL AID POSTS. 1. MARGARETTING HALL.(B. Section.)
                       2. Corner of INGATESTONE ROAD.(S.E. of black figures 230).(A. SECTION.)

B. Section will collect wounded FRESTLING HALL-RAMSET TYRELLS.

A. Section will collect wounded BUTTSBURY HALL-RAMSEY TYRELLS.

LIGHT DUTY MEN and MESS ORDERLIES will act as Patients.

SIGNALLERS will locate all positions, and keep Stations in communication.

SIGNALLERS and SANITARY SQUAD will proceed on their duties at the 1st. halt.

BUGLE CALLS."Rations"at 1.30 p.m.

S C H E M E .

An enemy force operating from the South East, has cut the Railway Line, and advanced towards MILL GREEN.

A. Friendly Force, attacking on MILL GREEN, has fought a successful action, and is pressing the enemy across the line, near INGATESTONE, and is advancing rapidly twards the area STOCK-BILLERICAY, leaving their wounded behind.

The 1st. Field Ambulance is ordered to move out, and deal with these cases.

Regimental Aid Posts are reported at:- MARGARETTING HALL.

Corner of INGATESTONE ROAD.S.E. of black figures 230.

             By Order.

Oaklands.   W.J.Hirst.

   January 5th. 1916.   Captain.R.A.M.C.(T). Section Officer.

APPENDIX 2.

=0=0=0=0=0-0-0=0=

Field Manoeuvres. 12th January 1916.

-0-0-0-0-0-0-0-0=

2/1st. South Midland Field Ambulance,

Oaklands,

Chelmsford.

Reference ½ inch Map.   Sheet 30.

SCHEME for Field Operations. Wednesday. January 12th. 1916.

A friendly Force has been manning the trenches at MOUNTNESSING, and has defended BRENTWOOD against an attack by shell fire and bombs. It is reported to the 2/Ist. South Midland Field Ambulance that a number of casualties have occurred, and that the wounded have been left in these trenches.

Sections "B" and "C" are therefore, instructed to proceed to the trench area, establish a Dressing Station near INGATESTONE VILLAGE at any suitable place, and an Advanced Dressing Sation near MOUNT-Nessing and to proceed with the work of rescuing the wounded.

MARCHING ORDERS.

The Ambulance will parade in full Marching Order - Overcoats rolled and worn.

STARTING POINT. O A K L A N D S.

TIME.   9 a.m.

Route.   By CHELMSFORD-BRENTWOOD MAIN ROAD.

SUPPLY.   Cooks will carry all Rations for the day.

DRESSING STATION. Any suitable place near INGATESTONE VILLAGE.

LIGHT DUTY MEN AND MESS ORDERLIES. These will act as Patients.

The SIGNALLERS will ocate all positions, and keep all Stations in communication.

BUGLE CALLS.   "Rations" - I.30 p.m.

Oaklands.   By Order.
   Chelmsford.   W.J.Hirst.
      January IIth. 1916.   Captain.R.A.M.C.(T).
                                         Section Officer.

APPENDIX 3.

-o-o-o-o-o-o-o-

Field Manoeuvres. 18th January 1915.

-o-o-o-o-o-o-o-

2/1st. South Midland Field Ambulance.

    Oaklands,

        Chelmsford.

Reference ½ inch Map. Sheet 30.

S C H E M E for Field Operations for "C" Section.

Tuesday. January 18th. 1916.

-o-o-o-o-o-o-o-o-o-o-o-

An enemy Force is located on the Ridge ALSTEADS FARM.
C. SECTION of the 1st. Field Ambulance are attached to a Unit who are fighting a successful action, and are driving the enemy from the Ridge, in the direction of GREAT DUNMOW.

M A R C H I N G   O R D E R S.

C. Section will parade in full Marching Order. Overcoats rolled and worn.

    Reveille. 6.50 a.m.

    Load Waggons. 7'0.a.m.

    Breakfast. 7.30 a.m.

STARTING POINT. OAKLANDS.

TIME. 8 a.m.

ROUTE. CHELMSFORD - WITHAM MAIN ROAD.

SUPPLY. Cooks will carry all Rations for the day.

DRESSING STATION. BOREHAM.

ADVANCED DRESSING STATION. RUNSELL GREEN.

DRESSING STATION advanced to LOWNS FARM at 11.30 a.m.

SIGNALLERS will locate positions and keep Stations in Communication.

TRANSPORT. 2 G. S. Waggons.

    1 Maltese Cart.

    1 Water Cart.

    2 Ambulance Waggons.

Note. The two Ambulance Waggons will be outside the Stores at 6.50 a.m.

By Order,

Oaklands,   W.J.Hirst.

  Chelmsford.   Captain.R.A.M.C.(T).

    January 17th. 1916.   Section Officer.

APPENDIX 4.

-o-o-o-o-o-o-

Field Manoeuvres, 21st. January 1916.

-o-o-o-o-o-o-

2/1st. South Midland Field Ambulance.

Oaklands,

Chelmsford.

Reference ½ inch Map.   Sheet 30.

MARCHING ORDERS.

    FRIDAY January 21st. 1916.

STARTING POINT.   OAKLANDS.

TIME.   8 a.m.

ROUTE.   Main Road WIDFORD-MARGARETTING-INGATESTONE- to MOUNTNESSING TRENCHES.

DRESSING STATION.   Village Hall. MOUNTNESSING.

SUPPLY.   Cooks will carry all food for the day.

HEADQUARTERS.   Village Hall. MOUNTNESSING II a.m. - 2 p.m.

SCHEME.   Collection of Wounded from the trenches at MOUNTNESSING, and conveyance to the Dressing Station at the Village Hall, MOUNTNESSING.

TRANSPORT.   The whole of the Transport belonging to "C" Section will be in readiness to move off at 8 a.m.

    By Order,

    W.J.Hirst.

Oaklands,   Captain.R.A.M.C.(T).

  Chelmsford.   Section Officer.

    January 20th. 1916.

APPENDIX 5.

-o-o-o-o-o-o-o-

Field Manoeuvres, 25th January 1916.

-o-o-o-o-o-o-o-

2/1st. South Midland Field Ambulance.

Oaklands.

Chelmsford.

Reference ½ inch Map.   Sheet 30.

S C H E M E for Field Manoeuvres. Tuesday. January 25th. 1916.

A Friendly Force is defending a line of Trenches MARGARETTING) WEST HANNINGFIELD.

Regimental Aid Post is reported at THE SHIP INN near WEST HANNINGFIELD HALLS.

"A" Section of the Ist. Field Amb. is ordered to proceed to collect the wounded, forming an Advanced Dressing Station at the lower end of GALLEYWOOD COMMON, and a Dressing Station near the Brick Works on GALLEYWOOD COMMON.

NOTE. The Dressing Station will be supervised by St.Sgt.Burling and Sgt Wheeldon and the A.D.S. by Sgt. Perry and Sgt. Cranwell.

M A R C H I N G   O R D E R S.

"A" Section will parade in full Marching Order - Overcoats rolled and worn, at 8.45 a.m.

STARTING PLACE. OAKLANDS.

TIME.	9 a.m.
ROUTE.	via WOOD STREET.
SUPPLY.	Cooks will carry all rations for the day.
SIGNALLERS.	Will locate all positions, and keep the Stations in communication.
TRANSPORT.	The whole of the Transport belonging to "A" Section will be in position, and ready to move off with the Troops at 9 a.m.
HEADQUARTERS.	This will be near the BRICK WORKS on GALLEYWOOD COMMON, close to MAIN ROAD CHELMSFORD-GALLEYWOOD-STOCK from II a.m. - I p.m.

By Oredr,

George Mackie.

Major.R.A.M.C.(T).

Officer Commanding.

2/Ist. South Mid. Field Amb.

Oaklands,
  Chelmsford.
    January 24th. 1916.

APPENDIX 10.

=O=O=O=O=O=O=

Field Manoeuvres. 26th January 1916.

=O=O=O=O=O=O=

2/1st. South Midland Field Ambulance.

Captain,

Commandant.

SPECIAL ORDERS FOR "A" SECTION.

WEDNESDAY, JANUARY 26TH, 1916.

REVEILLE.   5.30 a.m.

BATHING.   30 men will proceed to the Baths at 5.40 a.m.

               The remainder of the Section will bathe at 6.40 a.m.

O.C'S PARADE. 9 o'clock. "A" Section will parade in full Marching

               Order. (Old clothes to be worn.)

STARTING POINT. OAKLANDS.

TIME.   9.15 a.m.

ROUTE.   CHELMSFORD - INGATESTONE Main Road.

SUPPLY.   The Cooks will carry all Rations for the day.

TRANSPORT.   The whole of the Transport belonging to "A" Section

               will be in position at 9 a.m.

HEADQUARTERS. MOUNTNESSING. 11.30 - 1.30 p.m.

SCHEME.   "A" Section will practise the Collection of Wounded

               from the Trenches at MOUNTNESSING.

               By order.

               George Mackie.

Oaklands.   Major.R.A.M.C.(T).

   Chelmsford.   Officer Commanding.

      January 25th, 1916.   2/1st. South Mid. Field Amb.

CONFIDENTIAL.

WAR DIARY OF THE

2/1ST. SOUTH MIDLAND FIELD AMBULANCE.

MAY 1916.

31ST. MAY 1916.

Army Form C. 2118.

WAR DIARY
or
INTELLIGENCE SUMMARY.

Reference O.S. Map ½ in. Sheet 33.

(Erase heading not required.)

Instructions regarding War Diaries and Intelligence Summaries are contained in F.S. Regs. Part II. and the Staff Manual respectively. Title pages will be prepared in manuscript.

Place	Date	Hour	Summary of Events and Information	Remarks and references to Appendices
NO.1.CAMP. PERHAM DOWN.	1916. May 1.		Route March. No. 1767 St.Sgt. J. DIX transferred from "B" SECTION to Acting Staff Sgt. in Charge Transport.	See App 1. Auth. O.C. 2/1 S.M.F.A. F.E.U.
do.	May 2nd.		Routine Training. Practising "mobilisation loading" of waggons. Lecture on "Gas" by MAJOR HEWITT. NO. 4 CAMP. Officers and N.C.O's attended. No. 2120 PTE. A. YOUNG rejoined Unit, having been discharged from Munition Work.	Auth. A.DMS Tel. Messag F.E.U.
do.	May 3rd.		Routine Training. Section lectures on "Gas and Gas Helmets" by Officers. Helmet Drill.	F.E.U.
do.	May 4th.		Routine Training. - Digging operations continued. Capt. WAY.R.A.M.C.(T). left Unit to rejoin 5th. SOUTHERN GENERAL HOSPITAL. PORTSMOUTH.	Auth. A.DMS 4/5/16. F.E.U. See app.2. Auth. A.DMS Tel.Mge. F.E.U.
do.	May 5th.		Inspection of 61ST. (SOUTH MIDLAND) DIVISION on BULFORD FIELD by HIS MAJESTY THE KING. LIEUT. MANUEL R.A.M.C. reported to this Unit for duty from SLING HOSPITAL.	Auth. ADMS. 616.M/D.16 F.E.U.
do.	May 6th.		Routine Training. Medical Board held on NO.2120 DRIVER BEST. 2/3rd. SOUTH MIDLAND FIELD ART. BDE.	F.E.U.
do.	May 7th.		Church Parades. Routine Training. Lecture on "Discipline and Divisional Standing Orders" by the O.C.	
do. & HURSTBOURNE PRIORS.	May 8th.		Divisional Manoeuvres.	See app.3. F.E.U.
HAZELDOWN FARM. LONGSTOCK.	May 9th.		Divisional Manoeuvres.	See app.3. F.E.U.
MONXTON SANGUTS & NO.1.CAMP.PERHAM DOWN.	May 10.		Divisional Manoeuvres.	See app.3. F.E.U.

Army Form C. 2118.

WAR DIARY
or
INTELLIGENCE SUMMARY.

(Erase heading not required.)

Instructions regarding War Diaries and Intelligence Summaries are contained in F.S. Regs., Part II. and the Staff Manual respectively. Title pages will be prepared in manuscript.

Reference O.S. ½ inch Map. Sheet 33.

Place	Date	Hour	Summary of Events and Information	Remarks and references to Appendices
NO.1.CAMP. PERHAM DOWN.	1916. May 11.		Unloading and cleaning waggons. General Fatigues. Surplus clothing consigned to ARMY CLOTHING DEPOT. DEWSBURY.	G.O.C/A. Auth.O.O. Tidworth.
do.	May 12.		Routine Training. Digging Operations. OFFICER COMMANDING attended G.O.C's Conference on recent Divisional Field Operations at BHURTPORE BARRACKS. TIDWORTH.	Auth.ADMS 11.5.16. G.O.C/A.
do.	May 13.		Routine Training. Lecture by OFFICER COMMANDING. Examination for promotion of Nursing Orderlies.	G.O.C/A.
do.	May 14.		Church Parade. Competition for Intersectional Monthly Cup, given by the OFFICER COMMANDING for smartest section.	G.O.C/A.
do.	May 15.		Routine Training. A.D.M.S. 61st. (S.M.) Div. visited the Camp. No.2495 PTE. McINTYRE J. reported to O.C. 2/1ST. S.M.F.A. on his transference from 1/6th. (CYCLIST) BATTN. ESSEX REGT.	Auth. O.1/Richards G.O.C/A.
do.	May 16.		Routine Training.	G.O.C/A.
do.	May 17.		Routine Training. General Fatigues.	G.O.C/A.
do.	May 18.		Cleaning Camp preparatory to departure. A.D.V.S. 61ST. (S.M.) DIV. visited Camp and inspected horses.	G.O.C/A.
do.	May 19.		Divisional Route March.	see app. 4 G.O.C/A.
do.	May 20.		Cleaning and packing of waggons etc. preparatory to departure. General cleaning of Camp.	G.O.C/A.
do.	May 21.		Church Parade. – Parade of all ranks, and address by OFFICER COMMANDING on duty overseas. Reading of message from H.M. THE KING.	G.O.C/A.

Army Form C. 2118.

WAR DIARY
or
INTELLIGENCE SUMMARY.
(Erase heading not required.)

Reference Sheet 36 a.O.S.Map.
Edition 6.

Place	Date	Hour	Summary of Events and Information	Remarks and references to Appendices
NO.I.CAMP. PERHAM DOWN.	May 22.			See app.5. F.E.Cl.
HAVRE.	May 23.		The Ambulance moved to FRANCE.	
HAVRE.	May 24.			
	May 25.			
LE VERTBOIS FERME.	May 26.		General Fatigues. Cleaning farm and surroundings, and erecting temporary Camp. Interpreter reported. Camp visited by Staff Capt. 184TH.INFANTRY BRIGADE.	F.E.Cl.
do.	May 27th.		General Fatigues. Motor Ambulance Fleet arrived. 5 SIDDELEY DEASEY CARS. 2 FORD CARS. 2 MOTOR CYCLES. No.0.20051 SGT. JONES.W. and I Corporal and 12 men arrived. OFFICER COMMANDING visited A.D.M.S. 61ST. (SOUTH MIDLAND) DIVISION at ST. VENANT. Hospital ready for occupation. Route March ST. VENANT - MERVILLE under CAPT. H.N.BURROUGHES.	F.E.Cl. F.E.Cl.
do.	May 28th.		Church Parade, conducted by REV.T.BENNETT.C.F. General Fatigues. 2 Sick admitted to Hospital:- 1. GUNNER HAMMOND.B.D. "B" BATTERY. 306 BDE. R.F.A. 2. PRIVATE BRITT. F.W. 2/4TH. ROYAL BERKS REGT. Temporary Scabies Hospital opened in tents. 1 case of Scabies admitted from 305th. ART. BDE.	F.E.Cl.
do.	May 29th.		Routine Training. BRIGADIER GENERAL C.H.P.CARTER. C.B., C.M.G., visited and inspected Camp.	F.E.Cl.
do.	May 30.		Routine Training. - OFFICER COMMANDING visited HINGES to see FIELD CASHIER re payment of men. MAJOR GENERAL COLIN MACKENZIE.C.B. visited Camp. Route March. LE SART - MERVILLE - LES LAURIERS - LE VERTBOIS FERME.	F.E.Cl.
do.	May 30.		Routine Training. - Inspection of Transport by Officer from ARMY VETERINARY CORPS.61ST. DIV.	F.E.Cl.

May 31st. 1916.

F.Edwards
MAJOR.R.A.M.C.(T).
O.C., 2/1st. South Midland Field Ambulance.

CONFIDENTIAL.

2/IST. SOUTH MIDLAND FIELD AMBULANCE.

WAR DIARY, MAY 1916.

APPENDIX NO. 1

P.E. Mackie.
Major R.A.M.C.T.

SPECIAL ORDERS BY MAJOR GEORGE MACKIE.R.A.M.C.(T).
OFFICER COMMANDING. 2/IST.SO.MID.FLD.AMB.
NO. 1. CAMP. PERHAM DOWN.
MONDAY. MAY IST. 1916. MONDAY.

PARADES.

    7 a.m. Breakfast.

    7.30 a.m. Sick Parade.

    7.45 a.m. O.C's. Parade.

    8 a.m. Sections "A" and "B" will parade in full marching order. Waterbottles filled. Every available man will turn out. Haversack Rations will be taken in the Cooks' Waggon. (Section Sergeants will notify to the Quartermaster's Stores, the approximate number of men who will be on parade.)

    The Ambulance will move off for a Route March.

TRANSPORT.

    1 Ambulance Waggon.

    1 G.S. Waggon for Cooks.

SPECIAL NOTE.   "C" SECTION WILL TAKE OVER ALL CAMP DUTIES COMMENCING ON MAY IST.

By Order,

G.W. Mackie.

Major.R.A.M.C.(T).
Officer Commanding.
2/Ist. So.Mid.Field Ambulance.

No. 1 Camp. Perham Down.
Salisbury Plain.
April 30th.1916.

NARRATIVE OF ROUTE MARCH OF

2/IST. SOUTH MIDLAND FIELD AMBULANCE.R.A.M.C.(T).

MAY 1st. 1916.

Time.		Narrative.
8.0.		Sections "A" and "B" paraded in full Marching Order, with the following personnel:-

                  Officers. 6.
                  St.Sgts. 2.
                  Sergeants. 5.
                  Corporals. 4.
                  L/Cpls. 6.
                  Privates. 89.
                            112.

Haversack Rations were carried in Cook's Waggon.

	ROUTE.	The route taken was as follows:- PERHAM DOWN - TIDWORTH - SHIPTON BELLINGER - WEST CHOLDERTON - BULFORD - AMESBURY - STONEHENGE.
	HALTS.	SHIPTON BELLINGER 9 a.m.
		WEST CHOLDERTON. 9.50 a.m.
		BULFORD. 10.30 a.m.
		AMESBURY. 11.15 a.m.
12.5.		STONEHENGE was reached at 12.5 p.m.
12.30.		Issue of Haversack Rations.
13.45		Ambulance started homewards.
17.5.		Ambulance arrived in Camp.
	CASUALTIES.	Two men fell out on march:- (1) Sore feet. (2) Colic.
	WEATHER.	Fine. Bright sunshine practically whole of day.

G.W. Mackie
Major.R.A.M.C.(T).
O.C., 2/1st. So.Mid.Field Amb.

No. 1 Camp. Perham Down.
May 1st. 1916.

CONFIDENTIAL.

2/1ST. SOUTH MIDLAND FIELD AMBULANCE.

WAR DIARY. MAY 1916.

APPENDIX NO. 2.

Geo. Mackie.
Major. R.A.M.C.T.

SPECIAL ORDERS BY MAJOR GEORGE MACKIE.R.A.M.C.(T).

OFFICER COMMANDING. 2/IST. SOUTH MID.FLD.AMB.

NO. 1 CAMP. PERHAM DOWN.

FRIDAY. MAY 5TH. 1916.

&@&@&@&@&@&@&@&@&@&

HIS MAJESTY THE KING WILL INSPECT ALL UNITS OF THE 6IST. (SO.MID). DIVISION ON BULFORD FIELD THIS DAY.

BUGLE CALLS.
- 5.15 a.m. Reveille.
- 6.30 p.m. Retreat.
- 10.15 p.m. Lights Out.

PARADES.
- 5.45 a.m. Roll Call.
- 6.0 a.m. Breakfast.
- 6.45 a.m. The Ambulance will parade in full marching order. Oil sheets will be neatly folded and placed on top of the pack. Waterbottles will be filled. Identity discs will be worn. Patch pockets will contain first field dressings.
Every available man will turn out. Haversack rations will be carried. Each man should carry in his pack a clean pair of socks and a pair of canvas shoes.
- 6.50 a.m. All teams will be hooked in, and spare horses etc. ready to move off.
- 7.0 a.m. The Ambulance will move off.

By order,

T.E.Mackie

Major.R.A.M.C.(T).

O.C.2/Ist.So.Mid.Field Ambce.

No. 1 Camp. Perham Down.

May 4th. 1916.

NARRATIVE OF INSPECTION BY H. M. THE KING ON

FRIDAY, MAY 5TH, 1916.

TIME.	NARRATIVE.
6.45.	Ambulance paraded in full marching order, with following personnel:-

                Officers.   10.
                Staff Sgts.   3.
                Sergeants.   8.
                Corporals.   7.
                Lance Corporals. 5.
                Privates.   140.
                Total R.A.M.C. personnel 173.

The following Transport was taken with the Unit,
                Ambulance Waggons. 3.
                G.S. Waggons.   7.
                Limber Waggons.   4.
                Water Carts.   3.
                Maltese Carts.   1.
together with the requisite personnel under Sgt. Major DIX.

7.0.	The Ambulance moved out of Camp.
	ROUTE. via SHIPTON BELLINGER. - CHOLDERTON - BULFORD - BULFORD STATION - on to Field in rear of Station.
10.50.	The Ambulance arrived at the Inspection Ground, and took up its position.
12.15.	The Ambulance was inspected by H.M. THE KING.
131.30.	Hot dinner provided for the men of the Unit.
12.30.	March back to Camp commenced.
17.0.	The Ambulance arrived in Camp.
CASUALTIES.	Three men of the Unit fell out on march back to Camp:- (1.) Severe abdominal pains. (2.) Blistered feet. (3.) Effects of a broken leg.
WEATHER.	Fine and bright first, changeable and showery later.

                                        F.W. Mackie.
                                  Major. R.A.M.C. (T).
                                      Officer Commanding.

No. 1 Camp. Perham Down.   2/1st. Sputh Midland Field Ambce.

    May 5th. 1916.

CONFIDENTIAL.

2/IST. SOUTH MIDLAND FIELD AMBULANCE.

WAR DIARY. MAY 1916.

APPENDIX NO. 3.

Geo. Mackie
Major. R.A.M.C.T.

NARRATIVE OF DIVISIONAL FIELD OPERATIONS OF MAY 8TH, 9TH, and 10TH, 1916.

by 2/1st. South Midland Field Ambulance.

Reference O.S. ½ in. Map Sheet 33.

Time.	Movements.	Destination.	Summary of messages.		Casualties.	Remarks.
			Sent.	Received.		
1916.						
May 8th. 10.a.m.	Parade.					
10.20.	Ambulance marched off from Camp.			Divisional Orders and March Table received. 2/1st. Field Amb. attached to 184th. INF. BDE.		
10.24.	Ambulance took its place in Column in rear of CYCLISTS and ENGINEERS on PERHAM DOWN-SHODDESDON ROAD.	WEYHILL.				
11.10.				From A.D.M.S. No.1. DIV.HDQRS. at WHITE HART HOTEL.WHITCHURCH & that 2/1st.FLD.AMB. would open 1 Tent Sub-Division for sick of 184 INF.BDE.		
11.38.	Ambulance halted behind Column and reached WEYHILL late at;					
12.5	Ambulance arrived at	WEYHILL.				
13.5.	On main road to	ANDOVER.		From 184 INF. BDE. Billeting Party to meet STAFF CAPTAIN at X ROADS near DOWN HOUSE at once.		

Reference ¼ inch O.S. Map. Sheet 33.

Time.	Movements.	Destination.	Summary of messages. Sent.	Summary of messages. Received.	Casualties.	Remarks.
13.20.	CAPT.HIRST and Billeting party proceeded ahead to DOWN HOUSE.					
13.45.	Ambulance reached ANDOVER.					
14.55.	At Halt on Main Road to WHITCHURCH.					
15.5.	Ambulance moved off to MANOR FARM.			From Billeting Party giving destination as MANOR FARM. HURSTBOURNE PRIORS.		
16.0.	Ambulance arrived at MANOR FARM. CAPT. BURROUGHES left at HDQRS.184 INF.BDE. for instructions, and an Orderly detached to guide supply waggon.		G.M.1 and 2 sent to A.D.M.S.Parade State and Unit Orders and that Amb. arrived at MANOR FARM. Tent Sub-Division had been opened for sick and casualties. G.M.3. to HDQRS. 184 INF.BDE. giving location as MANOR FARM,S.side of Main ANDOVER—WHITCHURCH Road,opposite 2nd. R. in PRIORS.(HURSTBOURNE PRIORS)		2/5 GLOSTERS. 3. 2/1 BUCKS. 4. 1/3 FIELD CO. R.E's. 1. 2/1ST.S.M. 3. FLD.AMB.	
16.50.	Arrangements made for accomodation of Officers and men. Tents pitched for sick, and horses picketed in open.		G.M.4 to A.D.M.S. re R.A.P's.			
17.5.	Waggons concealed under trees.					
17.30.	CAPT. H.N.BURROUGHES reported from 184 INF. BDE. HDQRS.					Billeting Instructions.
18.0.	2 Cycle Orderlies sent to Hdqrs.184 INF.BDE.for messages. Casualties having been treated, began to rejoin their Units with attending Orderlies in charge. G.M. 5, 6 and 7 re above.					

Reference O.S. ½ inch Map. Sheet 33.

Time.	Movements.	Destination.	Summary of messages. Sent.	Summary of messages. Received.	Casualties.	Remarks.
May 8th. 18.30.	Mens's Dinner - first proper meal since 7.30 a.m. owing to the Ambulance having no Field Cooker.					
20.30.	Officers Dinner.			G.M.8 acknowled- ging receipt.	184 INF.BDE.Orders for May 9. Copy 7.	
20.45.	Marching orders May 9th. 1. 1 Bearer Sub-Division (less waggons) to follow Advance Guard at 9.0. 2. Billeting Party to meet Staff Captain at STAR AND GARTER HOTEL.ANDOVER at 10.0. 3. Field Ambulance (less 1 Bearer Sub-Division) to move off in place in Main Body at 9.46. A X Roads HURSTBOURNE PRIORS.					
22.45. May 9th. 1.26.	Orders altered. ½ Bearer Sub-Division to report to CAPT. CHURCH 2/1. BUCKS. Rd.Junction S. of E in MIDDLETON at 9.45.			From A.D.M.S.Disposal of men unable to march at X Roads HURSTBOURNE PRIORS to be picked up at 13.0 by Mechanical Transport.		
7.0.	Breakfast.					
7.30.			G.M.9 to A.D.M.S acknowledging receipt of inst- ructions re sick and Duplicate A. & D.Bk.for May 8.			
8.30.	½ Bearer Sub-Division "C" Section under CAPT.GREEN & ST.SGT.JACQUES paraded for duty with Advance guard.	Rd.Junction S. of E. in MIDDLETON.				
8.35.				From 184 INF.BDE. asking for Sanitary Officer for Billeting Party.		
8.53.			G.M.10 & 11 to 184 INF.BDE.re Billeting and detailing CAPT. STOBIE.			
9.5.	CAPT.STOBIE reported at HEADQUARTERS 184th. INFANTRY BRIGADE.					
9.20.	Parade.					
9.30.	Field Ambulance ready to move off at 9.43 in column.			Amended order of march from 184 INF.BDE.		

Reference ½ inch Map, Sheet 33.

Time.	Movements.	Destination.	Summary of messages. Sent.	Summary of messages. Received.	Casualties.	Remarks.
May 9th. 9.50.	Field Ambulance moved off.					
11.30.				From Billeting Party stating that destination was HAZELDOWN FARM. S. of L. in LONGSTOCK HOUSE.		
12.15.	Arrived at - - -	FULLERTON JUNCTION.				
13.0.	Haversack Ration.					
14.55.	Ambulance moved off to	HAZELDOWN FARM.				
16.5.	Ambulance arrived at	HAZELDOWN FARM.	O.M.12 & 13 to 184 INF.BDE.& A.D.M.S. reporting arrival and casualties picked up and dealt with en route		2/4 R.BERKS. 12. 2/4 O. & BKS. 4. 2/1 BUCKS. 3. 1/3RD.R.E's. 1. 2/1S.M.F.AMB. 5. 2/5 GLOSTERS. 12.	
17.30.	D.S. inspected by A.D.M.S. & A.A.& Q.M.G.61st. DIV.					
18.30.				From 184 INF.BDE. re Watering Places. Also re rations for May 10th.		
22.0.	Instructions received that Unit less ½ B.Sec.Bearer Sub-Division were to move off at 6.0 to join Advance Guard at 6.30 at RD. JUNCT. W. of D.in HAZELDOWN.			From Officer Commanding Advanced Guard, giving time of start.		
22.30.	Instructions received that ½ Bearer Sub-Division was to move off at 6.0 to join Advance Guard at 6.30 at RD. JUNCT. W. of D.in HAZELDOWN.					

Reference ½ inch O.S. Map. Sheet 33.

Time.	Movements.	Destination.	Summary of messages.		Casualties.	Remarks.
			Sent.	Received.		
May 10.						
I.O.						CAPT. STOBIE admitted No.5275 Pte MILLER 2/4 ROYAL BERKS to Hospital Tent suffering from suspected measles.
2.20.				From 184 INF.BDE. that Amb. was to move off at 3.16 instead of 7.16.		
3.24.	Ambulance ready to move off. Waited for 2/4 R.BERKS to pass, and waited in vain.					
3.50.	Ambulance called to move on independently.					
3.57.	Joined column behind R.F's.					
6.0.	Breakfast halt.	Field S. of SAXELEY FARM.				
7.0.	O.C. attended at HDQRS. 184 INF.BDE.at Head of Column and received Bde.Order 10.5.16.D.S. to be opened at X Roads S.E.of MONKTON OAKCUTS.			Verbal message from BDE.MAJOR 184 INF BDE.		
	Troops advancing to assault QUARLEY HILL during which an Advanced Dressing Station would be necessary near GRATELEY.					
7.15.	Breakfast.					
7.45.	Ambulance moved off. Advance blocked by 2/2nd. FIELD ARTILLERY BDE.					
8.30.	Ambulance moved to X Roads S.E.of MONKTON OAKCUTS.					
9.5.	D.S. formed for reception of patients and casualties picked up and treated.				2/5 GLOSTERS. 2/4 R.BERKS.	1. 11.

Reference 1 inch O.S. Map. Sheet 123.

Time.	Movements.	Destination.	Summary of Messages.		Casualties.	Remarks.
			Sent.	Received.		
May 10.						
9.15.	D.S.established at Rd. S.E.of MONKTON OAKCUTS.		To A.D.M.S. BLACK SWAN INN?MONKTON. and 184 INF.BDE. reporting D.S.established.			
9.30.	CAPT. JAMIESON proceeded to ROWBERRY FARM to see PTE.KEEVES of B.Coy.2/1 BUCKS BATTN. and reported same to A.D.M.S.					
10.15.	O.C.proceeded to GRATELEY to find position for Advanced D.Station.					
10.40.	"C" Section under CAPT.HIRST formed A.D.S. close to windmill at GRATELEY.					
11.30.	A.D.M.S. visited D.Stn.					
11.30.	"Stand fast" sounded and O.C. proceeded to point 500 on Main Rd. AMESBURY-WEYHILL to Conference.					
12.20.	Dinner.					
13.30.	Ambulance moved to GRATELEY to "pick up" "C" Section.					
15.0.	Ambulance moved off from GRATELEY to PERHAM DOWN.					
16.40.	Ambulance arrived in Camp, having left PTE.MILLER 2/4 BERKS at TIDWORTH HOSPITAL.					
	No. 1 Camp. Perham Down. May 11th.1916.					

...............Major.R.A.M.C.(T).
O.C., 2/1st. South Midland Field Ambulance.

CONFIDENTIAL.

2/1ST. SOUTH MIDLAND FIELD AMBULANCE.

WAR DIARY, MAY 1916.

APPENDIX NO. 4.

Geo. Mackie.
Major, R.A.M.C.T.

REPORT ON DIVISIONAL ROUTE MARCH. MAY 19TH. 1916.

2/1st. South Midland Field Ambulance.

FALL IN. In accordance with instructions received from 182nd. INFANTRY BDE. the 2/IST. FIELD AMBULANCE paraded at 6.20 a.m.

POSITION IN COLUMN. In rear of 1/3rd. R.E.

PLACE. At X Roads S.W. Corner of No. 3 CAMP. PERHAM DOWN.

TIME. 6.44 a.m.

RENDEZVOUS. BULFORD RANGE.

LIEUT. MANUEL was sent ahead of the Unit to meet the Staff Officer at the Halt, in accordance with orders received. A place for resting was allotted, and instructions received as to watering of horses and filling of water carts.

The Unit arrived at the halting place at 8.45 a.m. for one hour's rest. Some 7 minutes were lost in getting all the teams away to the watering place as owing to one horse being lame one scratch team was awkward, and held up the formation into line.

WATERING OF HORSE. The watering was however successfully accomplished, and all N.C.O's and Men received their Haversack Ratiobs in the allotted time. The Unit moved off at 9.47.

The Water Carts had a long way to go to the supply, and were ten minutes late in returning, but rejoined the Unit within 300 yards of the Halting Place with their horses in duly watered and their carts more than $\frac{3}{4}$ filled.

ARRIVAL OF UNIT IN CAMP. The rest of the march was accomplished in good time, and the Unit, after many halts to pick up stragglers and to assist the sick who had fallen out, reached PERHAM DOWN at 1.40 p.m.

T.E. Mackie.
Major. R.A.M.C.T.

CONFIDENTIAL.

2/1ST. SOUTH MIDLAND FIELD AMBULANCE.

WAR DIARY. MAY 1916.

APPENDIX NO. 5

Geo. Mackie
Major. R.A.M.C.T.

NARRATIVE OF THE EMBARKATION ETC. OF THE

2/IST. SOUTH MIDLAND FIELD AMBULANCE.

R.A.M.C.(T).

DATE AND TIME.	NARRATIVE?
MAY 27TH. 22nd	
10.0.	The Ambulance paraded. Personnel etc. as below:-
	Officers. 11. (Includes Chaplain.)
	Other Ranks. 218.
	4 Wheeled Vehicles. 14.
	2 Wheeled Vehicles. 4.
	Horses. Riding. 15.
	Horses Draught. 41.
10.30.	The Ambulance marched out of Camp.
11.0.	Halt at TIDWORTH CORNER.
11.8.	Arrived at TIDWORTH STATION?
12.5.	Loading of waggons etc. completed, and entrainment of men completed.
12.50.	Train moved off.
14.20.	Train arrived at SOUTHAMPTON.
15.5.	All waggons, horses etc and personnel detrained, and entrained on the S.S.PANCRAS, except 2 Officers, and 80 men sent by RAILWAY TRANSPORT OFFICER to cross on S.S.CONNAUGHT.
18.14.	Parade of the whole Ambulance.
18.25.	All personnel aboard.
20.0.	The S.S.PANCRAS left SOUTHAMPTON DOCKS.
May 23rd.	
6.0.	Arrival at LE HAVRE.
8.30.	Interview with A.M.L.O. Detached party of 2 Officers and 80men dis-embarked alongside from S.S.CONNAUGHT.
9.0.	All men disembarked from S.S.PANCRAS.
10.40.	All waggons off boat. Two horses had to be slung.

CASUALTIES.

1. None to personnel.
2. 1 Water Cart Tap. Broken off in hold by bad handling by stevedores
3. 1 G.S.Baggage Waggon. Swingle bar broken through slinging. badly by stevedores
4. 1 Ambulance Waggon had two tyres cut from dragging by Stevedores in hold.

The waggons were parked at the end of shed at the QUAY in the following order:- HEADQUARTERS. 6IST. DIVISION.
2/IST. FIELD AMBULANCE.
ROYAL ENGINEERS.

Date and Time.	Narrative.
May 23rd.	
12.0.	Dinner.
13.20.	The Ambulance marched off, from DOCKS at LE HAVRE.
16.0.	Arrival at NO. 2 CAMP. SANVIC. LE HAVRE.
	The OFFICER COMMANDING interviewed the CAMP COMMANDANT. Orders were received from Divisional Staff regarding move of Unit. - Entrain at 12.0 on the 24th. inst. Point 1. Rations to be drawn at 12.0 at Point 4.
May 24.	
5.30.	Reveille.
6.0.	Packing waggons. The OFFICER COMMANDING interviewed the CAMP COMMANDANT with Parade States etc.
9.40.	Parade of Ambulance and Inspection. Fall in of Transport. G.S.Waggons leading.
9.50.	Guide reported his arrival at Camp.
10.0.	The Unit moved off. Route via LE HAVRE. Halt before Station
11.30.	Loading and boxing done. Entirely by Unit.
12.0.	All horses and transport entrained.
12.10.	All personnel entrained.
14.43.	Train moved off.
May 25.	
12.45.	Arrived at ST. OMER. Orders received that Ambulance was to detrain at BERGUETTE.
13.45.	Unit arrived at BERGUETTE.
14.7.	All personnel, horses and transport dis-entrained. CAPT. HIRST detached at the STATION to accompany the STAFF CAPTAIN 184TH. INFANTRY BRIGADE and conducted to Billeting Area allotted to Unit.
15.0.	Unit paraded and marched off. Motor lorry collected coats, packs etc. of working party of 20 men, left at BERGUETTE for unlaoding HEADQUARTERS 61ST. DIVISION baggage. Ambulance proceeded to destination via ST. VENANT.
18.10.	The Ambulance arrived at LE VERTBOIS FERME.
20.30.	Orders received from HEADQUARTERS. 184TH. INFANTRY BDE. re supplies. Arrangements made for QUARTERMASTER and Supply Waggons to start at 7.30 a.m.

G.E.Mackie.

................Major.R.A.M.C.(T).

Officer Commanding.

2/1st. South Midland Field Amb

No.

25th. May 1916.

2/IST. SOUTH MIDLAND FIELD AMBULANCE.R.A.M.C.(T). 6Ist. (SOUTH MIDLAND) DIVISION.

OFFICERS PROCEEDING OVERSEAS ON MAY 22ND. 1916,

Consecutive numbers by ranks.	Rank.	Name.	
1.	Lieut. Col.	—	
1.	Major.	Mackie.	G.
2.	Major.	—	
1.	Captain.	Burroughes.	H.N.
2.	Captain.	Hirst.	H.N.
3.	Captain.	Green.	P.H.
1.	Captain.	Jamieson.	T.H.
2.	Captain.	Lander.	C.L.
3.	Captain.	Stobie.	W,
-.	Lieut.	Evans.	W.J.
-.	Lieut.	Manuel.	J.
1.	Lieut.& Qrmr.	Rivers.	W.S.

..................Major.R.A.M.C.(T).
Officer Commanding 2/1st. South Mid. Fld. Amb.

No. 1 Camp. Perham Down.
Salisbury Plain.
May 22nd. 1916.

LANDING RETURN.

(To be rendered in duplicate.)

No. of Report _____
(For use in 3rd Echelon, General Headquarters.)

TO BE FURNISHED BY ALL ARMS, SERVICES AND DEPARTMENTS TO THE MILITARY LANDING OFFICER AT THE PLACE OF LANDING FOR DESPATCH TO THE 3RD ECHELON, GENERAL HEADQUARTERS.

Name of Vessel **PANCRAS** Port of Embarkation _Southampton_ Date _22 May 1916_

Place _Southampton_ Date of Embarkation _22-5-16_

RETURN showing numbers RATIONED by, and Transport on charge of *_2/1'3 South Midland Field Ambulance_

Detail.	Personnel.								Animals.				Guns, carriages and limbers, showing description.	Ammunition wagons and limbers.	Machine Guns.	Horsed.		Motor cars.	Tractors.	Lorries.	Mechanical.				Motor bicycles.	Bicycles.	Remarks.
	Officers.	Warrant officers.	Serjeants.	Trumpeters, &c.	Corporals.	Bombardiers and 2nd corporals.	Privates, gunners and sappers.	Troopers or drivers.	Total all ranks.	Horses.			Mules.				4-wheeled.	2-wheeled.				Workshop trucks.	Water tanks.	Travelling vans.	Trailers.		
										Riding.	Draught.	Pack.															
Effective strength of unit or train-load on entrain-ing.	11		16	–	10	6	133	29	154				1				14	4								2	
Casualties during journey.																											
Total casualties ...																											
Landing strength ...																											
Wanting to complete.																											

* Insert name of unit, stating if complete or a trainload of the same.

† Details of casualties are to be shown on the back of this form.

K. Mackie. Signature of Commander.
Major: RAMC. T.
O.C. 2/1st Field Ambulance

N.B.—This return will be rendered in place of those mentioned in paragraph 1652, King's Regulations.

(2596)

61a (AN Division)

2/1st S.M. Field Ambulance

June 1916

61st (S.M.) Division

Vol 2

(South Midland) T.A.

CONFIDENTIAL.

WAR DIARY OF

2/IST. FIELD AMBULANCE.

61ST. DIVISION.

JUNE 1916.

June 1916

COMMITTEE FOR THE
MEDICAL HISTORY OF THE WAR
Date 31 AUG. 1915

Army Form C.2118.

WAR DIARY
or
INTELLIGENCE SUMMARY.

Reference Sheet 36a. O.S. France.

(Erase heading not required.)

Instructions regarding War Diaries and Intelligence Summaries are contained in F.S. Regs., Part II. and the Staff Manual respectively. Title pages will be prepared in manuscript.

Place	Date	Hour	Summary of Events and Information	Remarks and references to Appendices
LE BERTBOIS FERME. K.26.a.5.8.	1916. June 1st.		General fatigues. Organisation of hospital - Medical, Surgical and Isolation departments. Bathing in R. LYS. Instructions received re attachment for instruction of O.C. and "A" Section to 129 Field Amb.	F.B.M. ADMS 38 Div. 38.D.M./83a. Geo.A.
DO.	June 2nd.		General routine work.	F.B.M.
DO.	June 3rd.		Inspection of equipment. Gas Helmet parade, and inspection. "A" Section paraded in full marching order, without section equipment, and proceeded under O.C. to 129th. Field Ambulance, for seven day's instruction. Location ; - LA GORGUE. L.35.b.9.9. Personnel. Officers 4:- MAJOR MACKIE. G. CAPTAIN STOBIE. W. LIEUT. MANUEL. J. LT.& QRMR.RIVERS. W.S. Other ranks. 56.	
DO.	June 4th.		Routine work. Church Parade. Gas demonstration for 80 men of Unit.	Auth.184 INF BDE. No.G.7.
DO.	June 5th.		Routine work. Inspection of all mechanical transport.	
DO.	June 6th.		Routine work.	
DO.	June 7th.		Routine work. Gas demonstration for 80 men of Unit.	Auth.184 INF Bde.No.G.7.
DO.	June 8th.		Routine work.	
DO.	June 9th.		Routine work. Erection of Bath-house, and establishment of Baths for 184th. INF. BDE. commenced. Preliminary orders received for move of Unit with 184 INFANTRY BRIGADE. - Equipment packed. MAJOR MACKIE returned from LA GORGUE.	Auth.ADMS 6I DIV.& 184 IN BDE. HDQRS.

Army Form C. 2118.

WAR DIARY
or
INTELLIGENCE SUMMARY.

Reference Sheets 36 and 36a, France.

(Erase heading not required.)

Instructions regarding War Diaries and Intelligence Summaries are contained in F.S. Regs., Part II. and the Staff Manual respectively. Title pages will be prepared in manuscript.

Place	Date	Hour	Summary of Events and Information	Remarks and references to Appendices
LA GORGUE. L.34.b.6.2.	June 10.	10.	Return of "A" Section from LA GORGUE cancelled. Remainder of Unit moved off from LE VERTBOIS FERME at 10.22 a.m. in rear of 184TH. INF. BDE. O.C. met D.A.D.M.S. 61ST. DIVISION & A.D.M.S. 38TH. DIVISION at LA GORGUE and received instructions to take over Hospital at LA GORGUE L.34.b.6.2. and A.D.S. at LAVENTIE G.34.c.6.3. "A" SECTION after weeks' instruction, proceeded to LAVENTIE under CAPTAIN STOBIE and LIEUT. MANUEL and took over the A.D.S. During move in D.D.M.S and D.D.M.S. XI CORPS visited premises.	GEM. GEM.
do.	June 11th.		Cleaning premises, and Hospital generally. A.D.M.S. 61ST. DIVISION inspected Hospital.	GEM.
do.	June 12th.		Hospital work and routine organised. Further inspect on in detail, of latrines, ablution, and other sanitary arrangements revealed conditions so thoroughly insanitary that it was decided to reconstruct the whole system. - Work begun. 2 N.C.O.s and 17 men detailed for Guard and Fatigues at XI CORPS LAUNDRY, MERVILLE ROAD. Instruction parties of I Officer, I N.C.O. and 9 men every three days to be attached to "A" SECTION 38 DIV at A.D.S. to learn @front line" routine. NO. 2923 PTE. WALKER. S. 4TH. BEDS att. 2/1ST. BUCKS BATTN. admitted to Hospital, suffering from self-inflicted bullet wound of left foot.	GEM. Auth.ADMS SECTION 38 DIV M.75.
do.	June 13th.		Routine work. 9 men detailed for Water Duties under DIVISIONAL SANITARY OFFICER at LA GORGUE. 5 men do. do. do. at PONT DU HEM. 5 men do. do. do. at PONT DU RIGEIUL. Field General Court Martial held on No. 2923 PTE. WALKER S. 4TH. BEDS. att. 2/1ST. BUCKS BATTN.	Auth.DIV. SAN.OFF. 12/6/16. GEM.
do.	June 14th.		Routine work. Hospital and premises inspected by A.D.M.S. 61ST. DIVISION.	GEM.
do.	June 15th.		Routine work. I N.C.O. and I Water Cart detailed for duty at HEADQUARTERS . 182ND. INFANTRY BDE.	Auth.O.C. 2/I S.MFA GEM.
do.	June 16th.		Routine work. Reconstruction of Packstore.	GEM.

WAR DIARY
or
INTELLIGENCE SUMMARY.

Army Form C. 2118

Instructions regarding War Diaries and Intelligence Summaries are contained in F.S. Regs., Part II. and the Staff Manual respectively. Title pages will be prepared in manuscript.

Reference (Sheet 36a. O.S. France and
(Sheet 36. Edition 6. O.S. France.

(Erase heading not required.)

Place	Date	Hour	Summary of Events and Information	Remarks and references to Appendices
LA GORGUE. L.34.b.6.2.	1916. June 16.		No. 34 CPL. POULSON and No. 1846 PTE. BANNISTER W.A. reported for duty from BASE. Gas alarm 1.30 a.m. Notice received from HEADQUARTERS, 61ST. DIVISION, and HAEDQUARTERS, 184TH. INFANTRY BRIGADE. Men paraded smartly - alarm proved abortive, and at 2.15 a.m. the men were released to billets.	Auth.ADMS. 61 Div. Festu.
DO.	June 17.		Routine work. A.D.M.S. 61ST. DIVISION inspected Hospital Books.	Festu.
DO.	June 18.		15 men detailed for duty at CORPS LABOUR DEPOT under CAPATAIN GREEN. The G.O.C. 61st. DIVISION (MAJOR GENERAL COLIN MACKENZIE.C.B) visited and inspected Hospital and Camp.	ADMS. M/224. 17/6/16. Festu.
DO.	June 19.		Routine work. BRIGADIER GENERAL GORDON.C.M.G. 182ND. INFANTRY BRIGADE, visited and inspected the Hospital. MAJOR MACKIE (O.C. 1ST. FIELD AMBULANCE) appointed President of Divisional Amusements Committee. A.D.M.S. 61ST. DIVISION visited Hospital.	Festu.
DO.	June 20.		Routine Work. A.D.M.S. 61ST. DIVISION inspected Sanitary improvements.	Festu.
DO.	June 21.		Routine work.	Festu.
DO.	June 22.		Routine work. CAPTAIN BURROUGHES proceeded to A.D.S. LAVENTIE with "B" Section, and took Command, vice CAPT. STOBIE, and "A" SECTION returned to LA GORGUE.	Auth. O.C. 1st. Fld.Amb. Festu.
DO.	June 23.		No. 1993 PTE. WALKER S.L. and No. 1944 PTE. HUBBAND.L.C. reported for duty from the BASE. Routine work.	Auth.O.C. Re-inforcemnts Rouen.21/6/16 Festu.
DO.	June 24.		Routine work. D.D.M.S. and D.A.D.M.S. XI CORPS visited and inspected the Hospital, Stores, Orderly Room, Books, and general arrangements of the Ambulance.	Festu.
DO.	June 25.		Routine work. New Hut for sick and wounded Officers' completed, furnished, and occupied.	Festu.

Army Form C. 2118.

WAR DIARY
or
INTELLIGENCE SUMMARY.

(Erase heading not required.)

Reference { Sheet 36 a. O.S. France. and
{ Sheet 36. Edition 6. O.S. France.

Instructions regarding War Diaries and Intelligence Summaries are contained in F.S. Regs., Part II. and the Staff Manual respectively. Title pages will be prepared in manuscript.

Place	Date	Hour	Summary of Events and Information	Remarks and references to Appendices
GORGUE. 34.b.6.2.	1916. June 26.		Routine work. DIVISIONAL THEATRE opened with a Variety Entertainment, and Cinematograph show. The 1ST. FIELD AMBULANCE contributing its quota to both orchestra and entertainment.	Fol.A
DO.	June 27.		LIEUT. 7% QUARTERMASTER RIVERS appointed permanent Transport Officer to Unit. Routine work. Lecture by OFFICER COMMANDING. 2nd. (LONDON) CASUALTY CLEARING STATION to Regimental Medical Officers and Officers of all three Field Ambulances held at Officers Mess of 1ST. FIELD AMBULANCE.	Auth. DDMS XI Corps & ADMS 61 Dv
DO.	June 28.		Routine work.	Fol.A
DO.	June 29th.		Routine work. 32 Casualties admitted after a raid by party of 184TH. INFANTRY BRIGADE.	Fol.A
DO.	June 30.		Routine work. O.C. with A.D.M.S. 61ST. DIVISION visited LAVENTIE to seek another A.D.S. if the present one became untenable, owing to the shelling of the town. G.O.C. 61ST. DIVISION visited patients in the Hospital. Field General Court Martial held on No.3371 SGT. WHEELER 2/4 ROYAL BERKS. REGT. after admission with an accidental self-inflicted wound of left foot.	Fol.A

F. Walacki

Major. R.A.M.C.(T).

O.C., 2/1st. Field Ambulance. 61st. Division.

June 30th. 1916.

CONFIDENTIAL.

2/1ST. FIELD AMBULANCE. 61ST. DIVISION.

APPENDIX 1.

JUNE 1916.

SPECIAL ORDERS FOR SATURDAY. JUNE 10TH. 1916.

- 10.0 a.m.   The whole of the personnel at LE VERTBOIS FERME will parade in full marching order.
- 10.10 a.m. Inspectio by the Officer Commanding.
- 10.22 a.m. Move Off.

The Ambulance will fall in rear of 184th. INFANTRY BRIGADE.

SPECIAL NOTE.   Haversack Rations will be carried.
Waterbottles filled.
Oil Sheets will be neatly folded, and placed on top of packs.
It is particularly brought to the notice of all N.C.O and Men of the Unit that the whole of the farm premises are to be left in a perfectly clean and tidy manner. Reveille has been fixed for 5 a.m. in order that there may be ample time for final cleaning and tidying of the farm buildings etc. immediately prior to departure.
The O.C. is confident that all ranks will make it a point of honour that the Farm shall be left, if possible, in a tidier state than it was when the Unit took possession of the premises.

SPECIAL ORDERS FOR TENT SUB-DIVISION OF "A" SECTION.

- 5.30 a.m.   Reveille.
- 6.30 a.m.   Breakfast.
- 7 - 8 a.m. Cleaning and tidying of premises.
- 8.15 a.m.   Parade and Inspection by CAPT. STOBIE.
- 8.25 a.m.   "A" SECTION will march off to LA GORGUE.

"A" Section arrived at Headquarters of the 129th. Field Ambulance at 9.45 a.m. and then received orders to proceed to LAVENTIE G.34.c.6.3. and take over the Advanced Dressing Station vacated by the 130th. FIELD AMBULANCE.
11.15 a.m. "A" Section had established A.D.S. at above point.

"B" and "C" Sections arrived at LA GORGUE L.34.b.6.2. at 2.45 p.m. and took over the Headquarters vacated by the 130TH. FIELD AMBULANCE.

----

4 p.m. Tea.

4.30 - 10 p.m. General Fatigues. Moving in equipment, stores etc. and "fixing up" Hospital etc.

10.15 p.m. Lights Out.

G E Wackie

Major. R.A.M.C.(T).
Officer Commanding.
2/1st. Field Ambulance.
61st. Division.

June 10th. 1916.

61st Division

211 S.M. Field Ambulance

July 1916

COMMITTEE FOR THE
MEDICAL HISTORY OF THE WAR
Date 13 SEP. 1915

CONFIDENTIAL.

WAR DIARY.

OF

2/1 South Midland
1ST. FIELD AMBULANCE.

61ST. DIVISION.

JULY 1916.

WAR DIARY
or
INTELLIGENCE SUMMARY.
(Erase heading not required.)

Army Form C. 2118.

Reference O.S. Maps. (Sheet 36. N.W.)
FRANCE. (Sheet 36. N.E.)
(Sheet 36. S.E.)
(Sheet 36. A. S.W.)

Place	Date	Hour	Summary of Events and Information	Remarks and references to Appendices
LA GORGUE. L.34.b.6.2.	1916. July 1st.		Routine Work.	Returns.
do.	July 2nd.		Church Parade. Routine work.	Gestn.
do.	July 3rd.		Routine work. D.D.M.S. and D.A.D.M.S. XIth. Corps visited and inspected Hospital and Premises. A.A. & Q.M.G. 61st. DIVISION inspected Hospital and Premises.	Gestn.
do.	July 4th.		Routine work.	Gestn.
do.	July 5th.		Routine work.	Gestn.
do.	July 6th.		Routine work. Inspection of Hospital and Premises by MAJOR GENERAL COLIN MACKENZIE C.B., G.O.C. 61st. DIVISION. A.D.M.S. 61st. DIVISION visited Hospital. 61ST. DIVISION suddenly ordered to extend its Front. 184TH. INFANTRY BRIGADE moved down towards NEUVE CHAPELLE. - 1ST. FIELD AMBULANCE ordered to be ready to move at a moments notice. All preliminary arrangements made for the move - stores packed etc.	Gestn.
		5 p.m.	1ST. FIELD AMBULANCE ordered to "stand fast", and to take over LA FLINQUE A.D.S. with EPINETTE Collecting Post and WINCHESTER HOUSE R.A.P. from 3RD. FIELD AMBULANCE, who were ordered South to VIELLE CHAPELLE. - All necessary arrangements quickly carried out. - All cases - 17 sick and 3 wounded - admitted to this Hospital from the 3RD. FIELD AMBULANCE. "C" SECTION despatched, under CAPTAIN HIRST and CAPTAIN LANDER to take over LA FLINQUE A.D.S. as ordered.	
		8 p.m.	All fresh dispositions completed.	
do.	July 7th.		Routine work. 3RD. FIELD AMBULANCE having vacated their Hospital, a "Holding Party" was installed from the 1ST. FIELD AMBULANCE. No. 2405 PTE. CROSS. A.S. and 2406 PTE. CROSS. W.S. reported from BASE. LE HAVRE. for duty.	Gestn.
do.	July 8th.		Medical Inspection of all ranks. A.D.M.S. 61ST. DIVISION visited and inspected Hospital.	Gestn.

WAR DIARY
or
INTELLIGENCE SUMMARY.

(Erase heading not required.)

Army Form C. 2118.

Instructions regarding War Diaries and Intelligence Summaries are contained in F.S. Regs., Part II. and the Staff Manual respectively. Title pages will be prepared in manuscript.

Reference O.S. Maps. (Sheet 36a. NE.
(Sheet 36. NW.
(Sheet 36a. SE.
(Sheet 36a. SW.
FRANCE.

Place	Date	Hour	Summary of Events and Information	Remarks and references to Appendices
LA GORGUE. L.34.b.6.2.	1916. July 9th.		Church Parade. Routine work. "B" Section vacated A.D.S. LAVENTIE, and were replaced by "A" SECTION under CAPTAIN STOBIE. D.D.M.S. and D.A.D.M.S. XI CORPS visited Hospital. A.D.M.S. 61ST. DIVISION inspected Hospital.	F.E.A.
do.	July 10th.		Routine work.	F.E.A.
do.	July 11th.		Routine work.	F.E.A.
do.	July 12th.		Routine work. NO. 2099 PTE. ARMITT. E. REPORTED to 61ST. DIVISIONAL MINING DETACHMENT for temporary water duties. A.D.M.S. 61ST. DIVISION visited and inspected Hospital.	Auth.A.D.M. 11/7/16. F.E.A.
do.	July 13th.		Routine work. D.A.Q.M.G. 61st. DIVISION visited Hospital, Camp and Transport of the Unit.	F.E.A.
do.	July 14th.		Routine work. "C" SECTION under CAPTAIN HIRST vacated LA FLINQUE A.D.S. handing over to a party from 95th. FIELD AMBULANCE. 31ST. DIVISION.	F.E.A.
do.	July 15th.		Routine work. Warning for the Ambulance to be in readiness for "active operations" received, and necessary dispositions made. - Extension of accomodation at A.D.S. LAVENTIE and D.3. LA GORGUE arranged. D.D.M.S. XIth. CORPS inspected arrangements made at both places.	F.E.A.
do.	July 16th.		Secret instructions received re "active operations". All dispositions made. 2 Officers reported from 93rd. FIELD AMBULANCE. 31ST. DIVISION, (CAPT. WALKER and CAPT. FRASER) to assist the Medical Staff. NO.2223 PTE. MARTIN A. wounded. No.2226 PTE. CLAYDON.T. and NO.2223 PTE. MARTIN A. wounded.	See app.1. Auth.H.Q.6. DIV. (Auth. XI Corps. F.E.A. See app. 2.
do.	July 17th.		Routine work. - Active operations delayed, owing to mist etc. D.A.D.M.S. 1ST. ARMY visited Hospital.	F.E.A.

WAR DIARY
or
INTELLIGENCE SUMMARY.
(Erase heading not required.)

Instructions regarding War Diaries and Intelligence Summaries are contained in F.S. Regs., Part II. and the Staff Manual respectively. Title pages will be prepared in manuscript.

Army Form C. 2118.

Reference O.S. Maps. (Sheet 36. N.W.
FRANCE. (Sheet 36. N.E.
(Sheet 36a. S.E.
(Sheet 36a. S.W.

Place	Date	Hour	Summary of Events and Information	Remarks and references to Appendices
LA GORGUE. L.34.b.6.2.	1916. July 18th.		Active operations postponed. Specially detailed detachments returned to their ordinary posts. A.D.M.S. 61ST. DIVISION visited Hospital.	Festu.
do.	do. July 19th.		Secret instructions received that "active hostilities" were to commence, but that "zero" would not be before 11 a.m. 2 Bearer Sub-Divisions of 2ND. FIELD AMBULANCE together with two Officers, reported for duty at HEADQUARTERS. LA GORGUE. to relieve all available Stretcher Bearers of 1ST. FIELD AMBULANCE. Original orders from HEADQUARTERS to hold good. - Original dispositions as detailed under appendix 1 again made. - All men in position by 1.30 p.m. Artillery offensive began about midday. Casualties began to arrive at A.D.S. LAVENTIE about 2 p.m. D.M.S. 1ST. ARMY and A.D.M.S. 61ST. DIVISION visited HEADQUARTERS. LA GORGUE. and A.D.S. LAVENTIE and RED HOUSE. R.A.P. D.D.M.S. XITH. CORPS and D.A.D.M.S. XITH. CORPS visited LA GORGUE and LAVENTIE, and found work proceeding smoothly. Reception and evacuation of wounded continued all night. 860 cases dealt with at A.D.S. LAVENTIE from 2 p.m. 19th. inst. - 9 a.m. on 20th. Special Casualty Wires sent off from HEADQUARTERS. LA GORGUE at 9 p.m. (19th. inst) and 6.0 a.m. and 12 noon (20th. inst) D.A.D.M.S. 61ST. DIVISION at RED HOUSE, and A.D.M.S. 61ST. DIVISION visited LA GORGUE and LAVENTIE.	See app. 2. P.Festu. See app. 3. 4.
do.	do. July 20th.		Cases continued to arrive most of the day. Official notification received from A.D.M.S. 61ST. DIVN. to withdraw part of personnel in forward area, at 12.0 noon and remainder at 4.0 p.m. This was duly carried out. 2nd. FIELD AMBULANCE party returned to MERVILLE at 6.0 p.m. No casualties reported in 1ST. FIELD AMBULANCE personnel. Roll Call at 7.0 p.m. All personnel accounted for.	G.Festu.
do.	do. July 21st.		Cleaning Hospital etc. Routine work. Congratulatory messages received. Inspection of Hospital and Premises by:- 1. GENERAL SIR CHARLES MONRO.G.C.M.G.,K.C.B. Commanding 1ST. ARMY. 2. LIEUT. GENERAL SIR R.C.B.HAKING. K.C.B. Commdg. XI ARMY CORPS. 3. MAJOR GENERAL COLIN MACKENZIE.C.B. G.O.C. 61ST. DIV. 4. COLONEL R.H.FIRTH. D.D.M.S. XITH.	See app. 5. Festu.

WAR DIARY
or
INTELLIGENCE SUMMARY.
(Erase heading not required.)

Instructions regarding War Diaries and Intelligence Summaries are contained in F.S. Regs., Part II. and the Staff Manual respectively. Title pages will be prepared in manuscript.

Army Form C. 2118.

Reference O.S. Maps. (Sheet 36a. N.E.
FRANCE. (Sheet 36. N.W.
(Sheet 36a. S.E.
(Sheet 36a. S.W.

Place	Date	Hour	Summary of Events and Information	Remarks and references to Appendices
L.34.b.6.2. LA GORGUE.	1916. July 22nd.		Medical Inspection of all ranks. Routine work. Special message to 61st. DIVISION by SIR DOUGLAS HAIG. G.C.B., K.C.I.E., K.C.V.O., A.D.C., COMMANDER IN CHIEF. BRITISH ARMIES IN FRANCE. 2 reinforcements from BASE. LE HAVRE. No. 1927 PTE. FRENCH.W.E. and NO. 2461 PTE. TAYLOR.G.W. reported for duty.	See app. 5. *[sig]*
do. do.	July 23rd.		Routine work.	*[sig]*
do. do.	July 24th.		Routine work. A.D.M.S. 61ST. DIVISION inspected Hospital. No. 1874 L/CPL. BAKER. C. reported for duty with 94TH. FIELD AMBULANCE.	Auth.ADMS 61st, Div. *[sig]*
do. do.	July 25th.		Routine work. - 988 PTE. HODGETTS.G.H. A.S.C."attached" reported to R.T.O. LA GORGUE, to be sent to BASE HORSE TRANSPORT DEPOT. PTE. BENNETT. J. G. 1ST. FLD. AMB. struck off effective strength of Unit, reporting to A.D.M.S. 61ST. DIVISION permanently.	DO. *[sig]*
do. do.	July 26th.		Routine work.	*[sig]*
do. do.	July 27th.		Routine work. A.D.M.S. visited Hospital. Instructions received re prospective move of 1ST. FIELD AMBULANCE to MERVILLE.	*[sig]*
DO. do.	July 28th.		Routine work. O.C. visited CORPS REST STATION, OFFICERS' REST STATION and BATHS. MERVILLE, and CORPS SKIN DEPOT. REGNIER-LE-CLERC, and saw O.C. 2ND. FIELD AMBULANCE to arrange details of transference of the two Units. 20 N.C.O's and Men of the 1ST. FIELD AMBULANCE reported to O.C.2ND. FIELD AMB. at MERVILLE. 20 N.C.O's and Men of the 2ND. FIELD AMBULANCE reported to O.C.1ST. FIELD AMB. at LA GORGUE.	*[sig]*
do. do.	July 29th.		Routine work. 2ND. 50 N.C.O's and Men of the 1ST. FIELD AMBULANCE reported to O.C.XXX. FIELD AMB. at MERVILLE. 50 N.C.O's and Men of the 2ND. FIELD AMBULANCE reported to O.C.1ST. FIELD AMB. at LA GORGUE.	*[sig]*

WAR DIARY or INTELLIGENCE SUMMARY.

(Erase heading not required.)

Army Form C. 2118.

Reference O.S. Maps. (Sheet 36a. N.E.)
(Sheet 36. N.W.)
Sheet 36a. S.E.
(Sheet 36a. S.W.)
FRANCE.

Place	Date	Hour	Summary of Events and Information	Remarks and references to Appendices
L.34.b.6.2. LA GORGUE.	1916. July 30th.		Routine work. Church Parades. Parchments for meritorious conduct in the Field, from the G.O.C. 61ST. DIVISION, for 2226. PTE. CLAYDON. T. and 2223 PTE. MARTIN. A. of the 1ST. FIELD AMBULANCE, received from the A.D.M.S. 61ST. DIVISION. 1ST. FIELD AMBULANCE took over the SKIN HOSPITAL at REGNIER LE CLERCQ (Map reference K.34.d.8.8.) 2ND. FIELD AMBULANCE took over ADVANCED DRESSING STATION. LAVENTIE.	Gev.
L.34.b.6.2. LA GORGUE and K.29.d.1.9. MERVILLE.	July 31st.	4 p.m.	A.D.M.S. 61ST. DIVISION visited Hospital prior to departure of Unit from LA GORGUE. Move completed. D.D.M.S. XI CORPS and A.D.M.S. 61ST. DIVISION notified of arrival of Unit.	Gev.

G.E. Mackie.
Major. R.A.M.C.(T).
Officer Commanding.
1st. Field Amb. 61st. Division.

August 1st. 1916.

CONFIDENTIAL.

APPENDIX. 1.

2/1st. FIELD AMBULANCE.

61ST. DIVISION.

WAR DIARY. - JULY 1916.

ADVANCED DRESSING STATION. LAVENTIE.

MAJOR MACKIE.
CAPT. STOBIE.
LIEUT. EVANS.

STAFF SGT. BURLING.
STAFF SGT. ROBINSON.

MARSHAL.   SGT. CLEMENTS.

RECEIVING AND
DRESSING ROOM.   L/C AUSTIN.   CHAMBERLAIN.)
                 KAYE.   BLACKHAM.   )   SGT. JOHNSON 1/.
                 HAMAR.   CROSS.   )
                 SMOUT.   CROSS.   )

STRETCHER BEARERS.   HERBERT.
                     BAILEY.
                     SMITH, S.J.P.

COOKS.   HICKINBOTHAM and WATT.

LOADERS.   LOWE. E.   FLETCHER. W.
           LOWE. F.   FLETCHER. J.
           BRYAN.   GAFFRON.

ARMOURER SGT.   TO BE DETAILED.

STEEL SHELTER COLLECTING POST.

CAPTAIN HIRST.

NURSING ORDERLIES.   STRETCHER BEARERS.
     L/C. MILES.   CPL. BAKER.
     L/C. DUNN.   THICKETT.   LATHAM.
     WORT.   HUNT.   TOLLEY.

CYCLIST ORDERLY.   GILBERT. R.E.

RED HOUSE. REGTL. AID POST.

CAPTAIN GREEN.

NURSING ORDERLIES.   STRETCHER BEARERS.
   GOODE. J.   LOADERS.   SGT. PERRY.
   PARTINGTON.   PERRINS.   MULLETT.
   WILKINS.   LOXTON.   CROWDER.   MEREDITH.   SMITH. H.
                  PERRY.   BENNETT.   FIELD.   GOODE. W.
                  WALKER.   L/C.WARMINGTON.   WHITBY.   HOBSON.
RIFLE CLEANING ORDERLY.   GILKES.   TAYLOR. F.
  TO BE DETAILED.   BLUCK.   FORTNUM.

HOUGOMONT REGTL. AID POST.

NURSING ORDERLIES.   STRETCHER BEARERS.   WHEELED STRETCHER BEARERS.

   MOORE.   L/C. EVANS.   L/C. GREEN.   BEECH.
   WOOD.   HERCUS.   BATES.   L/C. BANNISTER.   BRITTEN.
   HODGETTS.   TAYLOR.   B.BECK.   CLINTON.   STINTON.
                     COTTERELL. GARVEY.   WHITE.   FOX.
                     DRAKE.   ASKEY.   LACEY.   BOTT.
                     HANDS.   THOMPSON.R.   MASON.   MANN.
                     WIGGINS.   MCINTYRE.   LINCOLN.   PRICE.
                                               GEOGHEGAN.   ASPINALL.
RIFLE CLEANING ORDERLY.   HARRISON.   WHITMORE.
  TO BE DETAILED.   COOPER.   MAISEY

J.E. Mackie
MAJOR R.A.M.C. (T)
OFFICER COMMANDING
2/1st SOUTH MID. FIELD AMBULANCE

S E C R E T.   MEDICAL ARRANGEMENTS.

MAIN DRESSING STATIONS.   IST. FIELD AMBULANCE.   LA GORGUE. L.34.b.6.2.
                          3RD. FIELD AMBULANCE.   LA GORGUE. L.35.b.9.9.

ADVANCED DRESSING STATION.   LAVENTIE.   C.34.c.6.3.

COLLECTING POST.   LAVENTIE EAST. M.5.c.7.9.

REGIMENTAL AID POSTS.   RED HOUSE. M.6.d.2.0.

                        HOUGOMONT. M.12.c.3.4.

In addition to the above it is proposed to utilize the DIVISIONAL THEATRE LA GORGUE for sitting and walking cases.

The personnel for this will be found by the O.C. 3RD. FIELD AMB.

One additional Officer and 12 Stretcher Bearers will be detailed for duty at each of the Regimental Aid Posts.

At the Collecting Post the personnel will be one Officer and eight men. In addition, 50 Stretcher Bearers will be detailed for duty with 20 Wheeled Stretchers, working between the Regimental Aid Posts and Advanced Dressing Stations.

At the A.D.S. it is proposed to utilize a Barn, and if necessary, the Goods Shed at the RAILWAY STATION. LAVENTIE, for walking and slightly wounded cases.

There will be available fourteen DEASEY MOTOR AMBULANCES and 4 FORD AMBULANCES. Two of these Cars will be retained at each of the Main Dressing Stations for the evacuation of urgent cases.

Empty cars will travel to LAVENTIE by road crossing RAILWAY and LA BASSEE ROAD, and loaded cars will return to Main Dressing Station via NOUVEAU MONDE and ESTAIRES.

Evacuation of wounded from trenches will be by GREAT NORTH ROAD and STRAND to RED HOUSE and HOUGOMONT respectively.

The fullest possible use will be made of the GREAT NORTHERN and GREAT CENTRAL Tram Lines.

@@@@@@@@@@@@@@@@@@@@@@@@@@@

SPECIAL ORDERS FOR THE 1ST. FIELD AMBULANCE

DURING ACTIVE OPERATIONS.

1. **PERSONNEL.** Personnel and disposition will be found on the attached form. In the event of any shortage, from exhaustion or casualty, the 3RD. FIELD AMBULANCE will supply the necessary personnel at short notice.

2. **DRESSINGS.** Extensive dressings will not be carried out at R.A.P's or the STEEL SHELTER or at the ADVANCED DRESSING STATION.
CAPTAIN STOBIE, CAPTAIN GREEN and CAPTAIN HIRST will see that the supply of 1st. Field Dressings, Shell Dressings, Splints etc. is ample at the A.D.S. RED HOUSE, HOUGOMONT and the STEEL SHELTER.
At least 1500 A.T.S. Phials will be available at Main Dressing Station before operations commence. - Captain BURROUGHES will arrange this, and will draw on the 3RD. FIELD AMBULANCE if necessary.

3. **COMMUNICATION.** Two Motor Cyclists L/CPL. SILVER and PTE. VAUGHAN will be stationed at the A.D.S. LAVENTIE at the disposal of the O.C.
One Cyclist (PTE. GILBERT. R.E.) will be stationed at the STEEL SHELTER. LAVENTIE EAST.

4. **REGULATION OF TRAFFIC.** For the regulation of traffic, and to control admissions and discharges and disposal of all patients as they arrive or depart, three Marshals and two Guides will be provided
   (a) at LA GORGUE.   STAFF SGT. JACQUES.
   Marshals (b) at A.D.S. LAVENTIE. SGT. CLEMENTS.
   (c) at RED HOUSE.   SGT. PERRY.

   Guides. (d) at HOUGOMONT.   PTE. BECK.
   (e) at STEEL SHELTER. PTE. GILBERT. R.E.

5. **LOCATION OF PATIENTS IN VARIOUS PLACES.**
Special orders are attached to indicate the precise method of admitting patients, so that all available accomodation maybe used to the best advantage.

6. **COOKING** will go on continuously, and a plentiful supply of boiling water will be ready. - The Cooks will work in relays of three for four hours at a time. Two Cooks, HICKINBOTHAM & WATT will work at the A.D.S.
No cooking will be done at the STEEL SHELTER.

7. **RELIEF FOR BEARERS.** This will be arranged by the Officer Commanding on report being brought in by the Motor Cyclists and Cyclist at intervals when called for.
20 men of the 3RD. FIELD AMBULANCE will be stationed at the STEEL SHELTER, and will be utilised as a FIRST RELIEF along the HOUGOMONT- RED HOUSE ROAD when considered necessary.

8. **CLERKS.** No clerking will be done forward of the Main Dressing Station. There, the arrangements for admission will be as at present in force under the charge of SGT. GREEN and all departures will be superintended by SGT. BICKELL.

9. **CONTROLLING OFFICER.**
If circumstances allow, CAPT. BURROUGHES will act as Controlling Officer at Main Dressing Station, and will be in charge of all Marshals, Clerks etc. and control all traffic, and all dispositions at LA GORGUE.

10. **SECTION IN READINESS.** "C" SECTION's stores will be packed and the loaded Waggons parked along with the baggage waggons (empty) in the rear of the main Dressing Station, so that, if necessary, the whole Section can move complete in 20 minutes.

EVACUATION. Motor Ambulances will go right up, and clear direct from
RED HOUSE if hostile shelling permits.
ROUTE.
(a) All Motor Ambulances will proceed from LA GORGUE via
RUE DE LA GENDARMERIE across the LA BASSEE ROAD, and thence
to LAVENTIE.
(b) The return journey will be via the SAILLY ROAD through
ESTAIRES and back to LA GORGUE via the PONT DE LA MEUSE.
Eight Horse Ambulance Waggons will be left in reserve behind
A.D.S. LAVENTIE for the removal of slighter cases.
All slight and walking cases will go to CAPTAIN HIRST at the
cSTEEL SHELTER at LAVENTIE EAST, and when he requires the Horse
Ambulance convoy, he will send PTE. GILBERT to the O.C. at the
A.D.S.LAVENTIE. - PTE. GILBERT will then return with the Convoy,
acting as guide.

DISCIPLINE. All ranks will remember that the only danger which can be foreseen
is overkeenness, and excess of zeal. - There will be no occasion
for any excitement or fuss, which can only lead to confusion.
All ranks are specially ordered to work silently and quickly,
and to stick to their own jobs absolutely, so that the wounded
men under their care may receive every attention possible.
Meals for personnel will be served where, and when possible.

AMMUNITION ETC. It is notified for information that an Armourer Sergeant has been
detailed for duty at the A.D.S. LAVENTIE and one "T.U." Man
for each of the R.A.P's. These men are detailed for the sole
purpose of cleaning rifles of wounded who may be brought there.
All arms, ammunition and bombs must be handed over at LAVENTIE to
the keeping of the Armourer Sergeant there.

Geo. Mackie.
MAJOR R. A. M. C. (T.)
OFFICER COMMANDING
2/1st SOUTH MID. FIELD AMBULANCE

HEADQUARTERS STAFF.

CAPTAIN BURROUGHES.
CAPTAIN LANDER.
CAPTAIN JAMIESON.
LIEUT. & QRMR. RIVERS.

Marshal.	STAFF SGT. JACQUES.
RECEIVING ROOM) AND UNLOADING) ORD'RLIES.)	To be detailed from personnel of the 2nd. Field Ambulance.
DRESSING ROOM.	CHAPPEL.) EDWARDS. F.T.) SGT. CRANWELL i/c. CHANCE.) BISSELL.)

CLERKS.
- ARRIVALS.   L/C. LOTHEIM.)
 JAMES.) SGT. GREEN i/c.
- DEPARTURES.   L/C. ALDRIDGE.)
 CARTWRIGHT. P.) SGT. BICKELL. i/c.
- A. & D. BOOK.   MIDDLETON.)
 THOMPSON. L.)

PACKSTORE.
    CPL. ROBERTS.
    CPL. SMITH.
    L/C. BANNISTER.
    RICKETTS.

HOSPITAL.
- WARDS 1 AND 2. SGT. SMITH i/c.   DENHAM.)   BRIGGS.)
                                           TRUEMAN.) Ward 1.   OWENS.) Ward 2.
- WARDS 3 AND 4. SGT. SITCH i/c.   GOODE. G.)   LINFORTH.)
                                           CLERKE.)Ward 3.   MASTERS.) Ward 4.
- TENTS.   CPL. HILLIAR i/c. Two 2ND. FLD. AMB. Orderlies to assist.
- SHELTERS.   SGT. WHEELDON i/c. ROGERS.
                            2 Men from 2ND. FIELD AMBULANCE.
- OFFICERS.   BROWN. S.
                 PALSER.

DISPENSERS.   SGTS. PARRY AND ROGERS.

SANITARY.   SGT. SIMPSON & PTE. ALLEN.

COOKS.   SGT. DIX. CPL. PEWSEY. WHITMARSH. EDWARDS. DUCKERIN. HEMMING & BROWN. H.

QUARTERMASTERS STORES. Q.M.S.TAYLOR. SGT. ATTRILL. BALL. BATE. CARTWRIGHT.P.

WATER CARTS.   GRAIN. SMITH.R.W.

WAGGON ORDERLIES.
    ROBERTS.   GRAY.
    GEORGE.   BRANT.
    NEWEY.   FLOYD.
    ELLIOTT.

F.W.Mackie
MAJOR R. A. M. C.
OFFICER COMMANDING
2/1ST SOUTH MID. FIELD AMBULANCE

CONFIDENTIAL.

APPENDIX. 11.

1ST. FIELD AMBULANCE.

61ST. DIVISION.

WAR DIARY. - JULY 1916.

1ST. FIELD AMBULANCE. - 61ST. DIVISION.

@"@"@"@"@"@"@"@"@"@"@"@"@"@"@"@"@"@"@"@

REPORT ON ACT OF GALLANTRY. JULY 16TH.

The following particulars of an incident showing gratifying devotion to duty on the part of two Stretcher Bearers of this Ambulance, are forwarded for your information, please.

On the evening of Sunday, July 16th. about 9.30 p.m.

No. 2226 PTE. CLAYDON. T.

and   No. 2223 PTE. MARTIN. A.S

were bringing a wounded man on a Stretcher from the R.A.P. at HOUGOMONT to RED HOUSE for evacuation, when a shell burst on the road, close to the Stretcher.

Fortunately, the patient escaped further injury, but both bearers were badly injured.

MARTIN suffered a bad wound of the chin, which fractured his jaw, and loosened most of his teeth, and CLAYDON received a large perfporating wound of the left forearm, and monor wounds of the face.

Both men, though bleeding profusely, retained their presence of mind, and continued to hold on to the stretcher, thus saving the patient from a dangerous fall. They also proceeded steadily along the road, endeavouring to bring theirpatient to a place of safety, and entirely disregarding their own condition.

They were soon relieved of their burden by others, but they refused to have their own wounds attended to, until they had been repeatedly assured that their patient had been safely transferred to the Ambulance Waggon.

In my opinion, they acted throughout with the most remarkable courage and coolness, and showed a most exemplary devotion to the wounded man who was in their charge.

@"@"@"@"@"@"@"@"@"@"@"@"@"@"@"@"@"@"@"@

T. E. Mackie.

MAJOR R. A. M. C. (T.)
OFFICER COMMANDING
2/1ST SOUTH MID. FIELD AMBULANCE

CONFIDENTIAL.

APPENDIX. III.

1st. FIELD AMBULANCE.

61ST. DIVISION.

WAR DIARY. - JULY 1916.

COPIES OF CASUALTY WIRES. - JULY 19TH. - 20TH.

1.

To: A.D.M.S. 6IST. DIVISION.   SENDERS NO.C.A.S. 1.

Admitted wounded 40 aaa remaining lying 20 sitting 15 unfit for transport nil aaa

9 p.m.   (sgd) H.N.BURROUGHES CAPT.R.A.M.C.(T).
IST. FLD. AMB. 6IST. DIVN.

2.

To: A.D.M.S. 6IST. DIVISION.   SENDERS NO.C.A.S. 2.

Admitted wounded 118 aaa remaining lying 15 sitting 20 unfit for transport 2 aaa

Admitted 2 German Prisoners wounded, remaining two aaa

6 a.m.   (sgd) H.N.BURROUGHES. CAPT. R.A.M.C.(T).
IST. FLD. AMB. 6IST. DIVN.

3.

To: A.D.M.S. 6IST. DIVISION.   SENDERS NO. C.A.S. 3.

Admitted wounded 60 aaa remaining lying 22 sitting 28 unfit for transport 2 aaa

12.0 noon.   (sgd) GEORGE MACKIE. MAJOR R.A.M.C.(T).
O.C. IST. FLD. AMB. 61 DIV.

4.

To: A.D.M.S. 6IST. DIVISION.   SENDERS NO. C.A.S. 4.

Admitted wounded 19 aaa remaining lying 24 sitting 52 unfit for transport nil aaa

8.45 p.m.   (sgd) GEORGE MACKIE.MAJOR.R.A.M.C.(T).

CONFIDENTIAL.

APPENDIX. IV.

1ST. FIELD AMBULANCE.

61ST. DIVISION.

WAR DIARY. - JULY 1916.

COPIES OF MESSAGES RECEIVED AFTER ACTIVE OPERATIONS.
JULY 19TH. - 20TH. 1916.

The following message from the GENERAL OFFICER COMMANDING IN CHIEF, BRITISH ARMIES IN FRANCE, is published for the information of all ranks:-

"Please convey to the troops engaged night 19/20 my appreciation of
"their gallant effort and thorough preparation made for it. I wish them
"to realise that their enterprise has not been by any means in vain,
"and that the gallantry with which they carried out the attack is
"fully recognised."

                           CHIEF.

                    (sgd) C.C.MARINDIN. Lieut. Colonel.
                       A.A. & Q.M.G. 61st. Division.

D.H.Q. 20/7/16.

    I have much satisfaction in publishing the following message from the Corps Commander:-

"G.R. 39. 20/7/16.
"I wish to convey to all ranks of your Division my appreciation of the
"gallant attack carried out yesterday by them. - Although they were
"unable to consolidate the ground gained, the effect on the enemy will
"be far reaching, and will prevent him from moving troops away from our
"front to the South. - I wish you all in your next attack a more
"complete and permanent victory, and that you may reap the full fruit
"of the energy and skill displayed by all Commands, and their Staffs
"in the execution of their tasks."

                    (signed) R.HAKING. Lieut. General.
                       Commanding. XIth. Corps.

20/7/16.

    The Division has not only fought gallantly, but all ranks of every arm and service have carried out in the most exemplary and devoted manner, working day and night, an amount of labour which has highly tested their endurance and discipline, and merits my unqualified praise.

                    (sgd) COLIN MACKENZIE. Major General.
                       Commanding 61st. Division.

To: O.C., 2/1ST. FIELD AMBULANCE.

    The D.D.M.S. XIth. CORPS has asked me to convey to all ranks his appreciation of the excellent work which they have done during the last 24 hours. - Will you please let this be known to all your Officers N.C.O's and Men.

                    (sgd) JAMES YOUNG. Colonel.
                      A.D.M.S. 61st. Division.

20/7/16.

To: O.C., 2/1ST. FIELD AMBULANCE.

    Will you please convey to your Officers, N.C.O's and men, including Mechanical and other Transport Drivers, my very high appreciation of the splendid way in which they carried out their duties during the recent operations.

    All ranks vied with each other, in displaying an untiring keenness in the performance of their respective duties, and showed the utmost care and consideration for their wounded comrades.

                    (sgd) JAMES YOUNG. Colonel.
                      A.D.M.S. 61st. Division.

20/7/16.

CONFIDENTIAL.

ooooooooooooooooooo of S.M. Div. Volume 4

Aug 1916.   Vol. 4

2/1 So. Midland F.A.

W A R   D I A R Y.

for the month of

A U G U S T   1 9 1 6.

R. Obder

1st. Field Ambulance. 61st. Divn.

September 1st. 1916.

-o-o-o-o-o-o-o-o-

COMMITTEE FOR THE
MEDICAL HISTORY OF THE WAR
Date -5 OCT.1915

Army Form C. 2118.

WAR DIARY
or
INTELLIGENCE SUMMARY.
(Erase heading not required.)

Reference O.S. Maps.
FRANCE. SHEET 36a, N.E.

Instructions regarding War Diaries and Intelligence Summaries are contained in F. S. Regs., Part II. and the Staff Manual respectively. Title pages will be prepared in manuscript.

Place	Date	Hour	Summary of Events and Information	Remarks and references to Appendices
K 29.d.1.9. MERVILLE. 1916	August 1st.		Routine Work. Cleaning premises and arranging Equipment etc. Inspection of premises at CORPS REST STATION, MERVILLE, CORPS SKIN DEPOT, REGNIER LE CLERC; and OFFICERS' REST STATION, CHATEAU DEMON by OFFICER COMMANDING. A.D.M.S. 61st DIVISION visited Hospital. CAPTAIN H.N.BURROUGHES temporarily detached, in charge OFFICERS' REST STATION. CAPTAIN W.J.HIRST and CAPTAIN W.STOBIE, temporarily detached in charge CORPS SKIN DEPOT.	Festu.
do.	August 2nd.		Arrangement of Personnel throughout various departments. G.E. XI Corps visited and inspected CORPS REST STATION.	Festu.
DO.	August 3rd.		Routine Work. D.D.M.S. XIth Corps visited and inspected Hospital. CAPTAIN ACHESON, R.A.M.C. transferred to CASUALTY CLEARING STATION, suffering from Debility following upon former Poliomyelitis anterior acuta.	Festu.
do.	August 4th.		Routine Work. Ventilation of Huts improved by extra louvre ventilation in ends of same.	Festu.
do.	August 5th.		Routine Work.	Festu.
do.	August 6th.		Routine Work. Church Parade. O.C. and 3 Officers attended special service commemorating 2nd Anniversary of Declaration of War, at BETHUNE.	Auth, A.D.M.S. 61st Div.
do.	August 7th.		Routine Work. Name of CORPS SKIN DEPOT changed to CORPS SCABIES DEPOT. A.D.M.S. 61st DIVISION visited and inspected premises. No, 1827 CORPORAL CLINTON, G.H. awarded MILITARY MEDAL for Gallantry at FAUQUISSART.	Festu. Auth.D.D.M.S. XIth Corps. Auth 61 Div Order, 252.
do.	August 8th.		Routine Work. Construction of Shelter Shed for patients and Dining Shelter for Nursing Personnel commenced. Staff Sergeant Major MARLOW No.2.CO, 61st DIVISIONAL TRAIN, reported for duty vice Staff Sergeant Major J.DIX, transferred to No.2.Co, A.S.C. for training.	Festu.

Army Form C. 2118.

WAR DIARY
or
INTELLIGENCE SUMMARY.
(Erase heading not required.)

Instructions regarding War Diaries and Intelligence Summaries are contained in F.S. Regs., Part II. and the Staff Manual respectively. Title pages will be prepared in manuscript.

Reference O.S. Maps. FRANCE. Sheet 36a, N.E.

Place	Date	Hour	Summary of Events and Information	Remarks and references to Appendices
K 29.d.1.9. MERVILLE.	1916. August 9th.		Routine Work. Cases received from 30th DIVISION for first time. Parade of "B" Section, BEARER SUB DIVISION complete under CAPTAIN BURROUGHES - All ranks warned to hold themselves in readiness to move off at 1 hours notice at any time.	F8th.
do	August 10th		Routine Work. D.A.D.M.S. XIth Corps visited and inspected premises.	F8th.
do	August 11th		Routine Work. CAPTAIN STOBIE proceeded to EDINBURGH on leave of absence for 7 days. LIEUT. W.J.EVANS detailed for duty at CORPS SCABIES DEPOT vice CAPTAIN STOBIE. 1640. SERGEANT SIMPSON detailed to attend GAS COURSE.	Auth A.D.M.S. 61 Div. F8th. Auth A.D.M.S. 61 Div. F8th.
do	August 12th		Routine Work. Picnic and sports for 150 convalescent patients held at LE VERTBOIS FARM, LE SART.	F8th.
do	August 13th		Routine Work. Church Parade. Shelter for patients completed.	
do	August 14th		Routine Work. D.A.D.M.S. XIth Corps visited and inspected premises. Light Weight Boxing Competition, 61st DIVISION at LA GORGUE won by 2093, PRIVATE WHITBY.G.	F8th.
do	August 15th		Routine Work. Fire Drill and Practice.	F8th.
do	August 16th		Routine Work. No 1768, PRIVATE BAKER,E.C. proceeded to BIRMINGHAM on special leave. No 1929, PRIVATE CROSS,E.M.C.) reported for duty from BASE. No 2341, PRIVATE JONES,W.E.)	Auth A.D.M.S. 61st Div. Auth A.D.M.S. 61st Div.
do				F8th.

Army Form C. 2118.

WAR DIARY
or
INTELLIGENCE SUMMARY.
(Erase heading not required.)

Instructions regarding War Diaries and Intelligence Summaries are contained in F.S. Regs., Part II. and the Staff Manual respectively. Title pages will be prepared in manuscript.

Map reference. Sheet 36a.
FRANCE.

Place	Date	Hour	Summary of Events and Information	Remarks and references to Appendices
MERVILLE. K.29.d.1.9.	1916. Aug. 17th.		Routine work. CAPT. EVANS. I.D., R.A.M.C. reported for duty from BASE. Construction of new latrines commenced.	Gista
do.	Aug. 18th.		Routine work. CAPTAIN STOBIE returned from leave and resumed duty at CORPS SKIN DEPOT. CAPTAIN BURROUGHES selected as M.O. i/c new XI CORPS OFFICERS' REST STATION at BUSNES CHATEAU. D.D.M.S. and D.A.D.M.S. XI CORPS visited and inspected premises. A.D.M.S. 61st. DIVISION visited and inspected premises.	Gista
do.	Aug. 19th.		Routine work. Daily cleaning party detailed from 1ST. FIELD AMBULANCE and Patients to prepare for occupation BUSNES CHATEAU.	Gista
do.	Aug. 20th.		Routine work. Church Parades.	Gista
do.	Aug. 21st.		Routine work. Incinerator rebuilt. Reconstruction of existing Bath-house commenced. Corps Rest Station selected as store for Corps Stretchers - stretchers brought into use as beds throughout the Rest Station. - All stretchers inspected, and broken ones removed, for despatch to D.A.D.O.S. 61ST. DIVISION for repair.	Gista
do.	Aug. 22nd.		Gas Helmet Inspection and parade, and Gas Helmet Drill under the O.C. and SGT. SIMPSON. 1851 L/CPL. AUSTIN. R.G. proceeded to LA GORGUE on Course of Instruction at Gas School. G.O.C. 61ST. DIVISION (MAJOR GENERAL COLIN MACKENZIE.C.B.,) visited the CORPS REST STATION. D.D.M.S. XI CORPS visited the Rest Station. Construction of new latrines completed. Rebuilding and extension of Bath-house at CORPS REST STATION commenced.	Auth.A.D.M.S 61st.Divn. Gista
do.	Aug. 23rd.		Routine work. - Gas Helmet Inspection and Parade for staff of Scabies Depot and Transport Sed. No. 1832 PTE. PEERS. A.E. reported for duty from No. 1 TERRITORIAL BASE DEPOT. No. 161791? DRIVER RIDLER. H.M.T. COY. A.S.C., taken suddenly ill.	Gista

T2134. Wt. W708-776. 500000. 4/15. Sir J. C. & S.

WAR DIARY
or
INTELLIGENCE SUMMARY.

(Erase heading not required.)

Army Form C. 2118.

Reference O.S. Map. Sheet 36a.
FRANCE.

Place	Date	Hour	Summary of Events and Information	Remarks and references to Appendices
MERVILLE. K.29.d.1.9.	1916. Aug. 24th.		Routine work. A.D.M.S. 61st. DIVISION visited and inspected Rest Station. 1828 CPL. CLINTON.C.H. decorated by LIEUT. GENERAL SIR G.A.ANDERSON,K.C.B. with the Military Medal at HINGES. No. 167917 DRIVER RIDLER H. evacuated to the Casualty Clearing Station.	Gotw.
do.	Aug. 25th.		Routine work. - Concert for patients held at CORPS REST STATION. Gas Helmet parade and Inspection, and practise for Batmen, cooks and details previously omitted.	Gotw.
do.	Aug. 26th.		Routine work. No.167917 DRIVER RIDLER. H.,M.T.,A.S.C. died in Hospital, after operation for abscess in gall bladder. Inspection of Transport by LIEUT. COL. HARRISON. O.C. 61ST. DIVL. TRAIN. D.M.S. 1ST. ARMY inspected Premises. -	See app. 1. Gotw.
do.	Aug. 27th.		Church Parade. - Routine work. No. 167917 DRIVER RIDLER H. buried in BRITISH CEMETERY. MERVILLE.	Gotw.
do.	Aug. 28th.		Routine work. - Rebuilding of Kitchens at SCABIES DEPOT commenced. LIEUT. EVANS. W.J. - 2014 SGT. SITCH. W.H. and No. 1851 L/CPL. AUSTIN. R.G. commenced a course of Physical Drill at LA GORGUE BAYONET FIGHTING SCHOOL. D.D.M.S. & D.A.D.M.S. XI CORPS visited and Inspected premises at OFFICERS' REST STATION, CORPS REST STATION and CORPS SCABIES DEPOT. - CAPT. EVANS.I.D. reported for duty from leave.	Auth.A.D.M.S. 61st.Div. Gotw.
do.	Aug. 29th.		Routine work. No. 1892 PTE. MAISEY W. evacuated to CASUALTY CLEARING STATION suffering from appendicitis. Picnic and sports held for 180 patients at LE VERTBOIS FARM. LE SART.	Gotw.
do.	Aug. 30th.		Routine work. - D.A.D.M.S. XI CORPS visited and inspected the Rest Station. Alteration and extension of water supply to C.R.S. commenced. - Concert for patients held at C.R.S.	Gotw.
do.	Aug. 31st.		Routine work. A.D.M.S. 61ST. DIVISION visited OFFICERS REST STATION., CORPS REST.STATION and CORPS SCABIES DEPOT.	Gotw.

September 1st. 1916.

Gotwarkie
Major.R.A.M.C.(T).
Officer Commanding.
1st. Field Amb. 61st. Division.

WAR DIARY

APPENDIX 1.

1st. Field Amb. 61st. Divn.

September 1st. 1916.

1ST. FIELD AMBULANCE. - 61ST. DIVISION.

1. The following remarks are the result of the Inspection of Transport by Lieut. Col HARRISON. Officer Commanding. 61st. Divisional Train.

2/1st. FieldAmbulance.

HORSES.
Well groomed, good condition, well shod.

HARNESS.
Good condition, thoroughly clean and well fitting. - With pads require a little adjusting.

VEHICLES.
Excellent, and kept in a thoroughly clean condition.

This was an extremely good turnout, and reflects great credit on all ranks.

28.8.16.

CONFIDENTIAL.

WAR DIARY. - SEPTEMBER 1916.

2/IST. FIELD AMBULANCE. - 61ST. DIVISION.

IN THE FIELD.

OCTOBER 1ST. 1916.

Army Form C. 2118.

WAR DIARY
or
INTELLIGENCE SUMMARY.

(Erase heading not required.)

Map reference. Sheet 36a.
FRANCE.

Place	Date	Hour	Summary of Events and Information	Remarks and references to Appendices
K.29.d.1.9. K.34.d.8.8.	1916. Sept. 1st.		Routine work. D.A.D.M.S., XI CORPS visited and inspected XI CORPS REST STATION and CORPS SCABIES DEPOT.	Foster
do.	Sept. 2nd.		Medical Inspection of all ranks. A.D.M.S. 61ST. DIVISION inspected CORPS REST STATION. Routine work. - Concert given for patients of the C.R.S. by members of the Unit.	Foster
do.	Sept. 3rd.		Church Parades. Routine work.	Foster
do.	Sept. 4th.		Routine work. A.D.M.S. 61ST. DIVISION inspected the CORPS REST STATION. CAPTAIN GREEN. P.H.) 2097. SGT. PERRY. A.) proceeded to 61ST. DIVISIONAL SCHOOL OF BAYONET FIGHTING AND PHYSICAL 1813. CPL. SMITH. J.C.) TRAINING for Course of Instruction. Reconstruction of drainage system at CORPS REST STATION begun by Sanitary Squad. - Arrangements made for construction of brick manholes, and the removal of all the decayed wooden joints.	Auth.A.D.M.S. 61st.Divn. Foster
do.	Sept. 5th.		General fatigues, and routine work. D.D.M.S., XI CORPS inspected the CORPS REST STATION. A.D.M.S., 61ST. DIVISION inspected the CORPS REST STATION and the CORPS SCABIES DEPOT. Alterations and reconstruction of Bath House completed.	Foster
do.	Sept. 6th.		Routine work. No. 020051. SGT. JONES. R.N. M.T., A.S.C. att. 1ST. FIELD AMB. 61ST. DIV. proceeded on seven days special leave of absence to ENGLAND. Reconstruction of Cook House at SCABIES DEPOT begun. Concert given to Patients at XI CORPS REST STATION.	Auth.H.Q. 61st. Div. Foster
do.	Sept. 7th.		General routine work. The A.A. & Q.M.G., 61ST. DIVISION (LIEUT. COL. C.G.MARINDIN) inspected XI CORPS REST STATION, and CORPS SCABIES DEPOT.	Foster

Army Form C. 2118.

WAR DIARY
or
INTELLIGENCE SUMMARY.
(Erase heading not required.)

Map reference. Sheet 36a.
FRANCE.

Place	Date	Hour	Summary of Events and Information	Remarks and references to Appendices
K.29.d.1.9. K.34.d.8.8.	1916. Sep.8th.		Routine work. A.D.M.S. 61ST. DIVISION inspected XI CORPS REST STATION. CAPTAIN I.D.EVANS. R.A.M.C. detailed for duty at, and proceeded to HEADQUARTERS of 3RD. FIELD AMBULANCE. 61ST. DIVISION. LA GORGUE. D.A.Q.M.G., 61ST. DIVISION (MAJOR E.P.BLENCOWE. D.S.O.) visited and inspected Horse Transport of the Unit at REGNIER-LE-CLERC. Sites for winter horse standings selected and passed. Question of overhead cover left over.	G9/a. Auth.H.Q. 61st. Divn. Auth.A.D.M.S. 61st. Divn. G9/a.
do.	Sep. 9th.		Routine work. HON. LIEUT. & QUARTERMASTER W.S.RIVERS proceeded to ENGLAND on seven days special leave. Cookhouse at CORPS SCABIES DEPOT with special oven completed. 1309. CPL. FORRESTER. F.G.) 2228. L/C. MILES. S.) detailed for duty at DIVISIONAL BATHS at PONT RIGUEIL. Special picnic and sports arranged for 180 patients of the CORPS REST STATION in a field near the town.	G9/a.
do.	Sep.10th.		Routine work. - Medical Inspection of all Ranks. Church Parades.	G9/a.
do.	Sep.11th.		Routine work. Physical Drill under specially trained Officers and N.C.O's recommenced for personnel of Unit. Reconstruction of Packstore at CORPS SCABIES DEPOT begun, and rearrangement of accomodation there, in huts and tents carried out, to put the Depot on its winter footing.	G9/a.
do.	Sep. 12th.		Routine work.	G9/a.
do.	Sep. 13th.		Routine work. D.D.M.S. and D.A.D.M.S., XI CORPS inspected CORPS REST STATION and CORPS SCABIES DEPOT. Reconstruction of Bath House and Medical Room at CORPS SCABIES DEPOT commenced.	G9/a.
do.	Sep. 14th.		Routine work. - A.D.M.S. 31ST. DIVISION inspected CORPS REST STATION. A.D.M.S. 61ST. DIVISION inspected CORPS REST STATION. 2278. SGT. GREEN. H. proceeded to 61ST. DIVISIONAL GAS SCHOOL for Course of Instruction. Reconstruction of Ablution House at CORPS REST STATION begun - Floor to be raised 10" and redrained into a new concrete culvert.	Auth.A.D.M.S. 61st. Divn. G9/a.

Army Form C. 2118.

WAR DIARY
or
INTELLIGENCE SUMMARY.
(Erase heading not required.)

Map reference Sheet 36a.
FRANCE.

Place	Date	Hour	Summary of Events and Information	Remarks and references to Appendices
K.29.d.1.9. K.34.d.8.8.	1916. Sep. 15th.		Routine work. D.A.D.M.S., XI CORPS inspected CORPS REST STATION.	F.6.a.
do.	Sep. 16th.		Routine work. D.M.S., FIRST ARMY (SURGEON GENERAL W.M.PIKE) accompanied by A.D.M.S. 61ST. DIVISION, visited and made an exhaustive inspection of the XITH. CORPS REST STATION, and CORPS SCABIES DEPOT. All new work, and all books and methods examined, and found satisfactory. LIEUT. HAGGARD (M.O. 1/c XI CORPS OFFICERS' REST STATION. MERVILLE) and five men of the 30TH. DIVISION reported back to their Units, on the departure of the 30th. DIVISION from the XI CORPS.	F.6.a. Auth.D.D.M.S. XI Corps.
do.	Sep. 17th.		Routine work. Church Parades. LIEUT. RIVERS reported his arrival, on returning from special leave. Holding Party of 1 N.C.O. and 3 men detailed from Unit, to take over the premises vacated by the 94TH. FIELD AMBULANCE. 31ST. DIVISION at CALONNE-SUR-LA-LYS.	F.6.a. Auth.A.D.M.S. 61st. Divn.
do.	Sep. 18th.		Routine work. Concert for patients at XI CORPS REST STATION given by Troupe belonging to 1ST. FIELD AMB. Medical Officer detailed to inspect billets daily in the MERVILLE area, and report on same. Medical Officer detailed to visit the sick daily of all troops quartered at LE FORET.	F.6.a.
do.	Sep. 19th.		General Fatigues, and routine work. The OFFICER COMMANDING visited D.M.S., FIRST ARMY at HEADQUARTERS. FIRST ARMY, LILLERS, to submit a suggestion for a new form of Trench Stretcher, and various other appliances as used in the 1ST. FIELD AMBULANCE. 61ST. DIVISION.	F.6.a.
do.	Sep. 20th.		Routine work. Arrangements made for the construction of a road, and other much needed improvements at CORPS SCABIES DEPOT - the completion of which had been delayed, owing to the impossibility of obtaining an adequate supply of timber. Water Supply organised and carried out by members of this Unit, at CORPS REST STATION, completed and in full working order.	F.6.a.

Army Form C. 2118.

WAR DIARY
or
INTELLIGENCE SUMMARY.
(Erase heading not required.)

Map reference Sheet 36a.
FRANCE.

Instructions regarding War Diaries and Intelligence Summaries are contained in F. S. Regs., Part II. and the Staff Manual respectively. Title pages will be prepared in manuscript.

Place	Date	Hour	Summary of Events and Information	Remarks and references to Appendices
K.29.d.1.9. K.34.d.8.8.	1916. Sep. 21st.		Routine work. A.D.M.S., 61ST. DIVISION inspected XI CORPS REST STATION. D.D.M.S. XITH. CORPS visited CORPS REST STATION. Winter Billet at REGNIER-LE-CLERC arranged for SCABIES DEPOT personnel, and men moved in.	Gsta.
do.	Sep. 22nd.		Routine work. D.A.D.M.S., XITH. CORPS visited CORPS SCABIES DEPOT. OFFICER COMMANDING interviewed the A.A.& Q.M.G. 61ST. DIVISION (LIEUT. COL. J.W.SINGLETON,D.S.O.) at DIVISIONAL HEADQUARTERS.	Gsta.
do.	Sep. 23rd.		Routine work. Concert for patients given at CORPS REST STATION given by Unit personnel, and attended also by the A.A.& Q.M.G. and A.D.M.S. 61ST. DIVISION.	Gsta.
do.	Sep. 24th.		Routine work. - Medical Inspection of all ranks. Church Parades. H.D.A.D.M.S., XITH. CORPS visited CORPS REST STATION.	Gsta.
do.	Sep. 25th.		General Routine work. D.A.D.M.S., XI CORPS inspected XI CORPS REST STATION. No. 1892 PTE. MAISEY. W. evacuated to No. 7 C.C.S. suffering from chronic appendicitis. No. 2405. PTE. CROSS. A.S.) No. 2406. PTE. CROSS. W.S.) No. 2061. PTE. CONNOR. J.H.) transferred to 3RD. FIELD AMB. 61ST. DIVISION.	Auth.A.D.M.S 61st. Divn.
do.	Sep. 26th.		Routine work. CAPTAIN LANDER. C.L. 1ST. FLD. AMB. 61ST. DIVN. proceeded on 7 days special leave of absence. Building of cookhouse, latrines and ablution house at OFFICERS REST STATION. BUSNES commenced by party from this Unit. Special picnic and sports arranged for 180 patients at CORPS REST STN. in a field near the town.	Auth.A.D.M.S 61st. Divn. Gsta.
do.	Sep. 27th.		Routine work. - D.A.D.M.S. XI CORPS inspected CORPS REST STATION. Continuation of constructional work at SCABIES DEPOT, and road making for the winter commenced at the CORPS REST STATION and the CORPS SCABIES DEPOT.	G.Eda.

Army Form C. 2118.

WAR DIARY
or
INTELLIGENCE SUMMARY.
(Erase heading not required.)

Map reference Sheet 36a.
FRANCE.

Instructions regarding War Diaries and Intelligence Summaries are contained in F.S. Regs. Part II. and the Staff Manual respectively. Title pages will be prepared in manuscript.

Place	Date	Hour	Summary of Events and Information	Remarks and references to Appendices
K.29.d.1.9.) K.34.d.8.8.)	1916. Sep. 28th.		Routine work. The OFFICER COMMANDING visited the OFFICERS' REST STATION. BUSNES. Painting and decorating of Hall at CORPS REST STATION undertaken by this Unit.	G.Sto.
do.	Sep. 29th.		Routine work. A.D.M.S. 31ST. DIVISION inspected the CORPS REST STATION. D.A.D.M.S. XITH. CORPS with CAPTAIN STOBIE.) and LIEUT. EVANS) 1ST. FIELD AMB. 61ST. DIVISION, held a Medical Board at the XI CORPS REST STATION on NO. 16870 PRIVATE CROSBY. W. 3RD. SOUTH LANCS REGT. attached 7TH. SOUTH LANCS REGIMENT.	G.Sto.
do.	Sep. 30th.		Routine work. CAPTAIN W.J.HIRST. R.A.M.C.(T). 1ST. FIELD AMB. 61ST. DIVISION detailed for duty with 382nd. BATTERY. ROYAL GARRISON ARTILLERY? and reported there for duty. Concert given for patients at CORPS REST STATION.	Auth.A.D.MS 61st. Divn. G.Sto.

Oct. 1st. 1916.

G.Stoobie
Major.R.A.M.C.(T).
Officer Commanding. 1st. Field Amb. 61st. Division.

140/1/88

Giards

21. U. Field Ambulance

Colab

COMMITTEE FOR THE
MEDICAL HISTORY OF THE WAR
Date ⁼2 DEC. 1916

WAR DIARY
or
INTELLIGENCE SUMMARY.
(Erase heading not required.)

Army Form C. 2118.

2/1 S.M. Fd Amb

Reference O.S. Maps. Sheets 36 and 36a.
FRANCE.

Vol 6

Place	Date	Hour	Summary of Events and Information	Remarks and references to Appendices
K.29.d.1.9. K.34.d.8.8.	1916. Oct. 1st.		Church Parades. Routine Work. D.A.D.M.S. XI CORPS inspected XI CORPS REST STATION. LIEUT. EVANS W.J., R.A.M.C. detailed for duty with, and proceeded to HEADQUARTERS, 3RD. FIELD AMBULANCE. 61ST. DIVISION, on reduction of Establishment.	Auth.A.D.M.S 61st. Divn. Fsth.
do.	Oct. 2nd.		Routine work. CAPTAIN HIRST. W.J., R.A.M.C.(T). reported for duty at XI CORPS SCABIES DEPOT, his own Unit having moved.	Fsth.
do.	Oct. 3rd.		Routine work. Concert given to patients at the CORPS REST STATION by the "PRISMATICS CONCERT PARTY" (the Pierrot Troupe of the 1ST. FIELD AMB.) attended by D.A.D.M.S. XI CORPS and other visitors from MERVILLE. D.D.M.S. and D.A.D.M.S. XI CORPS inspected the XI CORPS REST STATION. 12 vacancies for 5TH. DIVISION allotted to m at XI CORPS REST STATION. STAFF SGT. MAJOR DIX reported for duty at HEADQUARTERS vice STAFF SGT. MAJOR MARLOWE.	Fsth. Auth.D.D.M.S XI CORPS.
do.	Oct. 4th.		Routine work. Five men of the 5TH. DIVISION reported for duty as Staff at the OFFICERS' REST STATION. MERVILLE vice 31ST. DIVISION personnel returned to their Units. CAPTAIN LANDER. C.L., R.A.M.C.(T). reported his arrival from leave. Painting and redecoration of XI CORPS REST STATION Hall completed. OFFICER COMMANDING visited A.D.M.S. 61ST. DIVISION re preliminary preparations in view of possible early move of the Division.	Auth.D.DMS XI CORPS. Auth.A.D.M.S 61st. Divn Fsth.
do.	Oct. 5th.		Routine work. No. 2060 PTE. YOUNG. F. reported his arrival to HEADQUARTERS from the BASE.	Fsth.
do.	Oct. 6th.		Routine work. CAPTAIN HIRST. W.J., R.A.M.C.(T). detailed for duty with, and reported to HEADQUARTERS of 2ND. (LONDON) BATTERY. R.G.A. Whist Drive held for patients at XI CORPS REST STATION.	Fsth.

WAR DIARY
or
INTELLIGENCE SUMMARY.

(Erase heading not required.)

Army Form C. 2118.

Reference O.S. Maps, Sheets 36 and 36a. FRANCE.

Place	Date	Hour	Summary of Events and Information	Remarks and references to Appendices
K.29.d.1.9. K.34.d.8.8.	1916. Oct.7th.		Routine work. Concert for Patients at the XI CORPS REST STATION given by the 1ST. FIELD AMBULANCE Pierrot Troupe. - Attended by LIEUT. GENERAL SIR R.C.B. HAKING, K.C.B., (XI CORPS COMMANDER, the D.D.M.S. XI CORPS and other officers.	W/M
do.	Oct.8th.		Church Parade. CAPTAIN JAMIESON. W. R.A.M.C.(T). proceeded to ENGLAND on 9 days special leave of absence. CAPTAIN STOBIE. W., R.A.M.C.(T). proceeded to XI CORPS OFFICERS' REST STATION. MERVILLE, vice CAPTAIN JAMIESON.	Auth.A.D.M.S. 61st. Divn. W/M
do.	Oct.9th.		Routine work. THE OFFICER COMMANDING, and No. 2276 SGT. GREEN. H. attended Gas Lecture at DIVISIONAL GAS SCHOOL, LA GORGUE. Inspection of all kits, and refitting of equipment of Unit Personnel completed. Route March for Unit Personnel.	W/M
do.	Oct.10th.		Routine work. D.A.D.M.S., XI CORPS visited and inspected premises of XI CORPS REST STATION. The A.A. & Q.M.G., 61ST. DIVISION inspected premises of XI CORPS REST STATION. The OFFICER COMMANDING visited A.D.M.S., 61ST. DIVISION re further preparations for possible move of Division. Inspection and re-issue of gas helmets to Unit Personnel.	W/M
do.	Oct.11th.		No. 1851 L/CPL. AUSTIN. R.G. and No. 2192 L/CPL. EVANS. H. reported to OFFICER IN CHARGE. DIVISIONAL BATHS. LA GORGUE, for Course of Instruction in "Lice Detection." Routine work. Route march for Unit Personnel and Patients.	W/M
do.	Oct.12th.		Routine work. Equipment Inspections and re-fitting and repair of waggons commenced. - Horse clipping begun. Informal Concert for patients given at XI CORPS REST STATION.	W/M
do.	Oct.13th.		Routine work. CAPTAIN W.H.GILL.R.A.M.C.(T). reported for duty from the BASE. D.A.D.M.S., FIRST ARMY visited and inspected XI CORPS REST STATION. No. 2160 PTE. BATE. W.F. evacuated to No. 2 (LONDON) C.C.S. suffering from "Internal derangement of Right Knee joint"	Auth.A.D.M.S. 61st. Divn. W/M

Army Form C. 2118.

WAR DIARY
or
INTELLIGENCE SUMMARY.

Reference O.S. Maps Sheets 36 and 36a.
FRANCE.

(Erase heading not required.)

Instructions regarding War Diaries and Intelligence Summaries are contained in F.S. Regs., Part II. and the Staff Manual respectively. Title pages will be prepared in manuscript.

Place	Date	Hour	Summary of Events and Information	Remarks and references to Appendices
K.29.d.1.9. K.34.d.8.8. CROIX BARBEE.	1916 Oct. 14th.		Routine work. 2192 L/CPL. EVANS. H. and No. 2278 L/CPL. MILES. S. detailed for duty at DIVISIONAL BATHS. The OFFICER COMMANDING visited A.D.M.S., 61ST. DIVISION.	Auth.A.D.M.S. 61st. Divn.
do.	Oct. 15th.		Routine work. Church Parade. A.D.M.S., 61ST. DIVISION visited and inspected the XITH. CORPS REST STATION and the CORPS SCABIES DEPOT.	
do.	Oct. 16th.		Routine work. CAPTAIN BURROUGHES. H.N., R.A.M.C.(T). proceeded on 10 days special leave of absence. The OFFICER COMMANDING visited DIVISIONAL HEADQUARTERS, and also the A.D.M.S. 61ST. DIVISION. Night Route March for Unit Personnel.	Auth.D.DMS. XI CORPS
do.	Oct. 17th.		Routine work. Installation of new water supply at XI CORPS SCABIES DEPOT commenced. D.A.D.M.S., XI CORPS visited and inspected CORPS REST STATION and CORPS SCABIES DEPOT. No. 2351. PTE. PEARSON. J.H. reported for duty from 3RD. FIELD AMBULANCE 61ST. DIVISION. Concert given at XI CORPS REST STATION by the "PRISMATICS" (1ST. FIELD AMBULANCE Pierrot Troupe) and Orchestra.	Auth.A.D.M.S. 61st. Divn.
do.	Oct. 18th.		Routine work. D.A.D.M.S., XI CORPS visited and inspected XI CORPS REST STATION.	
do.	Oct. 19th.		Routine work. A.D.M.S. 61ST. DIVISION visited and inspected XI CORPS REST STATION. The OFFICER COMMANDING. (MAJOR GEORGE MACKIE) proceeded to ENGLAND on eight days special leave of absence. - CAPTAIN G.L.LANDER.R.A.M.C.(T) appointed Acting O.C. during the absence of the O.C. D.A.D.M.S. XI CORPS visited and inspected XI CORPS REST STATION.	Auth.ADMS 61 Div
do.	Oct. 20th.		Routine work. Route march for Unit personnel. Preliminary instructions for move of Unit received from A.D.M.S., 61ST. DIVISION. No. 2230. PTE. DRAKE. T.M. evacuated to No. 2 C.C.S.	

Army Form C. 2118.

WAR DIARY
or
INTELLIGENCE SUMMARY.
(Erase heading not required.)

Reference O.S. Maps. Sheets 36 and 36a.
FRANCE.

Place	Date	Hour	Summary of Events and Information	Remarks and references to Appendices
K.29.d.1.9. K.34.d.8.8.	1916. Oct. 21st.		Routine work. LIEUT. COL. MONTGOMERIE SMITH., O.C., 2/2ND. LONDON FIELD AMB. 56TH. DIVISION, reported for Course of Instruction, preparatory to taking over CORPS REST STATION from this Unit. Stoves for Unit personnel in Billets received and installed.	Apl.
do.	Oct. 22nd.		Routine work. Church Parades. D.D.M.S., XI CORPS visited and inspected XI CORPS REST STATION.	Apl.
do.	Oct. 23rd.		Routine work. A.D.M.S., 61ST. DIVISION inspected the Unit, - all men paraded in full marching order - together with all available Transport. Night Route March for Unit personnel. Painting of waggons ommenced.	Apl.
do.	Oct. 24th.		Routine work. Instructions as to actual date of move etc. received from HEADQUARTERS. Loading of waggons etc. practised. 52 patients of the 56th. DIVISION damitted to CORPS REST STATION. 5 Officers and 100 N.C.O's and men of the 2/2ND. (LONDON) FIELD AMB. 56TH. DIVISION arrived at the XI CORPS REST STATION.	Apl.
do.	Oct. 25th.		Routine work. Instruction of Officers and Men of the 2/2nd. (LONDON) FIELD AMB. in the duties of XI CORPS REST STATION proceeded with. THE ACTING OFFICER COMMANDING(CAPT. C.L.LANDER) proceeded to HEADQUARTERS, and interviewed the A.D.M.S. 61ST. DIVISION re impending move of UNIT. LIEUT. W.J.EVANS. R.A.M.C. 2/3RD. FIELD AMB. 61 DIV. attached 2/1ST. FIELD AMB. 61ST. DIV. for duty.	Auth.D.DMS. XI CORPS. Auth.A.DMS. 61ST. DIVN. Apl.

WAR DIARY
or
INTELLIGENCE SUMMARY.
(Erase heading not required.)

Army Form C. 2118.

Reference O.S. Maps. Sheets 36 and 36a.
F R A N C E.

Place	Date	Hour	Summary of Events and Information	Remarks and references to Appendices
K.29.d.1.9. K.34.d.8.8.	Oct.26th. 1916.		Routine work. A.D.M.S. 56TH. DIVISION inspected XI CORPS REST STATION. Administration of XI CORPS REST STATION handed over to O.C., 2/2ND. LONDON FIELD AMBULANCE. 56TH. DIVISION at 2.0 p.m. Concert given for patients at XI CORPS REST STATION by the Unit Troupe. A.D.M.S. 61ST. DIVISION visited CORPS REST STATION. Night route march for Unit personnel.	Auth.D.D.M.S. XI CORPS.
do.	Oct. 27th.		Routine work. — All men on detached "special duties" recalled to HEADQUARTERS. All waggons packed. D.D.M.S. XI CORPS inspected premises. Final instructions re impending move received from A.D.M.S. 61ST. DIVISION.	
do.	Oct. 28th.		The Ambulance marched off from MERVILLE to ROBECQ. — Route:- MERVILLE - PEGNIER - LE - CLERC CALONNE. - ROBECQ. No casualties of any description were sustained en route. ROBECQ was reached at 11.30 a.m. Hospital established at P.29.b.6.4. and A.D.M.S. 61ST. DIVISION and H.Q. 184 INF. BDE. advised. THE OFFICER COMMANDING reported his arrival on the expiration of his "special leave." CAPTAIN H.N. BURROUGHES reported his arrival on the expiration of his "special leave." CAPTAIN W.J.HIRST. reported for duty, from 150TH. BATTY, R.G.A.	Auth.A.D.M.S. 61st.Divn.
P.29.b.6.4.	Oct.29th.		Routine work. — Church Parade. CAPTAIN K.H.GILL evacuated to No. 2 (LONDON) C.C.S. suffering from Bronchitis. CAPTAIN P.H.GREEN granted "special leave" to proceed to LE TOURQUET. MAJOR GEORGE MACKIE having returned from leave of absence, resumed command of the ambulance. MAJOR GEORGE MACKIE promoted Temp. Lt. Col. whilst commanding 2/1ST. SO. MID. FIELD AMBULANCE. to date from August 22nd. 1916. THE OFFICER COMMANDING visited A.D.M.S. 61ST. DIVISION, and HEADQUARTERS. 184TH. INFANTRY BDE. A.D.M.S. 61ST. DIVISION visited Hospital.	Auth.A.D.M.S. 61st. Divn.
do.	Oct. 30th.		The O.C. visited D.D.M.S. XI CORPS and K.K. XI CORPS REST STATION to interview LIEUT. COL. MONTGOMERIE SMITH R.A.M.C.(T), now in command there. CAPTAIN C.L.LANDER.R.A.M.C.(T), detailed for temporary duty with 2/5TH. GLOSTER REGT. 184TH. INF. BRIGADE. O.C. and CAPTAIN BURROUGHES attended Conference at HEADQUARTERS. 184TH. INF. BDE. Preliminary instructions received for H.Q. 184TH. INF. BDE. of proposed move of Unit to AUCHEL area.	Auth.A.D.M.S. 61st. Divn.

Army Form C. 2118.

WAR DIARY
or
INTELLIGENCE SUMMARY.

(Erase heading not required.)

Reference O.S. Maps. Sheets 36 and 36a.
F R A N C E.

Place	Date	Hour	Summary of Events and Information	Remarks and references to Appendices
P.29.b.6.4.	1916. Oct. 31st.		Routine work. OFFICER COMMANDING and CAPTAIN BURROUGHES reconnoitred route of proposed march to AUCHEL. Cleaning and packing of equipment. Every member of Unit practised in application and use of New Box Respirator. Two Water Carts sent to S. VENANT to have new petrol tin carriers fitted. Alarm turn out. – Orders received at 5.25 p.m. from 184th. INFANTRY BDE. HDQRS. for emergency move. – All stores packed, and Unit moved off complete in every detail at 6.35 p.m. – Parade dismissed at 6.40 p.m.	Tsa

Pollacke
Lieut. Col. R.A.M.C.(T).
Officer Commanding. 2/1st. South Midland Field Ambulance.

In the Field.
October 31st. 1916.

105/1549

Capt Dixon

2/1st S.M. Field Ambulance

Nov 1916

COMMITTEE FOR THE
MEDICAL HISTORY OF THE WAR
Date -3 JAN. 1917

CONFIDENTIAL.

WAR DIARY.

of the

2/1ST. SOUTH MIDLAND FIELD AMBULANCE.R.A.M.C.(T).

DECEMBER 1916.

In the Field.

December 1st. 1916.

WAR DIARY
or
INTELLIGENCE SUMMARY.

Army Form C. 2118.

Reference O.S.Map. FRANCE. HAZEBROUK. 5a. Scale 1/100,000. and LENS. 11. 1/100,000.

(Erase heading not required.)

Instructions regarding War Diaries and Intelligence Summaries are contained in F.S. Regs. Part II. and the Staff Manual respectively. Title pages will be prepared in manuscript.

Place	Date	Hour	Summary of Events and Information	Remarks and references to Appendices
ROBECQ.	1916. Nov. 1st.		Routine work. Final packing of waggons etc. preparatory to move. Box respirator practice for all ranks. No. 2593. PTE. CLARKE. T.H. 2/3rd. FIELD AMB. fetched from BETHUNE.	Auth.A.D.MS 6Ist. Divn. do.
ROBECQ. RAIMBERT	Nov. 2nd.		The Ambulance moved off from ROBECQ as per March Table from 184 INF. BDE. at 8.58 a.m. leaving starting point at 9.9 a.m. Route:- ROBECQ - BUSNETTES - BAS RIEUX - HAUT RIEUX - BURBURE - RAIMBERT arriving at 1.30 p.m. Arrival reported to 184TH. INFANTRY BDE. H. QRS., AND A.D.M.S. 6IST. DIVISION. Casualties:- a. Unit:- 3. b. Picked up from other Units in Bde:- 24. Serious cases evacuated to Casualty Clearing Station at LOZINGHEM.	v. app. 1.
RAIMBERT ROCOURT.	Nov. 3rd.		Ambulance moved off from RAIMBERT and passed starting point at 9.34 a.m. as per 184 INF. BDE. March Table. Route:- RAIMBERT - AUCHEL - CALONNE RICOURT - DIVION - OURTON - LA THIEULOYE - ROCOURT, arriving at ROCOURT at 4.15 p.m. Arrival reported to 184TH. INFANTRY BDE. H.Q., and A.D.M.S. 6IST. DIVISION. Casualties:- a. Unit. 2. b. Picked up from other Units in Bde. 21. Serious cases evacuated to Casualty Clearing Station at S. POL. (No. I2 Stationary Hospital.)	v. app. 2.
ROCOURT. TINQUETTES.	Nov. 4th.		Ambulance moved off from ROCOURT at IO.40 a.m. and passed starting point, as per March Table at 11.0 a.m. proceeding via ROCOURT - MAGNICOURT - CHELERS - TINQUES to TINQUETTE, which was reached at 1.15 p.m. 184TH. INF. BDE. H.Q., and A.D.M.S. 6IST. DIVISION informed of arrival. Casualties:- a. Unit. 2. b. Picked up from other Units in Bde. 12. Serious cases evacuated to Casualty Clearing Station at S. POL.	v. app. 3.
TINQUETTE. ROZIERE.	Nov. 5th.		Ambulance moved off at 7.55 a.m. and passed starting point as per March Table at 8.2 a.m. proceeding via AVERDOINGT - where one G.S. Waggon front axle broke, and the waggon had to be left behind - GOUY-EN-TOURNOIS - MAGNICOURT-SUR-CAUCHE - HOUVAIN - HOUVIGNEUL to ROZIERE where it arrived at 12.45 p.m.	v. app. 4.

Army Form C. 2118.

WAR DIARY
or
INTELLIGENCE SUMMARY.
(Erase heading not required.)

Reference O.S. Map FRANCE.
LENS. 11. 1/100,000

Instructions regarding War Diaries and Intelligence Summaries are contained in F.S. Regs., Part II. and the Staff Manual respectively. Title pages will be prepared in manuscript.

Place	Date	Hour	Summary of Events and Information	Remarks and references to Appendices
TINQUETTE. ROZIERE.	1916. Nov. 5th.	(con)	184th. INFANTRY BDE. and A.D.M.S. 61ST. DIVISION duly informed of arrival of Unit. Casualties. a. Unit. Nil. b. Picked up from other Units in Bde. 7. Serious cases evacuated to Casualty Clearing Station. ST. POL. Damaged waggon, empty, reached ROZIERE at 2.15 p.m. and was sent on to Heavy Mobile Workshop at FREVENT, where the axle was reforged — the waggon returning to Unit at 2.0 a.m. on Novr. 6th — abandoned waggon load was fetched from AVERDOINGT by 10.0 p.m. and all waggons repacked during night. One Deasy Motor Ambulance having broken its differential driving cog, had to be towed.	76th
ROZIERE. NEUVILLETTE.	Nov. 6th.		Ambulance moved off complete, with repaired waggon fully loaded, and passed starting point as per March Table at 10.0 a.m, proceeding via REBREUVIETTE - BOUCQUE MAISON t o NEUVILLETTE, arriving at 12.15 p.m. H.Q., 184TH. INFANTRY BDE. and A.D.M.S. 61ST. DIVISION duly informed of arrival. All Officers and Men billeted. — Headquarters established, and Hospital opened at 3.0 p.m. Casualties. a. Unit. 1. b. Picked up from other Units in Bde. 9. Serious cases evacuated to Casualty Clearing Station at DOULLENS.	v. app. 5. 76th
NEUVILLETTE.	Nov. 7th.		Routine work. CAPTAIN JAMIESON. R.A.M.C.(T). detailed for temporary duty with 2/4TH. ROYAL BERKS. REGT.	Auth.A.D.MS 61st.Divn. 76th
NEUVILETTE.	Nov. 8th.		Routine work. An extra Hospital opened in barn close to THE CHATEAU, NEUVILLETTE. BRIGADIER GENERAL 184TH. INFANTRY BDE. (BRIG. GEN. HON. R. WHITE. C.M.G.) with the A.A.& Q.M.G. 61ST. DIVISION (LIEUT. COL. H.C. SINGLETON) and the D.A.Q.M.G. 61ST. DIVISION (MAJOR E.P. BLENCOWE) visited and inspected Hospital and Premises generally. CAPTAIN W. STOBIE. R.A.M.C.(T). detailed for temporary duty at A.D.M.S. Office. FROHEN-LE-GRAND, vice MAJOR W.J.HOYTEN.R.A.M.C.(T).; D.A.D.M.S. 61ST. DIVISION, reported sick. CAPTAIN T.M.JAMIESON R.A.M.C.(T) reported back to this Unit, the M.O. of 2/4 BERKS REGT. having recovered.	76th

WAR DIARY
or
INTELLIGENCE SUMMARY.
(Erase heading not required.)

Army Form C. 2118.

Reference O.S. Map. FRANCE.
LENS.11. 1/100.000.

Instructions regarding War Diaries and Intelligence Summaries are contained in F.S. Regs., Part II. and the Staff Manual respectively. Title pages will be prepared in manuscript.

Place	Date	Hour	Summary of Events and Information	Remarks and references to Appendices
	1916.			
NEUVILETTE.	Nov. 9th.		A.D.M.S. 61ST. DIVISION visited and inspected premises. D.A.D.M.S. 61ST. DIVISION evacuated to No. 19 CASUALTY CLEARING STATION. DOULLENS. Routine work. - Route March for Unit personnel. Repacking of Medical Store Waggons on a new system arranged and carried out.	Both
NEUVILETTE.	Nov. 10th.		Routine work. Church Parade with 2/5TH. GLOSTER REGT. OFFICER COMMANDING visited A.D.M.S. and D.A.Q.M.G. at HEADQUARTERS, 61ST. DIVISION.	Both
NEUVILETTE.	Nov. 11th.		Routine work. A.D.M.S. 61ST. DIVISION visited Unit, and with the OFFICER COMMANDING visited H.Q., 2/4 BERKS REGT. Daily Medical officer detailed for duty with 1/3RD. FIELD COY., R.E's. BOUQUEMAISON. No. 1892. PTE. MAISEY. W. and No. 2532.PTE. TAYLOR. E. reported from R.A.M.C. BASE DEPOT. ROUEN.	Auth.ADMS. 61ST. DIVN. Both
NEUVILETTE.	Nov. 12th.		Routine work. - Hospital premises enlarged and altered. - Road and path making continued. 3 Bearer Sub-Divisions ordered to parade and march to HDQRS. 61ST. DIVISION, to be conveyed to the Front for detached duty. "A" SECTION paraded under LIEUT. EVANS, "B" SECTION under CAPTAIN GREEN, and "C" SECTION under CAPTAIN JAMIESON, and marched off, 11/2 Officers, N.C.o's and Men reaching OCCOCHES, HEADQUARTERS 184TH. INFANTRY BRIGADE at 1.0 p.m. - There they were picked up at 2.15 p.m. by Motor Buses from DIVISIONAL HEADQUARTERS, and conveyed to BERTRANCOURT, reporting to O.C., 6TH. FIELD AMB. (Sheet 57D. J.33.a.3.7.) for duty. - There they found that they were quite unexpected, and no arrangements had been made for their reception, or feeding, or work.	v. app. 6. Auth.ADMS. 61ST. DIVN.
NEUVILETTE.	Nov. 13th.	2ND.	Routine work. OFFICER COMMANDING and CAPTAIN BURROUGHES having heard that the three Bearer Sub-Divisions had no food, went to BERTRANCOURT with their day's rations, which had not arrived on Nov. 12th. till after their departure. - They visited the OFFICER COMMANDING, 2ND. FIELD AMB. and the A.D.M.S. XXXX. DIVISION, who knew nothing of the matter. 6TH. Arrangements made for rationing the men while in that area. THE BRIGADIER GENERAL, 184TH. INFANTRY BDE. (BRIG. GEN. THE HON R. WHITE, C.M.G.) together with the BRIGADE MAJOR. 184TH. INFANTRY BDE. visited the Hospital premises.	Both
NEUVILETTE.	Nov. 14th.		Routine work. LIEUT. AND QRMR. W.S. RIVERS L. visited BERTRANCOURT with rations etc. for the three Bearer Sub-Divisions.	Both

WAR DIARY
or
INTELLIGENCE SUMMARY.

(Erase heading not required.)

Army Form C. 2118.

Reference O.S. Map. FRANCE.
LENS. 11. - 1/100,000.

Place	Date	Hour	Summary of Events and Information	Remarks and references to Appendices
NEUVILETTE.	1916. Nov. 15.		Routine work. Preparations made for impending move - waggons packed etc. BRIGADIER-GENERAL 184TH. INFANTRY BDE. (BR. GEN. HON. SIR R.WHITE. C.M.G.) visited and inspected the premises, Hospital etc.	
NEUVILETTE. ALBERT. BONNEVILLE.	Nov. 16.		Ambulance moved from NEUVILETTE at 10.16 a.m. and passed starting point as per march table at 10.27 a.m. proceeding via RISQUETOUT - HEM - FIENVILLERS - MONTRELET - BONNEVILLE, which was reached at 4.30 p.m. Arrival reported to H.Q., 184TH. INF. BDE. and A.D.M.S. 61st. DIVISION. Casualties. a:- Unit. 1. b:- Picked up from other Units in Brigade. 5. 4 serious cases evacuated to Casualty Clearing Station at VADENCOURT. Hospital established for reception of patients by 4.45 p.m.	
BONNEVILLE. VADENCOURT.	Nov. 17.		Ambulance moved from BONNEVILLE at 9.45 a.m. and passed starting point at 9.41 a.m. as per march table. Route:- BONNEVILLE - PUCHEVILLERS - CONTAY - VADENCOURT which was reached at 3.45 p.m. Arrival reported to HEADQUARTERS 184th. INFANTRY BDE. and A.D.M.S. 61st. DIVISION. Casualties. (a) Unit. 2. (b) Picked up from other Units in Bde:- 6. 3 serious cases evacuated to Casualty Clearing Station VADENCOURT. Information received from CAPT. JAMIESON.R.A.M.C.(T). that the Bearer Sub - Divisions at BERTRANCOURT had been specially commended by the O.C. VI FIELD AMBULANCE for their gallant conduct. They had been led by CAPTAIN P.H.GREEN over "No mans' land" behind the Infantry, as far as the 2nd. line German trenches, and the following were specially recommended for mention for very good work:- 1. CAPTAIN P.H.GREEN. A.H. 2. 2097. SGT. PERRY. 3. 2496. PTE. WHITHORNE. T. 4. 2092. PTE. WHITMARSH. A. 5. 1802. PTE. BLUCK. H. The recommendations were forwarded to the OFFICER COMMANDING. VI FIELD AMBULANCE. They suffered the following casualties:- Severely wounded. 2224. PTE. TAYLOR. G. Slightly wounded. (1.) 2235. PTE. MIDDLEMAN. C.C. 1. 1829. 1/C. ALDRIDGE. A.E. Wounded. (2) 2213. PTE. BLACKHAM. B. 2. 2088. PTE. CLINTON. W.H. (3) 2132. PTE. BECK. W. Of the above, PTES. TAYLOR, BLACKHAM and MIDDLEMAN were evacuated at once to Casualty Clearing Stn. The others were treated, and returned to duty.	

WAR DIARY
or
INTELLIGENCE SUMMARY.

(Erase heading not required.)

Army Form C. 2118.

Reference O.S. Map. FRANCE.
LENS.II. 1/100.000.

Instructions regarding War Diaries and Intelligence Summaries are contained in F.S. Regs., Part II. and the Staff Manual respectively. Title pages will be prepared in manuscript.

Place	Date	Hour	Summary of Events and Information	Remarks and references to Appendices
VADENCOURT.	1916. Nov. 18.		Routine work. OFFICER COMMANDING proceeded to BERTRANCOURT to investigate Casualties in personnel of the three Bearer Sub - Divisions. OFFICER COMMANDING visited H.Q. and A.D.M.S. 61ST. DIVISION. Preliminary orders for move of Unit to ALBERT received from H.Q., 184TH. INFANTRY BDE. CAPTAIN STOBIER.A.M.C.(T). detailed as tempy. M.O. to 2/4 OXFORD & BUCKS L.I. during the absence of CAPTAIN WORSLEY. R.A.M.C.(T). on leave.	FSW
VADENCOURT. ALBERT.	Nov. 19th.		Ambulance moved from VADENCOURT at 8.45 a.m. and passed starting point as per march table, proceeding via WARLOY - HENENCOURT - MILLENCOURT - ALBERT - BECOURT RD, which was reached at 1.20 p.m. Arrival reported to H.Q., 184TH. INF. BDE. and A.D.M.S. 61st. DIVISION. Casualties:- (a) Unit:- 1. (b) Picked up from other Units in Brigade. 4. Serious cases (two) evacuated to Casualty Clearing Station ALBERT. Great difficulty experienced in finding billets.- Ultimately men installed in a small camp for 48TH. DIVISION Reinforcements on ALBERT - BECOURT RD. 800 yards E. of ALBERT at X Roads, close to light railway. Sheet 57d. - Hospital premises secured in BECOURT RD. in ALBERT, in a disused house.	FSW
ALBERT.	Nov. 20th.		Routine work. 3 Bearer Sub-Divisions reported back to HEADQUARTERS from BERTRANCOURT by Motor Bus, under CAPTAIN JAMIESON, CAPTAIN GREEN and LIEUT. EVANS. The O.C. visited A.D.M.S. 18TH. DIVISION and O's C. 55th. and 59th. FIELD AMBCES re taking over Advanced Dressing Stations etc.- Preparations made for staffing all Aid Posts on both Evacuation Lines, behind the trenches to be occupied by the 184 INF. BDE. at midnight Nov. 21 - 22.	FSW
ALBERT.	Nov. 21st.		Routine work in Hospital and Camp. - O.C. met A.D.M.S. 61ST. DIVISION at Office of A.D.M.S. 18TH. DIVISION and explored the "forward area" with D.A.D.M.S. 18TH. DIVISION. As a result, the following dispositions for R.A.M.C. personnel were ordered, and were carried out entirely by 4 p.m. RIGHT SECTOR. Two R.A.P's:- 1. R.28.a.6.7. RIFLE TRENCH. 2. R.29.c.9.9. LANCASHIRE TRENCH.- These are about 100 yards apart,- I Relief Post at RIFLE DUMP at R.28.c.8.3. and are staffed by our Bearers. Stretcher cases are there also. Our men for Reliefs are there also. Stretcher cases are taken by tramway down to POZIERES cemetery post, staffed by men of this Unit under CAPTAIN BURROUGHES.	FSW

Army Form C. 2118.

WAR DIARY
or
INTELLIGENCE SUMMARY.
(Erase heading not required.)

Reference ALBERT Combined Sheet.
57d.S.E.
and 62d.N.E.

Place	Date	Hour	Summary of Events and Information	Remarks and references to Appendices
ALBERT.	1916. Nov.21.(con)		From POZIERES Cemetery cases brought by motor tramway to RED CROSS CORNER on main road ALBERT - BAPAUME just S. of POZIERES, and evacuated from there to Main Dressing Station by Motor ambulances. LEFT SECTOR. Regimental aid Post in ZOLLERN TRENCH and Bearers in ZOLLERN REDOUBT. R.27.a.I0.6. Relief Post in GRAVEL PIT. R.27.c.4.3. - Cases evacuated by Horse Tramway to DONNET POST via DANUBE TRENCH POST and thence by cars to AVELUY POST.	
ALBERT.	Nov. 22nd.		Routine work. - OFFICER COMMANDING visited H.Q., 61 DIV. and A.D.M.S. 61ST. DIVISION, and with D.A.D.M.S. 61ST. DIVISION visited AVELUY POST, THE CAB STAND, and DONNET POST. No. 1859 ST. SGT. JACQUES and 8 N.C.O's and Men of "C" Section returned to Headquarters after handing over DONNETS' POST to party from 2/3RD. FIELD AMB. 61ST. DIVISION. CAPTAIN HIRST and Bearers remained in the forward area for the night to introduce the Bearers of the 2/3RD. FIELD AMB. to their work, having orders to return to their Unit next morning, after having handed over all stores and fittings. No. 2132 PTE. BECK w. evacuated to C.C.S. suffering from wound in the forearm received on Nov. 16.	Auth.*ADMS. 61st.Divn.
ALBERT.	Nov. 23rd.		Routine work. - CAPTAIN HIRST and 36 Stretcher Bearers returned to H.Q. of the Unit after having been relieved at DONNETS POST by the 2/3RD. FIELD AMB. 61ST. DIVISION. OFFICER COMMANDING visited Advanced Dressing Station and Collecting Post, and confirmed the arrangements already made.	
ALBERT.	Nov. 24th.		OFFICER COMMANDING visited HEADQUARTERS and A.D.M.S. IIND CORPS and with D.A.D.M.S. 61ST. DIVISION went on to SENLIS to see D.D.M.S. IIND CORPS as to new position for ambulance, Head quarters, and possible lines of evacuation from POZIERES, this village having now passed out of the 61st. Divisional Area. - Instructions received to carry on for the present, and to extend billet premises in N.E. corner of ALBERT if possible.	
ALBERT.	Nov. 25th.		D.A.D.M.S. 61ST. DIVISION visited Advanced Dressing Station and Collecting Post. An Officer arrived in Camp from 48th. DIVISION, and removed all tents etc. from the Camp. Fresh billets found for part of personnel in ALBERT, and bell tents pitched for remainder. 1st. Relief Party sent to "forward area" and relieved bearers reported back to Camp.	

Army Form C. 2118.

WAR DIARY
or
INTELLIGENCE SUMMARY.
(Erase heading not required.)

Map reference ALBERT Combined Sheet.
57d. S.E.
and 62d. N.E.

Place	Date	Hour	Summary of Events and Information	Remarks and references to Appendices
ALBERT.	1916. Nov. 26th.		Routine work. - Headquarters of Ambulance, Officer Commanding, Orderly Room Staff and most of personnel moved to ALBERT to temporary billets. Instructions received from A.D.M.S. 61ST. DIVISION for move of Unit Headquarters to AVELUY POST. OFFICER COMMANDING visited A.D.M.S. 61ST. DIVISION at DIV. H.Q. and visited AVELUY POST, temporarily occupied by 2/3RD. FLD. AMB. 61ST. DIV. arranging to take over post tomorrow morning. Reliefs of officers and Men in the "forward area" carried out.	Fosta
ALBERT. AVELUY POST. Nov.27.			Routine work. - OFFICER COMMANDING and 24 N.C.O's and Men proceeded to AVELUY POST and established HEADQUARTERS and Hospital there. - Cleaning of Camp and site generally taken in hand. OFFICER COMMANDING visited Div. H.Q. and interviewed A.D.M.S. 61ST. DIV. and with D.A.D.M.S. returned to AVELUY POST. Arrangements commenced for developing the post into a Main Dressing Station.	Fosta
AVELUY POST. Nov. 28.			Routine Work. - D.D.M.S. and D.A.D.M.S. IV CORPS visited and inspected Camp. D.A.D.M.S. 61ST. DIV. visited and inspected Camp. CAPT. BURROUGHES and LIEUT. EVANS relieved at Advanced Dressing Stations by CAPT. HIRST & CAPT. GREEN. 4 Nissen Huts and 3 Hospital Marquees indented for, and arrangements made for their reception and erection. - Clearing up, and future arrangement of Camp proceeded with. Remainder of personnel, and all transport except Quartermaster's Stores and part of section equipment and Motor Transport Section arrived in Camp. - Horse Lines established, and Waggon Park arranged. Tents pitched for temporary shelter for part of personnel, and two "dug outs" taken over.	Fosta
AVELUY POST. Nov. 29.			Routine work. - Arrangements continued for developing post. - Attempts made to find accomodation for cars, and Mechanical transport section and Cars. Construction of underground hospital in hill side commenced, and a rail track begun, to bring patients from main road into Reception Hut and Hospital Tent. The following men were evacuated to Casualty Clearing Station:- 2088 PTE. COOPER. F. 2141. PTE. FLETCHER. W. 1927. PTE. FRENCH. W. 2113 PTE? HERBERT. C.A. 2090. PTE. MULLETT. J. and 2222 PTE. SMITH. H.	Fosta
AVELUY POST. Nov. 30.			Routine work. - CAPTAIN W.J. HIRST. No.1859 ST.SGT.JACQUES.J.H. No.2124 SGT. BICKELL.R.J.G. and No. 1846 B/CPL. BANNISTER proceeded on 10 days leave of absence. 184th. INFANTRY BDE. relieved from trenches by 183RD. INF. BDE. 1ST. FLD. AMB. provided two Ambulances for collection of patients on march back. Waggons returned at 4.30 a.m. Wooden parts of Nissen Huts drawn. No ironwork yet available. Non-arrival of marquees reported to A.D.M.S. 61ST. DIVISION.	Auth.ADMS. 61 Divn. Fosta

Fosta
Lieut. Colonel. R.A.M.C.(T).
Officer Commanding. 2/1.South Midland Field Amb.
December 1st. 1916.

WAR DIARY.

2/1ST. SOUTH MIDLAND FIELD AMBULANCE.

APPENDIX NO. 7.

In the Field.
December 1st. 1916.

SECRET.   Copy No. 14.

184TH. INFANTRY BRIGADE ORDER.

                                                           31/10/16.

Reference Maps.   1. On November 2nd. 1916, the 184th. Brigade Group
I/100.000.   will march to Area A. in accordance with table
                     overleaf, and Area A. Map attached.

                  2. There will be 15 minutes inetrval between Units.
                     All Units to halt 15 minutes before clock hour,
                     until clock hour.

                  3. Billeting Parties will take over Billets from 183rd.
                     Brigade Group in Area A. on the afternoon of the
                     1st. November.

                  4. On November 3rd. the 184th. Brigade Group will move to
                     the MONCHY BRETON Area.

                  5. On November 2nd. Divisional Headquarters will close
                     at S. VENANT at 10.0 a.m. and re-open at ROLLECOURT
                     at the same hour.

                  6. Brigade Headquarters will close at ROBECQ at 9.0 a.m.
                     November 2nd. and re-open at AUCHEL at the same hour.

                     ACKNOWLEDGE.
                                                (sgd) E.C.GEPP. Major.
                                                      Brigade Major.
                                                  184th. Infantry Brigade.
                     Issued at 9.0 p.m.

Unit.   From.   To.   Starting Point.

1ST. Fld.Amb.   ROBECQ.   RAIMBERT.   Cross Roads just N.
                                           of ROBECQ CHURCH.

Time.   Route.   Remarks.

9 - 9 a.m.   L'ECLEME - HAUT   An Ambulane Waggon will
                   RIEUX - VIEUX   be detailed to follow
                   RIEUX - BURBURE -   the rear Battalion on each
                   RAIMBERT.   Road.

W A R   D I A R Y.

2/1ST. SOUTH MIDLAND FIELD AMBULANCE.

APPENDIX NO. 11.

In the Field.

December 1st. 1916.

SECRET. Copy No. 14.

184TH. INFANTRY BRIGADE ORDER NO. 45.

2/II/I6.

Reference Maps
HAZEBROUK. 5a.
& LENS. 11.
I/I00.000.

1. On November 3rd 1916, the 184th. Brigde Group will march to Area B.1 in accordance with Table overleaf and Area B.1 Map attached.

2. The Brigade Group will march as a Briage, wth 2nd. Echelon of 1st. Line Transport bigaeded in order of march of Units under the Brigade Transport Officer.

3. The Column will halt at 12.45 p.m. and move on again at 2.0 p.m. Haversack ration will be taken. Cokkers will not be used until arrival in Billets.

4. On November 4th. 1916 the 184th. Bde. Group will move to CHELERS area.

5. Reference para. 5 of Bde. Order No. 44 Divisional Headquarters oves to CHELERS and not as stted therein.

6. Brigade Headquarters will close at AUCHEL at 9.0 a.m. November 3rd. and re-open at ORLENCOURT at the same hour.

ACKNOWLEDGE.

Issued at 6.30 a.m.

(sgd) E. C. GEPP. Major.
Brigade Major.
184th. Infntry Brigade.

Order of March of Units.	From.	To.	Starting Point.
IST. FLD. AMB.	RAIMBERT.	ROCOURT.	X RDS. 900ˣ N.W. of CAUCHY X Roads.

Time.	Route.	Remarks.
9.34 a.m.	AUCHEL - Road just W. of S. in ST. LEONARD -X Roads ¼ mile W. of S. in CALONNE-RIOUCART STATION - OURTON - ROCOURT.	Not to leave column E. of DIEVAL.

WAR   DIARY.

2/1ST. SOUTH MIDLAND FIELD AMBULANCE.

APPENDIX NO. III.

In the Field.
December 1st. 1916.

SECRET.   Copy No. 14.

                    184TH. INFANTRY BRIGADE ORDER.

                                             3/11/16.

Reference Maps.
LENS. 11.
1/100.000.

        1. On November 4th. 1916, the 184th. Infantry Brigade
           Group will move to Area B.3, in accordance with March
           Table overleaf, and area B.3 map attached.

        2. Divisional Headquarters will close at CHELERS at 11.0
           a.m. November 4th. and re-open at ROLLECOURT at the
           same hour.

        3. Brigade Headquarters will close at ORLENCOURT at 11.0 a.m.
           November 4th. at 11.0 a.m. and re-open at CHELERS the
           same hour.

           ACKNOWLEDGE.
                                   (sgd) E.C.OEPP. Major.
                                         Brigade Major.
                    Issued at 9.0 p.m.   184th. Infantry Brigade.

           Unit.   From.   To.   Starting Point.
           1ST. FIELD AMB. ROCOURT.   TINCQUETTE.   Road Junction
                                                     S. of T. in ROCOURT.

           Time.   Route.   Remarks.

           11.0.   MAGNICOURT-   -
                           CHELERS.

WAR DIARY.

2/1st. SOUTH MIDLAND FIELD AMBULANCE.

APPENDIX No. IV.

In the Field.
December 1st. 1916.

Copy No. 14.

SECRET.

184TH. INFANTRY BRIGADE ORDER NO. 47.

4/II/16.

Reference Map
LENS 11.
1/100.000.

1. On November 5th. 1916, the 184th. Brigade Group will move to Area C.3. in accordance with March Table overleaf, and Area C.3. Map attached.

2. Bde½ Headquarters will close at CHELERS at 7.15 a.m. on November 5th. after which hour reports will be sent to REBREUVE CHATEAU.

ACKNOWLEDGE.

Issued at 4.0 p.m.

(sgd) E.C.GEPP. Major.
Brigade Major.
184th. Infantry Brigade.

Unit.	From.	To.	Starting Point.
IST. F. AMB.	TINCQUETTE.	ROZIERE.	X RDS. on ARRAS - S. POL RD. E. of 2nd. L. in LE QUESNEL.

WAR DIARY.

OF "EVERY ENEMY GROUP WITH 4/5 BATT/S.
A. & S. HIGH'RS"

$\frac{4}{5}$

In the Field.
December 1st. 1916.

Copy No. 14.

SECRET.

184TH. INFANTRY BRIGADE ORDER NO. 48.

Reference Map
LENS 11.
1/100000.

5/II/16.

1. On November 6th. 1916, the 184 Brigade Group will move to area D.1. in accordance with March Table overleaf, and area D.1. Map attached.

2. All Units will be clear of the FREVENT – DOULLENS Road by 2.0 p.m.

3. Divisional Headquarters will close at ROLLECOURT at 11.0 a.m. November 6th. and reopen at the same hour at FROHEN-IE-GRAND.

4. Brigade Headquarters will close at REBREUVE at 9.0 a.m. on November 6th. after which hour reports to OCCOCHES.

ACKNOWLEDGE.

(sgd) E.C.GEPP. Major.
Brigade Major.
Issued at 5.0 p.m.   184th. Infantry Brigade.

Unit.	From.	To.	Starting Point.
IST. FIELD AMB.	ROXIERE.	NEUVILETTE.	REBREUVIETTE CH.

TIME.a.m.	Route.	Remarks.
10.0 a.m.	Rd. through Ist. R. in REBREUVIETTE-ARBRE-BOUCQUEMAISON.	A M.M.P. will be on FREVENT - ETREE RD. to show turning. An Ambulance Waggon will be detailed to follow L.T.M.

CONFIDENTIAL. 61st Div. 140/1990.

WAR DIARY.

2/IST. SOUTH MIDLAND FIELD AMBULANCE.R.A.M.C.(T).

DECEMBER 1916.

In the Field.
December 1916.

Army Form C. 2118.

WAR DIARY
or
INTELLIGENCE SUMMARY.

(Erase heading not required.)

Reference ALBERT Combined Sheet 57.d.S.E. and 62.d.N.E.

Instructions regarding War Diaries and Intelligence Summaries are contained in F.S. Regs., Part II. and the Staff Manual respectively. Title pages will be prepared in manuscript.

Place	Date	Hour	Summary of Events and Information	Remarks and references to Appendices
	1916.			
AVELUY POST.	Dec. 1st.		Routine work. – A.D.M.S. 61ST. DIVISION visited and inspected Hospital, and surrounding premises. OFFICER COMMANDING visited 61ST. DIVISIONAL HEADQUARTERS. Extra Marquee pitched for use as Hospital Office and Packstore. – General outline of Camp decided on.	Evtn.
AVELUY POST.	Dec. 2nd.		Routine work. – Construction of tramway commenced, for carriage of patients from Main Road to Receiving Tent – the pathway and steps being dangerous in frosty weather. Dug Out for Hospital continued, off main road – hewing out of the solid chalk. No. 1832 PTE. GOODE. W.H. evacuated to Casualty Clearing Station. T4/248654 DRIVER SEARS. P. No. 2 Coy. 61ST. DIVL. TRAIN att. 2/1ST.SO.MID.FLD.AMB. killed.	FnStn. See appl.
AVELUY POST.	Dec. 3rd.		Routine work. – D.A.D.M.S. 61ST. DIVISION visited Hospital. OFFICER COMMANDING visited and inspected Collecting Post,(RED CROSS CORNER,)&the Advanced Dressing Station. (POZIERES CEMETERY POST.) to see how the new tramway arrangements and construction were proceeding. T4/248654 DRIVER SEARS buried at AVELUY CEMETERY. The Quartermaster's Stores, and Mechanical Transport Billet at ALBERT heavily shelled. – No Unit casualties. – Serious damage caused to the framework of one of the SIDDELEY DEASEY Ambulances.	Evtn.
AVELUY POST.	Dec. 4th.		Routine work. – Further development of tramway, and also Hospital dug out. Wooden hut erected for use of three officers. – Dug out for Quartermasters stores commenced, behind present stores. – The personnel of the Quartermasters' Stores, and also all M.T. personnel and cars, vacated their billets at ALBERT, and rejoined the Unit at AVELUY POST. The OFFICER COMMANDING had a meeting with R.O.D. Officers to see if railway evacuation by power line could not be arranged direct from POZIERES CEMETERY. – constant hostile shelling in that area making evacuation there frequently very dangerous.	Evtn.
AVELUY POST.	Dec. 5th.		Routine work. – Relief parties sent to Advanced Dressing Station and R.A.P. and relieved bearers returned to Camp. – Bearer parties from Front Line to RIFLE DUMP heavily shelled. No casualties. D.A.D.M.S. 61ST. DIVISION inspected Hospital and Camp. Shelter at POZIERES Cemetery hit by hostile shell. – This shell, a "dud" exploded two derelict unused British shells, which had been left thereunmarked. – No casualties. Further conference with Railway Officers about possible wounded train service.	FnStn.

WAR DIARY
or
INTELLIGENCE SUMMARY.
(Erase heading not required.)

Army Form C. 2118.

Reference ALBERT Combined Sheets.
57.d.S.E. and 62.d.N.E.

Place	Date	Hour	Summary of Events and Information	Remarks and references to Appendices
AVELUY POST.	1916. Dec. 6th.		Routine work. - Duck boards laid on all paths round Camp area. Arrangements made for moving the horse lines to site on top of ridge facing the Hospital grounds. OFFICER COMMANDING visiting Advanced Dressing Station and Collecting Post etc. The G.O.C., 61ST. DIVISION, (MAJOR GENERAL COLIN MACKENZIE.C.B.) visited and inspected Hospital and Camp generally. Railway from road completed and used for the first time, for carriage of wounded.	G.B.McL
AVELUY POST.	Dec. 7th.		Routine work. - A.D.M.S. 61ST. DIVISION evacuated to Casualty Clearing Station. Reliefs arranged and carried out between M.O's at Dressing Station, and M.O's at A.D.S. and Collecting Post. Heavy hostile shelling of area round Camp this evening. No shells fell actually in Camp, but several very close. Casualties brought from CRUCIFIX CORNER etc. and treated in the tents during the shelling. - Subsequently all tents evacuated, and personnel and patients crowded the dug outs for the night. - The M.T. billet at AVELUY CHATEAU was also seriously damaged by an enemy shell. No casualties in Unit or attached personnel, but a Motor Bicycle belonging to the Unit which was standing outside was entirely destroyed.	G.B.McL
AVELUY POST.	Dec. 8th.		Routine work. The G.O.C., 61ST. DIVISION (MAJOR GEN. COLIN MACKENZIE.C.B.) visited and inspected Hospital, and discussed evacuation routes and condition of the forward area, and R.A.P's. The O.C. requested that the construction of a new A.D.S. N.W. of TULLUCH'S CORNER might be proceeded with, and POZIERES evacuated, as being too unsafe for retention of wounded, and accomodation being very inadequate. - Bearer parties from Front Line to RIFLE DUMP again heavily shelled. No casualties to Unit personnel. This evening the Camp was again shelled and several casualties were collected from the immediate neighbourhood, and treated. - Patients evacuated to C.C.S. between the attacks, and others housed as on previous night. New dug out at RED CROSS CORNER completed for M.T.personnel.	G.B.McL
AVELUY POST.	Dec. 9th.		Routine work. - Improvements and developments in Camp proceeded with. POZIERES CEMETERY POST and RED CROSS CORNER again shelled. - New M.T.Billet at RED CROSS CORNER destroyed by a direct hit. - No casualties. No.1811 ST.SGT.BURLING and No.2395 PTE.LOWE.F. returned from leave of absence.	G.B.McL

Army Form C. 2118.

WAR DIARY
or
INTELLIGENCE SUMMARY.
(Erase heading not required.)

Reference ALBERT Combined Sheets. 57.d.S.E. and 62.d.N.E.

Place	Date	Hour	Summary of Events and Information	Remarks and references to Appendices
	1916.			
AVELUY POST.	Dec.10th.		Routine work. - D.A.D.M.S. 61ST. DIVISION visited and inspected Camp and Hospital Premises. No. 2158 PTE. HERBERT. C.A. returned to the Unit from No. 9 Casualty Clearing Station. No. 542 ST.SGT.CLEMENTS proceeded to POZIERES CEMETERY POST as Staff Sgt. in Charge of the "forward area."	F.S.M.
AVELUY POST.	Dec.11th.		Routine work. - D.A.D.M.S. 61ST. DIVISION visited and inspected A.D.S. (POZIERES CEMETERY POST) and Collecting Post. (RED CROSS CORNER.) OFFICER COMMANDING visited and inspected A.D.S. and Collecting Post. Relief Party sent to POZIERES and RED CROSS CORNER, and relieved bearers returned to Camp. Party sent to BOUZINCOURT to fetch an additional Marquee for use at AVELUY POST. Hospital Marquees connected by canvas passages, thus allowing access from one to another under cover. Daily power trams for wounded arranged for from POZIERES to AVELUY POST.	Auth.ADMS 61st. Div. F.S.M.
AVELUY POST.	Dec.12th.		Routine work.- D.A.D.M.S. 61ST. DIVISION visited and inspected Hospital. OFFICER COMMANDING visited R.A.P. and A.D.S. etc. COLLECTING POT at REDCROSS CORNER again shelled. - No unit casualties. Marquee pitched for Hospital Office and Pack Store. No.1931 L/CPL. LOTHEIM.J. appointed Corperal vice No. 2070 CPL. WHITEHOUSE.J. evacuated to C.C.S.	F.S.M.
AVELUY POST.	Dec. 13th.		Routine work. - General constructional work carried on. - Duck Beards laid down in all parts of Camp. - Cook House pulled down, and re-erected in another part of Camp - brick fleering laid down for same. - No.T4/248643 DRIVER HUMPAGE.T. returned to duty from C.C.S.	F.S.M.
AVELUY POST.	Dec.14th.		Routine work. - CAPTAIN HIRST.W.J.; No.1859 ST.SGT.SGT.JACQUES.J.H., No. 2124 SGT.BICKELL.R.J.G. and No. 1846 L/CPL. BANNISTER.A. returned from leave of absence to ENGLAND. Dug Out in rear of Quartermasters' Stores completed, and further Dug Out for use of Quartermasters Stores Personnel commenced. CAPTAIN BANNERMAN. 2/2ND. SOUTH MIDLAND FIELD AMBULANCE reported for temporary duty with Unit.	F.S.M. Auth.A.DMS 61st. Div.
AVELUY POST.	Dec.15th.		Routine work. - Prev.L/Cpl.WHITEHOUSE.E. appointed Cpl. vice No.2072 L/CPL. FOXHALL evacuated to C.C.S. - Further developments and improvements in Camp area proceeded with. - Material for Nissen Huts received. - CAPTAIN GREEN.P.H., No.2148 Q.M.S.TAYLOR.W.H.; No.1931 CPL. LOTHEIM.J. and No.2216.PTE. CHAMBERLAIN.G. proceeded on 10 days leave of absence to ENGLAND. 2282	F.S.M. Auth.ADMS 61st.Div.

Army Form C. 2118.

WAR DIARY
or
INTELLIGENCE SUMMARY.
(Erase heading not required.)

Reference ALBERT Combined Sheets.
57.d.S.E. and 62.a.N.E.

Instructions regarding War Diaries and Intelligence Summaries are contained in F.S. Regs., Part II. and the Staff Manual respectively. Title pages will be prepared in manuscript.

Place	Date	Hour	Summary of Events and Information	Remarks and references to Appendices
AVELUY POST.	1916. Dec.16.		Routine work. - OFFICER COMMANDING visited DIVISIONAL HEADQUARTERS and A.D.M.S. 61ST. DIVISION. M.T. Section moved from Billet at AVELUY CHATEAU and installed in temporary shelter in Camp. Construction of Dug Out for M.T. Personnel commenced in quarry close to Camp. Personnel at Advanced Dressing Station and Regimental Aid Post changed, and relieved bearers reported back to Camp.	GStu
AVELUY POST.	Dec.17.		Routine work. - Preparations made for building two more steel shelter Dug Outs -- one in Camp for the Officers, and one for the M.T.Personnel as stated. Marquee Store Tent supplied by D.A.D.O.S. 61ST. DIVISION, at order of A.A.& Q.M.G. 61ST. DIVISION fetched from HEDAUVILLE. CAPTAIN HIRST.W.J. relieved LIEUT.W.JONES EVANS at POZIERES CEMETERY POST. POZIERES CEMETERY POST damaged by shell fire.	GStu
AVELUY POST.	Dec.18th.		Routine work. - Large Marquee pitched for reception of sick and wounded cases. Church Parade for patients and Unit Personnel. D.A.D.M.S. 61st.-DIVISION visited and inspected Camp and Hospital. Orders received from G.O.C., 61ST. DIVISION for OFFICER COMMANDING to proceed tomorrow to DIVISIONAL HEADQUARTERS to act as A.D.M.S., vice LT. COL. MOXEY. O.C., 2/3RD. FIELD AMB. gone home on leave.	GStu
AVELUY POST.	Dec.19th.		Routine work. - Orders to OFFICER COMMANDING cancelled on arrival of COLONEL CLAYTON, who reported at DIVISIONAL HEADQUARTERS as A.D.M.S. Division. CAPTAIN JAMIESON R.A.M.C.(T) proceeded to POZIERES to relieve CAPTAIN BANNERMAN, 2/2ND. S2M.FLD. AMB. who returned to his Unit. Construction of Steel Shelter for use of Officers at AVELUY POST commenced, and site for second steel shelter for M.T. Personnel decided on in Quarry close to Camp. Operating tent pitched in quarry as a temporary store for car accessories, petrol etc.	GStu
AVELUY POST.	Dec.20th.		Routine work. - OFFICER COMMANDING proceeded to DIVISIONAL HEADQUARTERS and interviewed A.D.M.S. and D.A.D.M.S. 61ST. DIVISION. - A.D.M.S. and D.A.D.M.S. 61ST. DIVISION subsequently visited and inspected Camp and Hospital Premises. Erection of Steel Shelter for use of M.T. personnel etc. commenced, after the quarry after the quarry had been suitably levelled. New Steel Shelter for use of Officers completed and brought into use.	GStu

Army Form C. 2118.

WAR DIARY
of
INTELLIGENCE SUMMARY.

Reference ALBERT Combined Sheets. 57.d.S.E. and 62.d.N.E.

(Erase heading not required.)

Instructions regarding War Diaries and Intelligence Summaries are contained in F.S. Regs., Part II. and the Staff Manual respectively. Title pages will be prepared in manuscript.

Place	Date	Hour	Summary of Events and Information	Remarks and references to Appendices
	1916.			
AVELUY POST.	Dec.21st.		Routine work. - Personnel at Advanced Dressing Station and Regimental Aid Post changed, and relieved Bearers reported back to Camp. Advanced Dressing Station at POZIERES CEMETERY POST heavily shelled - two direct hits on dug out. No casualties. Place reported unsafe. 1859 ST. SGT. BURLING proceeded to A.D.S. vice 587 ST. SGT. CLEMENTS who reported back to H.Q. Construction of underground Hospital continued. - Third room opened out. T4/243703 ST. SGT. MAJOR DIX. J.; No. 1875 PTE. ROGERS.A.E.; No. 2274 L/CPL.GREEN. E.B. and 73772 DRIVER ARMITAGE. E. reported back from leave of absence to ENGLAND.	RCW
AVELUY POST.	Dec.22nd.		Routine work. - Further improvements in Camp and Premises generally carried out. Construction of second steel shelter for M.T. and other N.C.O's continued. After heavy rain, dug outs in POZIERES CEMETERY POST badly flooded. - R.R's, 61ST. DIVISION commenced repairs to walls and pumps. Relief Post and Regimental Aid Post heavily shelled. - No Unit casualties.	RCW
AVELUY POST.	Dec.23rd.		Routine work. - D.D.M.S. IV CORPS (Acting D.M.S. Vth. ARMY) visited and inspected Camp, and Hospital premises, and expressed himself as satisfied with the constructional work achieved in the short time since last visit. OFFICER COMMANDING visited A.D.M.S. 61ST. DIVISION. Small relief party despatched to A.D.S. relieved bearers returning to Camp. Construction of Steel Shelters etc. continued. POZIERES CEMETERY POST again badly shelled. New dressing shelter destroyed.	RCW
AVELUY POST.	Dec.24th. CHRISTMAS EVE.		Routine work. - Divine Service for all ranks and for patients in Marquee at 6.30 p.m. Dug Out at POZIERES CEMETERY again damaged by a direct hit, flooding worse than before.	RCW
AVELUY POST.	Dec.25th. CHRISTMAS DAY.		Church Parade for all ranks at 9.0 a.m. Holiday for all ranks as far as possible. - Christmas Dinner for all ranks in Marquee at 1.0 p.m. 198 including patients, sat down. - Impromptu Concert in the evening.	RCW
AVELUY POST.	Dec.26th.		Routine work. - Construction of steel shelters at Main Dressing Station completed. - Erection of one Nissen Hut commenced. Entire Staff at ADVANCED DRESSING STATION, - RIFLE DUMP and REGIMENTAL AID POST relieved. Fresh party proceeded from Headquarters to take over, and relieved bearers reported back to Headquarters.	RCW

Army Form C. 2118.

WAR DIARY
or
INTELLIGENCE SUMMARY.

Reference ALBERT Combined Sheet. 57.d.S.E. and 62.d.N.E.

(Erase heading not required.)

Instructions regarding War Diaries and Intelligence Summaries are contained in F.S. Regs., Part II. and the Staff Manual respectively. Title pages will be prepared in manuscript.

Place	Date	Hour	Summary of Events and Information	Remarks and references to Appendices
	1916.			
AVELUY POST.	Dec.27th.		Routine work. - Religious service and Christmas Dinner for all ranks who were minding "forward area" on Christmas Day, - 48 sat down to dinner. CAPTAIN R. COX. R.A.M.C.(T) reported his arrival and was taken on the strength of the Unit. Dug Outs for M.T. Personnel finally completed and men moved in. POZIERES CEMETERY POST badly shelled in the evening, the enemy sent sending over "tear shells" All ranks forced to wear box respirators for two hours.	Auth.ADMS. 61 Diva. Fcolu.
AVELUY POST.	Dec.28th.		Routine work. - CAPTAIN P.H.GREEN reported his arrival back from leave of absence to ENGLAND. Hospital Dug Out continued and preparations made for tunnelling under road, and connecting Hospital Marquee and Hospital Dug Out by tram line through tunnel. Construction of new latrines with special incinerator begun at Main Dressing Station.	Fculu.
AVELUY POST.	Dec.29th.		Routine work. - GENERAL OFFICER COMMANDING, 61ST. DIVISION visited and inspected Camp and Hospital Premises. - Further developments and improvements in Camp proceeded with. No. 2148 Q.M.S.TAYLOR, No.1931 CPL. LOTHEIM and No. 2216 PTE. CHAMBERLAIN. G. returned from leave of absence to ENGLAND. POZIERES CEMETERY POST finally blown in by direct hit from German Shell. - Most Dressing Room at POZIERES CEMETERY POST finally blown in by direct hit from German Shell. - Most of the equipment destroyed and buried. Heavy evening bombardment. 9 direct hits on top of dug outs which showed signs of collapsing, - all were badly flooded.	Fculu.
AVELUY POST.	Dec.30th.		Routine work. - BRIGADIER GENERAL, 184TH. INFANTRY BDE. (BRIG. GEN. THE HON R.WHITE.C.M.G.,) visited and inspected Hospital and Camp premises. CAPTAIN JAMIESON reported back to Camp from ADVANCED DRESSING STATION. OFFICER COMMANDING visited A.D.M.S. and C.R.E. 61ST. DIVISION at DIV. H.Q. to report that POZIERES CEMETERY POST is uninhabitable. - Decided by A.D.M.S. and C.R.E. to evacuate the post, and retire to a new place, West of Main OVILLERS - TULLUCH CORNER ROAD, about 500 yards S. of TULLUCH CORNER.	Fculu.
AVELUY POST.	Dec.31st.		Routine work. - CAPTAIN HIRST and Staff from A.D.S. POZIERES CEMETERY POST after salving all equipment and stores that could possibly be saved, left their station and reported back to Camp. OFFICER COMMANDING met C.R.E. and A.D.M.S. 61ST. DIVISION at site of new A.D.S. - Plans decided on for construction of new A.D.S. and temporary arrangements made for carrying on whilst new place is being made ready. - D.A.D.M.S. 61ST. DIVISION visited and inspected Camp. Alterations to, and extension of Quartermasters Stores begun. - New latrines completed and brought into use.	Fculu.

Fculu,
Lt. Col. R.A.M.C.(T).
Officer Commanding. 2/1st.South Midland Field Ambulance.

December 31st. 1916.

APPENDIX 1.

WAR DIARY.

2/IST. SOUTH MIDLAND FIELD AMBULANCE,R.A.M.C.(T).

In the Field.

December 31st. 1916.

(C O P Y.)

To:

The Assistant Director of Medical Services.

61st. Division.

I greatly regret to have to report the following occurrence, which took place this day (December 2nd.)

We received a message from CAPTAIN STOBIE (Temp. M.O. 2/4th. OXFORD and BUCKS L.I.) asking us to remove 27 cases of so called "Trench Feet" and three other cases last evening.

As we had no accomodation here for these men, I arranged with the Officer in Charge, 3RD. FIELD AMBULANCE at "THE CAB STAND" to house these men for the night, and we would evacuate them through the Motor Ambulance Convoy today.

Owing to the shortage of accomodation at "THE CAB STAND" this morning, the Officer in Charge there asked me to remove some of the cases as soon as possible, before the M.A.C. clearance. - As we had no Motor Ambulance available, we despatched a Horsed Ambulance at 12.0 noon, with four horses, two drivers, and four leaders.

The hostile shelling of the village of AVELUY took place shortly after the waggon had left here. - The latter was halted in the village by one of the Traffic Control personnel, owing to the shelling in front. - After halting, the next shell exploded underneath the front pair of horses. - No. T4/2486/654 DRIVER SEARS. P. was killed, both his horses were killed, and also one of the wheeler pair. - No T4/248648 DRIVER LAWLER J. was wounded in the back and face, not seriously. - No 2530 PRIVATE HITCHMAN E.A. who was sitting on the front of the waggon was wounded, not seriously.

There are no other casualties to report.

(sgd) George Mackie. Lieut. Colonel. R.A.M.C.(T).

Officer Commanding. 2/1st. South Midland Field Ambce.

In the Field.

December 2nd. 1916.

Army Form C. 2118.

WAR DIARY
or
INTELLIGENCE SUMMARY.

(Erase heading not required.)

Reference ALBERT Combined Sheet
57.d.S.E. and 62.d.N.E.

Instructions regarding War Diaries and Intelligence Summaries are contained in F. S. Regs., Part II. and the Staff Manual respectively. Title pages will be prepared in manuscript.

Place	Date	Hour	Summary of Events and Information	Remarks and references to Appendices
AVELUY POST.	1917. Jan.1st.		Routine work. - Address by OFFICER COMMANDING to Unit and "attached" personnel. Unloading station, and motor bicycle shed at Railhead erected.	Folio
AVELUY POST.	Jan.2nd.		Routine work. - GENERAL OFFICER COMMANDING (MAJOR GENERAL COLIN MACKENZIE.C.B.,) called, and inspected the whole of the Hospital Premises, being greatly interested in the new tunnel to the dug outs.	Folio
AVELUY POST.	Jan.3rd.		Routine work. - Construction of new Advanced Dressing Station at HUN TANK commenced. Temporary shelter erected, and line of evacuation altered. Reconstruction of stores continued. No. 2043 ST.SGT.ROBINSON, H.F.; No. 2236 PTE. JAMES,E.A., No. 2351 PTE. PEARSON,J.H. and No. 2283 PTE. MACBETH, W. proceeded on 10 days leave of absence to ENGLAND. Telephone installed in Orderly Room.	Folio
AVELUY POST.	Jan. 4th.		Routine work. - Work at Advanced Dressing Station continued. Construction of Tunnel under main road progressing, and fresh railway line laid in Camp to connect up with proposed line in tunnel.	Folio
AVELUY POST.	Jan.5th.		General Routine work. - CAPTAIN H.N.BURROUGHES,R.A.M.C.(T). left Unit on appointment as OFFICER COMMANDING. 2/2ND. SOUTH MIDLAND FIELD AMBULANCE, with the rank of Lieut. Colonel. CAPTAIN COX. R.A.M.C.(T) reported for duty as temporary Medical Officer to OFFICER COMMANDING, 2/7TH. WARWICKS. Construction of second Nissen Hut for use of personnel commenced.	Auth.ADMS. 61st. Divn. do. Folio
AVELUY POST.	Jan.6th.		Routine work. OFFICER COMMANDING'S name found "mentioned in Despatches". No. 984 SGT. JOHNSON, H.; No. 1841 PTE. ATKINS, W.E.; No. 2289 PTE. THICKETT, A., and No. T.4/248648 PTE. WARD.W. A.S.C. att. 2/1st. S.M.F.AMB. proceeded on 10 days leave of absence to ENGLAND. Hostile bombardment of area round HUN TANK with gas shells during night. - Staff compelled to wear box respirators for over two hours. - One casualty, No. 1920 PTE. ELLIOTT, B.G. being slightly gassed. Constructional work continued there, and also in Camp at HEADQUARTERS.	Folio

Army Form C. 2118.

WAR DIARY
or
INTELLIGENCE SUMMARY.

Reference ALBERT Combined Sheet. 57.d.S.E. and 62.d.N.E.

(Erase heading not required.)

Place	Date	Hour	Summary of Events and Information	Remarks and references to Appendices
AVELUY POST.	1917. Jan.7th.		Routine work. - Church Parade for Patients and Unit personnel able to attend. All constructional work continued. Second Nissen Hut completed and occupied.	Pbl.
AVELUY POST.	Jan.8th.		Routine work. - Medical Inspection of all ranks at 7.0 a.m. BRIGADIER GENERAL, 184TH. INFANTRY BRIGADE (BRIG. GEN. THE HON R. WHITE.C.M.G.) and D.D.M.S. IV CORPS inspected the Hospital and Camp premises, the latter with a view to the eventual development of this post into a large Main Corps Dressing Station. D.A.D.M.S., 18TH. DIVISION visited Camp, preparatory to taking over the area. 1 DEASEY CAR reported from 2/3RD. FIELD AMBULANCE to be attached here, for purpose of evacuating sick and wounded from the left sector of the line. - DONNETS POST evacuated by 2/3 FIELD AMBULANCE. - THE OFFICER COMMANDING inspected NAB ROAD as far as GRAVEL PIT to see new route of evacuation to be followed by cars.	Auth ADMS 61st.Div. Pbl.
AVELUY POST.	Jan.9th.		Routine work. - Construction of railway and tunnel continued. Acting D.A.D.M.S. IV CORPS visited Camp to obtain plan and measurements of the ground. Construction of first steel shelter at HUN TANK completed, and shelter occupied. Unit notified that it was to be ready to receive and treat all "gassed" cases from IV CORPS front. Two tents arranged specially for such cases, and already existing preparations extended.	Auth ADMS 61st. Divn. Estu
AVELUY POST.	Jan.10th.		Routine work. - Constructional work continued in its various branches. OFFICER COMMANDING visited A.D.M.S. 61ST. DIVISION as instructed, subsequently visiting D.D.M.S. IVTH. CORPS to further discuss plans for the erection of a large Main Dressing Station at AVELUY POST. Instructions received that active operations were contemplated on Divisional Front. Arrangements developed to meet any possible contingency. REGIMENTAL AID POST and COLLECTING POST Staffs doubled, and a system of rapid reliefs arranged from HUN TANK. - Cooking apparatus etc. installed there. - Six wheeled stretchers posted at TULLUCH'S CORNER, in case railway line was blocked, and continuous car service for both lines organised. CAPTAIN CRAIG R.A.M.C.(T). with one DEASEY Car reported for temporary duty from 2/2nd. FLD. AMB. Two DEASEY CARS and one FORD CAR also reported from 2/3rd. FIELD AMBULANCE. CAPTAIN HIRST proceeded to HUN TANK.	Pbl. Auth.ADMS 61st. Divn.

Army Form C. 2118.

WAR DIARY
or
INTELLIGENCE SUMMARY.

(Erase heading not required.)

Reference ALBERT Combined Sheet.
57.d.S.E. and 62.d.N.E.
FRANCE, Lens 11. 1/100,000.

Instructions regarding War Diaries and Intelligence Summaries are contained in F.S. Regs., Part II and the Staff Manual respectively. Title pages will be prepared in manuscript.

Place	Date	Hour	Summary of Events and Information	Remarks and references to Appendices
AVELUY POST.	1917. Jan.11th.		Routine work. - Letter received from COLONEL JAMES YOUNG, A.M.S. late A.D.M.S. 61st. DIVISION congratulating the OFFICER COMMANDING and the Unit on its splendid record of work since landing in FRANCE. Military Operations proving to be of limited extent, the extra arrangements were cancelled at 7.0 p.m. and the extra cars reported back to their Units. CAPTAIN CRAIG, R.A.M.C.(T). reported back to 2/2nd. FIELD AMBULANCE.	GWh.
AVELUY POST.	Jan.12th.		Routine work. - LIEUT. W. JONES EVANS reported back from leave. Tunnel under Main Road almost completed and opened through into system of dug outs on the other side. - Construction of new Advanced Dressing Station continued.	GWh.
AVELUY POST.	Jan.13th.		Routine work. - CAPTAIN JAMIESON, R.A.M.C.(T). reported for duty to OFFICER COMMANDING. 2/4th. ROYAL BERKS REGT. for Temporary Duty as Medical Officer to the Battn. No. 2119 SGT. ROGERS. J.H., No. 2003 L/CPL. WARMINGTON.E. and No. 2179 PTE. DENHAM. F. proceeded on 10 days leave of absence to ENGLAND. CAPTAIN CHAPMAN, R.A.M.C. and 30 other ranks of the 54TH. FIELD AMBULANCE, 18th. DIV. reported to OFFICER COMMANDING to arrange taking over front line.	Auth. ADMS. 61st. Divn. GWh.
AVELUY POST.	Jan.14th.		All constructional work in Cam; completed as far as possible. - General Fatigues, cleaning Camp &c. Final packing of waggons, preparatory to move of Ambulance to Rest Area. Orders for march, and march table received from H.Q. 182nd. INFANTRY BRIGADE. Orders received from A.D.M.S. 61ST. DIVISION re evacuation of front line area, and handing over stores etc. to O.C. 54TH. FIELD AMBULANCE. CAPTAIN CHAPMAN taken round front area by O.C. - LEFT SECTOR. DANUBE TRENCH and GRAVEL PIT inspected, and arrangements made for relief of personnel of 2/3RD. FIELD AMBULANCE. RIGHT SECTOR. HUN TANK and RIFLE DUMP and R.A.P. inspected by CAPTAIN CHAPMAN in conjunction with CAPTAIN HIRST, and first reliefs arranged and sent up to their new positions. Half of Unit Personnel from front line reported back to Camp on relief. All Camp and area stores handed over.	V.app.ADMS. V.app 182 Inf. Bde. GWh.
AVELUY POST. VAL-DE-MAISON.	Jan.15th.		One Heavy Draught horse kicked in night, found with leg broken, destroyed by Veterinary Officer. Ambulance paraded at 9.30 a.m. but were were ordered to fall out by O.C. owing to hostile shelling of Camp area and adjacent roads. - One shell burst close to Camp, one fragment piercing Hospital Office tent. - No Casualties. 9.45 a.m. Unit moved off under CAPTAIN HIRST, CAPT.GREEN in charge of Transport.	GWh.

2353 Wt. W2544/1454 700,000 5/15 D.D.&L. A.D.S.S. Forms/C.2118.

Army Form C. 2118.

WAR DIARY
or
INTELLIGENCE SUMMARY.
(Erase heading not required)

Reference Map. FRANCE. LENS II.
1/100.000.

Instructions regarding War Diaries and Intelligence Summaries are contained in F.S. Regs., Part II. and the Staff Manual respectively. Title pages will be prepared in manuscript.

Place	Date	Hour	Summary of Events and Information	Remarks and references to Appendices
VAL-de-MAISON.	1917. Jan.15.(con).		Lieut. RIVERS proceeded in advance to act as Billeting Officer. O.C., remained behind, and interviewed O.C. 54TH. FIELD AMBULANCE on his arrival, personally handing over the Camp to him, and explaining the plans for the proposed development and construction of the Camp into a large Dressing Station, as ordered by D.D.M.S., IV CORPS. Remainder of Unit Personnel reported back from front line, and with the Sanitary and Cleaning Party, were sent on later in the day by Motor Lorry, with Unit blankets. Ambulance arrived at VAL-de-MAISON after a march of 16½ miles, being billeted in old Divisional Rest Stn. Route:- BOUZINCOURT-HEDAUVILLE-VARENNES-HARPONVILLE-TOUTENCOURT-PUCHEVILLERS-VAL-de-MAISON. Casualties:- (a) Unit. Nil. (b) Picked up from other Units. Three.	G.B.U. v. app. 182 Inf. Bde.
VAL-de-MAISON.	Jan.16th.		Unit rested. - Sick and Casualties collected from Units of 182nd. INFANTRY BRIGADE, and sent off to Casualty Clearing Station at PUCHEVILLERS. (Three cases so evacuated.) Heavy fall of snow and hard frost rendering adjacent roads very bad for traffic, the OFFICER COMMANDING decided to park the three heaviest G.S. Waggons in farm yard, in charge of Town Major and double the teams in the Horse Ambulances, which were likely to have a long and heavy days' work.	G.B.U.
VAL-de-MAISON. VACQUERIE.	Jan. 17th.		Unit marched off according to table, leaving VAL-de-MAISON at 1.15 p.m. passed starting point accurately at 1.16 p.m. and after a very delayed march, arrived safely at VACQUERIE at 7.10 p.m. Route:- FME du RUSEL - X Roads S. of last E. in AUCH MIN. de VALHEUREUX - CANDAS - FIENVILLERS - Road Fork S. of R. in VACQUERIE - VACQUERIE. Casualties:- (a) Unit. Two. (b) Picked up from other Units. Seven.	G.B.U. v. app. 182 Inf. Bde.
VACQUERIE. HANCHY.	Jan. 18th.		Ambulance paraded at 10.15 a.m. and marched off in heavy snow at 10.20 a.m. - March delayed owing to weather and bad roads, but Unit made good time, and arrived at HANCHY at 2.20 p.m. Route:- BEAUMETZ - LONGVILLERS - CRAMONT - HANCHY. Casualties:- (a) Unit. Nil. (b) Picked up from other Units. Five.	G.B.U. v. app. 182 Inf. Bde.
HANCHY. GUESCHART.	Jan. 19th.		Ambulance paraded at 7.30 a.m. and marched off according to March Table at 7.45 a.m. arriving at GUESCHART at 11.45 a.m. Route:- YVRENCH - MAISON PONTHIEU - GUESCHART. Casualties:- (a) Unit. Nil. (b) Picked up from Other Units. Four.	G.B.U. v. app. 182 Inf. Bde.

Army Form C. 2118.

WAR DIARY
or
INTELLIGENCE SUMMARY.
(Erase heading not required.)

Reference Map FRANCE. LENS.
1/100,000.

Instructions regarding War Diaries and Intelligence Summaries are contained in F.S. Regs., Part II. and the Staff Manual respectively. Title pages will be prepared in manuscript.

Place	Date	Hour	Summary of Events and Information	Remarks and references to Appendices
GUESCHART.	1917. Jan. 20th.		Ambulance rested, and gradually arranged their personnel in billets, which were cleaned. Fuel parties organised. - Cook-house, and temporary hospital and dressing room established. Latrines repaired and extended. - Recreation ground hired, and school room in village taken over for use in the evenings by men of the Unit. Horses rested, and waggons unpacked for checking and cleaning of section equipment. D.A.D.M.S. 61ST. DIVISION visited and inspected billets and premises.	F.J.M.
GUESCHART.	Jan. 21st.		Holiday for personnel. General fatigues.	F.J.M.
GUESCHART.	Jan. 22nd.		Construction of beds, and general cleaning up and improvement of billets continued. Three double teams of horses despatched to VAL-de-MAISON under STAFF SGT. MAJOR DIX, to bring on the waggons left there. CAPTAIN HIRST and three DEASEY MOTOR AMBULANCES proceeded to BOUZINCOURT to escort the 61ST. DIVISIONAL ARTILLERY to their Rest Area.	F.J.M.
GUESCHART.	Jan. 23rd.		General Fatigues and Recreation. - Constructional work continued. G.O.C. 61ST. DIVISION (MAJOR GENERAL COLIN MACKENZIE.C.B.) visited Camp, and inspected the Billets etc. - ST.SGT.MJR DIX reported back with 3 G.S.Waggons left behind at VAL-de-MAISON, all correct.	F.J.M.
GUESCHART.	Jan. 24th.		Fresh accomodation found for a small Hospital for Unit and local casualties. Arrangements made for putting in windows, and a stove, and re-flooring the barn. Improvement of billets continued. - Waggon cleaning commenced under difficulties, owing to the continued frost. CAPTAIN HIRST and I DEASEY Car arrived back, the other two cars having broken down, were left to be towed in by the Field Ambulance Workshop. O.C. visited the Field Ambulance Workshop at ST. RICQUIER to see the other Unit Ambulances under repair, and called upon A.D.M.S. 61ST. DIVISION at BRAILLY.	F.J.M.
GUESCHART.	Jan. 25th.		Routine work. - Repairs and general constructional work continued. Letter received from A.D.M.S. 61ST. DIVISION that G.O.C., VTH. ARMY had conferred 3 Military Medals on the following men of this Unit:- No. 2180 CORPORAL HILLIAR. J.T. - No. 1802 PTE. BLUCK. H. - and No. 2496 PRIVATE WHITHORN. T. and had arranged for two others viz.No. 2097 SERGEANT PERRY. A.H. and No. 2082 PRIVATE GOODE. G. to be mentioned in despatches.	F.J.M. v. app. 1.

2353 Wt. W2544/1454 700,000 5/15 L.D.&L. A.D.S.S./Forms/C. 2118.

Army Form C. 2118.

WAR DIARY
or
INTELLIGENCE SUMMARY.

Reference Map FRANCE. LENS II.
1/100,000.

(Erase heading not required.)

Instructions regarding War Diaries and Intelligence Summaries are contained in F. S. Regs., Part II. and the Staff Manual respectively. Title pages will be prepared in manuscript.

Place	Date	Hour	Summary of Events and Information	Remarks and references to Appendices
GUESCHART.	1917. Jan. 26th.		Routine work. - Baths for all ranks. CAPTAIN COX proceeded to 2/4th. OXFORD and BUCKS L.I. vice CAPTAIN STOBIE going on leave. This being cancelled later, CAPTAIN COX returned to Unit. LIEUT. W. JONES EVANS detailed for duty as Medical Officer to 61st. DIVL. AMMUNITION COLUMN vice CAPTAIN STAFFORD going on leave.	Auth A.D.M.S. 61st. Div. do. Refer
GUESCHART.	Jan. 27th.		Weekly Medical Inspection of all ranks. - Routine work. OFFICER COMMANDING visited Ordnance Workshop at CRECY with reference to repair of Unit waggons.	Refer
GUESCHART.	Jan. 28th.		Church Parade. - Routine work. The three recipients of the Military Medal having put, on their ribbons for the first time, were saluted by the whole Unit on parade.	Refer
GUESCHART.	Jan. 29th.		Routine work. A.D.M.S. 61ST. DIVISION visited village, and inspected Hospital premises.	Refer
GUESCHART.	Jan. 30th.		Routine work. Constructional work continued. - Wash-house for cooks erected outside present Cook-house. Canvas screens erected in billets. - Improvements to Hospital finished.	Refer
GUESCHART.	Jan. 31st.		Routine work. A.D.M.S. 61ST. DIVISION visited Village, and interviewed the OFFICER COMMANDING.	

Officer Commanding.

Lieut. Colonel. R.A.M.C.(T).
2/1st. South Midland Field Ambulance.

January 31st. 1917.

WAR DIARY

of the

2/1ST. SOUTH MIDLAND FIELD AMBULANCE.R.A.M.C.(T).

APPENDIX:- A.D.M.S. INSTRUCTIONS.

In the Field.
January 31st. 1917.

APPENDICES:- 182ND. INFANTRY BRIGADE ORDERS.

WAR DIARY

of the

2/1ST. SOUTH MIDLAND FIELD AMBULANCE. R.A.M.C.(T).

In the Field.

January 31st. 1917.

SECRET.
@@@@@@@@@@

61st. DIVISION R.A.M.C. ORDER. NO. 1208.

1. The 61st. Division (less Artillery) will be relieved by the 18th. Division (less Artillery) on January 15th. and January 16th. and will move to the MARIEUX AREA.

2. Advance parties from incoming Units will arrive as follows:-

   For 2/1st. Field Amb. from 54th. Field Ambulance on evening 13th. Jan
   For 2/2nd. Field Amb. from 55th. Field Ambulance on morning 14th. Jan
   For 2/3rd. Field Amb. from 56th. Field Ambulance on morning 15th. Jan

3. All details of the relief of personnel in the forward area will be arranged between O.C., 2/1st. Field Amb. and O.C., 54th. Field Ambce.

4. Separate instructions will be issued as to handing over of patients and stores.

5. The Field Ambulances less motor transport will move in accordance with attached march table.

6. The Sanitary Section will not move with the Division. - It will remain in the area, attached to 18th. Division, for period of one week.

7. On arrival in the MARIEUX area, Field Ambulances will be distributed as follows:-

GROUP.	UNIT.	BRIGADE AREAS.
182nd. Bde. Group. Under G.O.C. 182 Bde.	1st. Field Amb.	RUBEMPRE - LA VICOGNE.
183rd. Bde. Group. Under G.O.C. 183 Bde.	3rd. Field Amb.	BEAUQUESNE.
184th. Bde. Group. Under G.O.C. 184 Bde.	2nd. Field Amb.	PUCHEVILLERS.

Maps showing limits of Brigade areas have been issued.

8. Distances of 500 yards between Field Ambulances and Units in front will be maintained on the march into the MARIEUX AREA.

9. A.D.M.S. Office will close at BOUZINCOURT at 12.0 noon on 16th. January, and will re-open at same hour at MARIEUX.

(sgd) W.Wilson Clayton. Colonel.

A.D.M.S., 61st. Division.

January 13th. 1917.

Date.	Unit.	From.	To.	Route.	Remarks.
Jan. 15.	1st. F. Amb.	AVELUY POST.	VAL-de-MAISON.	BOUZINCOURT-HEDAUVILLE-VARENNES-HARPONVILLE-PUCHEVILLERS.	To follow Bn of 183 Bde. from huts at W.10.c.2.7.

C O P Y.

SECRET.   13.1.17.

    182nd. Infantry Brigade Order No. 71.

1. The 54th. Infantry Brigade will relieve the 182nd. Infantry Bde. in the front area on Jan. 15th. and 16th. in accordance with attached relief table:-
    On relief the Brigade will move to the RUBEMPRE - LA VICOGNE - Area en route to the BRAILLY area.
The Bde. Group will march from the RUBEMPRE area to CANDAS area on the 17th. inst.

2. Baggage Waggons will march with Ist. line Transport. They will report at Transport lines of Units at 4.0 p.m. the day before transport marches.

3. ROUTE.

    Ist. Field Amb. AVELUY POST → BOUZINCOURT - HEDAUVILLE → VARENNES -

                HARPONVILLE - TOUTENCOURT - PUCHEVILLERS - VAL-de-M'SON

4. TIME Ist. FIELD AMB. will start from AVELUY POST at 9.30 a.m. on the

    15th. January 1917.

                          (sgd) J.R.HEELIS. Major.
                          Brigade Major.
                          182nd. Infantry Bde.

13th. January 1917.

C O P Y.

SECRET. 14.1.17.

182nd. Infantry Brigade Order No. 72.

Reference. LENS Sheet 11. 1/100,000.

1. The Brigade Group will march on the 17th. January to the CANDAS Area, in accordance with March Table subjoined.
Route:- RUBEMPRE-TALMAS-LA VICOGNE-VERT GARLAND Fme.-Cross Roads just S. of last E. in ANCn. Min. de VALHEUREUX.

2. Units will march closed up, and normal halts will be observed.

3. Billeting Parties will meet the Staff Captain at CANDAS Church on the 17th. inst. at 11.0 a.m.

4. Baggage Waggons will accompany Units.

5. O.C., No. 2 Coy. 61st. Dicl. Train will send supply waggons, after refilling to billets of Units. - Guides will meet them outside billets, and guide them to their Q.M.Stores. Time for guides to meet waggons, will be notified by the Staff Captain to billeting parties.

6. O.C. 1st. Field Ambulance will arrange for one horse ambulance to follow 182nd. M.G.C. from TALMAS.

7. Brigade Headquarters close at RUBEMPRE at 11.30 a.m. and re-open at FIENVILLERS at the same hour.

8. ACKNOWLEDGE.

           (sgd) J.R.Heelis. Major.

           Brigade Major.

14.1.17.   182nd. Infantry Brigade.

ROUTE. 1st. Field Ambulance. Fme-du-RUSEL-X rds. S. of last E in AUCH MIN de VALHEUREUX - CANDAS - FIENVILLERS - VACQUERIE.
Time of starting:- 1.16 p.m. January 17th. 1917.

C O P Y.

SECRET.   16.1.17.

182nd. Infantry Brigade Order No. 73.

Reference LENS and ABBEVILLE Sheets. 1/100.000.

1. The 182nd. Brigade Group will march to the CANCHY area in accordance with March Tables attached.

2. Distances of 200 yards between Companies and 500 yards between Battalions will be maintained.

3. Baggage waggons will accompany Units. - Cookers will march with their Companies.

4. Billeting parties will meet the Staff Captain at CRAMONT CHURCH and CANCHY CHURCH on January 18th. and 19th. respectively at 10.0 a.m.

5. O.C., No. 2 Coy. Divl. Train will send supply waggons, after refilling to billets of Units. Guides will meet them outside billets, and guide them to their Quartermasters' Stores. Times for guides to meet waggons will be notified by Staff Captain to Billeting Parties.

6. O.C. 1st. Field Ambulance will arrange for one horse ambulance to follow each Battalion on the march.

7. Brigade Headquarters will close on January 18th. and 19th. at 11.30 a.m. and will re-open at the same hour at CRAMONT and CANCHY respective

8. ACKNOWLEDGE.

                                    (sgd) J.R.HEELIS. Major.

                                            Brigade Major.

16.1.17.   182nd. Infantry Brigade.

ROUTE.   1st. Field Amb. BEAUMETZ - LONGVILLERS - CRAMONT- HANCHY.
         Time of starting 10.42 a.m. January 18th. 1917.

         1st. Field Ambulance. YVRENCH - MAISON PONTHIEU - GUESCHART.
         Time of starting 7.30 a.m. January 19th. 1917.

WAR DIARY

of the

2/1ST. SOUTH MIDLAND FIELD AMBULANCE.

APPENDIX 1.

In the Field.
January 31st. 1917.

1.

IV Corps.   495/D.368.

Reference your 75/17.A. dated 19/1/17. - Under authority delegated in Military Secretary's letter No/MS/H 2260 G.H.Q. dated 2/6/16, I have awarded the Military Medal to the under named Non-Commissioned Officer and Men:-

    2180. Corporal Hilliar. H.T.) 2/1st. South Midland
    1802. Private   Bluck.   H.) Field Ambulance.
    2496. Private   Whithorn. T.) R.A.M.C.(T).

Will you kindly convey my congratulations to the recipients. I am of the opinion that the conduct of No. 2097 SGT. PERRY. A.H. and No. 2082 PTE. GOODE. G. would be more suitably dealt with by inclusion in despatches.

        (sgd)   G. Symmas. Captain, for
                      Lieutenant General.
21/I/17.   Commanding V Corps.

2.

To: Headquarters,
   61st. Division.

For information, with regard to your H.A.213 dated 17/I/17.

        (sgd)   L.C.D.Jenner. Major for
22/I/17.   D.A.A. & Q.M.G., IV Corps.

3.

To: A.D.M.S.
   61st. Division.

For information and necessary action, reference your 307/M/17 of the 12th. inst.

        (sgd)   N.C.Bennett. Captain.
D.H.Q.,
23/I/17.   D.A.A. & Q.M.G., 61st. Division.

4.

To: O.C.
   2/1st. Field Ambulance.

For information and return. - I congratulate the recipients.

        (sgd)   T.F.P.Breen. Captain for
                      Colonel. 61st. Division.

5.

To: A.D.M.S.
   61st. Division.

Returned herewith, please. - Thank you for your congratulations, which have been conveyed as requested. O.C. 2/1st. Fld.Amb.

CONFIDENTIAL.

WAR DIARY.

FEBR^URY 1917. FEBRUARY.

2/1ST. SOUTH MIDLAND FIELD AMBULANCE.R.A.M.C.(T).

(Volume 10)

2/1st. South Midland Field Ambulance.

In the Field.

March 1st. 1917.

COMMITTEE FOR THE MEDICAL HISTORY OF THE WAR
Date 4TH APR. 1917

61st Div
140/9—
Vol 10

Army Form C.2118.

WAR DIARY
or
INTELLIGENCE SUMMARY.
(Erase heading not required.)

Reference O.S. Maps. FRANCE.
LENS.11: 1/100,000.
ABBEVILLE. 1/100,000.

Place	Date	Hour	Summary of Events and Information	Remarks and references to Appendices
GUESCHART.	1918. Feb.1st.		General Fatigues. - A.D.M.S. 61ST. DIVISION visited village, and inspected Hospital and billets, cleaning and oiling of all waggons proceeded with, and results approved by A.D.M.S. PTES. STEADMAN and SANDERSON of this Unit sent to MOBILE ORDNANCE WORKSHOP near CRECY to assist in repair of waggons.	G.S.O.
GUESCHART.	Feb. 2nd.		General Fatigues. - Instructions for move of Ambulance to new area received from HEADQUARTERS, 182ND. INFANTRY BRIGADE. Two DEASEY MOTOR AMBULANCES returned to 61st. Divisional workshop where the other three were under repair, and five DAIMLER Ambulances reported to Unit for duty, complete with drivers, in exchange.	G.S.O.
GUESCHART.	Feb. 3rd.		General Fatigues. - Waggons loaded, and preparations for impending move continued. Advance Party despatched to new area with Medical Store Waggons, to prepare billets and Hospital for occupation.	G.S.O.
GUESCHART.	Feb. 4th.		General Fatigues. - Final cleaning up of all occupied premises and billets. Motor Lorry reported at 10.30 p.m. from O.C., 2/2ND. SOUTH MIDLAND FIELD AMBULANCE, for conveyance of patients, hospital stores etc. to new area.	G.S.O.
GUESCHART. VAUCHELLES-les-QUESNOY.	Feb. 5th.		Ambulance paraded at 6.55 a.m. and marched off at 7.5 a.m. - Passed starting point (cross roads ¼ mile N.E. of 2nd. E in FONTAINE-sur-MAYE) at 7.45 a.m. as per March Table. ROUTE :- CANCHY - X Roads at U in NEUILLY l'HÔPITAL - LE PLESSIEL - ABBEVILLE - VAUCHELLES-les-QUESNOY. VAUCHELLES was reached at 2.35 p.m. Unit Casualties on the march. Nil. Picked up from other Units. Nil. Hospital established for reception of patients.	v. app. 1. G.S.O.
VAUCHELLES-les-QUESNOY.	Feb. 6th.		General Fatigues. - Tidying and general renovation and cleaning of hospital premises. All billets thoroughly cleaned and made habitable.	G.S.O.
VAUCHELLES-les-QUESNOY.	Feb. 7th.		General Fatigues. - CAPTAIN A.P.THOMSON.R.A.M.C.,T.C. reported for duty from 308th.BDE.R.F.A. Arrival notified to A.D.M.S., 61ST. DIVISION. Following R.A.M.C. Orderlies reported with CAPTAIN THOMSON:- 2376. A/L.CPL. HAMPTON. V. 2481. PTE. HUTCHINGS. A.	G.S.O.

WAR DIARY or INTELLIGENCE SUMMARY.

(Erase heading not required.)

Army Form C.2118.

Reference U.S.Map. FRANCE.
ABBEVILLE.14. 1/100,000.

Place	Date	Hour	Summary of Events and Information	Remarks and references to Appendices
	1917.			
VAUCHELLES-les-QUESNOY.	Feb. 8th.		General Fatigues. - Continuation of cleaning and tidying of all premises, and fitting up of latrines and packstore etc. Waggons thoroughly cleaned and overhauled - two defective waggons despatched to Ordnance workshop, ABBEVILLE for repair.	G.W.Cr.
VAUCHELLES-les-QUESNOY.	Feb. 9th.		General Fatigues. - Letter received from O.C. 2/3rd. FIELD AMB. 61st. DIVISION stating that CAPTAIN JAMIESON.R.A.M.C.(T). had been evacuated to No. 2 STATIONARY HOSPITAL, ABBEVILLE, with Influenza. Preliminary notice of further move of Unit to new area received from HEADQUARTERS, 182 INF. BDE. LIEUT. W.JONES EVANS R.A.M.C. reported back for duty from 61st. DIVL. AMMN. COLUMN on return of CAPTAIN STAFFORD R.A.M.C. from leave.	G.W.Cr.
VAUCHELLES-les-QUESNOY.	Feb.10th.		General Fatigues. - The PRISMATICS Concert Party gave an Entertainment at VAUCHELLES which was attended by BRIGADIER GENERAL W.J.BLACKLOCK, D.S.O. (BRIGADIER COMMANDING 182ND. INFANTRY BRIGADE) and Staff. Small fire occurred at "THE CHATEAU" VAUCHELLES, in bedroom occupied by LIEUT. RIVERS,R.A.M.C.(T). H.Q. 182ND. INFANTRY BDE., A.D.M.S. 61ST. DIVN. and DIVISIONAL CLAIMS OFFICER duly notified.	G.W.Cr.
VAUCHELLES-les-QUESNOY.	Feb.11th.		General Fatigues. - Preparations for move continued. - Medical Store Waggons etc. packed. Preliminary Investigation as to cause of fire at "THE CHATEAU" VAUCHELLES held, and Court of Enquiry ordered for 10.0 a.m. tomorrow (the 12th. Feb.)	G.W.Cr.
VAUCHELLES-les-QUESNOY.	Feb. 12th.		General Fatigues.- Court of Enquiry held at HEADQUARTERS to investigate the fire which occurred at "THE CHATEAU" on the 10th. inst. PRESIDENT:- A Captain. 2/8th. Royal Warwicks Regt. MEMBERS:- A Subaltern. 2/5th. Royal Warwicks Regt. A Subaltern. 182nd. Machine Gun Company. A.D.M.S. 61ST. DIVISION visited VAUCHELLES and interviewed the OFFICER COMMANDING. - He inspected and reported very favourably on the condition of the transport of the Unit. All waggons finally loaded in preparation for the move of the Transport Section tomorrow to the new area. CAPTAIN THOMSON R.A.M.C.,T.C. appointed O.C.Transport during move.	G.W.Cr.

Army Form C. 2118.

WAR DIARY
or
INTELLIGENCE SUMMARY.
(Erase heading not required.)

Reference O.S. Map. FRANCE.
ABBEVILLE. No. 14.
AMIENS. No. 17.

Place	Date	Hour	Summary of Events and Information	Remarks and references to Appendices
VAUCHELLES-les-	1917. Feb.13.		General Fatigues. - Transport Section moved off at 7.45 a.m. under orders from 182ND. INFANTRY BRIGADE, two days ahead of Unit. ROUTE:- BELLANCOURT - AILLY - FLIXECOURT - ST. SAUVEUR. Marching Out State:- I Officer, I Warrant Officer, 47 N.C.O's and Men, 49 horses and all waggons and vehicles belonging to Unit.	G.S.M.
do.	Feb.14.		General Fatigues. - Cleaning and tidying of Camp and Hospital premises. Motor Lorry reported for duty to help to move hospital stores and blankets - all transport having gone off ahead of Unit.	G.S.M.
do. MARCELCAVE.	Feb.15.		Ambulance moved off from Camp at 8.45 a.m. and arrived at PONT REMY STATION at 10.15 a.m. Entrained at 11.15 a.m. and arrived at MARCELCAVE STATION at 3.15 p.m. Lorry left for PONT REMY at 9.0 a.m. with Hospital Stores etc. returning at 10.30 a.m. and left for MARCELCAVE at 11.0 a.m. OFFICER COMMANDING inspected all Brigade Area to see that all sick had been removed. Unit Casualties:- Nil.	Auth.ADMS. 61 Divn.
do.	Feb.16.		General Fatigues. - Repairs to Huts in Encampment, and adaptation of Huts for Scabies and ordinary Hospital cases. - D.A.D.M.S. 61 DIVISION visited and inspected Camp. CAPTAIN COX.R.A.M.C.(T). reported back from duty with the 2/4 OXFORD & BUCKS L.I. on return of CAPTAIN STOBIE.R.A.M.C.(T). from leave.	G.S.M.
do.	Feb.17.		General Fatigues. - Continuation of Camp and Hospital cleaning etc. OFFICER COMMANDING visited Divisional Headquarters and A.D.M.S. 61 DIVISION. D.A.D.M.S. 61ST. DIVISION visited Camp.	G.S.M.
do.	Feb.18.		Routine work. - Church Service in evening for Unit personnel along with 2/5 & 2/7 R.Warwicks Regt. Orders received that Unit was to remain in present billets irrespective of forward move of 182ND. INFANTRY BRIGADE.	Auth.ADMS. 61 Divn.
do.	Feb.19.		General Fatigues. - 182nd. INFANTRY BDE. moved off to forward area. 104th. INFANTRY BRIGADE arrived in Billeting Area, and part were accomodated in Camp.	G.S.M.

Army Form C. 2118.

WAR DIARY
or
INTELLIGENCE SUMMARY.

(Erase heading not required.)

Instructions regarding War Diaries and Intelligence Summaries are contained in F.S. Regs., Part II. and the Staff Manual respectively. Title pages will be prepared in manuscript.

Reference O.S. Map. FRANCE.
ABBEVILLE No. 14. 1/100,000.
AMIENS. No. 17. 1/100,000.

Place	Date	Hour	Summary of Events and Information	Remarks and references to Appendices
	1917.			
MARCELCAVE.	Feb.20th.		Routine work. - A.D.M.S. 61ST. DIVISION visited and inspected the Camp and Hospital.	GWM.
MARCELCAVE.	Feb. 21st.		Routine work. - OFFICER COMMANDING visited HEADQUARTERS. 61ST. DIVISION and interviewed A.A.& Q.M.G. and A.D.M.S. 61ST. DIVISION. CAPTAIN MONTGOMERY. A.; R.A.M.C.; (T.C.) and LIEUT. REGAN. T.E., R.A.M.C.(T.C.) reported their arrival and were taken on the strength of the Unit.	GWM. Auth. A.D.M.S. 61 Divn.
MARCELCAVE.	Feb.22nd.		Routine work.	RWM.
MARCELCAVE.	Feb. 23rd.		Routine work.	GWM.
MARCELCAVE.	Feb. 24th.		Routine work. - Concert by the "PRISMATICS" Troupe of the 2/1st. SOUTH MIDLAND FIELD AMB. OFFICER COMMANDING took up his duties as A.D.M.S. 61ST. DIVISION during the absence on leave of COLONEL CLAYTON.A.D.M.S. 61ST. DIVISION.	Auth.A.D.M 61 Divn. GWM.
MARCELCAVE.	Feb. 25th.		Routine work. - LIEUT. REGAN R.A.M.C.?T.C. reported for duty to A.D.M.S. 32nd. DIVISION and was struck off the strength of the Unit. Church Service for Unit Personnel. - Preliminary notice of move of Unit to GUILLACOURT received from A.D.M.S. 61ST. DIVISION.	GWM.
MARCELCAVE.	Feb.26th.		Routine work. - Nursing Sections of "A" and "B" Sections and Fatigue Party sent on to GUILLACOURT under CAPTAIN HIRST. - Hospital established for reception of patients by 2.0 p.m. Transport with Medical Store Waggons etc. moved off under CAPTAIN THOMSON. Concert by "THE PRISMATICS" given, attended by D.A.Q.M.G. and CAMP COMMANDANT 61 DIVL.H.Q.	GWM.
MARCELCAVE. GUILLACOURT.	Feb.27th.		Ambulance moved to GUILLACOURT under arrangements of A.D.M.S. 61 DIVISION. ROUTE:- MARCELCAVE - WIENCOURT - GUILLACOURT, which was reached at 2.45 p.m. - Unit Casualties:- NIL. Arrival reported to A.D.M.S. 61ST. DIVISION. - 61ST. DIVISIONAL REST STATION established for the reception of 100 patients. - Small Field Ambulance Hospital prepared for reception of local sick. - Scabies and Impetigo Hospital arranged close by, and arrangements made to billet whole personnel in vicinity in barns.	GWM.
GUILLACOURT.	Feb. 28th.		Routine work. - CAPTAIN P.H.GREEN.R.A.M.C.(T). appointed as Second in Command of 1ST. FIELD AMBULANCE. 61 DIVISION. - Total patients in residence in Hospitals:- 114.	Auth. 61 Divn.

Mwate
Lieut. Colonel, R.A.M.C.(T).
Officer Commanding. - 2/1st. South Midland Field Ambulance.R.A.M.C.(T).

February 28th. 1917.

CONFIDENTIAL.

W A R   D I A R Y.

2/1st. South Midland Field Ambulance, R.A.M.C.(T).

A P P E N D I X   1.

2/1st. South Midland Field Ambulance.

In the Field &

March 1st. 1917.

182nd. Infantry Brigade Order No. 74.   Copy No. 12.

February 3rd. 1917.

1. The 182nd. Infantry Brigade Group will march to the BELLANCOURT AREA on February 5th. 1917, in accordance with March Table attached:-
   ROUTE. :-
   Cross roads ¼ mile N.E. of Second E in FONTAINE-SUR-MAYE - Cross roads at U of NEUILLY l'HOPITAL - LE PLESSIEL - ABBEVILLE - BELLANCOURT.

2. Distances of 200 yards between Companies and 500 yards between Battalions will be kept on the march.

3. Baggage Waggons will march with Units.

4. Billeting parties will meet the Staff Captain at X roads ¼ mile west of VAUCHELLES-les-QUESNOY at 10.0 a.m. on Sunday, February 4th. They will remain in the new Billeting Areas. - The billeting areas are unoccupied, so there will be plenty of accomodation for Advance Parties or surplus stores if required.

5. Brigade Headquarters will close at CANCHY at 7.45 a.m. - Reports will be sent to head of column until 12.0 noon, after which hour, to BELLANCOURT.

6. Motor Ambulances will move independently.

7. Acknowledge.

                              (sgd) P.V.Davies. Captain.
                                       for Major.
Issued at 12.0 noon.   Brigade Major. 182nd. Infantry Brigade.

NAME OF UNIT.	DESTINATION.	STARTING POINT.	TIME.	ROUTE.
2/1st. Field Ambulance.	VAUCHELLES-les-QUESNOY.	¼ mile N.E. of second E in FONTAINE-sur-MAYE.	7.45 a.m.	Cross roads at U In NEUILLY l'HOPITAL - LE PLESSIEL - ABBEVILLE - VAUCHELLES-les-QUESNOY.

CONFIDENTIAL.

WAR DIARY.

of the

2/1ST. SOUTH MIDLAND FIELD AMBULANCE. R.A.M.C.(T).

for the month of M A R C H 1 9 1 7.

In the Field.

1st. April 1917.

No. 3. Vol. 3.

Army Form C. 2118.

WAR DIARY
or
INTELLIGENCE SUMMARY.
(Erase heading not required.)

Reference O.S. Map. FRANCE.
AMIENS. 17. 1/100,000.

Instructions regarding War Diaries and Intelligence Summaries are contained in F.S. Regs., Part II. and the Staff Manual respectively. Title pages will be prepared in manuscript.

Place	Date 1917	Hour	Summary of Events and Information	Remarks and references to Appendices
GUILLACOURT.	March 1.		Routine work. General Camp Cleaning, and renovation of Hospital premises. D.D.M.S. IV CORPS visited and inspected Camp and Hospital premises generally. CAPTAIN E.H.WOOD.R.A.M.C. reported for duty with the Unit.	Vide. Auth. ADMS. 61 Divn.
GUILLACOURT.	March 2.		Routine work. OFFICER COMMANDING visited DIVISIONAL HEADQUARTERS in his capacity as Acting A.D.M.S. CAPTAIN P.H.GREEN.R.A.M.C.(T). appointed "Second in Command" of the Unit. Construction of new latrines begun, and further cleaning of Hospital premises carried out.	Vide. Auth. ADMS. 61 Divn.
GUILLACOURT.	March 3.		Routine work. - OFFICER COMMANDING visited H.Q. as a/A.D.M.S. 61 DIVISION. OFFICER COMMANDING attended Conference of A.D's.M.S. IV CORPS at Corps Headquarters.	Vide.
GUILLACOURT.	March 4.		Routine work. - Premises secured for Officer's Hospital and Rest Station, and thoroughly overhauled and renovated. Church Parade for Unit personnel and patients able to attend. Instructions received from A.D.M.S. 61 DIVISION that a Medical Inspection Room was to be opened at WIENCOURT for the use of troops stationed there. OFFICER COMMANDING visited DIVISIONAL HEADQUARTERS.	Vide.
GUILLACOURT.	March 5.		Routine work. - CAPTAIN COX with a Corporal and two men proceeded to WIENCOURT and established a Medical Inspection Room at "THE CHATEAU" there as ordered by A.D.M.S. 61 DIVISION. Motor lorry proceeded to HEM DOULLENS, (the Depot of the BRITISH RED CROSS SOCIETY) and fetched Stores, Beds etc. for use at Hospital, Officers' Hospital etc. OFFICER COMMANDING visited DIVISIONAL HEADQUARTERS.	Vide.
GUILLACOURT.	March 6.		Routine work. - Motor lorry reported back from B.R.C.S. with stores for Hospitals. LT. COL SIR HEREWARD WAKE, BART., D.S.O., G.S.O.1, 61 DIVISION evacuated to NEW ZEALAND STATIONARY HOSPITAL, AMIENS. OFFICER COMMANDING visited DIVISIONAL HEADQUARTERS.	Vide.
GUILLACOURT.	March 7.		Routine work. Holding Party of two men despatched to take over Camp vacated at "CAMPE DES DAMES" GUILLACOURT. OFFICER COMMANDING visited DIVISIONAL HEADQUARTERS.	Auth. ADMS. 61 Divn. Vide.

Army Form C. 2118.

WAR DIARY
or
INTELLIGENCE SUMMARY.
(Erase heading not required.)

Reference O.S. Map. FRANCE.
AMIENS. 17. 1/100,000.

Instructions regarding War Diaries and Intelligence Summaries are contained in F.S. Regs., Part II. and Staff Manual respectively. Title pages will be prepared in manuscript.

Place	Date 1917.	Hour	Summary of Events and Information	Remarks and references to Appendices
GUILLACOURT.	March	8.	Routine work. LIEUT. GENERAL H.S. WOOLCOMBE, K.C.B., COMMANDING. IV CORPS made an exhaustive inspection of the Hospital premises, also Transport etc. OFFICER COMMANDING visited DIVISIONAL HEADQUARTERS. No.2233, PTE. CARTWRIGHT,O.W. reported for duty at Office of A.D.M.S. 61 DIVISION, and No. 2148 a/L/CPL. ROBERTS,W.H.S. reported for duty with this Unit. Officer's Rest Station opened and staffed throughout.	*signature* Auth. ADMS. 61 Divn.
GUILLACOURT.	March	9.	Routine work. OFFICER COMMANDING visited DIVISIONAL HEADQUARTERS. D.A.D.M.S. 61 DIVISION visited Hospital.	*signature*
GUILLACOURT.	March	10.	Routine work. - OFFICER COMMANDING. No. 1809 CPL. SMITH,J.C. and two men despatched to SAINS-en-AMIENOIS to act as "Holding Party" at a Camp vacated there.	*signature* Auth.ADMS 61 Divn.
GUILLACOURT.	March	11.	Routine work. - Voluntary Church Parade for Unit Personnel and patients able to attend. Medical Inspection of all ranks. OFFICER COMMANDING visited DIVISIONAL HEADQUARTERS.	*signature*
GUILLACOURT.	March	12.	Routine work. - OFFICER COMMANDING visited DIVISIONAL HEADQUARTERS and interviewed COLONEL J.PICKARD. (late O.C. 24 FIELD AMBULANCE) appointed A.D.M.S. 61 DIVISION. D.D.M.S. IV CORPS visited Hospital and inspected premises etc.	*signature*
GUILLACOURT.	March	13.	Routine work. - Constructional work proceeded with, in all branches. CAPTAIN E.H. WOOD,R.A.M.C. detailed for duty temporarily, as M.O. to 2/8 WARWICKS.	*signature* Auth. ADMS. 61 Divn. Auth. DGMS.
GUILLACOURT.	March	14.	Routine work. - LIEUT. W.JONES EVANS, R.A.M.C. appointed to rank of Temporary Captain on re-signing his contract.	*signature*
GUILLACOURT.	March	15.	Routine work. - A.D.M.S. 61 DIVISION visited Hospital and inspected all premises, Scabies and Impetigo Hospitals, Officers' Rest Station, Transport etc. CAPTAIN R. COX,R.A.M.C. detailed for duty temporarily,at IV CORPS SCHOOLS.	*signature* Auth. ADMS. 61 Divn.

Army Form C. 2118.

WAR DIARY
or
INTELLIGENCE SUMMARY.
(Erase heading not required.)

Reference O.S. Map. FRANCE.
AMIENS. 17. 1/100,000.

Place	Date	Hour	Summary of Events and Information	Remarks and references to Appendices
	1917.			
GUILLACOURT.	March 16.		Routine work. - D.A.D.M.S, 61 DIVISION visited Hospital. OFFICER COMMANDING visited DIVISIONAL HEADQUARTERS and interviewed the A.D.M.S. 61 DIVISION.	[sig]
GUILLACOURT.	March 17.		Routine work. - OFFICER COMMANDING interviewed A.D.M.S. 61 DIVISION at DIVISIONAL HEADQUARTERS in view of possible advance in near future. Preliminary arrangements made by A.D.M.S.	[sig]
GUILLACOURT.	March 18.		Orders received for new dispositions, from A.D.M.S. 61 DIVISION, 1ST. FIELD AMB. detailed to proceed to TOUR CARRE. - Party despatched under CAPTAIN THOMSON. DRESSING STATION established at TOUR CARRE, Relay Post at LIHONS, and an Advanced Dressing Station established at CHAULNES. CAPTAIN W.J.HIRST inspected all wells in CHAULNES area, and analysed contents, reporting back to TOUR CARRE at midnight. Relay Post established in TRIANGULAR WOOD. Communication and contact obtained with HEADQUARTERS 182 and 183 INFANTRY BRIGADES and some of the Artillery.	[sig]
GUILLACOURT.	March 19.		Dressing Station completed at CHAULNES and all country round explored. Bearers left at OMIECOURT and a further Advanced Dressing Stationed established at PERTAIN, under CAPTAIN THOMSON, and entirely staffed. OFFICER COMMANDING negotiated the possibilities of getting Transport through the old German Lines, to the Forward Area, via VERMANDOVILLERS, and by 6.0 p.m. 1 FORD Car, and 1 Limber Waggon got through to CHAULNES, and both pushed through to PERTAIN at once. Wheeled Stretchers which were sent through in a Maltese Cart were blocked en route, by the Artillery, as was also the second FORD Car which had been despatched by the O.C. - the latter vehicle having almost reached CHAULNES. D.A.D.M.S. visited all posts in the "Forward Area". 107 patients evacuated from 61 Divisional Rest Station to Casualty Clearing Station.	Auth. ADMS. 61 Divn.
GUILLACOURT.	March 20.		OFFICER COMMANDING visited HEADQUARTERS at GUILLACOURT and arranged to close Divisional Rest Station, Officers' Rest Station, Scabies and Impetigo Hospitals in accordance with A.D.M.S. orders. OFFICER COMMANDING visited A.D.M.S. 61 DIVISION at D.H.Q. afterwards proceeding through CHAULNES to PERTAIN, visiting all posts in "Forward Area" in order to inspect personnel and equipment, which was pushed through as fast as possible by the bearers. Four Marquees arrived for use at Advanced Dressing Station at PERTAIN. 2 FORD CARS, Maltese Cart and 2 Limber waggons, with stretchers etc. arrived at CHAULNES, for 61 DIVN. "Forward Area."	[sig] Auth. ADMS. 61 Divn.

Army Form C. 2118.

WAR DIARY
or
INTELLIGENCE SUMMARY.
(Erase heading not required.)

Reference O.S. Map. FRANCE.
AMIENS. 17; 1/100,000.

Instructions regarding War Diaries and Intelligence Summaries are contained in F.S. Regs., Part II. and the Staff Manual respectively. Title pages will be prepared in manuscript.

Place	Date	Summary of Events and Information	Remarks and references to Appendices
	1917. Mar.		
GUILLACOURT.	20 (con)	CAPTAIN THOMSON explored DRESLINCOURT and MORCHAIN and reconnoitred and marked out suitable dug outs for use as Advanced Dressing Stations in future, if necessary. FORD CAR service established from PERTAIN - CHAULNES as far as gap in road - from there, wheeled stretchers manipulated by bearers to the other side of gap - from thence DAIMLER Cars ran through LIHONS to TOUR CARRE and HARBONNIERES for conveyance of sick and wounded. GENERAL OFFICER COMMANDING. 61 DIVISION visited the ABvanced Dressing Station at PERTAIN. A.D.M.S. 61 DIVISION visited all posts in forward area, and called at TOUR CARRE on his way back. - No.2148 Q.M.S. TAYLOR detailed for duty at office of A.D.M.S. 61 DIVISION.	Auth.ADMS 61 Divn. Auth.ADMS. 61 Divn.
GUILLACOURT.	Mar.21.	Two packsaddles drawn from 2/2 FIELD AMBULANCE and brought into use. Report on wells in forward area received from A.D.M.S. 61 DIVISION. 1 DAIMLER CAR despatched to PERTAIN via ROSIERES - CHILLY - PUNCHY - FOURCHETTE - CURCHY - DRESLINCOURT and POTTE to try to get round by better road, than that formerly used, to forward area.	
GUILLACOURT. TOUR CARRE.	Mar.22.	OFFICER COMMANDING appointed Acting A.D.M.S. 61 DIVISION vice COLONEL J.PICKARD evacuated to Casualty Clearing Station. CAPTAIN P.H.GREEN.R.A.M.C.(T) assumed command of the Unit during the absence of the O.C. Headquarters of Unit moved from GUILLACOURT to TOUR CARRE. Holding Party left at "THE CHATEAU" under LIEUT. & QEMR W.S.RIVERS to supervise stores etc. left behind. The a/OFFICER COMMANDING visited all posts in the forward area, and found everything satisfactory, rations and supplies etc. being carried by Transport with considerable skill. Sick evacuated in cars via CHAULNES - LIHONS - TOUR CARRE - HARBONNIERES.	Auth.ADMS. 61 Div.
TOUR CARRE.	Mar.23.	Routine work. - The a/A.D.M.S. 61 DIVISION visited HEADQUARTERS? and inspected all posts in forward area subsequently, in company with the a/Officer Commanding.	
TOUR CARRE.	Mar.24.	Routine work. - D.D.M.S. IV CORPS visited and inspected HEADQUARTERS of Unit with D.A.D.M.S. 61 DIVISION. - All dispositions in Forward Area unchanged.	
TOUR CARRE.	Mar.25.	Routine work. - The a/OFFICER COMMANDING visited all posts in the forward area, finding everything correct. CAPTAIN THOMSON reconnoitred in BETHANCOURT with a view to established a further A.D.S. there.	
TOUR CARRE.	Mar.26.	Routine work. - LIEUT. RIVERS and party arrived at HEADQUARTERS from GUILLACOURT on completion of dumping stores there.	Auth.ADMS. 61 Divn.

A.5834 Wt.W4973/M687 750,000 8/16 D.D.&L. Ltd. Forms/C.2118/13.

Army Form C. 2118.

WAR DIARY
or
INTELLIGENCE SUMMARY.
(Erase heading not required.)

Reference O.S. Map. FRANCE.
AMIENS. 17. 1/100,000.

Instructions regarding War Diaries and Intelligence Summaries are contained in F.S. Regs., Part II. and the Staff Manual respectively. Title pages will be prepared in manuscript.

Place	Date	Hour	Summary of Events and Information	Remarks and references to Appendices
	1917.			
TOUR CARRE.	March 27.		Routine orders. – Preliminary orders received from A.D.M.S. 61 DIVISION for general move forward of the Ambulance. CAPTAIN THOMSON established an Advanced Dressing Station at BETHANCOURT, taking with him 1 Sergeant, and 10 men, – 1 Limber Waggon and 1 Water Cart. CAPTAIN R. COX reported back to Unit from IV CORPS SCHOOLS.	Auth. ADMS. 61 Divn. Auth. ADMS. 61 Divn.
TOUR CARRE. BETHANCOURT.	March 28.		Ambulance moved to BETHANCOURT. – Camp at TOUR CARRE struck at 1.0 p.m. – All Advanced Dressing Stations evacuated at the following hours:– LIHONS at 3.0 p.m. CHAULNES at 4.0 p.m. Above two parties joined the HEADQUARTERS party at PERTAIN, where tea was provided. The entire Ambulance moved from PERTAIN to BETHANCOURT at 6.30 p.m. the latter place being reached at 8.0 p.m. The whole move was carried out smoothly and satisfactorily. All ranks worked well, especially the Army Service Corps personnel, who carried much material from various centres. CAPTAIN THOMSON with 1 Sgt. 10 men, 1 Water Cart and 1 Limber waggon established an Advanced Dressing Station at MOLIGNEUX.	Auth. ADMS. 61 Divn.
BETHANCOURT.	Mar. 29.		Routine work. – Weather was extremely wet, practically the whole of the Camp being under water, great difficulty being experienced in getting constructional work done, owing to the weather, and also to the lack of building material. A.D.M.S. 61 DIVISION visited the Camp, and appeared pleased with the work which had been accomplished since the previous night. D.A.D.M.S. 61 DIVISION visited the Advanced Dressing Station at MOLIGNEUX under CAPTAIN THOMSON. Building at the A.D.S. proceeded with – a small hut being put up for the men, with cookhouse adjoining – a deep dug out being utilised for the Medical Inspection Room. All the country en route much devastated – villages burned – and trees chopped down indiscriminately. The bridges across the river at BETHANCOURT which had been blown up are now partly repaired. Cross Roads blown up in several places.	
BETHANCOURT.	Mar. 30.		Routine work. – D.D.M.S. IV CORPS inspected Camp and premises generally. Weather again seriously interfered with outdoor constructional work, although much was accomplished – an Orderly Room and Dispensary being built, and Latrines started upon. A roadway was also made leading from the road to the Camp. – Secret orders received from A.D.M.S. 61 DIVISION.	

2/8 WARWICKS on village of SOYECOURT.

Army Form C. 2118.

Reference Ordnance Map. FRANCE.
AMIENS.17. 1/100.000.

WAR DIARY
or
INTELLIGENCE SUMMARY.
(Erase heading not required.)

Instructions regarding War Diaries and Intelligence Summaries are contained in F. S. Regs. Part II. and the Staff Manual respectively. Title pages will be prepared in manuscript.

Place	Date	Hour	Summary of Events and Information	Remarks and references to Appendices
	1917.			
BETHENCOURT.	Mar.30. (con)		2/1ST. FIELD AMBULANCE detailed to assist 2/2ND. FIELD AMBULANCE in accomodating wounded if necessary. - All dispositions carried out for receiving 80 patients (wounded), and three large marquees pitched and fitted up. - During the evening no patients were received, but about 6.30 a.m. 12 wounded were received, this representing the total number of casualties admitted to Hospital on account of the attack on SOYECOURT.	MG
BETHENCOURT.	Mar.31.		Routine work. Large Marquee pitched for the use of Divisional Re-inforcements etc, passing through the village of BETHENCOURT. A.D.M.S. 61 DIVISION inspected Camp, and appeared pleased with the work accomplished since his last visit. Construction of latrines completed. - Packstore and Dispensary also completed. Construction of fresh billets for a large number of Unit personnel rendered imperative, owing to the instability of one of the large walls over a cellar in which the men were previously billeted - this causing great inconvenience to the already limited space available for patients, as a number of the men had to be placed temporarily in Hospital tents.	Auth.ADMS. 61 Divn. MG

Philip H. Green
Captain. R.A.M.C.(T).
a/Officer Commanding. - 2/1st.South Midland Field Ambulance.

April 1st. 1917.

CONFIDENTIAL.

WAR DIARY

of the

2/1ST. SOUTH MIDLAND FIELD AMBULANCE.

for the month of

APRIL 1917.

In the Field.
May 1st. 1917.

No. 4.
Volume 3.

WAR DIARY
or
INTELLIGENCE SUMMARY.

(Erase heading not required.)

Army Form C. 2118.

Reference Ordnance Map. FRANCE.
AMIENS. 17. 1/100,000.
S.QUENTIN. 18. 1/100,000.

Place	Date	Hour	Summary of Events and Information	Remarks and references to Appendices
BETHENCOURT.	April 1st. 1917.		Routine work. - General Constructional Work in Camp continued. - Large number of wounded passed through the Hospital. A.D.M.S. 61 DIVISION visited Hospital, and explained detailed orders for evacuation of wounded of 61st. DIVISION in case of an advance. - Hospital premises arranged as Main Dressing Station. CAPTAIN E.H.WOOD. R.A.M.C. detailed to assist 2/3rd. FIELD AMBULANCE during the "push".	Auth.ADMS. 61 Divn.
BETHENCOURT.	April 2nd.		Routine work. - Weather extremely tempestuous, causing the greatest difficulty in transport of patients. - Large number of wounded received and evacuated. Road for passage of Ambulances etc. in front of Hospital completed. D.D.M.S. IV CORPS visited Hospital, and expressed himself as well satisfied with all that he saw.	
BETHENCOURT.	April 3rd.		Routine work. - General constructional work continued. CAPTAIN MONTGOMERY.R.A.M.C. detailed as temporary M.O. to 2/6 GLOSTERS during the illness of CAPTAIN COLEMAN, R.A.M.C. A.D.M.S. 61ST. DIVISION visited and inspected Hospital and Premises. Hospital as now constructed, calculated to accomodate 100 wounded patients.	Auth.ADMS. 61 Divn.
BETHENCOURT.	April 4th.		Routine work. - Wet weather precluded any out of door constructional work. - Personnel employed checking and cleaning equipment, stores etc. OFFICER COMMANDING. 2/2nd. FIELD AMBULANCE visited Hospital. Large number of sick and wounded passed through the Hospital.	
BETHENCOURT.	April 5th.		Routine work. - Construction of Office for use of O.C. commenced, also erection of Packstore. OFFICER COMMANDING visited the Advanced Dressing Station at MOLIGNEUX and found everything quite satisfactory. One Horse Ambulance and One Daimler Ambulance despatched to 2/3rd. FLD. AMB. TREFCON. One Horse Ambulance and One Daimler Ambulance despatched to O.C. 2/2nd. FLD. AMB. TERTRY. Divisional Operation Order (R.A.M.C.) received from A.D.M.S. 61 DIVISION, arranging for evacuation of sick during forward move of 61ST. DIVISION. - 2/1ST. FIELD AMBULANCE taking no active part in advance, but acting as a Main Dressing Station. All Motor Ambulances held in readiness to clear cases from TERTRY and TREFCON.	Auth.ADMS. 61 Divn.

Army Form C. 2118.

WAR DIARY
or
INTELLIGENCE SUMMARY.
(Erase heading not required.)

Reference Ordnance Map. FRANCE.
AMIENS. 17. 1/100,000.
S.QUENTIN. 18. 1/100,000.

Instructions regarding War Diaries and Intelligence Summaries are contained in F.S. Regs., Part II. and the Staff Manual respectively. Title pages will be prepared in manuscript.

Place	Date	Hour	Summary of Events and Information	Remarks and references to Appendices
	1917.			
BETHENCOURT.	April 6th.		Routine work. - Construction of Pack Store completed. New Cook-House commenced. A large number of sick, but few wounded passed through Hospital. A.D.M.S. and D.A.D.M.S. 61 DIVISION visited and inspected Hospital and Premises, and expressed approval with the general arrangements, and constructional work completed. CAPTAIN THOMSON returned to Headquarters from A.D.S. MOLIGNEUX, and was replaced there by CAPTAIN HIRST.	pmg
BETHENCOURT.	April 7th.		Routine work. - All available tents and marquees prepared for anticipated operations tonight. D.D.M.S. IV CORPS and A.D.M.S. 61ST. DIVISION visited and inspected Camp. - D.D.M.S. IV CORPS suggested that all available space in the village etc, be utilised for reception of sick and wounded if necessary. - All arrangements completed by 6.0 p.m. Large number of wounded received during the evening.	pmg
BETHENCOURT.	APRIL 8th.		Routine work. - D.A.D.M.S. 61ST DIVISION visited Camp. Church Service for Unit Personnel and patients able to attend held morning and evening.	pmg
BETHENCOURT.	APRIL 9TH.		Routine work. - Preliminary notification of move of Division received from A.D.M.S. 61 DIVN. D.D.M.S. IV CORPS inspected Camp. CAPTAIN MONTGOMERY R.A.M.C. reported back for duty from 2/6 GLOSTERS on return of CAPT. COLEMAN.	pmg
BETHENCOURT.	APRIL 10th.		Routine work. - Severe weather prevented outdoor constructional work. Fair number of sick and wounded passed through the Hospital during the day. 3 N.C.O's and 22 Men detailed for duty with O.C. 107 FIELD AMBULANCE, NESLE and proceeded there.	Auth.ADMS. 61 Divn.
BETHENCOURT.	APRIL 11TH.		OFFICER COMMANDING visited A.D.S. at MOLIGNEUX. Preliminary building started for construction of Scabies Bath-house etc. A.D.M.S. and D.A.D.M.S. 61st. DIVISION inspected Hospital and Premises. CAPTAIN W.J.HIRST. R.A.M.C.(T). detailed as 61st. DIVL. SANITARY OFFICER during the absence of CAPTAIN DAVISON.R.A.M.C.(T). OFFICER COMMANDING visited ENNEMAIN with a view to establishing a Relay Post there for the collection of Brigade Sick quartered in that locality.	AUTH.ADMS. 61 Divn. do.
BETHENCOURT.	April 12th.		Routine work. - Constructional work at Scabies Bath-house proceeded with. D.D.M.S. IV CORPS inspected Hospital and Premises. THE OFFICER COMMANDING (LIEUT.COL.GEORGE MACKIE) returned to Unit from 61 DIVL HEADQUARTERS, on arrival of COL. CYRIL HOWKINS.A.M.S.	pmg

A5834 Wt.W4973/M687 759,000 8/16 D.D.&L.Ltd. Forms/C.2118/13.

Army Form C. 2118.

WAR DIARY
or
INTELLIGENCE SUMMARY.
(Erase heading not required.)

Reference Ordnance Map. FRANCE.
AMIENS. 17. 1/100,000.
S.QUENTIN. 18. 1/100,000.

Instructions regarding War Diaries and Intelligence Summaries are contained in F.S. Regs., Part II. and the Staff Manual respectively. Title pages will be prepared in manuscript.

Place	Date Hour 1917.	Summary of Events and Information	Remarks and references to Appendices
BETHENCOURT.	April 13th.	Routine Work. – OFFICER COMMANDING 3RD. FIELD AMBULANCE visited Hospital. Construction of Premises for Scabies Bath House continued.	
BETHENCOURT.	April 14th.	Routine work. – A.D.M.S. 61 DIVISION visited Hospital, and expressed himself satisfied with progress of work, constructional and otherwise. LIEUT. COLONEL MACKIE proceeded on 14 days leave of absence – CAPTAIN PHILIP GREEN continuing to act in the capacity of Officer Commanding.	Auth. ADMS. 61 Divn.
BETHENCOURT.	April 15th.	Routine work. Church services held for Unit personnel and patients able to attend.	
BETHENCOURT.	April 16th.	Routine work. – Scabies Bath House practically completed. D.D.M.S. IV CORPS inspected Hospital and all constructional work. D.A.D.M.S. 61 DIVISION also inspected Hospital. Hospital chosen as Scabies Depot for 61st. Division.	Auth. ADMS. 61 Divn.
BETHENCOURT.	April 17th.	Routine work. A.D.M.S. 61 DIVISION inspected the Unit on Parade, and congratulated all on their appearance and past record. He also inspected the Hospital and Premises, and expressed his entire satisfaction with all that he saw. – Scabies Department completed, and ready for reception of patients.	
BETHENCOURT.	April 18th.	Routine work.	
BETHENCOURT.	April 19th.	Routine work. Orders received from A.D.M.S. 61 DIVISION that 2/1ST. SOUTH MIDLAND FIELD AMBULANCE were to remain stationed at BETHENCOURT.	
BETHENCOURT.	April 20th.	Routine work. – Divisional Scabies Depot in full working order. Washing Room for dirty linen in course of construction. D.A.D.M.S. 61 DIVISION inspected the Hospital.	
BETHENCOURT.	April 21st.	Routine work. – Instructions received from A.D.M.S. 61 DIVISION that 1 Bearer Sub-Division (less Officer and Equipment) were to report for duty to the O.C. 2/3 FIELD AMBULANCE. FORRESTE.	

Army Form C. 2118.

WAR DIARY
or
INTELLIGENCE SUMMARY.

Reference Ordnance Map. FRANCE.
AMIENS. 17. 1/100.000.
S.QUENTIN. 18. 1/100.000.

(Erase heading not required.)

Instructions regarding War Diaries and Intelligence Summaries are contained in F.S. Regs., Part II. and the Staff Manual respectively. Title pages will be prepared in manuscript.

Place	Date 1917.	Hour	Summary of Events and Information	Remarks and references to Appendices
BETHENCOURT.	April 22nd.		Routine work. One Bearer Sub-Division reported for duty with 2/3rd. FIELD AMBULANCE in accordance with instructions received from A.D.M.S. 61 DIVISION. D.D.M.S. IV CORPS visited the Hospital and inspected same, also new Scabies Bath-House etc. and expressed his entire satisfaction with the work being done.	
BETHENCOURT.	April 23rd.		Routine work. D.A.D.M.S. 61 DIVISION inspected Camp and Hospital.	
BETHENCOURT.	April 24th.		Routine work. OFFICER COMMANDING attended Conference at Office of A.D.M.S. 61 DIVISION. Construction of airtight chamber for reception of "CLAYTON" Disinfector completed.	
BETHENCOURT.	April 25th.		Routine work. OFFICER COMMANDING proceeded to Headquarters 2/3RD. FIELD AMBULANCE at FORRESTE, and visited detached Bearers at FORRESTE - SAVY - HOLNON etc. attached to 2/3 FIELD AMBULANCE. The majority of the Stretcher Squads of this Ambulance are on detached duty at HOLNON and FAYET. No. 435312 PTE. MASTERS, W.A. of this Unit seriously wounded. CAPTAIN THOMSON, A.P., R.A.M.C. proceeded on leave of absence. (CAPT. HIRST.W.J. reported back. (from duty with DIV.SAN.Sec.	Auth. ADMS. 61 Division.
BETHENCOURT.	April 26th.		Routine work. A.D.M.S. 61 DIVISION visited and inspected the Hospital and Camp generally. Notification received that this Hospital was constituted XX KKFKK SCABIES DEPOT. for all cases occurring in IV CORPS area.	Auth. DDMS. IV CORPS.
BETHENCOURT.	April 27th.		Routine work. CAPTAIN MONTGOMERY, R.A.M.C. detailed to act as Medical Officer daily to the French Civilian Population at ROUY-LE-GRAND and ROUY-LE-PETIT. OFFICER COMMANDING visited and inspected the Relay Post at MOLIGNEUX. CAPTAIN W.J.HIRST detailed as Medical Officer to Troops of the ROYAL FLYING CORPS stationed at MOLIGNEUX and District. Further latrines and ablution benches for patients completed.	Auth. ADMS. 61 Division. do.

Army Form C. 2118.

WAR DIARY
or
INTELLIGENCE SUMMARY.
(Erase heading not required.)

Instructions regarding War Diaries and Intelligence Summaries are contained in F. S. Regs., Part II. and the Staff Manual respectively. Title pages will be prepared in manuscript.

Reference Ordnance Map. FRANCE.
AMIENS.I7. 1/100,000.
S.QUENTIN. 1/100,000.

Place	Date	Hour	Summary of Events and Information	Remarks and references to Appendices
	1917.			
BETHENCOURT.	April 28th.		Routine work. All constructional work in Camp continued. a/OFFICER COMMANDING visited 3rd. FIELD AMBULANCE and proceeded to "Forward Area" visiting "Detached Bearer Sub-Division" at HOLNON - SAVY and S.16.c.c.	
BETHENCOURT.	April 29th.		Routine work. D.D.M.S. IV CORPS inspected Camp and Hospital. Church Parade held for Unit Personnel and all Patients able to attend.	
BETHENCOURT.	April 30th.		Routine work. "CLAYTON DISINFECTOR" fetched from 91st. FIELD AMB. at LANGUEVOISIN, and placed in airtight chamber provided for its reception. - Disinfector in full working order by 3.0 p.m. a/OFFICER COMMANDING visited DIVISIONAL HEADQUARTERS and interviewed A.D.M.S. 6I DIVISION.	Auth. DDMS. IV Corps.

Philip H. Green

Captain. R.A.M.C.(T).

a/Commanding. - 2/Ist. South Midland Field Ambulance, 6I Division.

May Ist. 1917.

CONFIDENTIAL.

W A R   D I A R Y.

of the

2/1ST. SOUTH MIDLAND FIELD AMBULANCE.

for the month of MAY 1917.

In the Field.

May 31st. 1917.

COMMITTEE FOR THE
MEDICAL HISTORY OF THE WAR
Date   10 JUL.1917

Number 5.
VOLUME 3.

Army Form C. 2118.

WAR DIARY
or
INTELLIGENCE SUMMARY.
(Erase heading not required.)

Instructions regarding War Diaries and Intelligence Summaries are contained in F.S. Regs., Part II. and the Staff Manual respectively. Title pages will be prepared in manuscript.

Reference Ordnance Maps. FRANCE.
AMIENS. 17. 1/100.000.
S.QUENTIN. 18. 1/100.000.

Place	Date	Hour	Summary of Events and Information	Remarks and references to Appendices
	1917.			
BETHENCOURT.	May 1st.		LIEUT. COL. GEORGE MACKIE.R.A.M.C.(T). having returned from leave of absence resumed command of the Unit. O.C. inspected Unit and all premises built during his absence. - Bath house for Scabies patients finished and in use. - Officers' Bath Room & nearing completion. Alterations in Quartermaster's Stores commenced.	Festa.
BETHENCOURT.	May 2nd.		General Routine work. - OFFICER COMMANDING visited A.D.M.S. 61 DIVISION. - Arrangements made to allow CAPTAIN W.J.HIRST. R.A.M.C.(T) to go to DIV. H.Q., as Acting A.D.M.S. during the absence of CAPTAIN T.F.P.BREEN.R.A.M.C. on leave. Construction of open air shed commenced, for open air and sunlight treatment of skin infections O.C. visited Relay Post at MOLIGNEUX. CAPTAIN E.H.WOOD reported back for duty from 2/3 FLD. AMB. O.C. inspected Transport Section of the Unit.	Festa.
BETHENCOURT.	May 3rd.		Officer's Bath House finished and in use. - Further alterations in Camp mapped out, including draining of effluent pond from Bath houses. - New Mess Room for Officers begun. "B" Section bearers proceeded to 2/3 FIELD AMBULANCE at FORRESTE to relieve "C" Section Bearers who had been there for eight days. OFFICER COMMANDING visited No. 21 CASUALTY CLEARING STATION. NESLE to enquire into the Dental treatment of Troops. - Open air shed completed, and Scabies Camp moved to new site.	Festa.
BETHENCOURT.	May 4th.		Routine work. - All spare men engaged on constructional work. "C" Section bearers reported back from "the line."	Festa.
BETHENCOURT.	May 5th.		Routine work. - New Dressing Room built. - Alterations to, and extensions of Cook-house begun. Fly proof chamber for meat finished in stores.	Festa.
BETHENCOURT.	May 6th.		Routine work. - OFFICER COMMANDING visited the Relay Post at MOLIGNEUX. Church Parade for Unit Personnel and patients able to attend.	Festa.
BETHENCOURT.	May 7th.		Routine work. - OFFICER COMMANDING visited 2/3rd. FIELD AMBULANCE at FORRESTE, to inspect work done by "B" Section.	Festa.
BETHENCOURT.	May 8th.		Routine work. - D.D.M.S. IV CORPS inspected Hospital and premises. New pathway constructed from main entrance into Camp leading to Orderly Room, Dressing Room etc. CAPTAIN A.P.THOMSON. R.A.M.C. reported back from leave.	Festa.

A 5834 Wt. W 4973/M687 750,000 8/16 D.D. & L. Ltd Forms/C.2118/13

Army Form C. 2118.

WAR DIARY
or
INTELLIGENCE SUMMARY.

Reference Ordnance Maps. FRANCE.
AMIENS.17. 1/100,000.
S.QUENTIN. 18. 1/100,000.

(Erase heading not required.)

Instructions regarding War Diaries and Intelligence Summaries are contained in F.S. Regs., Part II. and the Staff Manual respectively. Title pages will be prepared in manuscript.

Place	Date Hour	Summary of Events and Information	Remarks and references to Appendices
BETHENCOURT.	May 9th. 1917.	Routine work. - All constructional work carried on. Extension of Quartermasters' Stores finished. - No.T4/248641 DRIVER FRANKLIN, J.H.,A.S.C. proceeded on 10 days leave of absence.	Fiota.
BETHENCOURT.	May 10th.	Routine work. A.D.M.S. 61st. DIVISION inspected Camp and Hospital. Extension of Officers' Mess continued. - No. 435416 PRIVATE ASKEY, A. proceeded on 10 days leave of absence.	Fiota.
BETHENCOURT.	May 11th.	Routine work. - OFFICER COMMANDING visited DIVISIONAL H.Q. and attended A.D.M.S's conference. Officers Mess completed. - OFFICER COMMANDING visited 3RD. FIELD AMBULANCE.	Fiota.
BETHENCOURT.	May 12th.	Routine work. - Preliminary Orders received from A.D.M.S. 61 Division regarding move. - Ambulance ordered to proceed to MESNIL-ST-NICAISE tomorrow. All Scabies cases discharged to their Units. - All other cases disposed of as follows:- if fit, sent back to their Units, if unfit to march - evacuated to C.C.S. Party of 34 N.C.O's and Men reported back at Headquarters from duty with the 2/3 FIELD AMBULANCE. OFFICER COMMANDING proceeded to NESLE and interviewed D.D.M.S. IV CORPS and Staff Captain, 184 INFANTRY BRIGADE. Relay Post at MOLIGNEUX closed, and all Staff with equipment etc. reported back to Headquarters.	v.app.1. Fiota.
BETHENCOURT. MESNIL-ST-NICAISE.	May 13th.	Camp cleaned and left in thoroughly tidy condition. Ambulance left BETHENCOURT at 1.15 p.m. and arrived at MESNIL-ST-NICAISE at 2.45 p.m. Usual notifications sent to A.D.M.S. 61 DIVISION and HEADQUARTERS. 184 INFANTRY BRIGADE. CASUALTIES: (a) Unit:- Nil. (b) Picked up from other Units. Nil. Hospital established by small Advance Party who came by Motor Ambulance, and ready for reception of patients by 1.0 p.m. Transport Section under CAPTAIN A.P.THOMSON. R.A.M.C.(T) remained behind in Camp at BETHENCOURT.	Fiota.
~~BETHENCOURT~~ MESNIL-ST-NICAISE.	May 14th.	General tidying and cleaning of Camp premises. Orders for move tomorrow to RIVERY area received from HEADQUARTERS. 184 INFANTRY BRIGADE. Transport Section started for RIVERY. ROUTE:- MESNIL-ST.-NICAISE - MANICOURT - CURCHY - FONCHES - FRANSART - ROUVROY - WARVILLERS which was reached at 11.45.a.m. Transport remained here for night. D.D.M.S. IV CORPS inspected Camp vacated at BETHENCOURT and expressed his appreciation of work which had been done by the Ambulance. CAPTAIN E.H.WOOD.R.A.M.C. detailed for further period of duty with 2/3rd.FLD.AMB.and proceeded to FORRESTE.	v. app. 2. v.app.3. Fiota. Auth.ADMS. 61 Divn.

A.5834 Wt. W.4973/M687 750,000 8/16 D.D. & L.Ltd. Forms/C.2118/13.

Army Form C. 2118.

WAR DIARY
or
INTELLIGENCE SUMMARY.
(Erase heading not required.)

Instructions regarding War Diaries and Intelligence Summaries are contained in F.S. Regs., Part II. and the Staff Manual respectively. Title pages will be prepared in manuscript.

Reference Ordnance Maps: FRANCE.
AMIENS. 17. 1/100.000.
LENS. II. 1/100.000.

Place	Date	Hour	Summary of Events and Information	Remarks and references to Appendices
MESNIL-ST-NICAISE. RIVERY.	May 15th. 1917.		Ambulance moved to RIVERY by train as follows:- Left MESNIL at 7.40 a.m. and marched to NESLE which was reached at 8.15 a.m. Train left NESLE Station at 9.15 a.m. and reached LONGEAU Station at 11.45 a.m. Ambulance marched from there to RIVERY which was reached at 1.0 p.m. No Unit or Brigade Casualties during journey. - Usual notifications sent to A.D.M.S. and H.Q. 184 INFANTRY BRIGADE. - Hospital established and ready for reception of patients by 1.30 p.m. Transport Section under CAPTAIN THOMSON left WARVILLERS at 6.15 a.m. and proceeded via BEAUFORT - le QUESNEL to DOMART-sur-la-LUCE which was reached at 11.30 a.m. where Transport was halted until following day.	Feth.
RIVERY.	May 16th.		General tidying and cleaning of Camp and Hospital. - Kit Inspection. - Short Route March in morning. - CAPTAIN A. MONTGOMERY. R.A.M.C. detailed for duty as temporary M.O. to 2/1 BUCKS.BN. A.D.M.S. 61 DIVISION visited and inspected Hospital and premises. Orders for move of Ambulance tomorrow to LA VICOGNE received from 184 INFANTRY BRIGADE. Billeting party consisting of CAPTAIN EVANS R.A.M.C. and Billeting Sgt. proceeded there. Transport Section arrived in Camp at 11.30 a.m. ROUTE :- via ST. NICHOLAS STATION - LONGEAU - AMIENS - RIVERY. No casualties to personnel, horses or waggons.	Auth.ADMS 61 Divn. v. app 4. Feth.
RIVERY. LA VICOGNE.	May 17th.		Ambulance marched to LA VICOGNE as follows :- Left RIVERY at 5.40 a.m. proceeding via AMIENS - POULAINVILLERS - VILLERS BOCAGE - TALMAS - LA VICOGNE which was reached at 11.45 a.m. Unit Casualties:- Nil. Picked up from other Units. Three. Usual notifications sent to A.D.M.S. 61 DIVISION and H.Q., 184 INFANTRY BDE. Hospital established and ready for reception of patients by 12.0 noon. A.D.M.S. 61 DIVISION inspected Hospital and Camp premises generally. CAPTAIN W. HIRST R.A.M.C.T. rejoined Unit on return of D.A.D.M.S. 61 DIVISION from leave. LIEUT. M.S. MUNRO R.A.M.C. joined this Unit, and was taken on strength of Officers from this date. CAPTAIN W.J. HIRST. R.A.M.C. (T) detailed as Sanitary Officer for TALMAS area.	Feth. Auth.ADMS. 61 Divn.
LA VICOGNE.	May 18th.		General tidying and cleaning of whole of Hospital and Camp area. All waggons washed and cleaned. - All Section equipment cleaned and checked. A.D.M.S. 61 DIVISION visited and inspected Camp.	Feth.
LA VICOGNE.	May 19th.		General Routine work. - Ambulance proceeded on Route March to NAOURS in afternoon, and visited "LES SOUTERRAINS" in that village.	Feth.

WAR DIARY
or
INTELLIGENCE SUMMARY.

(Erase heading not required.)

Army Form C. 2118.

Reference Ordnance Maps. FRANCE.
AMIENS. 17. 1/100.000.
LENS. 11. 1/100.000.

Place	Date	Hour	Summary of Events and Information	Remarks and references to Appendices
LA VICOGNE.	May 20th.		Routine work. Notification of impending move received from HEADQUARTERS. 184 INFANTRY BRIGADE. DIVISIONAL GAS OFFICER lectured to all ranks of the Unit, and tested all Box Respirators in improvised Gas Chamber.	v. app. 5. F.E.M.
LA VICOGNE. HEM.DOULLENS.	May 21st.		Ambulance moved to HEM. DOULLENS. Started at 5.50 a.m. ROUTE :- VERT GALAND Fm. - BEAUVAL - GEZAINCOURT - BRETEL - HEM.DOULLENS, which was reached at 10.30 a.m. CASUALTIES. (a) Unit:- Nil. (b) Picked up from other Units. Three. Usual notifications sent to A.D.M.S. 61 DIVISION and H.Q. 184 INFANTRY BRIGADE. Hospital ready for reception of patients by 11.0 a.m. A.D.M.S. and D.A.D.M.S. 61 DIVISION visited and inspected Hospital and Premises. General cleaning and tidying of camp. - Bathing Parade.	F.E.M.
HEM.DOULLENS.	May 22nd.		Routine work. - Notification received from HEADQUARTERS. 184 INFANTRY BRIGADE that Unit would move tomorrow to BARLY.	v. app. 6.
HEM.DOULLENS. BARLY.	May 23rd.		Ambulance moved to BARLY. Started at 4.45 a.m. ROUTE:- DOULLENS - LUCHEUX - HUMBERCOURT - WARLUZEL - WARLUZEL - SOMBRIN - BARLY which was reached at 10.40 a.m. CASUALTIES. (a) Unit:- Nil. (b) Picked up from other Units. Eight. Usual notifications sent to A.D.M.S. 61 DIVISION and H.Q., 184 INFANTRY BRIGADE. Hospital established and ready for reception of patients by 11.0 a.m. A.D.M.S. and D.A.D.M.S. 61 DIVISION visited and inspected Hospital and Camp Premises. Notification of move of Unit to DUISANS area received from H.Q., 184 INFANTRY BRIGADE.	F.E.M.
BARLY. DUISANS.	May 24th.		Ambulance moved to DUISANS. Started at 9.30 a.m. ROUTE :- FOSSEUX - WANQUETIN - WARLUS - DUISANS. Latter place reached at 1.30 p.m. Usual notifications sent to A.D.M.S. 61 DIVISION and H.Q. 184 INFANTRY BRIGADE. - Hospital established and ready for reception of patients by 2.0 p.m. CASUALTIES. (a) Unit:- Nil. (b) Picked up from other Units. Two. A.D.M.S. 61 DIVISION visited and inspected Camp and Hospital premises etc.	v. app. 7. F.E.M.
DUISANS.	May 25th.		General Routine work. - Camp cleaning and tidying etc. CAPTAIN W.J.HIRST.R.A.M.C.(T) appointed Auth ADMS Area Sanitary Officer. - O.C. attended Conference at Office of D.D.M.S. VI CORPS.	61 Divn. F.E.M.

WAR DIARY
or
INTELLIGENCE SUMMARY.

(Erase heading not required.)

Army Form C. 2118.

Reference Ordnance Map FRANCE.
1/100,000. LENS.11.
Also Ordnance Maps. FRANCE.
1/40,000 Sheets 51.b. and 51.c.

Place	Date	Hour	Summary of Events and Information	Remarks and references to Appendices
	1917.			
DUISANS.	May 26th.		Routine work. - A.D.M.S. 61 DIVISION visited and inspected Camp and Hospital premises. All baths etc. brought by Motor Lorry from HEM and dumped at Camp.	Fisth.
DUISANS.	May 27th.		Routine work. - Church Parades for whole of Unit Personnel.	Fisth.
DUISANS.	May 28th.		Routine work. - A.D.M.S. 61 DIVISION visited Camp. Advance information received of impending move of 184TH. INFANTRY BDE. into line. 2/1ST. FIELD AMBULANCE to take over area at present occupied by 48th. FIELD AMBULANCE. HEADQUARTERS to be at TILLOY H.37.d.1.4. Two Advanced Dressing Stations. Right Sector. Caves at MARLIERE.N.17.d.2.4. Left Sector. N.11.b.2.8. CAR POSTS. Right at N.15.d.3.9. Left at N.4.b.3.8. O.C. visited O.C. 48th. FIELD AMBULANCE and discussed arrangements. O.C. visited 49th. FLD. AMB. at HOPITAL ST. JEAN, ARRAS to act as Divisional Main Dressing Station.	Fisth.
DUISANS.	May 29th.		O.C. with CAPTAIN HIRST R.A.M.C.(T) and CAPTAIN THOMSON.R.A.M.C.(T) inspected new area, including Advanced Dressing Stations and Regimental Aid Posts. Arrangements concluded for relief of bearers in line by an Advance Party on May 30th, and by complete personnel on June 1st. Transport, except one Limber waggon and three water carts to be parked on RACE COURSE, ARRAS. O.C. visited A.D.M.S.61 DIVISION and reported progress. - O.C. visited C.R.E. 61 DIVISION to discuss alterations in land at Left A.D.S. by R.E. 56th. DIVISION. - General Routine work.	Fisth.
DUISANS.	May 30th.		Routine work. - Packing of equipment. - Advance party went "up the line" under CAPTAIN W.J. HIRST, and was divided between the two sides, to learn routes, and also to act as Guides. O.C. met Brigade Regimental Medical Officers, and went over all Medical arrangements with them and Staff Captain.	Fisth.
DUISANS.	May 31st.		OFFICER COMMANDING and LIEUT. & QR MR. W.S.RIVERS.R.A.M.C.(T). visited HEADQUARTERS, 48th. FIELD AMBULANCE, and settled all final details of taking over the line. Bearers to be sent up today, so as to effect relief first relief in darkness. OFFICER COMMANDING visited A.D.M.S. 61 DIVISION to report.	Fisth.

May 31st, 1917.

GMacke

Lieut. Colonel. R.A.M.C.(T).
2/1st. South Midland Field Ambulance.

2/1ST. SOUTH MIDLAND FIELD AMBULANCE.
@"@"@"@"@"@"@"@"@"@"@"@"@"@"@"@

A P P E N D I X / .

WAR DIARY.

MAY 1917.

SECRET.

184th. INFANTRY BRIGADE ORDER. NO. 95.

Reference Maps. 1/100.000.
S. QUENTIN.
1/100.000. AMEINS.

1. The Brigade will march tomorrow (13th. inst(to the NESLE area via. FORESTE-DOUILLY-MATIGNY-BUNY-VOYENNES.

2. 200 yards distance will be maintained between Companies and 300 yards between Battalions.

3. There will be a halt from 6.15 - 7.15 a.m. for breakfast.

4. Cookers will march in rear of Companies, and one Water Cart in rear of each half Battalion.

5. A Representative will be left to hand over all Maps, Sketches Defence Scheme etc. to the French, and to show them to their Billets.

6. Brigade Headquarters will close at GERMAINE at 6.0 a.m. and re-open in NESLE area on conclusion of march.

7. ACKNOWLEDGE.

Issued at 2.0 p.m.

(sgd) G. MOORE.
Captain.
Brigade Major.
184th. Infantry Bde.

NOTE. 2/1st. FIELD AMBULANCE will march independently of Brigade - starting about 1.0 p.m. from BETHENCOURT.

2/1ST. SOUTH MIDLAND FIELD AMBULANCE.
=================================

APPENDIX 2.

WAR DIARY.

MAY 1917.

SECRET.

184TH. INFANTRY BRIGADE ORDER No. 96.

Reference Map　　　　　　　　　　　　　　　　May 14th. 1917.
1/100,000.
AMIENS.

1. The Brigade will march to NESLE Station tomorrow in accordance with the attached table, and will entrain there.
   There will be no halts on the march from billets to NESLE STATION irrespective of time of start. Companies will march at 200 yards distance.

2. On reaching LONGEAU, the Brigade will detrain. Guides from Billeting parties will meet their respective Units at LONGEAU STATION and lead them to their new billets.

3. Brigade Headquarters will close at NESLE at 7.0 a.m. Reports will be sent to Railway Station NESLE from 7.0 a.m. - 9.15 a.m.
   After detraining at LONGEAU, to LONGEAU STATION until such time as place of new Brigade Headquarters is notified, after which time to new Brigade Headquarters.

4. Acknowledge.

Timetable.

1ST. FIELD AMBULANCE.	STARTING POINT.	TIME.
	X ROADS at CHURCH. MESNIL-ST-NICAISE.	7.20 a.m.

ROUTE. Direct through E. of MESNIL-LE-PETIT.

TRAIN LEAVES NESLE STN.　　　9.15 a.m.

UNIT WILL ARRIVE AT STN.　　　8.15 a.m.

Issued at 4.0 p.m.

　　　　　　　　　　　　　　(sgd) G. MOORE. Captain.
　　　　　　　　　　　　　　　　　Brigade Major.
　　　　　　　　　　　　　　　184 Infantry Brigade.

2/1ST. SOUTH MIDLAND FIELD AMBULANCE.
=-=-=-=-=-=-=-=-=-=-=-=-=-=-=-=-=-=

APPENDIX 3.

WAR DIARY.

MAY 1917.

184 Infantry Brigade No. Q.169.

ADMINISTRATIVE ORDERS FOR MOVE OF TRANSPORT TO RIVERY AREA.

1. The Transport of the Brigade Group will move on the 14th. inst. to WARVILLERS and ROUVROY via CURCHY - FONCHE - FRANSART.

2. On the 15th. inst. to DOMART-sur-la-LUCE via BEAUFORT and le QUESNEL.

3. One the 16th. inst. to RIVERY via ST. NICHOLAS STATION - LONGEAU - AMIENS - RIVERY.

4. Units will march in the following order, with 200 yards between Units.

        184th. Machine Gun Company (pass starting point 6.30 am
        2/4 Royal Berks.
        No. 4 Coy. Divl. Train.
        Brigade Headquarters.
        2/5 Glosters.
        479 Field Coy. R.E's.
        2/4 Oxfords.
        2/1 Bucks.
        184 L.T.M.B.
        1st. Field Ambulance.

5. $\frac{1}{4}$ hour halts will be observed throughout.

6. Each waggon will carry one petrol tin (full) per horse.

7. One mounted N.C.O. from each Unit will proceed direct to ROUVROY and meet the Interpreter at the Church at 7.30 a.m. This procedure will be followed on each day of the move.

8. The total number of personnel and horses reported by you as going by road should be adhered to as far as possible, as rations have been asked for on this basis.

9. During the move of the Transport, strict March Discipline will be maintained, and Officers in Charge of Units will issue instructions that no water is to be drunk by the men unless it has been ascertained that it is fit for drinking, or has been put through a water cart. Billets will be left scrupulously clean, and all necessary fire precautions will be taken.

10. Billeting certificates will be made out by the Interpreter, and the duplicates returned to Staff Captain's Office at the end of the journey, for transmission to Officer in Charge, Branch Requisition Office.

11. Any animals which have to be left behind on the journey, will be left with the Maire of the village, with a paper showing day handed in. The Officer leaving the animal will report location to this Office immediately on arrival in the new area.

                        (sgd) A. BICKNELL. Captain.
                             Staff Captain.
                       184th. Infantry Brigade.

B.H.Q.,
13.5.17.

2/1ST. SOUTH MIDLAND FIELD AMBULANCE.
==============================

A P P E N D I X 4.

WAR DIARY.

MAY 1917.

184TH. INFANTRY BRIGADE ORDER NO. 97.

Reference Map.
LENS. 1/100,000.
AMIENS. 1/100,000.

May 16th, 1917.

1. The Brigade will march tomorrow (the 17th. inst.) to the TALMAS area, via POULANVILLERS, in accordance with March Table below.

2. 500 yards distance will be maintained in rear of each Battalion, 479 Field Coy. R.E's, and No. 4 Coy. Divisional Train - 10 yards between Companies - and 25 yards between 184 Machine Gun Company, and 184 L.T.M.B. 50 yards between 184 Machine Gun Company and 479 Field Company R.E's.

3. There will be a halt of 10 minutes before each clock hour, and a halt from 6.50 a.m. to 7.50 a.m. for breakfasts.

4. Transport will march in the usual echelons in rear of Battalions, but with Cookers in front of the 1st. line Transport, followed immediately by Water Carts.

5. Brigade Headquarters will close at RIVERY tomorrow at 4.0 a.m. after which reports will be sent to head of column until after the march, after which to Brigade Headquarters, REGENT STREET. TALMAS.

6. ACKNOWLEDGE.

Issued at 3.0 p.m.

(sgd) G. MOORE. Captain.
Brigade Major.
184th. Infantry Brigade.

		STARTING POINT.	TIME.
TIMETABLE.	IST. FIELD AMBULANCE.	Road junction ½ mile S.E. of E. in Citadelle.	6.15 a.m.

ROUTE.   AMIENS - POULANVILLERS - VILLERS BOCAGE - TALMAS - LA VICOGN

2/2nd. SOUTH MIDLAND FIELD AMBULANCE.

WAR DIARY.

APPENDIX 5.

MAY 1916.

184 INFANTRY BRIGADE ORDER NO. 98.

REFERENCE MAP
LENS. 1/100.000.   May 20th. 1917.

1. The Brigade will march tomorrow 21st. to the OCCOCHES area, via BEAUVAL, in accordance with subjoined March Table.

2. 500 yards distance will be maintained in rear of each Battalion, 479 Field Coy. R.E's, and No. 4 Co. Divisional Train - 10 yards between Companies, and 25 yards between 184 Machine Gun Company, and 184 L.T.M.B.; 50 yards between 184 L.T.M.B. and 479 Field Coy. R.E's.

3. There will be a halt of 10 minutes before each clock hour, and a halt from 6.50 a.m. to 7.50 a.m. for breakfasts.

4. Transport will march in the usual echelons in rear of Battalions, but with cookers in front of the 1st. line Transport followed immediately by Water Carts.

5. BRIGADE HEADQUARTERS will close at TALMAS at 4.0 a.m. after which reports to BRIGADE HEADQUARTERS? marching in front of the BUCKS, until the conclusion of the march, when Brigade Headquarters will re-open at OCCOCHES.

6. <u>ACKNOWLEDGE</u>.

		STARTING POINT.	TIME.
<u>TIMETABLE</u>.	1ST. FIELD AMBULANCE.	Road junction TALMAS BEAUVAL rd, with road to ROSEL FM. 500 yds. N. of LA VICOGNE.	6.15 am

ROUTE.:-   BEAUVAL - GEZAINCOURT - BRETEL - HEM.DOULIENS.

                        (sgd) G. Moore, Captain.
                              Brigade Major.
                        184th. Infantry Brigade.

2/2nd. SOUTH MIDLAND FIELD AMBULANCE.
="

APPENDIX 6.

WAR DIARY.
MAY 1917.

184 INFANTRY BRIGADE ORDER NO. 99.

May 22nd. 1917.

Reference Map.
LENS.1/100,000.

1. The Brigade will march tomorrow (the 23rd. inst) to the SOMBRIN-FOSSEUX area, in accordance with the attached March Table, in two columns.

2. 500 yards distance will be maintained in rear of each Battalion, and in rear of the 479 Field Coy. R.E's - 10 yards between Companies, 100 yards in rear of the 184th. L.T.M.B. and No. 524 Coy. Divisional Train.

3. Transport will march in the usual echelons in rear of Battalions, but with Cookers in front of the first line transport, followed immediately by the Water Carts.

4. There will be a halt of 10 minutes before each clock hour.
There will not be any long halt.
Haversack rations will be carried.

5. On arrival at GRANDE RULLECOURT the 1/5 D.C.L.I. will come under the orders of the 183 INFANTRY BRIGADE.

6. Brigade Headquarters will close at OCCOCHES CHATEAU at 4.0 a.m. and re-open at BARLY at the same hour.
During the march, reports to be sent to the head of the 479 Field Coy. R.E's.

7. ACKNOWLEDGE.

		STARTING POINT.	TIME.
TIMETABLE.	1ST. FIELD AMBULANCE.	Level crossing on the HEM GEZAINCOURT road 600 yards N. of D. in CITADELLE.	5.15 a.m.
ROUTE.		DOULIENS - LE MARAIS - SEL - GROUCHES - LUCHEUX - HUMBERCOURT - COULIEMONT - SOMBRIN - BARLY.	

(sgd) G. MOORE. Captain.
Brigade Major.
184th. Infantry Brigade.

184TH. INFANTRY BRIGADE ORDER NO. 100.

Reference Map IENS.
1/100.000.
                May 23rd. 1917.

1. The Brigade will march tomorrow (the 24th. inst.) to the DUISSANS area. in accordance with subjoined table.

2. 500 yards distance will be maintained between each Battalion, and in rear of the 479 Field Company R.E's; 10 yards between Companies, 100 yards in rear of the 184 L.T.M.B. and No. 524 Coy. Divisional Train.

3. Transport will march in the usual Echelons in rear of Battalions, but with cookers in front of the 1st. Line Transport, followed immediately by the Water Carts.

4. There will be a halt of 10 minutes before each clock hour, and there will not be any long halt.
Haversack rations will be carried.

5. BRIGADE HEADQUARTERS will close at BARLY at 6.30 a.m. and will re-open at DUISANS at the same hour.
During the march reports to be sent to the Head of the Column.

	STARTING POINT.	TIME.
TIMETABLE:- 1ST. FIELD AMBULANCE.	Road junction BAVINCOURT-BARLY Road.	9.50 a.m.

ROUTE:- FOSSEUX - WANQUETIN - WARLUS - DUISANS.

                (sgd.) G. MOORE. Captain.
                    Brigade Major.
              184th. Infantry Brigade.

2/1ST. SOUTH MIDLAND FIELD AMBULANCE.
=====================================

APPENDIX 7.

WAR DIARY.
MAY 1917.

CONFIDENTIAL.

WAR DIARY OF

2/1st SOUTH MIDLAND FIELD AMBULANCE.

FROM:- 1st JUNE, 1917 - 30th JUNE, 1917.

VOLUME 3. NUMBER 6.

In the field.
30.6.1917.

WAR DIARY
or
INTELLIGENCE SUMMARY.

(Erase heading not required.)

Army Form C. 2118.

Reference Ordnance Maps FRANCE.
1/100,000 LENS 11.
1/40,000 Sheets 51b and 51c.

Place	Date	Summary of Events and Information	Remarks and references to Appendices
DUISANS TILLOY.	1917 June 1st.	Ambulance moved to forward area and established Headquarters at TILLOY(H37.d.1.4.). Two Advanced Dressing Stations. Right Sector at MARLIERE CAVES (N 17.d.2.4.). Officers–CAPTAIN THOMSON. Left Sector at GUN PITS just S. of ARRAS – CAMBRAI main road. (N 4.b.2.8.) Officers. CAPTAIN HIRST, LIEUTENANT MUNRO. Transport except that actually in use, parked on RACE COURSE, ARRAS. Taking over complete by 5.0 p.m. without incident, and reported to A.D.M.S. 61st Division and HEADQUARTERS, 184th INFANTRY BRIGADE.	Feu.
TILLOY.	June 2nd.	O.C. visited RIGHT ADVANCED DRESSING STATION, MARLIERE CAVES. Saw CAPTAIN THOMSON and all the men at work. Night Relief from R.A.P. had just come in. Evacuation Route satisfactory from RIGHT R.A.P. at GUEMAPPE. Regimental Stretcher Bearers Route in finding R.A.P. rather long and exposed but fairly easy to follow. Gas Case Tent fitted up. CAPTAIN HIRST at GUN PITS heavily shelled. 435297, PRIVATE B.L.LINCOLN, 2/1st SOUTH MIDLAND FIELD AMBULANCE buried by a direct hit on top of one of the Gun Pit shelters. Pinned under the collapsed framework and only rescued after very great trouble and danger to the following party:- CAPTAIN HIRST.R.A.M.C.T., 435282, SERGEANT A.H.PERRY, 435306, PRIVATE D.TAPPER, 435391, PRIVATE J.WIGGINS,435348, PRIVATE J.F.CAVE, 437115, PRIVATE C.W. HARRISON. PRIVATE LINCOLN was returned to Headquarters.	Feu.
TILLOY.	June 3rd.	O.C. visited GUN PITS and saw CAPTAIN HIRST and LIEUTENANT MUNRO. Shelling hard. Found 1 Gun Pit knocked in. GERMAN GUN unearthed and made visible in left pit. This was covered with blankets and camouflaged during night by 435488 PRIVATE E.P.PERRY and 435094 L/CPL R.AUSTIN. CAPTAIN HIRST reports 435282 SERGEANT A.H.PERRY, 355306 PRIVATE D.TAPPER, 435391 PRIVATE J.WIGGINS,435348 PRIVATE J.F.CAVE and 437115 PRIVATE C.W.HARRISON for meritorious conduct. 1 STEEL SHELTER and Dressing Room commenced owing to the prevalence of splinters from high Shrapnel bursting over the Camp at TILLOY. Report from CAPTAIN THOMSON about possibility of trench railway, former Hun Track, being used for wounded from A.D.S. to Car post, Right Sector. Canadian Engineers assistance secured, also a track proposed down the inclined slide at entrance to CAVES. A.D.M.S. 61st Division, COLONEL SINGLETON, BRIG. GENERAL SPOONER visited Camp. MAJOR WHITWELL, O.C. 478 COMPANY R.E's reports GUN PITS unrepairable at present and a "Death Trap"	Feu.
TILLOY.	June 4th.	A.D.M.S. 61st Division, called. O.C. visited CAPTAIN HIRST – all well. – O.C. visited CAPTAIN THOMSON who reports Railway repaired and in working order.– used this morning ⅔ track down CAVE slide nearly finished. Windlass and rope sent up- also Timber. Railway blown up in afternoon but repaired at once by Engineers. GUN PITS heavily shelled – No direct hits. 1 STEEL SHELTER finished – Dressing Room framework done. Construction of 2nd STEEL SHELTER begun. Orderly Officers' hut constructed out of sunken tent.	Feu.

WAR DIARY
or
INTELLIGENCE SUMMARY.
(Erase heading not required.)

Army Form C. 2118.

Reference Ordnance Maps FRANCE.
1/100,000 LENS11
1/40,000 Sheets 51b, 51c.

Place	Date	Summary of Events and Information	Remarks and references to Appendices
TILLOY.	1917. June 5th.	O.C. visited GUN PITS to look for possible new position for A.D.S. D.A.D.M.S. 61st Division visited camp. O.C. arranged with C.R.E. 61st Division to have a splinter proof Shelter erected on S. side of CAMBRAI ROAD near the Car Stand for shelter for Car drivers and orderlies and a possible refuge when the GUN PITS are being shelled. 435282 SERGEANT A.H.PERRY wounded. Following recommendations forwarded to A.D.M.S. 61st Division. CAPTAIN W.J.HIRST, R.A.M.C. 435282 SERGEANT PERRY.A.H. DISTINGUISHED CONDUCT MEDAL, 435306, PRIVATE D.TAPPER and 435391 PRIVATE J.WIGGINS, MILITARY MEDAL. Heavy Barrage 8.0 p.m. Air Fight. German Aeroplane brought down in flames. British Airman, 2/LIEUTENANT STEVENSON killed. LIEUTENANT MUNRO returned from duty at A.D.S. GUN PITS? and CAPTAIN MONTGOMERY reported to A.D.S. GUN PITS for duty. 435270 PRIVATE G.GOODE and 435429 PRIVATE H.BISSELL taken on strength of this Unit from Base.	F.S.M.
TILLOY.	June 6th.	A.D.M.S. 61st Division called. Also D.A.D.M.S. 61st Division. Routine work. Evacuation of line from both Sectors working smoothly - a good deal of promiscous shelling of back areas and a good deal of counter battery shelling by the enemy, much of it close to both our A.D.S's. O.C. visited Right A.D.S. MARLIERE with D.A.D.M.S. 61st Division and inspected all improvements made there by CAPTAIN THOMSON - area quiet. -Sanitary conditions satisfactory- Railway down into CAVE with Windlass in constant use - 3 new carrying trucks working in and along line and a self balancing truck constructed for use in the inclined part.	F.S.M.
TILLOY.	June 7th.	O.C. visited GUN PITS and inspected new shelter at Car Stand on road side - digging finished - work impossible except in the dark - Shelter half completed - New shelters in camp and being rapidly Sandbagged. Left area quieter today than since we took over. Area round RIGHT A.D.S. heavily shelled. 437389 L/CPL HAMPTON, 435071 PRIVATE H.BLUCK, 435284 PRIVATE E.ARMITT, and 435566 PRIVATE T.WHITHORN brought down severe Abdominal Case through German Barrage.	F.S.M.
TILLOY.	June 8th.	Camp shelled by High Velocity gun, 8.30 a.m.- Shelters nearing completion - New roads almost completed - new incinerator built - 184th Warning Order for move received. O.C. 2/2nd LONDON FIELD AMBULANCE called and made arrangements for carrying out relief of this Ambulance. Visited forward posts and arranged details of reliefs. G.O.C. 61st Division, visited and inspected Camp. Advance parties of 2/2nd LONDON FIELD AMBULANCE arrived and went up the line, both Sectors.	v App 1. for instructions re move.
TILLOY.	June 9th.	2 Bearer Sub - divisions arrived under 3 Officers of 2/2nd LONDON FIELD AMBULANCE. O.C. visited A.D.M.S. 61st Division and inspected Unit Transport. Relief of Line commenced and carried out in the Evening and night successfully - no asualties. 437389 L/CPL HAMPTON, 435071 PRIVATE H.BLUCK 435284 PRIVATE E.ARMITT and 435566 PRIVATE T.WHITHORN recommended for gallant conduct in bringing down a severe Abdominal Case through a German Barrage.	F.S.M.
TILLOY. BERNEVILLE.	June 10th.	All personnel back from line. Stores returned less Wheeled Stretchers and 1 Operating Tent. O.C. visited BERNEVILLE and arranged Billets. Quiet day not much shelling.	F.S.M.

Army Form C. 2118.

WAR DIARY
or
INTELLIGENCE SUMMARY.

Reference Ordnance Maps FRANCE. 1/100,000 LENS 11.
1/40,000 Sheets 51b and 51c.

(Erase heading not required.)

Place	Date 1917.	Hour	Summary of Events and Information	Remarks and references to Appendices
TILLOY. BERNEVILLE.	June 10th.		Handed over to O.C. 2/2nd LONDON FIELD AMBULANCE at 12.0 noon. Transport left at 12.40 p.m. Ambulance marched off at 2.30 p.m. Arrived BERNEVILLE at 5.35 p.m. Casualties NIL. Usual notifications sent to A.D.M.S. 61st Division, and Headquarters 184th Infantry Brigade. Hospital opened and ready for reception of patients immediately.	Capt A. F.tu.
BERNEVILLE.	June 11th.		Holiday. A.D.M.S. 61st Division visited and inspected Camp.	F.tu.
BERNEVILLE.	June 12th.		Routine work. Physical Drill started. Concert Party rehearsing. O.C. visited A.D.M.S. 61st Division who proceeded on leave. Also visited 61st Divisional Headquarters, C.R.E. 61st Division and VI Corps Rest Station. Horsed Ambulance Waggon reported back from 307 Bgde R.F.A. 435282 SERGEANT A.H.PERRY, 435306, PRIVATE D.TAPPER and 435391 PRIVATE J.WIGGINS awarded MILITARY MEDALS.	Auth VI Corps R.O. No 2284.
BERNEVILLE.	June 13th.		Routine Work.	
BERNEVILLE.	June 14th.		Routine work. OFFICER COMMANDING, took over duties as A/A.D.M.S. 61st Division during absence on leave of A.D.M.S. 61st Division. Medical Board held at BERNEVILLE to medically examine and report on personnel required to form the 651st Divisional Employment Company, Labour Corps, which is allotted to this Division. PRESIDENT, Lieut.Col G.MACKIE, D.S.O., A/A.D.M.S. 61st Division. CAPTAIN BREEN, D.A.D.M.S. 61st Division, and CAPTAIN P.H.GREEN, R.A.M.C.T.	Auth. 61st D.R.O. 1206. 13,6,17. F.tu.
BERNEVILLE.	June 15th.		Routine Work. Medical Board continued.	F.tu.
BERNEVILLE.	June 16th.		Routine Work. Medical Board continued.	F.tu.
BERNEVILLE.	June 17th.		Routine work. 9.15 a.m. Inspection of Transport Section - Horses and Waggons by OFFICER COMMANDING. Church Parades - 9.10 a.m. Medical Board continued.	F.tu.
BERNEVILLE.	June 18th.		Routine Work. 5.35 a.m. Medical Inspection of all ranks by OFFICER COMMANDING.	F.tu.
BERNEVILLE.	June 19th.		Routine work. LIEUTENANT MUNRO, R.A.M.C.T. transferred to A.D.M.S. 3rd Division to replace CAPTAIN VICKERS, R.A.M.C.T. attached 2/? ROYAL WARWICKSHIRE REGIMENT. Open Air Swimming Bath opened at BERNEVILLE.	F.tu.
BERNEVILLE.	June 20th.		Routine Work. LIEUTENANT A.D.GORMAN reported for duty. Orders received re impending move of Division to HESDIN AREA.	vide App.??
BERNEVILLE.	June 21st.		61st Division entrainment order received. 61st Division R.A.M.C. order received.(Order 33, Copy) ADMINISTRATIVE ADDENDUM to Brigade Warning Order received.	vide App. 3,4,5.
BERNEVILLE.	June 22nd.		Unit Transport moved by road under CAPTAIN THOMSON, R.A.M.C.T. to ROUGEFAY, stopping night of 22/23rd June, 1917 at REBREUVE? Map Reference LENS 11, 1/100,000.	F.tu.
BERNEVILLE. ROUGEFAY.	June 23rd.		Unit entrained GUOY EN ARTOIS, at 9.0 a.m.Detrained AUXI LE. CHATEAU at 2.30 p.m. Marched to ROUGEFAY arriving 4.30 p.m. Hospital opened and ready for reception of patients immediately. Usual notifications forwarded to 184th INFANTRY BRIGADE and A.D.M.S. 61st Division.	F.tu.

WAR DIARY
or
INTELLIGENCE SUMMARY.

(Erase heading not required.)

Reference Ordnance Maps, FRANCE 1/100,000 LENS 11. Army Form C. 2118.

Place	Date 1917.	Hour	Summary of Events and Information	Remarks and references to Appendices
ROUGEFAY.	June 24th,		Routine work. A.D.M.S. 61st Division returned from leave of absence. A.D.M.S. 61st Division called and gave instructions for this Unit to open a Divisional Skin Hospital. Construction of Hospital and Baths commenced. Fatigue parties detailed to clean village and drains.	
ROUGEFAY.	June 25th.		Routine work. Construction of Hospital and Baths continued.	
ROUGEFAY.	June 26th.		Routine work. Orders received from A.D.M.S. 61st Division re move to BACHIMONT. Billeting Officer v App 6. LIEUTENANT W.S.RIVERS, R.A.M.C.T. secured all billets at BABHIMONT for reception of Ambulance next day. CAPTAIN W.J.HIRST, R.A.M.C.T. attended conference at A.D.M.S. 61st Division Office. 11.30 p.m. Order received from A.D.M.S. 61st Division cancelling previous one and ordering Unit to move to FROHEN LE GRAND.	
ROUGEFAY.	June 27th.		One G.S. waggon loaded with all Tents etc, and "C" Section Tent Sub - division moved off at 7.30 a.m. to FROHEN LE GRAND via AUXI LE CHATEAU. 9.30 a.m. Unit Transport moved off independently under CAPTAIN A.P.THOMSON R.A.M.C.T. and marched to FROHEN LE GRAND via AUXI LE CHATEAU. 9.30 a.m. Unit personnel moved off under CAPTAIN W.J.HIRST, R.A.M.C.T. Arrived FROHEN LE GRAND at 3.0 p.m. Hospital opened and ready for the reception of patients immediately. Usual notifications forwarded to A.D.M.S. 61st Division, and 184th INFANTRY BRIGADE.	v App 7.
FROHEN LE GRAND.	June 28th.		Routine work. Preparing Hospitals and Grounds. CAPTAIN W.J.HIRST, R.A.M.C.T. examined Water Cart of the 184th MACHINE GUN COMPANY and reported on same to A.D.M.S. 61st Division. CAPTAIN THOMSON? R.A.M.C.T. attended conference at 2/2nd SOUTH MIDLAND FIELD AMBULANCE re R.A.M.C. sports.	
FROHEN LE GRAND.	June 29th.		Routine Work.	
FROHEN LE GRAND.	June 30th.		Routine Work.	
	JUNE 30th, 1917.			

Signed

Lieut Colonel:R.A.M.C.T.

COMMANDING. 2/1st SOUTH MIDLAND FIELD AMBULANCE.

SECRET.
APPENDIX 1.
COPY.

The 61st Division (less Artillery) will be relieved on 10/11th June by the 56th Division.

The Advanced Dressing Stations (N17 d.2.2.) and (N11.a.7.6.) TILLOY,(H 31 d.2.4.,) Hopital St Jean and Convent ARRAS will be taken over by daybreak June 11th. Details to be arranged by O's.C.concerned.

The 2/1st Field Ambulance will be associated with the 184 Brigade Group.

           Sgd.   C.HOWKINS. Col A.M.S.
                        A.D.M.S. 61st Division.

8.6.1917.

30.6.1917.
                     Lieut Colonel:R.A.M.C.T.
COMMANDING. 2/1st SOUTH MIDLAND FIELD AMBULANCE.

APPENDIX. 2

COPY.

D.M. 208.

61st Div. Wire begins aaa YThe Division will move to WILLEMAN area 5 miles East of HESDIN on 22nd and 23rd aaa 183rd Brigade group by bus on 22nd 184th Brigade by bus and 182 group by train on 23rd aaa Transport will move by road two days match, probably one day before their groups. aaa ends aaa.

From:- Medical, 61st Division.

Sgd). T.F.P.BREEN, Capt.

R.Mackie.
Lieut Col:R.A.M.C.T.

30.6.1917.   COMMANDING. 2/1st SOUTH MIDLAND FIELD AMBULANCE.

2/1st Field Ambulance.   SECRET.   WARNING ORDER.   G.160.

----

1. 184th BRIGADE GROUP, less 184 L.T.M.B. and 1/5 D.C.L.I. and plus 478 Field Coy R.E. will move on 22nd and 23rd inst to WAVANS AREA in accordance with March Table attached.

Sgd).. J.R.WHARTON Capt,
A/Brigade Major. 184th Infantry Bgde.

20.6.17.

MARCH TABLE.

Serial No	Date	Troops	From	To	Remarks
3.	23rd.	184 Bgde group.	BERNEVILLE.	WAVANS area. En-Bgde H.Qrs at CHATEAU de BEAUVOIN.	By train. train FOSSEUX Loop(Q.1.a.) Sheet 51c. Detrain AUXI.

R.Mackie.
Lieut Col:R.A.M.C.T.
COMMANDING. 2/1st SOUTH MIDLAND FIELD AMBULANCE.

30.6.1917.

APPENDIX 3.   A.D.M.S. 955/4/17, 21.6.17.

COPY.

<u>2/1st Field Ambulance.</u>

<u>ENTRAINMENT ORDERS</u>.

Units will entrain in accordance will table below.

G.O.C'S BRIGADE GROUPS will issue orders:-
    (a) as to which Units of their Group entrain on which of the two trains allotted to their group.
    (b) Route and Rendezvous etc for troops entraining.

23rd. 1st Portion. 184 Bgde group.	TrainNo 3.	Entrain FOSSEUX loop. (Q.1.a.)	Time of departure. 10.a.,.	Detrain. AUXI LE CHATEAU. about 2.p.m.

Sgd. T.F.P.BREEN Capt for
Lieut Col: A/A.D.M.S. 61st Division.

21.6.1917.

[signature]

Lieut Col:R.A.M.C.T.
30.6.1917.   O.C. 2/1st SOUTH MIDLAND FIELD AMBULANCE.

SECRET.   APPENDIX 4.   Copy.9.
                              COPY.

ADMINISTRATIVE ADDENDUM TO 184 BRIGADE WARNING ORDER G.160, 20.6.17.

ENTRAINMENT.
1. 184th Infantry Brigade Group and 478 Field Coy R.E. will entrain as
   follows:-
     1st Train leaving at 10.a.m.
         4 R.BERKS.
         2 BUCKS.
         479 FIELD COY.R.E.
         2/1st FIELD AMBULANCE.
         478 FIELD COY R.E.

   Billeting parties composed as under will proceed on 22nd by bus or lorry.
   They will carry Rations for 22nd and 23rd.
   2/1st FIELD AMBULANCE.   1 Officer or N.C.O.

   The billeting areas are allotted as follows:-
   2/1st FIELD AMBULANCE.   ROUGEFAY.

   Brigade Group transport will move by road on 22nd inst and night 22/23rd.
   Transport will billet at REBREUVE, BOURET area.

21.6.1917.   Sgd: A.BICKNELL, Captain. Staff Captain.
Copy 9 to 1st Fld Ambce.   184th Infantry Brigade.

                                        R.O.Mackie
                                        Lieut Col:R.A.M.C.T.
30.6.1917.   Commanding. 2/1st SOUTH MIDLAND FIELD AMBULANCE..

APPENDIX 5.

SECRET.   Copy.
                                                    COPY 1.

            61st DIVISION.R.A.M.C. ORDER No 33.   21.6.1917.

1. The Division(less artillery) will move by road and rail to the
    WILLEMAN - FROHEN area on 21st, 22nd and 23rd June.
2. The Field Ambulances will remain grouped as at present, and will come
    under the orders of their Group Commanders.
3. Motor Transport willmove under orders of O.C's Field Ambulances.
4. On arrival in new area O's C Field Ambulances will arrange to collect
    sick from their Group area.
5. O.C. 2/1st Field Ambulance will, in addition collect sick from the
    Divisional Engineers area.
6. All maps Vl Corps area in possession of Field Ambulanees will be retained
7. The A.D.M.S. Office will close at WARLUS at 11.0 a.m. on June 23rd and
    re-open at the same hour at WILLEMAN.
8. ACKNOWLEDGE.
Issued at 1.0 p.m.   Sgd. T.F.P.BREEN Capt for
                                  Lieut Col: A/A.D.M.S. 61st Division.

Copies No 1 to 2/1st Field Ambulance.

                                        [signature]
                                        Lieut Col:R.A.M.C.T.
30.6.1917.   COMMANDING. 2/1st SOUTH MIDLAND FIELD AMBULNCE.

APPENDIX 6.　　　　　　　　　　　　　　A.D.M.S. 955/4/17, 26.6.17.
　Copy.

SECRET.

To:- 2/1st Field Ambulance.

　　　　　The following moves will take place tomorrow (June 27th). 2/1st Field Ambulance from ROUGEFAY to BACHIMONT, to clear ROUGEFAY by 9.a.m. Report arrival.

26.6.17.　　　　　　　　　Sgd.　C.HOWKINS. Col:A.M.S.
　　　　　　　　　　　　　　　　A.D.M.S. 61st Division.

　　　　　　　　　　　　　　　　[signature]
　　　　　　　　　　　　　　　Lieut Col:R.A.M.C.T.
　　　　COMMANDING. 2/1st SOUTH MIDLAND FIELD AMBULANCE.
30.6.1917.

APPENDIX 7.

SECRET. COPY. A.D.M.S. 955/4/17, 26.6.17.

To:- Officer Commanding.
       2/1st Field Ambulance.

              There is no objection to your moving tomorrow to FROHEN LE GRAND in place of the Battalion which is moving out. Inform your associated Brigade etc.

                          Sgd. C. HOWKINS. Col:A.M.S.
26.6.1917.   A.D.M.S. 61st Division.

[signature]
Lieut Colonel:R.A.M.C.T.

30.6.1917.   COMMANDING. 2/1st SOUTH MIDLAND FIELD AMBULANCE.

140/298

2/1st South Midland F.A.

COMMITTEE FOR THE
MEDICAL HISTORY OF THE WAR
Date 10 SEP. 1917

Medical
96/15

C O N F I D E N T I A L.

WAR DIARY OF THE

2/1st SOUTH MIDLAND FIELD AMBULANCE,

61st DIVISION.

FROM: 1st JULY, 1917 to 31st JULY, 1917.

VOLUME 3. BOOK 7.

B.E.F.

SUMMARY OF MEDICAL WAR DIARIES OF

2/1st S.M.F.A. 61st Div. 8th Corps, 5th ARMY.
from 26.7.17.

19th Corps from August 15th.
5th Corps from Sept. 7th.

To 17th Corps, 3rd Army 18.9.17.

Western Front Operations - "July - Sept. 1917.

O.C. - Lt.Col. Mackie, D.S.O. (T).

SUMMARISED UNDER THE FOLLOWING HEADINGS :-
Phase "D 1". Passchendaele Operations, "July-Nov. 1917"
(a) - Operations commencing 1.7.17.

B.E.F.

1.

2/1st (S.M.) F.A. 61st Div. 8th Corps. 5th ARMY. WESTERN FRONT.
July-Nov.1917.

Officer Commanding - Lt.Col. G. Mackie D.S.O. (T).

19th Corps from Aug. 15th.

PHASE "D"1. Passchendaele Operations, July -Nov. 1917.

(a) - Operations commencing 1/7/17.

Headquarters at Broxeele.

July 26th.   Moves.   ) Unit arrived in 8th Corps Area from 6th Corps
             Transfer.)
             1st ARMY.

B.E.F.

1.

2/1st S.M. F.A. 61st Div. 8th Corps. 5th ARMY. WESTERN FRONT. July-Nov.1917.

Officer Commanding - Lt.Col. G. Mackie D.S.O. (T).

19th Corps from Aug. 15th.

PHASE "D"1. Passchendaele Operations, July - Nov. 1917.

(a) - Operations commencing 1/7/17.

Headquarters at Broxeele.

July 26th. Moves.) Unit arrived in 8th Corps Area from 6th Corps
Transfer.)
1st ARMY.

WAR DIARY
or
INTELLIGENCE SUMMARY.

Army Form C. 2118.

MAP REFERENCE: LENS 11, 1/100,000.
ORDNANCE MAPS, FRANCE.

(Erase heading not required.)

Place	Date 1917.	Hour	Summary of Events and Information	Remarks and references to Appendices
FROHEN le GRAND.	JULY 1st.		Routine work. - A.D.M.S. 61st DIVISION visited and inspected CAMP - Fitting of SCABIES HOSPITAL commenced.	Gorm.
FROHEN le GRAND.	JULY 2nd.		Routine work. -	Gorm.
FROHEN le GRAND.	JULY 3rd.		Routine work - Field Training - Improvising Equipment. OFFICER COMMANDING visited 61st DIVISIONAL HEADQUARTERS.	Gorm.
FROHEN le GRAND.	JULY 4th.		Routine work - 184th INFANTRY BRIGADE HORSE SHOW held - No: 17159, QUARTERMASTER SERGEANT G.JONES reported from A.D.M.S. 61st DIVISION to take over duties as SERGEANT MAJOR of this Unit.	Auth. D.M.S. 3rd ARMY. Gorm.
FROHEN le GRAND.	JULY 5th.		Routine work till 12.0 noon. - Unit Sports held in the afternoon.	Gorm.
FROHEN le GRAND.	JULY 6th.		Routine work.	Gorm.
FROHEN le GRAND.	JULY 7th.		Routine work. - Field Training for Officers and other ranks.	Gorm.
FROHEN le GRAND.	JULY 8th.		Routine work. - Medical Inspection of all ranks by OFFICER COMMANDING. - All Iron Rations, Steel Helmets, Gas Helmets etc inspected.	Gorm.
FROHEN le GRAND.	JULY 9th.		Routine work - Field Operations.	Gorm.
FROHEN le GRAND.	JULY 10th.		ROUTINE WORK. Route March, 9.30 a.m. - 12.0 noon. - LIEUTENANT A.D.GORMAN, R.A.M.C. (S.R.) struck off the strength of this Unit, on proceeding to report to D.D.M.S., HAVRE, for duty.	A.D.M.S Auth: 61st DIV. Gorm.
FROHEN le GRAND.	JULY 11th.		Routine work - Special Inspection of, and practice with, Gas Helmets. - Field work during supposed Gas attack.	Gorm.
FROHEN le GRAND.	JULY 12th.		Routine work. - List of honorary unpaid promotions for good service, published in Unit Orders.	Gorm.
FROHEN le GRAND.	JULY 13th.		Routine work. - N.C.O's and men mentioned in Unit Orders for good work - OFFICER COMMANDING met all Regimental Medical Officers of the 184th INFANTRY BRIGADE, re Regimental Stretcher Bearers Sports, and for the Tactical Scheme ordered for 184th INFANTRY BRIGADE Medical Officers under OFFICER COMMANDING, 2/1st SOUTH MIDLAND FIELD AMBULANCE.	Gorm.

WAR DIARY
or
INTELLIGENCE SUMMARY.

REFERENCE ORDNANCE MAP, FRANCE   Army Form C. 2118.
SHEET: LENS 11, 1/100,000.

(Erase heading not required.)

Instructions regarding War Diaries and Intelligence Summaries are contained in F.S. Regs., Part II and the Staff Manual respectively. Title pages will be prepared in manuscript.

Place	Date 1917.	Hour	Summary of Events and Information	Remarks and references to Appendices
FROHEN le GRAND.	JULY 14th.		Routine work. — 3 Medical Officers and 1 Sanitary N.C.O. visited Sanitary Exhibition at ST POL. → OFFICER COMMANDING visited A.D.M.S. 61st DIVISION, re Tactical Scheme for Regimental Medical Officers of the 184th INFANTRY BRIGADE. — CAPTAIN W.J.EVANS, R.A.M.C. inspected and reported on the Water Cart of the 184th MACHINE GUN CORPS.	Eastu
FROHEN le GRAND.	JULY 15th.		Routine work. — Medical Inspection of all ranks. — Church Parade, 6.30 p.m. — CAPTAIN W.J.HIRST R.A.M.C.T. proceeded on leave of absence to ENGLAND.	Eastu Authi: A.D.M.S. 61st Div: Eastu v. Appx 1
FROHEN le GRAND.	JULY 16th.		Tactical Scheme carried out by "A" and "B" Sections, 2/1st SOUTH MIDLAND FIELD AMBULANCE. — Regimental Medical Officers of 184th INFANTRY BRIGADE present. — A.D.M.S. 61st DIVISION inspected arrangements with OFFICER COMMANDING.	Eastu
FROHEN le GRAND.	JULY 17th.		Routine work. — Night Operations.	Eastu
FROHEN le GRAND.	JULY 18th.		Routine work. — 61st DIVISIONAL RACE MEETING. — Officers, N.C.O's and men of this Unit took and active part in the function.	Eastu
FROHEN le GRAND.	JULY 19th.		Routine work. — Stretcher Bearer competition for Regimental Stretcher Bearers held at DIVISIONAL HEADQUARTERS under A.D.M.S. 61st DIVISION. — Judged by Officers of the Field Ambulances under D.A.D.M.S. 61st DIVISION. Prizes presented by MAJOR GENERAL COLIN MACKENZIE, G.O.C. 61st DIVISION.	Eastu
FROHEN le GRAND.	JULY 20th.		Routine training. — 61st DIVISIONAL ADMINISTRATIVE INSTRUCTION, No: 1, received, re move of DIVISION from WILLERMAN area.	Pestu
FROHEN le GRAND.	JULY 21st.		Field Operations - Unit attended special manoeuvres with 184th INFANTRY BRIGADE to test the results of the training, while BRIGADE has been in the rest area. — Inspected by BRIGADIER GENERAL, the HON R. WHITE, COMMANDING, 184th INFANTRY BRIGADE and G.O.C. 61st DIVISION.	Pestu
FROHEN le GRAND.	JULY 22nd.		Routine training. Advance party instructions received from 184th INFANTRY BRIGADE and A.D.M.S. 61st DIVISION.	Pestu

Army Form C. 2118.

WAR DIARY
or
INTELLIGENCE SUMMARY.

(Erase heading not required.)

REFERENCE ORDNANCE MAPS, FRANCE.
SHEETS, LENS 11, 1/100,000 and
HAZEBROUCK, 5a.

Instructions regarding War Diaries and Intelligence Summaries are contained in F. S. Regs., Part II. and the Staff Manual respectively. Title pages will be prepared in manuscript.

Place	Date 1917.	Hour	Summary of Events and Information	Remarks and references to Appendices
FROHEN LE GRAND.	JULY 23rd.		Routine work. SERGEANT ROBINSON, 2/1st SOUTH MIDLAND FIELD AMBULANCE proceeded to BROXEELE AREA as billeting N.C.O.	Capt.M.
FROHEN LE GRAND.	JULY 24th.		Routine training.	Capt.M.
FROHEN LE GRAND.	JULY 25th.		Routine work. D.A.D.M.S. 61st DIVISION called. - Final preparations made for move from WILLERMAN AREA.	Fd.M.
			Unit Transport fell in at 8.15 p.m. Moved off at 8.30 p.m. Unit personnel fell in at 10.15 p.m. and moved off at 10.30 p.m., marching to AUXI LE CHATEAU.	
FROHEN LE GRAND. AND BROXEELE.	JULY 26th.		Entrained at AUXI LE CHATEAU at 2.0a.m. - Detrained ST OMER at 7.45 a.m. Marched to BROXEELE, arriving at 1.30 p.m. - Tented Hospital pitched and ready for reception of patients immediately - Usual notifications sent out to A.D.M.S. 61st DIVISION, and HEADQUARTERS, 184th INFANTRY BRIGADE.	Fd.M. Fd.M.
BROXEELE.	JULY 27th.		Routine work. D.D.M.S. VIIIth CORPS, and A.D.M.S. 61st DIVISION, visited and inspected Camp and Hospital. CAPTAIN A.P. THOMSON, R.A.M.C.T. sent to No: 7 Hospital, MALASSISE, with P.U.O.	Fd.M.
BROXEELE.	JULY 28th.		Routine work. OFFICER COMMANDING, OFFICERS AND GAS N.C.O.'s of this Unit attended Lecture at 184th BRIGADE HEADQUARTERS, on the new German Gas. OFFICER COMMANDING attended Conference at A.D.M.S. OFFICE, 61st DIVISION HEADQUARTERS, ZEGGARS CAPPEL.	Fd.M.
BROXEELE.	JULY 29th.		Routine work. - Medical Inspection of all ranks - Church parade, 9.0 a.m. OFFICER COMMANDING visited HEADQUARTERS, 184th INFANTRY BRIGADE.	Capt.M.
BROXEELE.	JULY 30th.		Routine work. - OFFICER COMMANDING visited HEADQUARTERS, 184th INFANTRY BRIGADE. CAPTAIN W.JONES EVANS, R.A.M.C. proceeded to 2/8th ROYAL WARWICKSHIRE REGIMENT as M.O. during absence on leave of CAPTAIN VICKERS, R.A.M.C.	Auth A.D.M.S 61st Div.
BROXEELE.	JULY 31st.		Routine work. OFFICER COMMANDING visited HEADQUARTERS, 184th INFANTRY BRIGADE. Demonstration of THOMAS' SPLINT by OFFICER COMMANDING. CAPTAIN A. MONTGOMERY, R.A.M.C. proceeded to ENGLAND on 1 months Special leave of Absence.	Auth. A.D.M.S. 61st Div.

31st JULY, 1917.

G. Ewart
Lieut Colonel: R.A.M.C.T.
COMMANDING. 2/1st SOUTH MIDLAND FIELD AMBULANCE.

"A" Form.
MESSAGES AND SIGNALS.

Army Form C.2121 (in pads of 100). No. of Message ....

Prefix .... Code .... m.	Words	Charge	This message is on a/c of:	Recd. at .... m.
Office of Origin and Service Instructions.	Sent		.... Service.	Date ....
	At .... m.			From ....
	To			
	By		(Signature of "Franking Officer.")	By ....

TO — Addressed all Medical Officers, 184 Bde Group, also M.O. R.E's and M.O. D.C.L.I.

Sender's Number.	Day of Month.	In reply to Number.		
* G.M. 502	15th.			A A A
A	tactical	scheme	will	be
carried	out	tomorrow	Monday	16th
inst	from	10.30 a.m.	till	3.0 p.m.
by	order	of	A.D.M.S.	61st
Division	a.a.a.	Will	you	kindly
meet	me	at	10.30 a.m.	at
N.W.	corner	of	BOIS de la	JUSTICE
on	AUXI-LE-	CHATEAU- QUOEUX road		about
400	yards	S.	of	final
E	in	EPINE	map	reference
sheet	LENS	X1	1	in
100,000	a.a.a.			

From 2/1st South Mid. Field Ambulance.
Place
Time

The above may be forwarded as now corrected. (Z)

Censor.

Lt. Col. R.A.M.C.T.
Signature of Addresser or person authorised to telegraph in his name.
Commanding 2/1st Sth. M. Fld Amb.

TACTICAL EXERCISE

for

Regimental Medical Officers,

of

184th INFANTRY BRIGADE, R.E's and D.C.L.I.

Monday, July 16th 1917.

Map reference - FRANCE - Sheet LENS 11 - Scale 1 to 100,000.

SCHEME.

1. A Hostile force which has been defeated in the region of the HESDIN - FREVENT Road is retreating on ABBEVILLE and is at present in strength on the high ground S.W. of AUXI LE CHATEAU but is still holding the Valley of the River AUTHIE and is still N. of the main road DOULIENS - FROHEN LE GRAND - AUXI LE CHATEAU - LE PONCHEL.

2. The Attacking force, of which the 61st DIVISION is part, is holding the line :-

    VAULX - BUIRE AU BOIS - VILLERS L'HOPITAL and is pushing on. It reaches and consolidates the ridge -

    VAULX - S.W. corner of BOIS DE LA JUSTICE - NOEUX on the morning of Monday, July 16th, establishing a strong point in the crater and trenches W. of the main road -

    AUXI LE CHATEAU - QUOEUX awaiting the arrival of Heavy Artillery.

-o-o-o-o-o-o-o-o-o-o-o-o-o-o-o-o-o-o-o-o-o-

TACTICAL EXERCISE.

Summary of position

taken from extracts from:- 61st Division Orders.
184th Infantry Brigade Orders.
R.A.M.C. Orders by A.D.M.S. 61 Div.

-o-o-o-o-o-o-o-o-o-o-o-o-o-o-o-o-o-o-o-o-o-

1. The 184TH INFANTRY BRIGADE is responsible for the line from the L in PT. PONCHEL through S.W. corner of BOIS DE LA JUSTICE to the S in BOIS D'AUXI.

2. This is a 2 Battalion front - the dividing line being the main road AUXI LE CHATEAU - QUOEUX.

3. The two roads -
    AUXI LE CHATEAU - VACQUERIE LE BOUCQ and
    AUXI LE CHATEAU - BUIRE AU BOIS
   HAVE been badly mined and are impassable.

4. The 2/1ST SOUTH MIDLAND FIELD AMBULANCE is at HARAVESNES and has orders to follow the 184TH INFANTRY BRIGADE closely - evacuating wounded after 10am July 16th to a temporary C.C.S. at QUOEUX.

5. The road AUXI LE CHATEAU - QUOEUX is open.

ORDERS BY LIEUT: COLONEL GEORGE A. MACKIE. D.S.O., R.A.M.C.T.

COMMANDING. 2/1st SOUTH MIDLAND FIELD AMBULANCE.

MONDAY.   JULY 16th, 1917.

DUTIES.
Medical Officer i/c Hospital for week. — Captain Green.
Medical Officer i/c Scabies for week. — Captain Evans.
Orderly Officer for week. — Captain Montgomery.
Orderly Transport Officer. — Captain Thomson.
Orderly Sergeant. — Sergeant Perry.
Orderly Bugler. — Bugler Loxton.

ROUTINE.
5.30 a.m. — Reveille.
5.50 a.m. — Tea and Biscuits.
6.0 – 6.30 a.m. — Physical Drill, "C" Section. "A" and "B" load Waggons.
7.0 a.m. — Breakfast.
7.30 a.m. — Unit Sick Parade.
8.0 – 9.30 a.m. — 1st parade – C Section – general fatigues.
10.0 – 12.noon. — 2nd parade – C section – general fatigues.
12.20 p.m. — Dinner.
2.30 p.m. — C Section, till dismissal – general fatigues.
4.30 p.m. — Tea.
6.0 p.m. — Parade for Guard and Picquet (Orderly Officer
9.0 p.m. — Lights Out.

SPECIAL ORDERS FOR FIELD OPERATIONS, JULY 16th, 1917.

The Ambulance, less C Section, will parade at 8.15 a.m. for Field Operations.

Move off. 8.30 a.m.

"A" Section under CAPTAIN THOMSON and "B" Section under CAPTAIN GREEN, will parade complete.

DRESS. Marching Order, less Pack, with Steel Helmets, P.H. Helmet and Waterproof Sheet.

RATIONS will be carried on Cooks' Limber. Water Bottles will be filled by Ss

TRANSPORT. "A" SECTION will take its complete Transport, plus Cooks Limber and less Horse Ambulance Waggon. Water Cart to be filled.

"B" SECTION will take its complete Transport, with Water Cart filled. Baggage Waggon will carry only 1 Operating Tent, 2 Bell Tents and 2 Wheeled Stretchers.

ROUTE. FROHEN LE GRAND – AUXI – LE – CHATEAU – QUOEUX. The halting place on the road to QUOEUX will be marked.

RETURN. March will be timed for return to Headquarters by 4.15 p.m.

SCHEME.

The Ambulance is supposed to be in support of 184th INFANTRY BRIGADE, which is holding a position on the ridge facing AUXI – LE – CHATEAU from the North.

"A" SECTION will be shown a site where they will establish a main Dressing Station (Tented) and prepare for dressing wounded, Operations etc.

"B" SECTION will be shown another site further forward where they will establish an Advanced Dressing Station, using Tents if necessary. They will not unpack their MEDICAL STORE WAGGON unless specially ordered.

The Regimental Medical Officers of te 184th INFANTRY BRIGADE will be present and will see the Ambulance at work.

Dinner will be served at "A" Section Post at 1.15p.m, for all personnel of both Sections, except Transport and Nursing Details of "B" Section (up to 20 individuals) who will be catered for at the Advanced Dressing Station.

CONFIDENTIAL.

WAR DIARY OF THE

2/1st SOUTH MIDLAND FIELD AMBULANCE.

61st DIVISION.

AUGUST 1st, 1917 — AUGUST 31st, 1917.

VOLUME 3.   BOOK 8.

COMMITTEE FOR THE
MEDICAL HISTORY OF THE WAR
Date -1 OCT.1917

B.E.F.

SUMMARY OF MEDICAL WAR DIARIES OF

2/1st S.M.F.A. 61st Div. 8th Corps, 5th ARMY.
from 26.7.17.

19th Corps from August 15th.
5th Corps from Sept. 7th.

To 17th Corps, 3rd Army 13.9.17.

Western Front Operations - "July - Sept. 1917.

O.C. - Lt.Col. Mackie, D.S.O. (T).

SUMMARISED UNDER THE FOLLOWING HEADINGS :-
Phase "D 1". Passchendaele Operations, "July-Nov. 1917"
(a) - Operations commencing 1.7.17.

Aug. 1st-14th. Operations R.A.M.C. Routine and Training.

15th.   Transfer.) To Wattou and transferred to 19th Corps with
        Moves.   )
        61st Division.

B.E.F.

2/1st S.M.F.A. 61st Div. 19th Corps. 5th ARMY. WESTERN FRONT
July-Nov./17

Officer Commanding - Lt.Col. G. Mackie D.S.O.(T).

5th Corps from Sept. 7th.

PHASE "D" 1. Passchendaele Operations ,"July-Nov.1917".

(a) - Operations commencing 1/7/17.

Headquarters at Wattou.

Aug. 15th.	**Transfer.** Transferred to 19th Corps. Moves to Wattou.
	Moves. Detachment. 3 T.S.D's to 19th Corps W.W.C.P.
16th.	50 S.B's to 108th Field Ambulance.
17th.	24 Bearers to 2/3rd S.M.F.A.
18th.	**Moves.** To G.11.a.4.6. (Sheet 28).
20th.	**Moves.**) H.8.a.9.9. (Sheet 28).
	Medical Arrangements.) To VLAMERTINGHE MILL and took over 19th C.W.W.C.P. from 112th F.A. and MOATED FARM from 113th F.A. 16th Div.
21st.	**Medical Arrangements.** MOATED FARM opened as Rest Station for Neurasthenic cases.
22nd.	**Operations.** Attack commenced on 19th Corps front towards St. JULIAN - ZONNEBEKE Road, 61st Div. on left, 15th Division on right.
	Casualties. Wounded began to arrive 7 a.m. and continued all day.
23rd.	16 & 1207 wounded passed through during past 24 hours.
27th.	**Casualties** R.A.M.C. O & 1 wounded.
Sept. 7th.	**Transfer.** Unit transferred with 61st Division to 5th Corps.

Sept. 7th. Transfer. Unit transferred with 61st Division to 5th Corps.

Aug. 1st-14th. Operations R.A.M.C. Routine and Training.

15th. Transfer.) To Wattou and transferred to 19th Corps with
       Moves.   ) 61st Division.

B.E.F.

2/1st S.M. F.A. 61st Div. 19th Corps. 5th ARMY. WESTERN FR
                                                        July-Nov./
Officer Commanding - Lt.Col. G. Mackie D.S.O.(T).

5th Corps from Sept. 7th.

PHASE "D" 1. Passchendaele Operations ,"July-Nov.1917".

  (a) - Operations commencing 1/7/17.

Headquarters at Watou.

Aug. 15th.   Transfer. Transferred to 19th Corps. Moves to Watou.
             Moves. Detachment. 3 T.S.D's to 19th Corps W.W.C.P.
     16th.   50 S.B's to 108th Field Ambulance.
     17th.   24 Bearers to 2/3rd S.M.F.A.
     18th.   Moves. To G.11.a.4.6. (Sheet 28).
     20th.   Moves.   ) H.8.a.9.9. (Sheet 28).
             Medical Arrangements.)
                                To VLAMERTINGHE MILL and took over
             19th C.W.W.C.P. from 112th F.A. and MOATED FARM from
             113th F.A. 16th Div.
     21st.   Medical Arrangements. MOATED FARM opened as Rest Station
             for Neurasthenic cases.
     22nd.   Operations. Attack commenced on 19th Corps front
             tpwards St. JULIAN - ZONNEBEKE Road 61st Div. on left
             15th Division on right.
             Casualties. Wounded began to arrive 7 a.m. and continued
             all day.
     23rd.   16 & 1207 wounded passed through during
             past 24 hours.
     27th.   Casualties R.A.M.C.O & 1 wounded.

WAR DIARY or INTELLIGENCE SUMMARY.

Army Form C. 2118.

REFERENCE MAPS
FRANCE.
FRANCE AND BELGIUM, HAZEBROUCK. 5a.
BELGIUM, Sheet 27.
BELGIUM, Sheet 28.

(Erase heading not required.)

Instructions regarding War Diaries and Intelligence Summaries are contained in F.S. Regs., Part II. and the Staff Manual respectively. Title pages will be prepared in manuscript.

Place	Date 1917	Hour	Summary of Events and Information	Remarks and references to Appendices
BROXEELE.	AUG: 14th.		Routine work. OFFICER COMMANDING visited XIX Corps 2 CORPS MAIN DRESSING STATIONS and XIXth CORPS WALKING WOUNDED COLLECTING POST. All waggons packed in readiness for move. March Tables for Unit and Transport received from HEADQUARTERS, 184th INFANTRY BRIGADE.	Ce/M.
BROXEELE. WATOU.	AUG: 15th.		Unit personnel entrained at ARNEKE at 4.40 a.m. - Detrained at ABEELE at 8.30 a.m. - Arrived WATOU at 11.30 a.m. Usual notifications of arrival sent to A.D.M.S. 61st DIVISION and to HEADQUARTERS, 184th INFANTRY BRIGADE. Instructions received from A.D.M.S. 61st DIVISION TO SEND IMMEDIATELY 3 TENT SUB DIVISIONS and 3 CLERKS to XIXth CORPS WALKING WOUNDED COLLECTING POST. Transport arrived at WATOU at 6.0 p.m. having started from BROXEELE at 6.0 p.m.	Ce/M.
WATOU.	AUG: 16th.		OFFICER COMMANDING visited A.D.M.S. 61st DIVISION and XIXth CORPS WALKING WOUNDED COLLECTING POST. 50 STRETCHER BEARERS sent to 108th FIELD AMBULANCE under instructions received from D.D.M.S., XIXth CORPS.	Ce/M.
do Sheet 28. G,11,a.4.6.	AUG: 17th.		D.D.M.S. XIXth CORPS visited and inspected camp. OFFICER COMMANDING visited Forward area with D.A.D.M.S. 61st DIVISION. Instructions received from A.D.M.S. 61st DIVISION for move of Unit to G,11,a.4.6. (Sheet 28). Instructions received from A.D.M.S. 61st DIVISION to send 24 Bearers to be attached to the 2/3rd SOUTH MIDLAND FIELD AMBULANCE.	Ce/M.
do.	AUG: 18th.		Remaining personnel moved to G,11, a.4.6. (Sheet 28). Hospital opened for Sick of 182nd and 184th INFANTRY BRIGADES. Notifications of arrival sent to A.D.M.S. 61st DIVISION and HEADQUARTERS, 184th INFANTRY BRIGADE.	Ce/M.
DO.	AUG: 19th.		Orders received from A.D.M.S. 61st DIVISION, for move of Unit to take over the XIXth CORPS WALKING WOUNDED COLLECTING POST, VLAMERTINGHE MILL, Reference Sheet 28, H,8,a.9.9.	Ce/M.
H,8,a.9.9.	AUG: 20th.	7.45 a.m. 9.0 a.m.	Transport moved off. Unit personnel proceed to H,8,a.9.9. and took over XIXth CORPS WALKING WOUNDED COLLECTING POST from OFFICER COMMANDING, 112th FIELD AMBULANCE and MOATED FARM from OFFICER COMMANDING, 113th FIELD AMBULANCE,/6th DIVISION. D.D.M.S., XIXth CORPS called and sanctioned proposed alterations to Structure and system of disposing of Patients.	Ce/M.
do.	AUG: 21st.		Reconstruction of Hospital premises commenced. Medical Orders received re coming attack by 61st and 15th DIVISIONS. A.D.M.S. and D.A.D.M.S. 61st DIVISION visited and inspected premises. CAPTAIN P.H. GREEN, R.A.M.C.T. took over Rest Hospital for Neurasthenic cases at MOATED FARM.	Ce/M.
DO.	AUG: 22nd.	7.0 a.m.	D.D.M.S. XIXth CORPS visited and inspected the alterations which were practically complete by A.D.M.S and D.A.D.M.S. 61st DIVISION, A.D.M.S. 15th DIVISION, visited and inspected Camp. G.O.C., XIXth CORPS, and A.A.& Q.M.G. 61st DIVISION visited and inspected premises. New Sanitary System erected and opened at MOATED FARM. An attack was made on the XIXth CORPS front towards the ST JULIEN - ZONNEBEKE Road. 61st DIVISION on Left, 15th DIVISION on right.	Ce/M.

Army Form C. 2118.

WAR DIARY
or
INTELLIGENCE SUMMARY.

(Erase heading not required.)

REFERENCE MAP. FRANCE. HAZEBROUCK 5A.

Place	Date 1917	Hour	Summary of Events and Information	Remarks and references to Appendices
BROXEELE	AUG: 1st.		Routine work. OFFICER COMMANDING visited HEADQUARTERS, 184th INFANTRY BRIGADE, to arrange about Tactical Training Scheme.	Cash.
BROXEELE	AUG: 2nd.		Routine training and work. Special training in Field work with Gas Helmets and Box Respirators.	Cash.
BROXEELE	AUG: 3rd.		OFFICER COMMANDING visited XVIII and XIX CORPS MAIN DRESSING STATIONS, in forward area.	Cash.
BROXEELE	AUG: 4th.		Routine work.	Cash.
BROXEELE	AUG: 5ht.		Church Parade for all ranks at 9.0 a.m. OFFICER COMMANDING visited HEADQUARTERS 61st DIVISION. Special Training of M.T. and H.T. Drivers wearing Box Respirators.	Cash.
BROXEELE	AUG: 6th.		Routine work. OFFICER COMMANDING visited HEADQUARTERS, 184th INFANTRY BRIGADE.	Cash.
BROXEELE	AUG: 7th.		Routine work. OFFICER COMMANDING visited HEADQUARTERS, 184th INFANTRY BRIGADE.	Cash.
BROXEELE	AUG: 8th.		Routine training. 184th INFANTRY BRIGADE PRACTICE TRENCH ATTACK carried out. 2/1st SOUTH MIDLAND FIELD AMBULANCE represented by "G" SECTION under CAPTAIN W.J.HIRST, R.A.M.C.T. A.D.M.S. 61st DIVISION inspected Ambulance posts. OFFICER COMMANDING inspected arrangements made by the REGIMENTAL MEDICAL OFFICERS. Gas Alarm for M.T's at 11.0 p.m. Motor Ambulance Cars driven in and out of camp in dark, to test capability of driving in dark while wearing Box Respirators.	Cash.
BROXEELE	AUG: 9th.		Routine work. OFFICER COMMANDING reported to A.D.M.S. 61st DIVISION on his inspection of arrangements made by REGIMENTAL MEDICAL OFFICERS during the Tactical scheme.	Cash.
BROXEELE	AUG: 10th.		Routine work. Gas Alarm for H.T. Drivers at 11.0 p.m. Horses harnessed in dark without lights by A.S.C. Personnel wearing Box Respirators. Warning Order received from HEADQUARTERS, 184th INFANTRY BRIGADE for probable move of the Brigade, 13th and 14th AUGUST, 1917. A.D.M.S. 51st DIVISION	Cash.
BROXEELE	AUG: 11th.		Routine work. OFFICER COMMANDING visited HEADQUARTERS, 61st DIVISION. visited and inspected Camp.	Cash.
BROXEELE	AUG: 12th.		Routine work.	Cash.
BROXEELE	AUG: 13th.		Routine work. G.O.C., 61st DIVISION visited Camp. Orders re move of the Division received from A.D.M.S. 61st DIVISION and HEADQUARTERS, 184th INFANTRY BRIGADE.	Cash.

Army Form C. 2118.

WAR DIARY
or
INTELLIGENCE SUMMARY.

(Erase heading not required.)

MAP REFERENCE. BELGIUM SHEET 28.

Place	Date 1917	Hour	Summary of Events and Information	Remarks and references to Appendices
H.8.a.9.9.	AUG 22nd. (contd)		Good progress was made but casualties began to arrive by 7.0 a.m. and continued all day, — a large number of minor importance being due to Machine Gun bullets.	Eden
do.	AUG 23rd		D.D.M.S., XIXth CORPS called and inspected the premises and particularly the alterations at MOATED FARM. D.A.D.M.S., 61st DIVISION called. Total number of Walking Wounded passed through this CORPS WALKING WOUNDED COLLECTING POST during the past 24 hours OFFICERS 16, OTHER RANKS, 1207.	Eden
d..	AUG 24th.		A.D.M.S. 61st DIVISION visited and inspected camp. CAPTAIN F.J.CAHILL, U.S.M.C. reported here for duty. 435364, PRIVATE E.PARTINGTON, recommended for the immediate reward of the MILITARY MEDAL, for gallant conduct and devotion to duty in rescuing and dressing wounded men, under close shell fire, on the night 20th/21st AUGUST, 1917.	Eden
do.	AUG 25th.		Routine work. D.D.M.S. XIXth CORPS visited and inspected premises. Medical Board held on all A.S.C. personnel, both HORSE and MECHANICAL TRANSPORT, attached to this Unit, to allot them to their respective categories as regards fitness for active service with Infantry Units.	Eden
do.	AUG 26th.		A.D.M.S. 61st DIVISION visited camp. OFFICER COMMANDING visited HEADQUARTERS, 184th INFANTRY BRIGADE. D.D.M.S., XIXth CORPS visited and inspected premises. CAPTAIN W.JONES EVANS, R.A.M.C., rejoined from leave and went as Medical officer to the 2/6th GLOUCESTER REGIMENT.	Eden
do.	AUG 27th.		A.D.M.S. 61st DIVISION called. D.D.M.S., XIXth CORPS called and inspected MOATED FARM with a view to its being eventually made the site of the XIXth CORPS MAIN DRESSING STATION, should it be moved forward in the event of an advance. 435318, PRIVATE W.SPAULL returned from forward area. Wounded, Shrapnel, Head.	Eden
do.	AUG 28th.		A.D.M.S. 61st DIVISION visited camp. Preliminary arrangements made for alterations of MOATED FARM with a view to its conversion later on into a CORPS MAIN DRESSING STATION. Structural alterations at VLAMERTINGHE MILL continued. Clerks' office extended and much constructional work completed.	Eden
do.	AUG 29th.		A.D.M.S. and D.A.D.M.S., 61st DIVISION visited and inspected this camp and MOATED FARM.	Eden

WAR DIARY
or
INTELLIGENCE SUMMARY.
(Erase heading not required.)

Army Form C. 2118.

MAP REFERENCE : BELGIUM.
SHEET 28.

Place	Date 1917.	Hour	Summary of Events and Information	Remarks and references to Appendices
H,8,a,9,9.	AUG 30th.		D.A.D.M.S., 61st DIVISION visited and inspected camp and premises. CAPTAIN W.J.HIRST, R.A.M.C.T. proceeded to 2/5th ROYAL WARWICKSHIRE REGIMENT, for duty as Medical Officer. New road for lorries, under construction. 6 Riding Horses from the 2/1st SOUTH MIDLAND FIELD AMBULANCE, 6 from the 2/2nd SOUTH MIDLAND FIELD AMBULANCE and 5 from the 2/3rd SOUTH MIDLAND FIELD AMBULANCE transferred to 306 BRIGADE, R.F.A. under orders from A.D.M.S. 61st DIVISION through A.D.M.S. 61st DIVISION.	Ealm Ealm
do.	AUG 31st.		A.D.M.S. 61st DIVISION called. LIEUTENANT S.MILLER, U.S.M.C., proceeded to 2/8th WORCESTERS for temporary duty as Medical Officer. OFFICER COMMANDING visited HEADQUARTERS, 183rd INFANTRY BRIGADE, and BATTALIONS which had just come out of forward area.	

Wallacke.

LIEUTENANT COLONEL: R.A.M.C.T.

COMMANDING. 2/1st SOUTH MIDLAND FIELD AMBULANCE.

31st AUGUST, 1917.

CONFIDENTIAL.

WAR DIARY.   2/1st SOUTH MIDLAND FIELD AMBULANCE.

61st DIVISION.

From: 1st SEPTEMBER, 1917 - 30th SEPTEMBER, 1917.

VOLUME 3.   BOOK, 9.

COMMITTEE FOR THE
MEDICAL HISTORY OF THE WAR
Date -5 NOV.1917

B.E.F.

2/1st S.M.F.A. 61st Div. 5th Corps. 5th ARMY. WESTERN FRONT
July-Nov.1917
Officer Commanding - Lt.Col. G. MACKIE D.S.O.(T).

17th Corps. III. ARMY from 18th Sept.

PHASE "D" 1. Passchendaele Operations, "July-Nov. 1917".

(a) - Operations commencing 1/7/17.

Headquarters at Broxeele.

Sept. 7th.	Transfer. Unit transferred with 61st Division to 5th Corps.
13th.	Casualties R.A.M.C. Capt.W.J. Evans attached 2/6th Glosters died of wounds.
15th.	Medical Arrangements. C.W.W.C.P. handed over to 1st S.A.F.A. 9th Div.; MOATED FARM handed over to 1/3rd Lancs. F.A. 55th Division.
	Moves. To TRAPPIST FARM.
17th.	Moves. To WORMHOUDT.
18th.	Moves and) Unit transferred to 17th Corps III. ARMY Transfer.) and moved to Duisans.

B.E.F.

2/1st S.M. F.A. 61st Div. 5th Corps. 5th ARMY. WESTERN FRONT
July-Nov.1917

Officer Commanding - Lt.Col. G. MACKIE D.S.O.(T).

17th Corps. III. ARMY from 18th Sept.

PHASE "D" 1. Passchendaele Operations,"July-Nov. 1917".
(a) - Operations commencing 1/7/17.

Headquarters at Broxeele.

Sept. 7th.	Transfer. Unit transferred with 61st Division to 5th Corps.
13th.	Casualties R.A.M.C. Capt.W.J. Evans attached 2/6th Glosters died of wounds.
15th.	Medical Arrangements. C.W.W.C.P. handed over to 1st S.A.F.A. 9th Div. MOATED FARM handed over to 1/3rd Lancs. F.A. 55th Division.
	Moves. To TRAPPIST FARM.
17th.	Moves. To WORMHOUDT.
18th.	Moves and Transfer.) Unit transferred to 17th Corps III. ARMY and moved to Duisans.

Army Form C. 2118.

WAR DIARY
or
INTELLIGENCE SUMMARY.
(Erase heading not required.)

Instructions regarding War Diaries and Intelligence Summaries are contained in F.S. Regs., Part II. and the Staff Manual respectively. Title pages will be prepared in manuscript.

MAP REFERENCE. BELGIUM. Sheet 28.

Place	Date 1917.	Hour	Summary of Events and Information	Remarks and references to Appendices
H.S.,9.9.	Sept 1st.		Routine work. New incinerator built in camp grounds. A.D.M.S. 61st DIVISION and A.D.M.S. 59th DIVISION visited and inspected premises.	
do	Sept 2nd.		Routine work. A.D.M.S. 61st DIVISION visited the MILL and MOATED FARM.	
do	Sept 3rd.		Routine work. CAPTAIN J.N.GRIFFITHS,R.A.M.C., CAPTAIN W.D.DUNLOP, R.A.M.C. and CAPTAIN B. WALLACE, R.A.M.C. reported fro duty and were taken on the strength of this Ambulance.	
do	Sept 4th.		A.D.M.S. 61st DIVISION called and inspected premises. Conference of all Quartermasters of the 61st DIVISION held at VLAMERTINGHE MILL, presided over by A.D.M.S. 61st DIVISION.	
do	Sept 5th.		D.D.M.S. 19th CORPS and D.A.D.M.S. 61st DIVISION visited and inspected premises. LIEUTENANT F.M.BISHOP, R.A.M.C. reported for duty and was taken on the strength of this Unit.	
do	Sept 6th.		D.D.M.S. 19th CORPS, A.D.M.S. 42nd DIVISION and D.A.D.M.S. 61st DIVISION called and inspected camp both at the MILL and MOATED FARM. CAPTAIN W.SPEEDY, R.A.M.C. reported for duty and was taken on the strength of this Unit.	
do	Sept 7th.		D.D.M.S. 5th CORPS, A.D.M.S. 61st DIVISION, D.A.D.M.S. 61st DIVISION and A.A.&.Q.M.G. 61st DIVISION, visited and inspected premises.	
do	Sept 8th.		Routine work. A.D.M.S. 61st DIVISION called.	
do	Sept 9th.		Routine work. A.A.&.Q.M.G., 61st DIVISION, A.P.M. 61st DIVISION, and D.A.D.M.S. 61st DIVISION visited and inspected camp and grounds during the day.	
do	Sept 10th.		Routine work. OFFICER COMMANDING visited 61st DIVISION HEADQUARTERS, and A.D.M.S. and D.A.D.M.S. 61st DIVISION visited and inspected structural alterations at VLAMERTINGHE MILL and MOATED FARM.	
do	Sept 11th.		Routine work. Preliminary instructions regarding the Medical Relief of 61st DIVISION received from A.D.M.S. 61st DIVISION. CAPTAIN J.L.WHATLEY, R.A.M.C. struck off the strength of this Unit on transfer to the Base.	

WAR DIARY or INTELLIGENCE SUMMARY.

(Erase heading not required.)

MAP REFERENCES. BELGIUM. Army &c., C. 2118. Sheet 27.

Place	Date 1917.	Hour	Summary of Events and Information	Remarks and references to Appendices
H.8.a.9.9.	Sept 12th.		Routine work. A.D.M.S. 9th DIVISION visited and inspected VLAMERTINGHE MILL AND MOATED FARM. A.D.M.S. and D.A.D.M.S. 61st DIVISION visited and inspected premises.	
do	Sept 13th.		Routine work. CAPTAIN W. JONES EVANS R.A.M.C. 2/1st SOUTH MIDLAND FIELD AMBULANCE attached as Regimental Medical Officer to 2/6th BATTALION GLOUCESTER REGIMENT, died of wounds at ADVANCED DRESSING STATION, WIELTJE. The body brought to VLAMERTINGHE MILL for burial under Unit arrangements.	
do	Sept 14th.		CAPTAIN W. JONES EVANS.R.A.M.C. buried in Cemetery at H.8.c.3.2. Service conducted by CAPTAIN the REV J.P.MILUM, C.F. and attended by all officers and available personnel of the 2/1st SOUTH MIDLAND FIELD AMBULANCE.	
do and TRAPPIST FARM.	Sept 15th.		2/1st SOUTH MIDLAND FIELD AMBULANCE relieved at VAMERTINGHE MILL by 1st SOUTH AFRICAN FIELD AMBULANCE, 9th DIVISION and at MOATED FARM by 1/3rd LANCASHIRE FIELD AMBULANCE, 55th DIVISION. 2/1st SOUTH MID. AND FIELD AMBULANCE evacuated and proceeded to TRAPPIST FARM, arriving there at 12.0 noon. Usual notifications forwarded to A.D.M.S. 61st DIVISION and HEADQUARTERS, 184th INFANTRY BRIGADE. CAPTAIN J.N.GRIFFITHS. R.A.M.C. struck off strength of Unit on transfer to 62 H.A.G.	
TRAPPIST FARM.	Sept 16th.		Routine work. CAPTAIN W.D.DUNLOP.R.A.M.C. struck off strength and attached to 2/8th ROYAL WARWICKSHIRE REGIMENT as Medical Officer. CAPTAIN W.SPEEDY.R.A.M.C. struck off strength and attached to 2/5th GLOUCESTER REGIMENT as Medical Officer. LIEUTENANT E.V.WHITAKER. M.O.R.C., U.S.A. struck off strength on transfer to 2/2nd SOUTH MIDLAND FIELD AMBULANCE. LIEUTENANT F.M.BISHOP.R.A.M.C. struck off strength and attached to 2/4th GLOUCESTER REGIMENT as Medical Officer.	
WORMHOUDT.	Sept 17th.		2/1st SOUTH MIDLAND FIELD AMBULANCE proceeded by march route to WORMHOUDT area, arriving at new camp at 1.15 p.m. Hospital opened and notification sent to A.D.M.S. 61st DIVISION and HEADQUARTERS, 184th INFANTRY BRIGADE.	
do	Sept 18th.		Routine work. D.A.D.M.S. visited camp. Orders received from A.D.M.S. 61st DIVISION re entraining for new area.	

WAR DIARY
or
INTELLIGENCE SUMMARY.

Army Form C. 2118.

MAP REFERENCE. FRANCE.
HAZEBROUCK. 5A.
Sheets 51 B and 51 C.

Place	Date 1917.	Hour	Summary of Events and Information	Remarks and references to Appendices
WORMHOUDT.	Sept 19th.		Unit entrained at ESQUELBECQ at 17.10 under orders from HEADQUARTERS, 184th INFANTRY BRIGADE. No casualties.	PHG
DUISANS. L.W. Central.	Sept. 20th.		Unit detrained at AUBIGNY at 4.30 a.m. and proceeded to DUISANS by march route.	PHG
do	Sept. 21st.		A.D.M.S. 61st DIVISION visited and inspected camp. OFFICER COMMANDING proceeded on 14 days special leave of absence to UNITED KINGDOM. CAPTAIN PHILIP.H.GREEN. R.A.M.C.T. assumed command of the Ambulance.	PHG
do	Sept. 22nd.		Routine work. D.A.D.M.S. 61st DIVISION visited premises.	PHG
do	Sept. 23rd.		CAPTAIN PHILIP.H.GREEN.R.A.M.C.T. ACTING OFFICER COMMANDING, visited all advanced posts in the new area.	PHG
do	Sept. 24th.		"C" SECTION under CAPTAIN W.J.HIRST.R.A.M.C.T. proceeded to ST NICHOLAS to act as holding party and to take over all advanced posts. ACTING OFFICER COMMANDING visited all forward posts.	PHG
ST NICHOLAS. G.16.c.5.9.	Sept. 25th		"A" and "B" SECTION and TRANSPORT proceeded to ST NICHOLAS and took over from 53rd FIELD AMBULANCE, 17th DIVISION. Transfer complete by 2.0 p.m. Notifications sent to A.D.M.S. 61st DIVISION and HEADQUARTERS, 184th INFANTRY BRIGADE. Notification received from HEADQUARTERS 61st DIVISION, that the GENERAL OFFICER COMMANDING, 61st DIVISION had awarded Parchments for gallantry to the following N.C.O. and man. 435347 A/CORPORAL J.T.HILLIAR and 435264, PRIVATE E.PARTINGTON, both of this Unit.	Auth. 61st Div. Q 596 24/9/17. PHG
do	Sept 26th.		Routine work. A.D.M.S. 61st DIVISION visited all forward posts with CAPTAIN PHILIP.H.GREEN, R.A.M.C.T. A/COMMANDING, 2/1st SOUTH MIDLAND FIELD AMBULANCE.	PHG
do	Sept 27th.		Routine work. A.D.M.S. 61st DIVISION visited and inspected premises.	PHG

Army Form C. 2118.

WAR DIARY
or
INTELLIGENCE SUMMARY.

MAP REFERENCE. Sheet 51 B.

(Erase heading not required.)

Place	Date	Hour	Summary of Events and Information	Remarks and references to Appendices
ST NICHOLAS. G.16.c.5.9.	Sept 28th. 1917.		Routine work. 3 NISSEN HOSPITAL HUTS drawn and erection commenced.	PMG
do.	Sept 29th.		Routine work. A/OFFICER COMMANDING, visited all forward posts. Framework of 1 Hut completed.	PMG
do.	Sept 30th.		Routine work. 1 NISSEN HOSPITAL HUT completed. 435525, PRIVATE J.SOCKETT, R.A.M.C.T., 2/1st SOUTH MIDLAND FIELD AMBULANCE, awarded MILITARY MEDAL for gallantry. Authority Divisional Routine order No: 1358, dated 29-9-1917. Construction of NISSEN HOSPITAL HUTS continued.	PMG

Philip Green

CAPTAIN: R.A.M.C.T.

A/COMMANDING. 2/1st SOUTH MIDLAND FIELD AMBULANCE.

CONFIDENTIAL.

WAR DIARY.

2/1st SOUTH MIDLAND FIELD AMBULANCE.

61st DIVISION.

From: 1.10.1917 to 31.10.1917.

Volume 3.   Book 10.

Army Form C. 2118.

WAR DIARY
or
INTELLIGENCE SUMMARY.
(Erase heading not required.)

MAP REFERENCE. Sheet 51 B.

Instructions regarding War Diaries and Intelligence Summaries are contained in F. S. Regs., Part II. and the Staff Manual respectively. Title pages will be prepared in manuscript.

Place	Date 1917.	Hour	Summary of Events and Information	Remarks and references to Appendices
ST NICHOLAS. G.16.c.5.9.	Oct 1st.		Routine. Work. Cleaning and altering premises and general constructional work continued.	
do	Oct 2nd.		Routine work. A.D.M.S. 61st Division, visited premises.	
do	Oct 3rd.		Routine work. A.D.M.S. 61st Division called.	
do	Oct 4th.		Routine work. A/ OFFICER COMMANDING visited all forward posts. D.D.M.S. 17th CORPS, visited and inspected premises. A.A.&.Q.M.G. 61st Division visited camp.	
do	Oct 5th.		Routine work. A.D.M.S. 61st Division visited premises.	
do	Oct 6th.		A.D.M.S. 61st Division visited and inspected premises. Erection of Nissen Hospital Hut completed.	
do	Oct 7th.		Routine work. OFFICER COMMANDING returned from leave of absence and resumed command of the Unit. CAPTAIN P.H.GREEN.R.A.M.C.T. proceeded to the 2/5th BATTN: GLOUCESTERSHIRE REGIMENT for temporary duty as Medical Officer.	
do	Oct 8th.		Routine work. OFFICER COMMANDING took over duties of Acting A.D.M.S. 61st Division while the A.D.M.S. is on leave of absence in England.	
do	Oct 9th.		OFFICER COMMANDING visited 61st Divisional Headquarters - D.D.M.S. 17th CORPS visited Camp. OFFICER COMMANDING inspected all forward posts on Left Sector of Divisional front. Construction begun of the 3rd Nissen Hut, made out of portions of the other two which were both built short.	

WAR DIARY
or
INTELLIGENCE SUMMARY.

Army Form C. 2118.
MAP REFERENCE SHEET 51 B.

(Erase heading not required.)

Place	Date 1917.	Hour	Summary of Events and Information	Remarks and references to Appendices
ST NICHOLAS. G.16.c.5.9.	Oct 10th.		Routine work. OFFICER COMMANDING visited Divisional Headquarters, before inspecting all forward posts on Right Sector of Divisional Front.	Taylor
do	Oct 11th.		Routine work. OFFICER COMMANDING visited Divisional Headquarters and 17th CORPS, Headquarters. - also interviewed Traffic Officer of 31st Light Railway Co as to the provision of covered trucks for winter work - and Officers of the Inland Water Transport re heating of the Barges used for Transport of Wounded.	Taylor
do	Oct 12th.		Routine work. Nissen Hut completed and occupied. Sanitary arrangements for camp completed, including covered Ablution House.	Taylor
do	Oct 13th.		Routine work. OFFICER COMMANDING visited forward area to arrange development of the R.A.P. at TRIPLE ARCH into and Advanved Dressing Station.	Taylor
do	Oct 14th.		Routine work. Work on roads round and near Unit Transport lines being actively proceeded with.	Taylor
do	Oct 15th.		Routine work. OFFICER COMMANDING visited Divisional Headquarters and Forward area. Unit Quartermaster's Stores rebuilt.	Taylor
do	Oct 16th.		Routine work. Damaged house in Camp area rebuilt as a Billet for M.T. Personnel. Construction of a closed in Garage for the Ambulance cars begun.	Taylor
do	Oct 17th.		Routine work. OFFICER COMMANDING visited all forward posts.	Taylor

WAR DIARY
or
INTELLIGENCE SUMMARY.

(Erase heading not required.)

Army Form C. 2118.

MAP REFERENCE SHEET 51 B.

Place	Date 1917.	Hour	Summary of Events and Information	Remarks and references to Appendices
ST NICHOLAS. G.16.c.5.9.	Oct 18th.		D.M.S. 3rd ARMY, visited and inspected the Unit and Camp, expressing himself satisfied with the constructional work done.	Cmdr
do	Oct 19th.		Routine work. OFFICER COMMANDING visited and inspected all forward posts.	Cmdr
do	Oct 20th.		Routine work. Construction of Bath House for Unit personnel commenced at ST NICHOLAS. Request received from 61st DIVISION "Q" that the Unit would undertake the design and construction of a forward Bath House for the Division, in a ruined factory at ATHIES. CAPTAIN A.F.L.SHIELDS. R.A.M.C.(.S.R.) and CAPTAIN F.H.NOLAN.R.A.M.C.(.T.C.) reported here for duty from the Base.	Cmdr
do	Oct 21st		Routine work. A.D.M.S. 61st DIVISION returned from leave. OFFICER COMMANDING visited Divisional Headquarters. CAPTAIN P.H.GREEN.R.A.M.C.T. proceeded on leave of absence to England. Divisional Forward Baths at ATHIES LOCK designed and work begun.	Cmdr
do	Oct 22nd.		Routine work. OFFICER COMMANDING visited Divisional Headquarters and ATHIES LOCK.	Cmdr
do	Oct 23rd.		Routine work. OFFICER COMMANDING visited all forward posts. A.D.M.S. 61st DIVISION visited camp.	Cmdr
do	Oct 24th.		Extra N.C.O's and Bearers sent to reinforce all advanced posts in view of impending operations. OFFICER COMMANDING visited all forward posts and remained at TRIPLE ARCH with CAPTAIN W.J.HIRST.R.A.M.C.T., to see how evacuation worked during active operations. Cases were removed satisfactorily.	Cmdr
do	Oct 25th.		OFFICER COMMANDING visited Divisional Headquarters and new Bath house at ATHIES LOCK.	Cmdr

Army Form C. 2118.

WAR DIARY
or
INTELLIGENCE SUMMARY.

MAP REFERENCE SHEET 51B.

(Erase heading not required.)

Instructions regarding War Diaries and Intelligence Summaries are contained in F. S. Regs., Part II. and the Staff Manual respectively. Title pages will be prepared in manuscript.

Place	Date 1917.	Hour	Summary of Events and Information	Remarks and references to Appendices
ST NICHOLAS. G.16.c.5.9.	Oct 26th.		Routine work. OFFICER COMMANDING forward area and found the main road FEUCHY - FAMPOUX had been blown up. Traffic resumed as usual in the evening.	
do	Oct 27th,		OFFICER COMMANDING visited and inspected all forward posts with a view of further active operations being suggested. OFFICER COMMANDING visited 183 INFANTRY BRIGADE HEADQUARTERS with reference to Medical arrangements for their impending raid - operations postponed. D.A.D.M.S. 61st Division visited camp.	
do.	Oct 28th.		The Divisional Commander inspected the new Baths at ATHIES LOCK.	
do	Oct 29th.		OFFICER COMMANDING visited TRIPLE ARCH to see how work was progressing. D.A.D.M.S. 61st DIVISION visited camp.	
do	Oct 30th,		OFFICER COMMANDING visited Baths at ATHIES with D.A.D.M.S. 61st Division. The baths were used today for the first time, 97 men being bathed and receiving new clean clothing.	
do	Oct 31st.		Routine work. OFFICER COMMANDING visited all forward posts.	

31.10.1917.

G. Wackis.

Lieut. Col: R.A.M.C.T.
COMMANDING. 2/1st SOUTH MIDLAND FIELD AMBULANCE.

Medical / VII 19

no. 578

Confidential

War Diary of
2/1st South Midland Field Ambulance
From 1st November 1917 to 30th November 1917.

Volume 3.   Book II.

COMMITTEE FOR THE
MEDICAL HISTORY OF THE WAR
Date 17 JAN. 1918

17

Army Form C. 2118.

WAR DIARY
or
INTELLIGENCE SUMMARY

(Erase heading not required.)

Map Reference. Sheet 51 B

Place	Date 1917	Hour	Summary of Events and Information	Remarks and references to Appendices
ST NICHOLAS G.16.C.5.9.	November 1st		Routine work.	C.13
- do -	November 2nd		Routine work. Distribution of Parchments for Gallantry, by Major General COLIN MACKENZIE, G.O.C., 61st Division at LEWIS BARRACKS, ARRAS. H35347, A/CORPORAL J.T. HILLIAR and H35264, PRIVATE E. PARTINGTON, both of this Unit received Parchments at this parade.	
- do -	November 3rd		Routine work. Construction of Bath House for Unit personnel proceeded with. Officer Commanding visited all forward posts.	
- do -	November 4th		BRIG: GEN: The Hon: R. WHITE. Commanding 184th INFANTRY BRIGADE visited & inspected camp. Fitting of new Containers for Small Box Respirators commenced.	
- do -	November 5th		Routine work.	
- do -	November 6th		Routine work. Bath House for Unit personnel completed and in use. Officer Commanding's Billet and private office nearing completion.	
- do -	November 7th		Routine work. Third Army Instructor in Catering visited Headquarters. 2/3rd SOUTH MIDLAND FIELD AMBULANCE. CAPTAIN P.H. GREEN, SERGT. W. DIX, CORPORAL PEWSEY and PRIVATE H. BROWN, detailed to attend for instruction.	
- do -	November 8th		Routine work. System of pipes laid in camp to convey water to the Ablution Bench.	
- do -	November 9th		Routine work. CAPTAIN W.J. HIRST, R.A.M.C.T. proceeded on leave of absence to England.	
- do -	November 10th		Routine work. Officer Commanding: Billet and private office completed & occupied.	

WAR DIARY or INTELLIGENCE SUMMARY

Army Form C. 2118.

Map Reference Sheet 57 B.

Place	Date 1917	Hour	Summary of Events and Information	Remarks and references to Appendices
G 16. c.5.9.	November 11th		Routine work. Officer commanding visited all forward posts.	Esher
-do-	November 12th		Routine work.	Esher
-do-	November 13th		Routine work. CAPTAIN E.F. O'CONNOR, R.A.M.C.(T.C.) reported to duty from Base. CAPTAIN A.P. THOMPSON, R.A.M.C.T. reported back from leave of absence in England.	Esher
-do-	November 14th		Routine work. CAPTAIN A.P. THOMPSON, R.A.M.C.T. detailed to report for duty as Medical Officer to the 2/6th Battn. ROYAL WARWICKSHIRE REGIMENT, 61st DIVISION. CAPTAIN H.F. NOLAN, R.A.M.C. struck off strength of Unit on proceeding to HAVRE.	Esher auth. A.D.M.S. 61st Div.
-do-	November 15th		Routine work. Special rearrangement of personnel in forward area during raid by 2/1st Battn. BUCKS REGIMENT.	Esher
-do-	November 16th		Routine work. Officer commanding visited all posts in forward area.	Esher
-do-	November 17th		Routine work. 1 Nursing Sergeant, Nursing Orderlies and extra stretcher bearers sent to forward posts during raid by 2/4th Battn. OXFORD & BUCKS LIGHT INFANTRY.	Esher
-do-	November 18th		Routine work. CAPTAIN E.F. O'CONNOR, 1 Nursing Sergeant + 13 O.R. proceeded to No. 3 C.C.S. for temporary duty.	Esher
-do-	November 19th		Routine work. Special rearrangement of personnel in forward posts during raid by 2/4th Battn. OX. & BUCKS LIGHT INFANTRY. Officer Commanding attended Conference at Office of A.D.M.S. 61st DIVISION, at 2.30 p.m.	Esher

Army Form C. 2118.

Map Reference:- Sheet 51 B.

WAR DIARY
or
INTELLIGENCE SUMMARY
(Erase heading not required.)

Instructions regarding War Diaries and Intelligence Summaries are contained in F.S. Regs., Part II. and the Staff Manual respectively. Title Pages will be prepared in manuscript.

Place	Date 1917	Hour	Summary of Events and Information	Remarks and references to Appendices
C.16.c.5.9.	November 20th		Routine work. Suggestion made by QUARTERMASTER. - HON: LIEUT. W.S. RIVERS, 2/1st SOUTH MIDLAND FIELD AMBULANCE, re Inhalation Bags, adopted by 61st DIVISION. "Q".	Enter
-do-	November 21st		Routine work. Special rearrangement of personnel in forward posts during raid by 2/1st BATTN. BUCKS REGIMENT. H35127, CORPORAL J.C. SMITH taken on strength of Unit from Base.	Enter
-do-	November 22nd		Routine work.	Enter
-do-	November 23rd		Routine work. Construction of special covered Ambulance truck for evacuation of wounded by railway commenced.	Enter
-do-	November 24th		Routine work.	Enter
-do-	November 25th		Routine work. CAPTAIN P.H. GREEN, R.A.M.C.T. proceeded to 2/4th GLOUCESTERSHIRE REGIMENT for temporary duty as Medical Officer. 1st LIEUT. E.O. PETERSON. M.O.R.C., U.S.A. } reported for duty from the Base & were taken on 1st LIEUT. N.S. GARRISON. M.O.R.C., U.S.A. } strength of Unit. 1st LIEUT. J.R. SANDFORD. M.O.R.C., U.S.A. }	Auth: ADMS. 61st DIV. Auth: ADMS. 61st DIV. Enter
-do-	November 26th		Routine work. Q-35005, CPL (A/SGT) H.G. WHEELDON. proceeded to the R.A.M.C. Base Depot, ROUEN, for transfer to the Home Establishment for duty. Authority Third Army A/9/9746.	Enter
-do-	November 27th		Routine work. Warning order re immediate move of Division received from A.D.M.S., 61st Division R.A.M.C. Order Jo. 141, also received from A.D.M.S., 61st DIVISION.	Enter
-do-	November 28th		Routine work. CAPTAIN P.H. GREEN, R.A.M.C.T. returned to Unit from temporary duty as Medical Officer to the 2/4th GLOUCESTERSHIRE REGIMENT. Cleaning & loading of equipment.	Enter

Army Form C. 2118.

WAR DIARY
or
INTELLIGENCE SUMMARY

(Erase heading not required.)

Map Reference. Sheet 51 B

Instructions regarding War Diaries and Intelligence Summaries are contained in F. S. Regs., Part II. and the Staff Manual respectively. Title Pages will be prepared in manuscript.

Place	Date 1917	Hour	Summary of Events and Information	Remarks and references to Appendices
G.16.C.59.	November 29th		Routine work. Waggons completely loaded & packed in readiness to move. Officer commanding visited all forward posts & handed over to the O.C. 47½ Field Ambulance. 15th Division.	PW
-do-	November 30th		Clearing of billets & camp surroundings preparatory to vacating same.	PW
		8.10 a.m.	Unit Transport moved off to proceed to new area by road.	
		3.30 p.m.	Unit personnel entrained at ARRAS STATION & proceeded to new area by rail.	

J.S. Mackie

Lieut Col. Ramlet
Officer Commanding. 2/1st South Mid. Fd. Ambulance.

30th November 1917.

CONFIDENTIAL

WAR DIARIES

of

MEDICAL UNITS 61 DIVISION.

December 1st to December 31st 1917.

Diaries enclosed :-

A.D.M.S., 61 Div.
2/1 South Mid.Field Amb.,
2/2 South Mid.Field Amb.,
2/3 South Mid.Field Amb.,

Colonel A.M.S.
A.D.M.S., 61 Division.

31/12/17.

COMMITTEE FOR THE
MEDICAL HISTORY OF THE WAR

Date 29 JAN.1918

Medical

14

WO 20

14/2/18

Confidential
War Diary
of the
2/1st South Midland Field Ambulance.
61st Division.
from 1/12/1917 to 31/12/1917.
Volume 12.
Book 2

COMMITTEE FOR THE
MEDICAL HISTORY OF THE WAR
Date —1 FEB. 1918

Army Form C. 2118.

WAR DIARY
or
INTELLIGENCE SUMMARY
(Erase heading not required.)

Map Reference Sheet 57c.

Place	Date 1917	Hour	Summary of Events and Information	Remarks and references to Appendices
BAPAUME	December 1st		After detraining at BAPAUME, the Unit proceeded in motor ambulance lorries to an unknown destination. Released at ROYAULCOURT and marched back to BERTINCOURT, arriving there 2.30 a.m. 1-12-1917. H35157. PRIVATE (T/CORPORAL) E.M.C. CROSS, R.A.M.C. 2/1st S.M.F. AMBULANCE died of wounds at 19 C.C.S. and was buried there this morning.	G.F.M.
BERTINCOURT	December 2nd		Unit remained in reserve at BERTINCOURT, with all equipment etc. packed and ready to move forward at a moment's notice. Under instructions from A.D.M.S. 61st DIVISION 28 N.C.O's & men proceeded to the forward area to act as bearers. 4 Clerks were also detailed for duty at Nos 21 & 48 C.C.S. YTRES. 13 N.C.O's & men proceeded to H.S. C.C.S., YTRES, for nursing duties. Officer commanding visited HEADQUARTERS 61st DIVISION to obtain information relative to the situation following upon the enemy attack yesterday. Arrangements still uncertain and no new ground gained of final duty and location of the 2/1st S.M. FIELD AMBULANCE.	G.F.M.
BERTINCOURT	December 3rd		Unit moved to another camp in the same area (BERTINCOURT) and remained packed and in reserve. Notification received from A.D.M.S. 61st DIVISION that the 2/1st S.M. FIELD AMBULANCE was to take over IIIrd Corps Main Dressing Station from the 61st FIELD AMBULANCE, 20th DIVISION. Remainder of bearers detailed for duty in the forward area. MORC., U.S.A. detached by A.D.M.S. 61st DIVISION for duty in the forward area, under Officer Commanding 2/3rd S.M. FIELD AMBULANCE. LIEUT. GARRISON.	G.F.M.
VIS. C.S.S.	December 4th		Officer Commanding proceeded to the IIIrd Corps Main Dressing Station, in advance of unit. Personnel proceeded by march route, arriving at IIIrd Corps Main Dressing Station at 1.30 p.m. This Station togs taken over from the 61st FLD AMBULANCE. 20th DIVISION. at noon 2.05 p.m. A.D.M.S. 61st DIVISION notified. D.D.M.S. IIIrd Corps visited premises. CAPTAIN W.J. HIRST, R.A.M.C.T. reported back from leave of absence in England. CAPTAIN P.H. GREEN, R.A.M.C.T. appointed Commanding Surgeon to IIIrd Corps Main Dressing Station. LIEUT. L. DAY, R.A.M.C.T. reported for temporary duty from the 2/3rd S.M. FIELD AMBULANCE.	G.F.M.

2449 Wt. W14957/M90 750,000 1/16 J.B.C. & A. Forms/C.2118/12.

Army Form C. 2118.

WAR DIARY
or
INTELLIGENCE SUMMARY
(Erase heading not required.)

Reference Map 5%.

Place	Date 1917	Hour	Summary of Events and Information	Remarks and references to Appendices
V.15.c.5.5.	December 5th		A.D.M.S., IIIrd CORPS, visited and inspected premises. Officer commanding visited HEADQUARTERS, 61st DIVISION. Alterations to Camp structure and arrangements commenced. 3 complete squads for day and night work in the 8 dressing rooms organised and started off on their duties on short tours of duty. Mr Squad organised to look after all Board cars, as a separate duty. Based cases removed to a special hut and temporary arrangements made for their reception pending alterations. Camp surrounding heavily shelled throughout the afternoon and evening with Gas and High explosive. No casualties among personnel.	CWM
— do —	December 6th.		Camp bombed by hostile aircraft at 3.0am. this morning. No casualties among personnel. A.D.M.S. IIIrd CORPS visited and inspected premises. Alterations to camp continued within the instructions of Officer Commanding. 2/1st SOUTH MIDLAND FIELD AMBULANCE Officers etc collected from B.R.C.S. Station at SAPIGNIES, and distributed in all waiting and dressing huts. Cleaning of Camp area continued.	CWM
— do —	December 7th.		A.D.M.S. VIIth CORPS, visited and inspected camp, with D.D.M.S. IIIrd CORPS. Gas Ward — Treatment room and bathroom fitted up. 3 complete dressing circuits finally organised and fitted up, each one complete in itself with Reception, Operating and evacuation rooms. LIEUT L. DAY, R.A.M.C., T.C. evacuated sick to C.C.S.	CWM
— do —	December 8th.		A.D.M.S. 36th DIVISION, A.D.M.S. 61st DIVISION and D.D.M.S, IIIrd CORPS visited and inspected Camp and premises. Structural alterations of premises continued. T/245643. DRIVER F. HUMPAGE, and PRIVATE (A/V/CA) A. ASKEY, #35, in charge of a Horsed Ambulance Waggon evacuating wounded between BEAUCAMP — TRESCAULT, severely wounded by shell fire. 2 Horses killed. T/245643. DRIVER F. HUMPAGE died of wounds later at No. 21. C.C.S.	CWM

Army Form C. 2118.

Map Reference ....

WAR DIARY
or
INTELLIGENCE SUMMARY
(Erase heading not required.)

Instructions regarding War Diaries and Intelligence Summaries are contained in F.S. Regs., Part II. and the Staff Manual respectively. Title Pages will be prepared in manuscript.

Place	Date 1917	Hour	Summary of Events and Information	Remarks and references to Appendices
V.18.C.5.5.	December 9th.		Officer commanding visited Nos. 21 and 48 C.C.S.s + HEADQUARTERS, 61st DIVISION. A.D.M.S. 61st DIVISION and D.D.M.S. IIIrd CORPS visited and inspected premises. T/8/28648, DRIVER F. HUMPAGE, buried at YTRES - party of N.C.O.s men attached to H.Q. C.C.S., attending. Bearer party of 17 N.C.O.s men returned from forward area for a rest. Warning order received of impending relief of 6th DIVISION by 19th DIVISION, with consequent alteration in personnel attached to IIIrd CORPS M.D. STATION. MAJOR MURRAY, S.A.F.A. 9th DIVISION, called re the establishing of a new IIIrd C.M.D.S. at NURLU, to take the place of the present one which is to be evacuated.	Taylor
- do -	December 10th.		D.D.M.S. IIIrd CORPS and A.A.+Q.M.G. 61st DIVISION visited inspected camp. A.R.M.S. 61st Division. No casualties amongst personnel. D.D.M.S. Lieut Colonel Hugh Eagleson + 86th Field S.M.F. Ambulance called regarding new method of evacuating wounded from TRESCAULT area + HAVRINCOURT WOOD by Decauville Railway. First train arrived this evening at 7.40 p.m. with 50 cases.	Taylor
- do -	December 11th.		A.D.M.S. 61st DIVISION and D.D.M.S. 3rd Corps visited and inspected camp. General cleaning of camp + premises.	Taylor
- do -	December 12th.		20 N.C.O.s men returned from work in the forward area + were replaced by an equal number of N.C.O.s men from Headquarters. These men were very exhausted after shelter bearing among the bad conditions prevailing in our indefinite front, consequent on the recent Enemy "Break through". Conditions now more normal. A new line established + ordinary trench warfare resumed.	Taylor
- do -	December 13th.		G.O.C. 61st DIVISION visited and inspected this Evening Mallon. D.D.M.S. 3rd CORPS, visited Camp. All work now going on satisfactorily. All departments entirely reorganised + the whole place working automatically. Fewer casualties coming through as the line improves is becoming quieter.	Taylor

Army Form C. 2118.

Map Reference Sheet 57c.

WAR DIARY
or
INTELLIGENCE SUMMARY
(Erase heading not required.)

Place	Date	Hour	Summary of Events and Information	Remarks and references to Appendices
V.18.c.55.	1917 December 14th		Brigrs 3rd, 5th & 7th Corps visited - inspected the 3rd C.M.D.S. to be ready to evacuate, when the 3rd Corps area is taken over by the 5th & 7th Corps. Officer Commanding visited HEADQUARTERS, 61st DIVISION	E.W.R.
- do -	December 15th		3rd C.M.D.S. handed over to O.C. 27th FLD AMBULANCE as from 12. 0% hour. Arrangements made to evacuate all casualties & patients now in 3rd CORPS to ROYAUCOURT, and then of the 7th CORPS to TINCOURT. - So this Station gradually drops out of action.	E.W.R.
LECHELLE	December 16th		Unit proceeded by march route to LECHELLE, taking over Field Ambulance site there as a Hor. Billet	E.W.R.
- do -	December 17th		Routine work.	E.W.R.
- do -	December 18th		Routine work. Warning order received that the 63rd (R.N) Division would relieve 61st DIVISION in the line on 23rd inst. that the Division would move back on relief 3 with 2/1st S.M.F.A, attached again to the 184th INFANTRY BRIGADE.	E.W.R.
- do -	December 19th		Routine work.	E.W.R.
- do -	December 20th		Routine work. 20 N.C.O's & men reported back from the line for duty.	E.W.R.
- do -	December 21st		Officer Commanding visited HEADQUARTERS, 61st DIVISION regarding Arrangement move & disposal. finding out that the Division is destined for XVII CORPS, 3E ARMY.	E.W.R.
- do -	December 22nd		Officer Commanding visited Divisional Headquarters re impending move. March tables received from 184th INF: BRIGADE	E.W.R.
- do -	December 23rd		CAPTAIN P.H. GREEN, R.A.M.C. + billeting party proceeded to new area. Preparations for move completed. All wagons loaded, checked & reported	E.W.R.

Army Form C. 2118.

WAR DIARY
or
INTELLIGENCE SUMMARY

(Erase heading not required.)

Map Reference AMIENS (N).
Scale 1:100000

Instructions regarding War Diaries and Intelligence Summaries are contained in F.S. Regs., Part II. and the Staff Manual respectively. Title Pages will be prepared in manuscript.

Place	Date 1917	Hour	Summary of Events and Information	Remarks and references to Appendices
CAPPY-SUR-SOMME	December 24th		Unit proceeded by train from YPRES Station & detrained at LE PLATEAU, near MARICOURT, & marched from there to CAPPY-SUR-SOMME. Hospital opened for the reception of Brigade Sick. Transport proceeded by road. Owing to the bad state of the surface could not complete the journey & bivouacked for the night near CLERY in a series of old dug-outs.	E.O.R.
-do-	December 25th		Transport arrived in camp at 1.45 P.M. A.D.M.S. 61st DIVISION visited & inspected premises. Arrangements made for the reception of Divisional Scabies cases.	E.O.R.
-do-	December 26th		Routine work. Captain O'CONNOR R.A.M.C. proceeded to D.D.M.S. 18th CORPS for temporary duty. G.O.C. 184th INFANTRY BRIGADE visited & inspected premises.	E.O.R.
-do-	December 27th		N.C.O.s & men reported back to duty from No. 3 C.C.S. GREVILLERS. A.D.M.S. 61st DIVISION visited Camp. Men's Christmas Dinner held. Military Entertainment.	E.O.R.
-do-	December 28th		Routine work. D.A.D.M.S. 61st DIVISION visited Camp.	E.O.R.
-do-	December 29th		LIEUT E.O. PETERSON M.O.R.C. U.S.A. proceeded to 2/4th Ox & Bucks LIGHT INFANTRY for temporary duty as Medical Officer. Warning Order re move of Division & march tables received from 184th INFANTRY BRIGADE.	E.O.R.
-do-	December 30th		Routine work. Church Parade. Officer Commanding visited nurses with STAFF CAPTAIN, 184th INFANTRY BRIGADE & established Brigade Hospital at ROZIERE-SUR-SANTERRE Hospital.	E.O.R.
ROZIERE-SUR-SANTERRE	December 31st		Unit with transport proceeded by march route to ROZIERE-SUR-SANTERRE. Hospital established & usual notifications sent out.	E.O.R.

31/1/7

Sewacki
Lieut Col RAMC
O.C. 2/1st S.M.F Ambulance

MEDICAL

VII 21/24

COMMITTEE FOR THE
MEDICAL HISTORY OF THE WAR
Date 8 APR. 1918

Confidential

War Diary

of

2/1st South Midland Field Ambulance

61st Division

From 1st January 1918 to 31st January 1918

Volume 4   Book 1.

Army Form C. 2118.

WAR DIARY
or
INTELLIGENCE SUMMARY.

(Erase heading not required.)

Map Reference
France Sheet 66 E
" 66 d.

Instructions regarding War Diaries and Intelligence Summaries are contained in F. S. Regs., Part II. and the Staff Manual respectively. Title pages will be prepared in manuscript.

Place	Date 1918	Hour	Summary of Events and Information	Remarks and references to Appendices
ROZIÈRE	January 1st.		New Years Day parade and inspection by Officer commanding. Cleaning of premises and organisation of Hospital in ÉCOLE DES FILLES, ROZIÈRE. A.D.M.S. 61st Division inspected premises	Capt/in
do	January 2nd.		Routine work and training. Officer Commanding attended Conference at ARMY. 61st DIVISION, Office at HARBONNIÈRES. Cleaning and checking of all Unit equipment preparatory to next move	Capt/in
do	January 3rd.		Routine work and duties. Continuation of refitting etc.	Capt/in
do	January 4th.		Routine work. A.D.M.S. 61st DIVISION visited and inspected Camp premises. CAPTAIN A.P. THOMSON, R.A.M.C.T. awarded MILITARY CROSS for work on the CAMBRAI FRONT. Officer commanding addressed the men on the history of the War - the present European situation and the necessity for complete victory before any further talk of peace.	Capt/in
do	January 5th.		A.D.M.S. 61st DIVISION visited and inspected Hospital. Orders received from A.D.M.S. 61st DIVISION that the Division would move on the 7th inst. towards the ST QUENTIN front	Capt/in
do	January 6th.		Officer commanding visited the new forward area with 184th INFANTRY BRIGADE Staff and inspected all the French medical arrangements. March tables received from HEADQUARTERS. 184th INFANTRY BRIGADE, instructing Unit to proceed to its former Camp at BETHENCOURT-SUR-SOMME.	Capt/in
BETHENCOURT SUR SOMME C 23 d.12.3.	January 7th.		Unit proceeded by march route from ROZIÈRE to BETHENCOURT-SUR-SOMME through LIHONS - CHAULNES - OMIÉCOURT - PERTAIN and MORCHAIN. Arriving at 4.10 p.m. Usual notifications sent out. G.O.C. 184th INFANTRY BRIGADE visited & inspected Camp.	Capt/in
do	January 8th.		Officer Commanding visited HEADQUARTERS 61st DIVISION, 184th INFANTRY BRIGADE. all posts in the C.M. Sector forward area, which 181th INFANTRY BRIGADE is to take over. Medical posts at MAISSEMY located and inspected and all minor posts at VILLECHOLLES - MARTEVILLE - MAISON de GARDE - ATTILLY and VILLEVEQUE.	Capt/in

Army Form C. 2118.

WAR DIARY
or
INTELLIGENCE SUMMARY.
(Erase heading not required.)

Map Reference. France
Sheet 66d.

Instructions regarding War Diaries and Intelligence Summaries are contained in F. S. Regs., Part II. and the Staff Manual respectively. Title pages will be prepared in manuscript.

Place	Date	Hour	Summary of Events and Information	Remarks and references to Appendices
BETHENCOURT SUR SOMME and LANCHY	January 9th 1918	4.0 pm.	Unit proceeded by march route to new area. Eventually arriving at LANCHY at 4.0 pm. Small parties of N.C.O's and men immediately proceeded to the medical posts now under administration of the French, to learn routes of evacuation in detail. Subsequently, to act as guides. Orders received from A.D.M.S. 61st DIVISION. To prepare to establish small isolated aid posts in the area behind the left sector of the divisional front, where help could be given in case of hostile bombing raids.	CWM
LANCHY	January 10th		Advancing party of hub de. CAPTAIN W.J. HIRST, R.A.M.C. with N.C.O's & bearers proceeded to forward area with the Officer Commanding & were delegated by him to the various posts & installed. Arrangements made for taking over all medical posts completely. Officer Commanding visited all the village again in connection with billeting the Ambulance main body & establishing the small bombing aid posts. D.A.D.M.S. 61st DIVISION. visited & inspected Camp.	CWM
do	January 11th		Unit transport rejoined from BETHENCOURT-SUR-SOMME. All medical posts in forward area completely staffed & evacuation of sick resumed taken over from the French. MILITARY MEDAL awarded to 435244. SERGEANT H.F ROBINSON, R.A.M.C. Authority D.R.O. 1583, dated 10-1-1918. PARCHMENT given by G.O.C. 61st DIVISION awarded to M2/167834. DRIVER W BUTCHER, M.T. A.S.C. attached to this Unit. Authority 61st DIVISION, G.390. Studied map & plan of evacuation system with plans of suggested bombing aid posts forwarded to A.D.M.S. 61st DIVISION.	CWM
do	January 12th.		Officer commanding visited HEADQUARTERS, 184th INFANTRY BRIGADE & forwarded on & settled finally the location of all aid posts - their respective staffs - completed arrangements for the medical service of the left sector of the Divisional area, held by the 184th INFANTRY BRIGADE. Alterations to present Camp site at LANCHY begun and request sent to HEADQUARTERS, 61st DIVISION that the Unit might be allowed to remain here in the absence of a suitable location further forward.	CWM
do	January 13th.		Officer Commanding visited HEADQUARTERS, 61st DIVISION, Horse Ambulance, Motor Ambulance. Circuit organised and established. Horsed Ambulance calling daily at all bombing aid posts & evacuating sick from the 183rd Brigade waggon lines to the Divisional Motor Bearing Station. GERMAINE. Unit turned out of billets to make room for the Divisional Artillery playing towards the front. GERMAINE. Headquarters 2/3rd FIELD AMBULANCE. remaining at LANCHY in Charge of bearers posts, proceeded with reference to above. Officer Commanding visited C.R.A. 61st DIVISION.	CWM

A5834 Wt. W4973/M687 750,000 8/16 D. D. & L. Ltd. Forms/C.2118/13.

WAR DIARY or INTELLIGENCE SUMMARY

Army Form C. 2118.

Map Reference - France - Sheet 62d

Place	Date 1918	Hour	Summary of Events and Information	Remarks and references to Appendices
LIANCHY E.2.b.4.2.	January 14th.		Officer Commanding visited all forward posts. LIEUT. W. S. RIVERS, R.A.M.C.T. returned from leave of absence in the United Kingdom. Medical Inspection Room & billets for bar drivers and orderlies begun at MARTEVILLE.	Enclr. Enclr.
- do -	January 15th.		Officer Commanding visited all forward posts. 307th Brigade R.F.A. personnel & waggon lines moved forward this day. The few French officers left here vacated their billets and handed them over to this Unit.	Enclr.
- do -	January 16th.		Unit Personnel returned to LIANCHY from Headquarters. 123rd FIELD AMBULANCE. GERMAINE. Improved system of Sanitation, latrines etc. immediately commenced. Duckboards laid down & a complete hack made round camp. Officer Commanding visited all bombing dugouts. Headquarters 184th INFANTRY BRIGADE. 435246. PRIVATE T. A. GEOGHEGAN, severely injured owing to the collapse of the gable end of a ruined house. He was evacuated to the Divisional main Dressing Station, 123rd FIELD AMBULANCE, suffering from the following injuries:- Compound fracture Right leg, Lower third. Compound fracture , Left leg, Lower Third. Severe bruise & abrasions, head. Severe general bruising.	Enclr.
- do -	January 17th.		Officer Commanding visited forward area. D.A.D.M.S. 61st DIVISION visited LIANCHY. Bath House erected at MAISSEMY EAST and made ready for the use of cases of "Mustard Gas" poisoning. Improvements in all the billets & posts of the Unit taken in hand.	Enclr.
- do -	January 18th.		Officer Commanding visited all bombing dugouts. Alterations & improvements to the existing system of Sanitation proceeded with. A.D.M.S. 61st DIVISION visited and inspected Camp. Officer Commanding visited Headquarters. 182th INFANTRY BRIGADE. Cultivation of 1 acre of ground at this Camp, to provide troops with vegetables etc in the coming Spring & Summer proposed & preparation of the ground commenced.	Enclr.
- do -	January 19th.		A.D.M.S. 61st DIVISION. visited Camp re establishing a Divisional Scabies Centre at Unit Headquarters. Officer Commanding visited HEADQUARTERS. 61st DIVISION. Bell Tents, Marquees etc picked for the accommodation of Scabies patients. Plans of bath house completed. Collecting of salvaged materials for construction begun. New Medical Inspection room completed at MARTEVILLE and hand standing for Cars platform &c.	Enclr.

WAR DIARY or INTELLIGENCE SUMMARY

Army Form C. 2118.

Map Reference: France. Sheet 66d.

Place	Date 1918	Hour	Summary of Events and Information	Remarks and references to Appendices
LANCHY E.12.c.6.8	January 20th		Officer commanding visited all forward posts, bombing and posts etc. and attended conference at the office of the A.D.M.S. 61st Division. Baths tubs brought from Unit Group for use in Scabies Bath house. 2/4th ROYAL BERKSHIRE REGIMENT being on parade on the main road suffered some casualties and were removed by our new much a short but sharp bombardment. MAISSEMY village shelled.	E.M.
do	January 21st		Routine work. Preparations of the hospital made for the reception of scabies. Raw Meade. Officer commanding worked parties etc. uncomplicated mumps etc.	E.M.
do	January 22nd		Officer commanding visited all Ambulance detached posts & A.D.S. Roading post at MAISSEMY. Following N.C.O.'s & men of this Unit received Ribbon to the MILITARY MEDAL from the Divisional Commander:-
A35244, SERGEANT H. F. ROBINSON. M.M.
A35262, CPL (A/SGT) A. H. PERRY. M.M.
A35391, PTE (A/CPL) J. WIGGINS. M.M.
H35625, PTE   J. SOCKETT. M.M.
H35306, PTE   D. TAPPER. M.M.
111760, DRIVER T. C. SHORROCKS. M.M.	E.M.
do	January 23rd		Routine work. Baths house for Scabies designed & preparations made for its erection. Saw till 41 Motor Buses and cyclists commenced at MARTEVILLE.	E.M.
do	January 24th		Routine work. Officer Commanding visited detached posts & A.D.S. with CAPTAIN W. STOBIE R.A.M.C. M.D.F.D.M.S. 61st Division. General tidying up of premises & enlargement of points peri. Inches withdrawn continued.	E.M.
do	January 25th		L.D.M.S. XVIIth CORPS, accompanied by A.D.M.S. 61st Division, visited inspected camp & premises. Plans for erection of Scabies hospital "Bath house" submitted & approved. Suggestion made to increase accommodation by makeshift lab. of 45 Couples live a Divisional Rest Station. Preceded Stained at MARTEVILLE begun. Dug outs for projection?	E.M.

WAR DIARY
or
INTELLIGENCE SUMMARY.
(Erase heading not required.)

Army Form C. 2118.

Reference Map France Sheet 66a.

Place	Date 1918	Summary of Events and Information	Remarks and references to Appendices
LANCHY E.2.b.u.5	January 26th	Routine work. Collection of Salvaged material continued, towards the erection of huts etc necessary for the housing of Scabies + Infectious cases.	
-do-	January 27th	Officer Commanding visited all forward posts + prospected Beauville Railway tracks with a view to their being utilised for evacuation of wounded from forward area. 182nd INFANTRY BRIGADE relieved 182nd INFANTRY BRIGADE in left sector of Divisional front. Officer Commanding visited 184th INFANTRY BRIGADE HEADQUARTERS at BEAUVOIS. 452282 Cpl (T/Sgt) A.H. PERRY R.A.M.C. promoted to rank of T/Sgt with pay from 24-12-17. vice H35028, Sgt S.W. SIMPSON R.A.M.C.T. evacuated sick to England. Authority A/DMS/1450/1976e4. 23/1/15. H25368 Pte/Cpl H EVANS R.A.M.C.T Mentioned in Despatches 3rd Army Supplement to London Gazette, 21/12/1917. No.30446.	
-do-	January 28th	Officer Commanding visited all forward posts + saw G.O.C. 182nd INFANTRY BRIGADE at BRIGADE HEADQUARTERS, MAISON de GARDE. Repair + erection of huts for the accommodation of Scabies patients commenced.	
-do-	January 29th	Officer Commanding visited all ambulance posts + HEADQUARTERS, 61st DIVISION. 1 Sergeant + 15 men proceeded to 173rd Tunnelling Company. S.A.V.Y. for duty in connection with the construction of Medical posts in the new defence line.	
-do-	January 30th	Routine work. A.D.M.S. + A/D.A.D.M.S. 61st DIVISION, inspected R.A.P's + Relay Posts in left sector.	
-do	January 31st	Officer Commanding visited R.Q.S + all Relay Posts + R.A.P's in left + right sectors. Medical inspection of all ranks Rank 6 + each now placed in Category "A" or "B".	

G.E. Mackie
Lieut Col R.A.M.C
O.C 2/3rd N. J Ambulance

CONFIDENTIAL.

WAR DIARY

of the

2/1st SOUTH MIDLAND FIELD AMBULANCE.

from

1st FEBRUARY, 1918 to 28th FEBRUARY, 1918.

VOLUME 4.   BOOK 2.

---0---0---0---0---0---0---0---0---0---0---0---0---

WAR DIARY *or* **INTELLIGENCE SUMMARY**

(Erase heading not required.)

Army Form C. 2118.

MAP REFERENCE SHEET 62c.

Place	Date 1918.	Hour	Summary of Events and Information	Remarks and references to Appendices
LANCHY. W.26.d.4.5.	February 1.		Officer Commanding visited all Ambulance detached posts and completed the medical examination of the N.C.O's and men on detached duty.	Vide.
do.	Feb: 2nd.		A.D.M.S. 61st DIVISION and D.A.D.M.S., XVlllth CORPS visited and inspected Camp.	Vide.
do.	Feb: 3rd.		Officer Commanding visited Divisional Headquarters and D.D.M.S. at XVlllth CORPS Headquarters re proposed Officers Corps Rest Station at TIRLANCOURT and received orders to inspect the Chateau and Farm and prepare to organise and open there a Rest Station for 40 Officers and 300, O.R. D.A.A.G., XVlllth CORPS visited and inspected Camp.	Vide.
do.	Feb: 4th.		Officer Commanding with LIEUT W.S.RIVERS, R.A.M.G.T. proceeded to inspect Officers Rest Station at TIRLANCOURT CHATEAU. Officer Commanding visited D.D.M.S. XVlllth CORPS and reported on the Chateau and his proposed system of organising and running the Corps Rest Station. Indent for necessary stores and furnishing submitted by QUARTERMASTER and Non: LIEUT W.S.RIVERS.R.A.M.C.T.	Vide.
do.	Feb: 5th.		Officer Commanding visited all forward posts. Gardening and preparation of ground in vicinity for agricultural purposes continued. Erection of Bath House for Scabies proceeded with.	Vide.
do.	Feb: 6th.		Officer Commanding attended Conference at Office of D.D.M.S. XVlllth CORPS to hear an account of the new scheme of evacuation of wounded, whereby the Main Dressing Stations are to be abolished and the Advanced Dressing Stations placed farther back than formerly so as to be out of reach of continuous shell fire during an engagement so that more complete work might be done there. From these Stations evacuation of wounded to be straight to C.C.S. Officer Commanding visited Ambulance bombing aid posts and MARIEVILLE to prospect there for site for the new Dressing Station necessitated by the immediate adoption of the above system.	Vide.
do.	Feb: 7th.		Officer Commanding visited all forward posts and then attended Conference at Office of A.D.M.S. 61st DIVISION and reported that site for Left Sector Dressing Station would be MARIEVILLE with the present Headquarters at LANCHY in reserve. Framework of Bath House for Scabies erected and laying of brick walls commenced. 435358, A/L/CPL EVANS, promoted to rank of A/Cpl with pay from 24.12.1917. Auth D.G.M.S./B/1450/2035, dated 3.2.1918.	Vide.

Army Form C. 2118.

WAR DIARY
or
INTELLIGENCE SUMMARY

MAP REFERENCE SHEET 62c.

(Erase heading not required.)

Instructions regarding War Diaries and Intelligence Summaries are contained in F. S. Regs., Part II. and the Staff Manual respectively. Title Pages will be prepared in manuscript.

Place	Date 1918.	Hour	Summary of Events and Information	Remarks and references to Appendices
LANCHY. W.26.d.4.5.	Feb: 8th.		Officer Commanding assumed duties of A/A.D.M.S. 61st DIVISION during absence on leave of COLONEL C.HOWKINS, D.S.O., A.M.S. A.D.M.S., 61st DIVISION. D.A.D.M.S. 61st DIVISION visited Camp.	[sig]
do.	Feb: 9th.		Officer Commanding visited Headquarters, 61st DIVISION, and all posts in Forward area. Railway Truck for Stretcher cases completed and sent forward for immediate use. Officer Commanding visited D.D.M.S. XVIIth CORPS to arrange for supply of steel shelters to extend accomodation at MARTEVILLE and ETREILLERS.	[sig]
do.	Feb:10th.		Officer Commanding visited Headquarters, 61st DIVISION and Headquarters, XVIIIth CORPS. Gardening and Agricultural work pursued at LANCHY. Construction of Bath house proceeded with.	[sig]
do.	Feb: 11th.		Officer Commanding visited Headquarters, 61st DIVISION and all the Ambulance bombing aid posts in the forward zone. Preparation of 1 acre of ground for cultivation of vegetables proceeded with and the advice of the Divisional Agricultural Officer asked as to quantity of seeds etc required for the area put under cultivation.	[sig]
do.	Feb: 12th.		Officer Commanding attended at XVIIIth CORPS SCHOOL OF INSTRUCTION TO R MEDICAL OFFICERS at HAM to deliver the first of a series of three lectures on the Medical Diseases of the War. Officer Commanding visited Headquarters, 61st DIVISION in pursuance of his duties as A/A.D.M.S. 61st DIVISION. CAPTAIN P.H.GREEN, R.A.M.C.T. visited all forward posts and inspected the Railway system of evacuation from FRESNOY TO MAISSEMY.	[sig]
do.	Feb: 13th.		Officer Commanding gave 2nd lecture of above series. Officer Commanding visited Headquarters, 61st DIVISION. D.D.M.S., XVIIIth CORPS visited and inspected Camp and with D.A.M.S., 61st DIVISION. A.A. & Q.M.G. 61st DIVISION visited and inspected &mp and Transport Lines. Officer Commanding gave a lecture to N.C.O's and men proceeding to forward area on the tactical situation at present and in case of hostile attack on this front.	[sig]

WAR DIARY or INTELLIGENCE SUMMARY

(Erase heading not required.)

Army Form C. 2118.

MAP REFERENCE SHEET 62c.

Place	Date 1918	Hour	Summary of Events and Information	Remarks and references to Appendices
LANCHY. W.26.d.4.5.	Feb: 14th.		Officer Commanding gave 3rd and last Lecture on the Medical Diseases of the War. Officer Commanding visited Headquarters, 61st DIVISION. Information received from Medical Officer 1/5th GORDON HIGHLANDERS, 61st DIVISION that left battalion R.A.P. had been moved to the QUARRY, FRESNOY. CAPTAIN W.J.HIRST, R.A.M.V.T. inspected the new post to arrange transference of Ambulance bearers and material. Officer Commanding visited MAISSEMY posts to see "B" Section personnel in forward posts relieved by men of "A" Section. Wheels obtained from R.E's for construction of a second ambulance trolley for evacuation of wounded. Instructions received from A.D.M.S., 61st DIVISION to transfer LIEUT E.O.PETERSON, M.O.R.C., U.S.A.S. to 258 TUNNELLING COMPANY at VRAIGNES.	
do.	Feb: 15th.		Officer Commanding visited Headquarters, 61st DIVISION and attended Conference at Office of D.D.M.S., XVIIIth CORPS. Construction of second truck for railway evacuation begun. Constructional work at LANCHY and MARTEVILLE proceeded with. Lecture by Officer Commanding to R.A.M.C. Nursing personnel. CAPTAIN P.H.GREEN, R.A.M.C.T. prospected the whole of the DECAUVILLE railway system and found some parts of the track bad and urgently requiring ballasting.	
do.	Feb: 16th.		Officer Commanding visited Headquarters, 61st DIVISION and inspected work at forward posts. Plans for Dressing Station at MARTEVILLE finally completed.	
do.	Feb: 17th.		Officer Commanding accompanied D.D.M.S., XVIIIth CORPS on tour of inspection of all Field ambulance posts in the forward area, and submitted plans of Dressing Station at MARTEVILLE. These were approved. — work proceeded with.	
do.	Feb: 18th.		Officer Commanding visited D.D.M.S., XVIIIth CORPS, Headquarters 61st DIVISION and forward posts in MAISSEMY. Ground for cultivation manured and prepared. Divisional Agricultural Officer inspected proposed garden site and estimated quantities of seeds and plants required to stock the area.	
do.	Feb: 19th.		Officer Commanding visited Headquarters, 61st DIVISION. Additional men sent to MARTEVILLE to assist in construction of new Dressing Station. Trenches dug in this camp for shelter for patients and personnel from hostile bombing raids. Huts projected in accordance with Divisional Orders.	

WAR DIARY or INTELLIGENCE SUMMARY.

Army Form C. 2118.
MAP REFERENCE SHEET 62c.

Place	Date 1918	Hour	Summary of Events and Information	Remarks and references to Appendices
LANCHY. W.26.d.4.5.	Feb: 20th		Officer Commanding visited Headquarters, 61st DIVISION and D.D.M.S. XVIIIth CORPS at CORPS HEADQUARTERS? HAM, with reference to the new medical arrangements made necessary by the alteration in the Divisional area and consequent contraction of the Divisional Front. Officer Commanding met A.D.M.S. 1st CAVALRY DIVISION and discussed and settled the mutual use of the MAISSEMY - VILLECHOLLES route of evacuation for the Left Sector. Improvements at LANCHY camp continued and collection of one Steel Shelter at MARTEVILLE begun.	
do.	Feb: 21st.		Officer Commanding visited Headquarters, 61st DIVISION, and all forward posts and inspected MAISON de GARDE - FRESNOY road for evacuation purposes. Road fairly good but route very exposed for daylight work. Medical personnel of new mounted troops which are to take over the most northerly part of our Divisional area arrived at MAISSEMY and were taken round the area by CAPTAIN P.H.GREEN, R.A.M.C.T. and installed in their aid posts. CAPTAIN W.J.HIRST, R.A.M.C.T. and CAPTAIN P.H.GREEN, R.A.M.C.T. reconnoitred the new FRESNOY route of evacuation.	
do.	Feb 22nd.		Officer Commanding visited Headquarters, 61st DIVISION, and attended Conference at Office of D.D.M.S., XVIIIth CORPS. Officer Commanding visited all forward posts. Officer Commanding visited G.O.C., 61st DIVISION and reported on the new evacuation routes from the Divisional Front.	
do.	Feb 23rd.		Officer Commanding visited Headquarters, 61st DIVISION and inspected new and proposed site for Dressing Station for Right Sector, near ETREILLERS. Officer Commanding visited MARTEVILLE with CAPTAIN P.H.GREEN, R.A.M.C.T. and inspected constructional work there.	
do.	Feb 24th.		Officer Commanding visited new RAILWAY CHANGING STATION at GUN PITS POST (R.18.a.5.8.) and all the constructional work at MARTEVILLE. CAPTAIN A.F.L.SHIELDS, R.A.M.C.(S.R.) reported back for duty from 25th Entrenching Battalion. CAPTAIN W.STOBIE, R.A.M.C.T. struck off strength of Unit on transfer to 41 C.C.S. at CUGNY. Authority A.D.M.S. 61st DIVISION 374/60 dated 24.2.1918.	
do.	Feb 25th.		Officer Commanding visited A.D.M.S. 61st DIVISION at Divisional Headquarters. A.D.M.S. 61st DIVISION visited and inspected Camp. CAPTAIN P.H.GREEN, R.A.M.C.T. met A.D.M.S. 1st CAVALRY DIVISION at MAISSEMY and handed over the post there.	

Lieut Col: R.A.M.C.T.
O.C. 2/1st SOUTH MIDLAND FIELD AMBULANCE.

WAR DIARY
or
INTELLIGENCE SUMMARY.
(Erase heading not required.)

MAP REFERENCE. SHEET 62c.
Army Form C. 2118.

Place	Date	Hour	Summary of Events and Information	Remarks and references to Appendices
	1918.			
LANCHY. W.26.d.455.	Feb:26th.		LIEUT COLONEL GEORGE MACKIE,D.S.O., R.A.M.C.T. having proceeded on leave of absence CAPTAIN PHILIP.H.GREEN, R.A.M.C.T. assumed command of the Ambulance. A/Officer Commanding visited all forward posts. Working party at MARTEVILLE doubled in order to expedite completion of new A.D.S. there. New Walking Wounded Posts taken over at R.30.d.5.5. on the MAISON de GARDE-MAISSEMY road. Construction of new Walking Wounded Collecting Post commenced at R.34.b.10.4.	
do.	Feb: 27th.		A/Officer Commanding visited MARTEVILLE and all forward posts. Construction of new A.D.S. at MARTEVILLE proceeding satisfactorily.	
do.	Feb: 28th.		Consulting Physician, FIFTH ARMY visited and inspected Camp. A.D.M.S. 61st DIVISION visited and inspected Camp and premises. A/Officer Commanding visited all forward posts and inspected constructional work at MARTEVILLE.	

28:2:19 18;

Geo. Green

CAPTAIN: R.A.M.C.T.
A/OFFICER COMMANDING. 2/1st SOUTH MIDLAND FIELD AMBULANCE.

Medical Vol 23

140/849

Confidential

War Diary
of
2/1st South Midland Field Ambulance,
61st Division
from
1-3-1918 to 31-3-1918.
Book 3.
Volume H.

COMMITTEE FOR THE
MEDICAL HISTORY OF THE WAR
Date 12 MAY 1918

WAR DIARY or INTELLIGENCE SUMMARY.

Army Form C. 2118.

MAP REFERENCE SHEET 62c.

(Erase heading not required.)

Place	Date 1918.	Summary of Events and Information	Remarks and references to Appendices
LANCHY. W.26.d.4.5.	MARCH 1st.	A/OFFICER COMMANDING visited all posts in the forward area. Warning order received re impending German attack. All Medical posts in LEFT SECTOR evacuated and personnel withdrawn to new A.D.S., MARTEVILLE. Construction of posts at MAISON de GARDE and Z.63 expedited. Site for Headquarters in case of retirement selected at QUIVIERES. A.D.M.S. 61st DIVISION confirmed and approved of arrangements made.	AMS
do	MARCH 2nd.	A/OFFICER COMMANDING visited HEADQUARTERS, 61st DIVISION and all forward posts.	AMS
do	MARCH 3rd.	A/OFFICER COMMANDING visited new A.D.S. at MARTEVILLE and inspected constructional work there and at the WALKING WOUNDED COLLECTING POST. Bath House and large Hut fitted up at LANCHY for reception of patients should it be necessary to move A.D.S. here.	AMS
do	MARCH 4th.	A/OFFICER COMMANDING visited HEADQUARTERS 61st DIVISION and proceeded to inspect constructional work at A.D.S., MARTEVILLE.	AMS
do	MARCH 5th.	A.D.M.S. 61st DIVISION visited and inspected camp and premises. A/OFFICER COMMANDING visited all forward posts. CAPTAIN D.B.I.HALLETT, R.A.M.C.(T.G.) taken on strength under instructions received from A.D.M.S. 61st DIVISION.	AMS
do	MARCH 6th.	CAPTAIN A.F.L.SHIELDS, R.A.M.C.(S.R.) struck off strength of Unit on transfer to 25th Entrenching Battalion, for duty as Medical Officer. A/OFFICER COMMANDING visited HEADQUARTERS, 61st DIVISION and then proceeded to all forward posts and inspected constructional work done at WALKING WOUNDED COLLECTING POSTS and at A.D.S., MARTEVILLE.	AMS
do	MARCH 7th.	A/OFFICER COMMANDING visited HEADQUARTERS, 61st DIVISION, and then inspected all forward posts.	AMS
do	MARCH 8th.	A/OFFICER COMMANDING visited all forward posts.	AMS
do	MARCH 9th.	Routine work at LANCHY. A/OFFICER COMMANDING visited and inspected all posts in the forward area.	AMS
do	MARCH 10.	A/OFFICER COMMANDING visited all forward posts. A.D.M.S. 61st DIVISION and G.O.C., 184th INFANTRY BRIGADE visited and inspected camp and premises.	AMS

Army Form C. 2118.

WAR DIARY
INTELLIGENCE SUMMARY.

MAP REFERENCE. SHEET 62c.

(Erase heading not required.)

Instructions regarding War Diaries and Intelligence Summaries are contained in F.S. Regs., Part II. and the Staff Manual respectively. Title pages will be prepared in manuscript.

Place	Date	Hour	Summary of Events and Information	Remarks and references to Appendices
LANGHY. W.26.d.4.5.	1918. MARCH 11th.		A/OFFICER COMMANDING attended Conference at Office of D.D.M.S., XVIIIth CORPS. A/OFFICER COMMANDING accompanied D.D.M.S., XVIIIth CORPS on tour of inspection of all posts in forward area.	
do	MARCH 12th.		CAPTAIN J.T.O'BOYLE, R.A.M.C. struck off strength of Unit on transfer as Medical Officer to the 14th Brigade, R.G.A. CAPTAIN J.MANUEL, M.C., R.A.M.C. taken on strength of Unit. A.D.M.S. 61st DIVISION and SECRETARY, WARWICKSHIRE TERRITORIAL FORCE ASSOCIATION visited and inspected premises. A/OFFICER COMMANDING visited FRANCILLY SELENCY to reconnoitre route of evacuation from ENGHIEN REDOUBT.	
do	MARCH 13th.		A/OFFICER COMMANDING visited all posts in the forward area.	
do	MARCH 14th.		A/OFFICER COMMANDING visited and inspected all forward posts. CAPTAIN J.MANUEL, M.C., R.A.M.C.T. posted for temporary duty with the 2/7th ROYAL WARWICKSHIRE REGIMENT.	
do	MARCH 15th.		A/OFFICER COMMANDING visited all posts in the forward area and inspected all Ambulance Bombing Aid Posts. Work at A.D.S., MARTEVILLE and at the WALKING WOUNDED COLLECTING POSTS proceeding satisfactorily.	
do	MARCH 16th.		A/OFFICER COMMANDING visited forward area. Notification received from A.D.M.S., 61st DIVISION that LIEUTENANT COLONEL GEORGE MACKIE, D.S.O., R.A.M.C.T. had arrived in AMIENS.	
do	MARCH 17th.		LIEUTENANT COLONEL GEORGE MACKIE,D.S.O., R.A.M.C.T. having returned from leave of absence to the United Kingdom, assumed command of the Ambulance from this date.	

WAR DIARY or INTELLIGENCE SUMMARY.

(Erase heading not required.)

Army Form C. 2118.

MAP REFERENCE. SHEET 62c

Place	Date 1918	Summary of Events and Information	Remarks and references to Appendices
LANCHY. N.26.d.4.6	March 18th.	CAPTAIN P.H. GREEN, R.A.M.C.T. proceeded on 14 days leave of absence to the United Kingdom. Officer Commanding visited forward posts & inspected all work done there during his leave. Found that excellent progress had been made in the erection of the Steel Shelter Messing Station at MARTEVILLE and also in the underground gallery. There, a new shell proof dugout dressing room, 16ft by 14ft had been dug, timbered and lined, 28ft below the surface & was ready for use. Two new dugouts for use as a Bearer forward base and as a Walking Wounded collecting post had been dug and built on the VILLECHOLLES – MAISON de GARDE road and were staffed and occupied. Two new posts had been taken over, cleaned and occupied between this place and FRESNOY QUARRY.	G.60/u
do	March 19th.	Officer Commanding visited Headquarters, 61st DIVISION & forward posts at MARTEVILLE and inspected all details of recent construction and alterations. Improvements at Headquarters, LANCHY continued	G.60/u
do	March 20th.	Officer Commanding attended conference at office of A.D.M.S. 61st DIVISION. Then visited all posts in forward area and, in view of the rumours which had been gathered from German prisoners recently taken, which suggested that an attack on a large scale might begin between March 20th & 21st on our own front, warned all parks to be ready. All forward posts were put in complete readiness for active operations.	G.60/u
do	March 21st.	Very intense German bombardment started at 4.30 a.m. First casualties received at LANCHY at 5.0 a.m. were from the 2/4th R BERKS who were billeted in Huts at UGNY. Officer Commanding immediately proceeded to and remained at MARTEVILLE. Weather:- Very misty. Body work of 140/167224. Driver W. BUTCHER'S FORD AMBULANCE Car was blown off by a shell, on the MAISON de GARDE road. Although he had been gassed, he drove the Car to MARTEVILLE, procured a saw, removed the shattered body work & after a brief rest insisted on carrying on. His Car was again hit & a patient – M35302 Pte H GRAY, he orderly, were killed & Driver BUTCHER badly wounded. All day a steady stream of wounded arrived at ADS MARTEVILLE & were evacuated in accordance with the Divisional System to C.C.S. H.P.M. Walking wounded were taken to the W.W.C.P. at VAUX.	G.60/u

WAR DIARY
or
INTELLIGENCE SUMMARY.
(Erase heading not required.)

Army Form C. 2118.

Map Reference. Sheet 62c.
AMIENS. 17.

Place	Date 1918	Hour	Summary of Events and Information	Remarks and references to Appendices
LANCHY and "Y"	March 22nd		Very misty night which lasted until about 2.0 p.m. Heavy German Barrage still continued. Large masses of Infantry pushed forward. British troops retiring on MARTEVILLE which had to be evacuated. Owing to the rapid advance of the enemy. LANCHY had to be evacuated + the Unit, less a small A.D.S. Staff marched to Y, arriving there about 6.0 p.m.	Feb.
"Y" and CREMERY	March 23rd		"Y" evacuated at 1.0 a.m. All cases moved to BETHENCOURT and dumped there in order to get all over the SOMME as quickly as possible. BETHENCOURT cleared later in the night. Flying Stations evacuated + burned. Unit proceeded in acquiring a stock of badly needed petrol before all was destroyed. Unit proceeded direct to CREMERY and Officer Commanding went to Headquarters. 61st DIVISION 2/N.60b 1.15 men of the Unit, reported as missing believed prisoners. 2 Ambulance Cars with drivers + orderlies also missing. Details. FRESNOY party captured in front German rush, except 3 men who were able to get away by the Lannoy Road to MAISON de GARDE. CARS. Little is known about these. They were clearing wounded very late, to H.Q. and apparently after the C.C.S. were closed, they cleared to NOYON and were either destroyed by Shellfire or captured returning towards H.Q., after enemy patrols had pushed further forward than was known.	Feb.
CREMERY and ROUVROY	March 24th		Officer Commanding visited Brigade Transport Lines at MANICOURT, CURCHY and HERLY, and got into touch with Infantry who were in front of MESNIL St NICAISE. Informed by A.D.M.S. 61st DIVISION that this Unit had now passed under orders of 7 A.D.M.S. 20th DIVISION, and that we were in reserve to his A.D.S. at MESNIL St NICAISE. The O.C. lived in vain to locate this A.D.S. and established contact with our own Infantry direct – opened a Collecting Post at CURCHY and an A.D.S. at CREMERY, from which cases were evacuated to HARGICOURT. The O.C. got into touch with M.O. 1/5th GORDONS + M.O. 1/8th ARGYLL + SUTHERLAND HIGHLANDERS. Heavy baggage and Headquarters ordered back to ROUVROY and reported arrival there at 8.30 p.m. Tent bivouac + all available transport went forward with CAPTAIN W.J. HIRST, from CREMERY and cleared all wounded that could be reached after fight at DRESLINCOURT.	Feb.
ROUVROY and BEAUFORT	March 25th		Further party of bearers sent to CURCHY area at 8.0 a.m. O.C. worked forward area + Headquarters, 61st DIVISION. CAPTAIN P.H. GREEN, reported back from leave having been recalled to AMIENS 61st DIVISION. Unit ordered to proceed forthwith to BEAUFORT. After being shelled out of CURCHY and the infantry having fallen back, our Staff retired by CREMERY + FRESNOY to ROYE. French troops were digging a position in front of CREMERY village, but had their own Medical Staff + Organisation + did not require our help, therefore as no British troops could now be identified on our immediate front, the details of 1/5 GORDONS + 1/8 A.S.H. having moved S.E. to NESLE area, our A.D.S. ceased to function. A small party remained at CREMERY till 9 p.m. when they were shelled out of that village + a pool was established at once behind back or FRESNOY to ROYE Road at 11.15 p.m. and was hit by heavy shells that had to be abandoned. The M.O. + personnel reported back to BEAUFORT at 11.50 p.m.	Feb.

WAR DIARY or INTELLIGENCE SUMMARY

Army Form C. 2118.

MAP REFERENCE. SHEET 62c AMIENS. 17.

Place	Date 1918	Hour	Summary of Events and Information	Remarks and references to Appendices
BEAUFORT and MAILLY-RAINEVAL	March 26th		Patrols during night having failed to find any wounded, either French or British, or to get in touch with any Artillery or Infantry in from of ROUVROY, CAPTAIN P.H. GREEN, R.A.M.C. - CAPTAIN W.J. HIRST, R.A.M.C.T. went off in a Daimler car with CORPORALS J.W. ROBERTS + R. RUSTIN, to reconnoitre the area. Finding ROUVROY village empty, they pushed on and suddenly encountered enemy outposts on ROUVROY - FRESNOY road. The car was badly damaged. Driver WALMSLEY and Orderly Pte MAISEY, got into a trench on the S. side of the road. The others into one on the N. side of the road. After one ineffectual attempt to restart the car, which came again under Machine Gun fire, the driver + orderly ran for BOUCHOIR, where they rejoined the Unit. The 2 Officers + 2 NCOs were reported to ANSUES 61 DIVISION as missing, believed prisoners. way to LE QUESNEL, where they reported by a Staff Car driver, found their car driver. Unit ordered to move to MEZIÈRES and establish an A.D.S. on the MAISON BLANCHE - MEZIÈRES road. This was carried out by 1.30pm. Orders were then received to move to MAILLY-RAINEVAL where the Unit reported at 6.25pm. Headquarters at Sebastopol farm on the MAILLY - LOUVRECHY road and a post established in MAILLY village which was full of French 102nd Chasseurs a pied. Bordeacl made with Medecin chef du Regiment and a party of NCOs + Bearers attached to him for duty.	G. Lt. Col.
MAILLY and COTTENCHY	March 27th		Orders received for Unit to move to COTTENCHY where we arrived at 4.0 pm. Headquarters at the Chateau in place. Last left at MAILLY with 102nd Chasseurs a pied.	G. Lt. Col.
COTTENCHY and HAILLES	March 28th		Unit received orders to proceed to HAILLES. Billets taken over from 1/3rd FIELD AMBULANCE. Arrangements made to collect and deal with sick from the Divisional Transport lines at HAILLES. The O.C. visited AUBERCOURT - Advanced Depot of Medical Stores at BOVES, to collect all available dressings material. Also 61 Bde of Divisional Headquarters, VILLERS BRETTONEUX - visited the A.D.S. 39th DIVISION at O.C. arranged for temporary occupation of huts as a Walking Wounded Dump at BOVES. Also the use of 2 Ammunition lorries to clear cases there during the night, en route for M.A.M.P.S which was a very long journey of one stretch.	
HAILLES + BOVES	March 29th		Orders received + Unit moved to BOVES, arriving at 1 p.m. Dressing Station opened at III Trd J of the church. This was to work in conjunction with - as a relief to the A.D.S. being run by the 2/3rd FIELD AMBULANCE at GENTELLES + MARCELCAVE. Cases from all divisions in the area arrived in large numbers + were evacuated as well as possible to M.A.M.P.S. Detachment left at MAILLY with the French, reported back to Headquarters. LIEUT G.L. GELL R.A.M.C. (T.F.) + LIEUT H.E. THOMPSON, R.A.M.C. (T.C.) taken on strength of Unit.	G. Lt. Col.

Army Form C. 2118.

WAR DIARY
or
INTELLIGENCE SUMMARY.

(Erase heading not required.)

MAP REFERENCE.
AMIENS. 17.

Place	Date 1918	Hour	Summary of Events and Information	Remarks and references to Appendices
BOVES.	March 30th.		Work continued at Dressing Station. BOVES. 3 Horse Ambulances were held in readiness to proceed under instructions from ADMS. 61 Division. Bearers on receipt of further orders.	Tester.
BOVES	March 31st		Work continued at Dressing Station. BOVES. Large numbers of wounded from all Divisions in the area treated & evacuated to C.C.S. NAMPS.	Tester.

T.G. Mackie
Lieut Colonel. RAMC.
O.C. 2/1st South Midland Field Ambulance.

MEDICAL.

9 WM 24

16/2900

COMMITTEE FOR THE
MEDICAL HISTORY OF THE WAR
Date -6 JUN 1918

CONFIDENTIAL.

WAR DIARY of the

2/1st SOUTH MIDLAND FIELD AMBULANCE.

from

1st APRIL, 1918 to 30th APRIL, 1918.   VOLUME 4.

BOOK 4.

WAR DIARY
or
INTELLIGENCE SUMMARY.
(Erase heading not required.)

Army Form C. 2118.

MAP REFERENCE. AMIENS.17. DIEPPE.16.

Place	Date 1918	Hour	Summary of Events and Information	Remarks and references to Appendices
BOVES.	APRIL 1st.		Work at BOVES continued. Large number of casualties cleared from the attack on HANGARD WOOD by the 3rd CAVALRY DIVISION. Sites occupied by 50th DIVISION and 20th DIVISION FIELD AMBULANCES in BOVES vacated - taken over and held by us on behalf of A.D.M.S. 18th DIVISION whose Field Ambulances arrived later in the day, occupied these places with us and carried on the clearance of all wounded in conjunction with our men.	Cox/W
-do-	APRIL 2nd.		BOVES work continued as above in conjunction with the 18th DIVISION. A.D.M.S. 18th DIVISION moved one Field Ambulance to ST ACHEUL- AMIENS and opened a Dressing Station there for Stretcher Cases - also a Walking Wounded Station at ST NICHOLAS on the other side of the river - thus opening a new line of evacuation direct through AMIENS and cutting out our Station at BOVES. HEADQUARTERS, 61st DIVISION moved from BOVES.	Cox/W
-do- AVELESGES.)	APRIL 3rd.		Unit evacuated BOVES and marched to PICQUINY and after commandeering 4 Motor Lorries from another Division embussed for AVELESGES arriving there at 6.0 p.m. Transport reported in complete at 10.0 p.m., thus accomplishing the whole move, a distance of 41 Kilometres, in one day. Hospital opened for Brigade Sick.	Cox/W
AVELESGES.	APRIL 4th.		All waggons unpacked and a beginning made with examination of all kit and equipment to assess damage and deficiencies sustained in the great battle. Indents forwarded for all articles required to make up men's and other losses. Clearing of waggons and equipment begun. Officer Commanding visited 184th BRIGADE HEADQUARTERS at THAILLY CHATEAU. CAPTAIN J.MANUEL.M.C. appointed temporary second in command of Unit - CAPTAIN E.F.O'CONNOR, apointed O.C. "A" Section and LIEUT; G.L.GALL, O.C. "C" Section.	Cox/W
do	APRIL 5th.		Officer Commanding with CAPTAIN J.MANUEL.M.C. visited Headquarters 184th INFANTRY BRIGADE- also Headquarters of the 2/5th GLOUCESTERS, 2/4th OXFORD AND BUCKS LIGHT INFANTRY and 2/4th ROYAL BERKS, and inspected the billets and all sanitary arrangements. Brigade Sick round established and cases collected from Brigade area.	Cox/W
do	APRIL 6th.		Clearing of waggons and equipment continued. Officer Commanding visited Headquarters, 61st DIVISION. D.A.D.M.S. 61st DIVISION visited Officer Commanding re establishing a Divisional Scabies Centre here. Preliminary arrangements made - site chosen. Baths found and tents pitched.	Cox/W
do	APRIL 7th.		Routine work. A.D.M.S. 61st DIVISION informed that we were ready to receive from 12 - 20 Scabies patients.	Cox/W

WAR DIARY or INTELLIGENCE SUMMARY.

MAP REFERENCE. DIEPPE. SHEET 36 A.

Army Form C. 2118.

Place	Date 1918.	Hour	Summary of Events and Information	Remarks and references to Appendices
AVELESGES.	APRIL 8th.		Routine work. Missing Officers Kits forwarded to Base via R.T.O. ABBEVILLE. Orders re establishing Scabies centre cancelled. Re-equipment of Unit proceeded with. Headquarters, 184th INFANTRY BRIGADE and Billets of Brigade Units visited and inspected by Officer Commanding and CAPTAIN J.MANURL.M.C.	Cols.
DO	APRIL 9th.		CAPTAIN A.P.THOMSON, R.A.M.C.T, rejoined Unit on return from leave. Orders received that the Division would entrain for an unknown destination on the 10th inst. Preparations made for an early departure on the 10th inst.	Cols.
DO & SEUX.	APRIL 10th.		Unit marched to SEUX and billeted there for the Day at the CHATEAU, and thence marched to St ROCHE Station, AMIENS. Second march begun by Transport at 9.0 p.m. and personnel at 11.0 p.m. to St ROCHE Station, AMIENS.	Cols.
IN TRAIN.	APRIL 11th.		Unit reached entraining point without incident. All troop trains 3 hours late. Entraining completed and train left about 8.30 a.m. Owing to a train having been hit by hostile shells and the permanent way damaged S. of CHOCQUES, the Unit train was diverted to the coast via BOULOGNE and CALAIS and did not arrive at BERGUETTE until 16 hours after schedule time. Officer Commanding proceeded to BERGUETTE by Car with LIEUT & Q.M. RIVERS and arrived at AIRE at 8.0 a.m. Visited Headquarters, 61st DIVISION and then proceeded to BERGUETTE as detraining Officer for the Station. Information received from 184th BRIGADE HEADQUARTERS that Ambulance would billet at ASILE des ALIENES, St VENANT.	Cols.
St VENANT.& BERGUETTE.	APRIL 12th.		Unit detrained at BERGUETTE station and marched to ASILE des ALIENES, St VENANT where billets had been obtained for them. Orders received to open a Divisional Main Dressing Station there. Hospital and grounds heavily shelled from 8.0 - 9.0 a.m. SERGEANT DIX.W., CORPORAL PEWSEY.R., PRIVATE EDWARDS.W.H. and PRIVATE COTTERILL.F. wounded and evacuated to C.C.S. Bearers sent to assist R.M.O's of the Battalions in 184th INFANTRY BRIGADE. Remainder of Transport and personnel less "B" Section evacuated ST VENANT and moved to LE PERRIERE afterwards proceeding on to BERGUETTE where a Divisional Main Dressing Station was established in the Schools, S. of the Church. Advanced Dressing Station formed at the Asylum, instead of a Main Dressing Station owing to its proximity to the fighting line. CAPTAIN A.P.THOMSON.M.C. and CAPTAIN J.MANURL.M.C. Left in charge. Officer Commanding visited A.D.S. and Headquarters, 184th INFANTRY BRIGADE in the afternoon to make final arrangements regarding evacuation of wounded.	Cols.

Army Form C. 2118.

WAR DIARY
or
INTELLIGENCE SUMMARY.
(Erase heading not required.)

MAP REFERENCE SHEET 36 A.

Instructions regarding War Diaries and Intelligence Summaries are contained in F.S. Regs., Part II. and the Staff Manual respectively. Title pages will be prepared in manuscript.

Place	Date 1918.	Hour	Summary of Events and Information	Remarks and references to Appendices
BERGUETTE.	APRIL 12th		CAPTAIN J.MANUEL.M.C. located and got into touch with all R.A.P's of 184th INFANTRY BRIGADE. A.D.M.S. 61st DIVISION visited A.D.S. regarding the new dispositions of the Field Ambulances.	Cover
do	APRIL 13th		Officer Commanding visited A.D.S. and Headquarters, 61st DIVISION. A.D.M.S. 61st DIVISION visited A.D.S. and M.D.S. A.D.S. again shelled in the night - no casualties. A good number of wounded collected from our Divisional Front and evacuated by M.A.C. Cars to C.C.S. Arrangements made to open a bathing centre for "Mustard Gas" cases at the A.D.S. as a certain amount of gas shelling was taking place against the batteries round the asylum.	Cover
do	APRIL 14th		D.D.M.S. XIth CORPS visited and inspected Camp, and issued instructions that about 1000 Lunatics were to be evacuated from the Asylum, ST VENANT and entrained at BERGUETTE. He asked for assistance in the entraining of these lunatics. CAPTAIN A.P.THOMSON.M.C. and CAPTAIN J.MANUEL.M.C. with personnel of "B" Section at ST VENANT arranged the loading of these patients into lorries etc and LIEUTENANT & Q.M.W.S.RIVERS, with small staff of N.C.O's and men were in attendance at BERGUETTE Station. Town of ST VENANT heavily shelled and roads impassable for cars. CAPTAIN F.R.MACDONALD.R.A.M.C. reported for duty.	Cover
do	APRIL 15th		LIEUTENANT RIVERS and staff worked throughout the night on the unloading of lunatics from the lorries- finding temporary shelter for them - feeding them and finally entraining them. The work was carried out quickly and smoothly and the train finally despatched at 2.5p.m. although it was loaded by 9.0 a.m. Officer Commanding received congratulatory messages from D.D.M.S. XIth CORPS and LIEUT:COL:ACLAND TROYTE, XIth CORPS STAFF, and was informed by the D.D.M.S. XIth CORPS that the action of the 2/1st SOUTH MIDLAND FIELD AMBULANCE in this matter would be brought to the notice of the CORPS and DIVISIONAL COMMANDERS. D.D.M.S. XIth CORPS and A.D.M.S. 61stDIVISION visited and inspected M.D.S. Officer Commanding visited A.D.S., ST VENANT and found all quiet but 2 direct hits were registered on the hospital buildings immediately he had left. No casualties. BERGUETTE Station shelled during the afternoon. Contact established with all R.M.O's and extra bearers sent to M.O. 2/4th OXFORD & BUCKS LIGHT INFANTRY as he expected active operations. 2 Medical Officers reported for temporary duty at M.D.S. They were sent under instructions from D.D.M.S. XIth CORPS.	Cover
do	APRIL 16th		Officer Commanding visited Headquarters 61st DIVISION and A.D.S. ST VENANT. D.A.D.M.S. 61st DIVISION visited M.D.S. 3 direct hits registered on A.D.S. Ford Ambulance Car circuit started at night. Car stationed at LES AMUSOIRES and evacuating to A.D.S. via ROBECQ and ST FLORIS roads to save long carry.	Cover

Army Form C. 2118.

WAR DIARY
or
INTELLIGENCE SUMMARY.
(Erase heading not required.)

MAP REFERENCE. SHEET 36A.

Place	Date 1918.	Hour	Summary of Events and Information	Remarks and references to Appendices
BERGUETTE.	APRIL 17th.		Officer Commanding visited A.D.S. and Headquarters 61st DIVISION to find out possible new site for an A.D.S. ASYLUM no longer possible, owing to heavy and constant shelling and owing to its now having been converted into 184th BRIGADE HEADQUARTERS, Infantry Billets and an Artillery Observation Post established on the roof. "G" Staff decided that in present circumstances all Administrative Services should be W. of LA BASSEE Canal. New site chosen near Eastern end of GUARBECQUE village and approved by A.D.M.S. 61st DIVISION who visited and inspected M.D.S. and then proceeded to the new site. Tents used by Portuguese troops at the ASYLUM taken down, moved to new site and arrangements made for their erection.	Coster
do.	APRIL 18th.		Officer Commanding visited new A.D.S. and party began the erection of the tents. Evacuation of A.D.S. at the ASYLUM begun. 435132, PRIVATE W.MAISEY, 435311, PRIVATE FLETCHER.W. Wounded and evacuated to C.C.S. 435402, PRIVATE F.TAYLOR, killed in action. 437389, PRIVATE (A/U/L/CPL E.V.HAMPTON, died of wounds at the M.D.S.	Coster
do.	APRIL 19th.		Long range shelling of GUARBECQUE. Several casualties amongst Artillery. A.D.S. at ASYLUM vacated leaving only Bearer Post and 1 Car there. Temporary A.D.S. formed at P.15.a.0.5. pending the erection of Marquees and Tents at new A.D.S. O.18.b.1.4. Erection and preparation of new A.D.S. rapidly pushed forward. A.D.M.S. 61st DIVISION visited and inspected M.D.S. A.A.& Q.M.G. 61st DIVISION visited M.D.S. re the feeding arrangements. Buffet instituted to provide special food and drinks for patients.	Coster
do	APRIL 20th.		Front very quiet - very few wounded arriving at M.D.S. Large amount of material and stores salved from the ASYLUM, ST VENANT and brought to our new A.D.S. which was almost ready for reception. Officer Commanding visited all forward posts and relived the personnel.	Coster
do	APRIL 21st.		A.D.M.S. 61st DIVISION and D.D.M.S. XIth CORPS notified that our new A.D.S. at O.18.b.1.4. was open as from 2.0 p.m. Officer Commanding visited A.D.S. A.D.M.S. 61st DIVISION visited the A.D.S. and Officer Commanding proceeded to the A.D.S. and warned the Officers in charge to be prepared for possible large number of casualties.	Coster

Army Form C. 2118.

SHEET. 36A.

WAR DIARY
or
INTELLIGENCE SUMMARY

(Erase heading not required.)

Instructions regarding War Diaries and Intelligence Summaries are contained in F. S. Regs., Part II and the Staff Manual respectively. Title Pages will be prepared in manuscript.

Place	Date 1918.	Hour	Summary of Events and Information	Remarks and references to Appendices
BERGUETTE.	APRIL 22nd.		Heavy reciprocal Artillery activity throughout night. No Infantry attack developed on our Divisional front. Officer Commanding visited A.D.M.S. 61st DIVISION and then proceeded to inspect new A.D.S. Warning order received from Brigade that 2/5th GLOUCESTERS and 1 Battalion of the 4th DIVISION would attack at 4.30 a.m. 23rd inst. Officer Commanding visited A.D.S. re this attack and arranged disposition of Stretcher Bearers, Cars etc. New evacuation route organised through ROBECQ village - which is directly behind the part of the line which is to be assaulted. Special Car Loading Post established and all bearer parties suitably reinforced.	
do	APRIL 23rd.		Attack successfully carried out according to plan. Medical arrangements worked well. Casualties began to arrive at M.D.S. by 8.0 a.m. 23 wounded prisoners of war received at M.D.S. and wire sent to XIth Corps "A" giving names and particulars of regiment etc of these prisoners. Officer Commanding visited A.D.S. D.D.M.S. XIth CORPS, A.A.&Q.M.G. 61st DIVISION and A.D.M.S. 61st DIVISION visited and inspected M.D.S. and A.D.S. CAPTAIN A.P.THOMSON.M.C. and CAPTAIN J.MANUEL.M.C. visited all 184th INFANTRY BRIGADE's R.A.P's after the action and reported all wounded had been cleared in a very short time.	
do	APRIL 24th.		Officer Commanding visited A.D.S. and CAR LOADING POSTS. Alterations and extensions at A.D.S. begun. 4 Tents in all now erected:- 1 for Administration, Feeding etc, 1 for Walking Wounded and Sick and 1 for use as a Dressing Room. The 4th was erected as a billet for the Staff - there being no other habitation available.	
do	APRIL 25th.		Officer Commanding visited A.D.S. Improvements there continued steadily. "B" Section personnel at A.D.S. relieved and their places taken by "C" Section. A.D.M.S. 61st DIVISION visited and inspected M.D.S. D.R.O. 1704 dated 25.4.1918, received, notifying the following awards :- 435358 CORPORAL H.EVANS,) 435407, PRIVATE MEREDITH.W.H.) Awarded MILITARY MEDAL by the CORPS COMMANDER. 437115, PRIVATE HARRISON.C.W.)	
do	APRIL 26th.		Officer Commanding with CAPTAIN J.MANUEL,M.C. visited CAR LOADING POSTS. A.D.M.S. 61st DIVISION visited and inspected M.B.S. and A.D.S.	

Form C. 2118.

WAR DIARY
or
INTELLIGENCE SUMMARY

MAP REFERENCE SHEET 26 A.

(Erase heading not required.)

Instructions regarding War Diaries and Intelligence Summaries are contained in F.S. Regs, Part II. and the Staff Manual respectively. Title Pages will be prepared in manuscript.

Place	Date 1918	Hour	Summary of Events and Information	Remarks and references to Appendices
BERGUETTE.	APRIL 27th.		Heavy shelling of ST.VENANT village with MUSTARD GAS. A good many casualties from the 1/5th GORDONS who were billeted in the town were brought down and treated at the M.D.S. Vicinity of A.D.S. shelled during evening - One N.C.O. bruised - no other casualties.	[initials]
do	APRIL 28th.		Front quiet. A few more gassed cases from ST.VENANT arrived and were treated here. D.D.M.S. XIth CORPS visited and inspected M.D.S. and A.D.S. CAPTAIN A.P.THOMSON, M.C. proceeded on 14 days special leave of absence to the United Kingdom. A.D.M.S. 61st DIVISION visited A.D.S. with O.C. and selected a site at the GUARBECQUE Baths in which to establish a Divisional forward gas centre. Carpenters began work at once so that the place could be ready for use at once.	[initials]
do	APRIL 29th.		A.D.M.S. 61st DIVISION visited and inspected M.D.S. Officer Commanding visited A.D.S. and all 184th INFANTRY BRIGADE R.A.P's. Heavy shelling of the ROBECQ area and of the ROBECQ - BUSNES Evacuation route, especially round New 184th INFANTRY BRIGADE HEADQUARTERS at P.27.b.2.3. Work at Gas Centre continued.	[initials]
do	APRIL 30th.		A.D.M.S. 61st DIVISION and Officer Commanding proceeded to 184th Advanced Brigade Headquarters and arranged a new car post in BUSNES village and decided to attach 1, N.C.O. and 2 Stretcher Bearers with Stretchers and Dressings to 184th INFANTRY BRIGADE HEADQUARTERS. Forward Gas Centre opened for treatment of all cases brought in.	[initials]

G.E.Mackie.

Lieut Col:R.A.M.C.T.
Commanding. 2/1st SOUTH MIDLAND FIELD AMBULANCE.

MEDICAL

Vol. 25
14 9/2983

CONFIDENTIAL. — 61st Div.

WAR DIARY

of

2/1st SOUTH MIDLAND FIELD AMBULANCE

from

1st MAY, 1918 to 31st MAY, 1918.

VOLUME 5.

BOOK 4.

—o—o—o—o—o—o—o—o—o—o—o—o—o—o—o—o—o—o—o—

COMMITTEE FOR THE
MEDICAL HISTORY
Date 9 JUL 1918

Army Form C. 2118.

WAR DIARY
or
INTELLIGENCE SUMMARY

(Erase heading not required.)

MAP REFERENCE .. SHEET 36a.

Place	Date 1918.	Hour	Summary of Events and Information	Remarks and references to Appendices
BERGUETTE. O.16.c.7.8.	MAY 1st.		Officer Commanding visited Advanced Dressing Station, Car Loading Posts and all R.A.P's of the 184th INFANTRY BRIGADE. A.D.M.S. 61st DIVISION visited and inspected M.D.S. and A.D.S. Evacuation Route from forward area altered on account of hostile shelling of ROBECQ village and adjacent roads. Road from ROBECQ to the CANAL so badly damaged as to be impassable by car. Forward Gas Centre at GUARBECQUE opened for the reception of cases.	Estu
-do-	MAY 2nd.		Officer Commanding visited and inspected A.D.S. 22 Reinforcements arrived and taken on the strength. New relay posts established along the evacuation route. CARVIN FARM- LES AMUSOIRES -Car Loading Post on BUSNES-St VENANT Main road. Repairs to track carried out and temporary bridges over streams constructed.	Estu
-do-	MAY 3rd.		Officer Commanding visited all forward posts. A.D.M.S. 61st DIVISION visited M.D.S. Further reorganisation of evacuation system in forward area owing to continued shelling of roads. Cars at P.15.a.Q.5. and at Headquarters 184th INF:BRIGADE at P.27.b.2.4. Relay Car at BUSNES Church where an extra Field Ambulance Aid Post has been established. Officer Commanding saw G.O.C. 184th INFANTRY BRIGADE who concurred in new arrangements.	Estu
-do-	MAY 4th.		Officer Commanding with CAPTAIN J.MANUEL.MC, visited all forward posts. D.D.M.S. XIth CORPS and A.D.M.S. 61st DIVISION visited and inspected M.D.S. All R.M.O's of 184th INFANTRY BRIGADE seen and told of new evacuation system.	Estu
-do-	MAY 5th.		Officer Commanding visited A.D.S. and accompanied A.D.M.S. 61st DIVISION on a tour of inspection of all the Ambulance posts. Protection and defences of various posts improved.	Estu
-do-	MAY 6th.		Officer Commanding visited forward area. A.D.M.S. 61st DIVISION visited and inspected M.D.S. Evacuation of wounded very unsatisfactory owing to the sudden withdrawal of all M.A.C. Cars which had hitherto been stationed at our A.D.S's.	Estu
-do-	MAY 7th.		Officer Commanding visited all forward posts and R.A.P's of 184th INFANTRY BRIGADE. A.D.M.S. 61st DIVISION visited and inspected M.D.S. Officer Commanding attended conference at office of A.D.M.S. 61st DIVISION. Officer Commanding visited Headquarters, 184th INFANTRY BRIGADE and discussed possible preventive measures against Trench Foot.	Estu

Army Form C. 2118.

WAR DIARY
or
INTELLIGENCE SUMMARY

REFERENCE. MAP. SHEET. 36a.

(Erase heading not required.)

Instructions regarding War Diaries and Intelligence Summaries are contained in F. S. Regs., Part II. and the Staff Manual respectively. Title Pages will be prepared in manuscript.

Place	Date 1918.	Hour	Summary of Events and Information	Remarks and references to Appendices
BERGUETTE. O.16.c.7.8.	MAY 8th.		M.D.S. very quiet. Officer Commanding visited A.D.S. and fell forward posts during morning. Activity on front confined to desultory shelling.	Eely
-do-	MAY 9th.		Officer Commanding attended conference at office of A.D.M.S. 61st DIVISION and received information regarding possibility of big German attack on adjacent front. Officer Commanding visited HEADQUARTERS, 184th INFANTRY BRIGADE and saw G.O.C. to discuss necessary arrangements to meet all contingencies. Officer Commanding handed over BUSNES CHATEAU to a CANADIAN FIELD AMBULANCE and explained system of evacuation to them in detail. Officer Commanding visited A.D.S. in evening re the German attack. Extra bearers sent forward - Advanced Gas Centre and M.D.S. made ready to deal with large number of wounded. No attack developed.	Eely
-do-	MAY 10th.		Officer Commanding visited all forward posts. A.D.M.S. 61st DIVISION visited and inspected premises. CAPTAIN J.MANUEL.MC awarded BAR to MILITARY CROSS. M2/167834, DRIVER W.BUTCHER, M.T., A.S.C. attached to this Unit awarded DISTINGUISHED CONDUCT MEDAL. Authority for these awards:- D.R.O. 1747 dated 10.5.1918.	Eely
-do-	MAY 11th.		A.D.M.S. 61st DIVISION visited and inspected M.D.S. Officer Commanding visited all forward posts. Sector very quiet - Emergency forward arrangements cancelled and extra bearers returned to Headquarters. Protective trench for defence against shelling or bombing raids completed at A.D.S.	Eely
-do-	MAY 12th.		Officer Commanding visited forward area. Whole sector very quiet - few casualties coming in. Reconstruction of Dispensary and Medical Inspection room at M.D.S. begun. Arrangements made to develop new system of latrines with immediate incineration of all refuse.	Eely
-do-	MAY 13th.		M.D.S. and A.D.S. inspected by D.M.S., 1st ARMY. Captain J.B.MACDONALD.R.A.M.C. proceeded to take temporary command of 57 Sanitary Section.(Auth: A.D.MMS.374/1096). Notification received that the 2/4th OXFORD & BUCKS LIGHT INFANTRY, 61st DIVISION would raid the enemy lines at 11.55 p.m. Extra bearers sent forward and the usual emergency arrangements carried out in case a large number of casualties required evacuating.	Eely

Army Form C. 2118.

WAR DIARY
or
INTELLIGENCE SUMMARY

MAP REFERENCE. SHEET 36a.

(Erase heading not required.)

Instructions regarding War Diaries and Intelligence Summaries are contained in F.S. Regs., Part II. and the Staff Manual respectively. Title Pages will be prepared in manuscript.

Place	Date 1918.	Hour	Summary of Events and Information	Remarks and references to Appendices
BERGUETTE. O.16.c.7.8.	MAY 14th.		Officer Commanding visited A.D.S. and Car Loading posts and HEADQUARTERS, 184th INFANTRY BRIGADE. Raid made by 2/4th O.B.L.I. entirely successful - 2 unwounded prisoners captured and no casualties caused to the raiding party. Extra bearers withdrawn from line. Alternative route of evacuation through HAMET BILLET and across CANAL at O.12.c.8.5. reconnoitred.	Colu
-do-	MAY 15th.		Officer Commanding visited Headquarters, 61st DIVISION, Headquarters, 184th INFANTRY BRIGADE and all forward posts. Concentrated area shoot by the enemy on area of CANAL BRIDGE at P.27.b.3.5. and Headquarters, 184th INFANTRY BRIGADE. 1 DAIMLER CAR damaged but no casualties to our personnel. Shrapnel over Hospital at M.D.S. during afternoon.	Colu
-do-	MAY 16th.		Position of car at Headquarters, 184th INFANTRY BRIGADE altered - It has been sent back to Farm at P.27.c.8.9. from where it can be called up to Brigade Headquarters by telephone.	Colu
-do-	MAY 17th.		A.D.M.S. 61st DIVISION visited and inspected premises. Officer Commanding visited Headquarters 184th INFANTRY BRIGADE and Ambulance forward posts and found all correct.	Colu
-do-	MAY 18th.		A.D.M.S. 61st DIVISION visited and inspected A.D.S. and M.D.S. A.D.S. shelled during day.	Colu
-do-	MAY 19th.		Officer Commanding visited all posts and Headquarters, 184th INFANTRY BRIGADE. A.D.S., GUARBECQUE and neighbourhood shelled again this morning by H.V.Gun - no casualties to personnel. Application to C.R.E. 61st DIVISION for a Steel Shelter as an emergency Dressing Room met with reply that none are available at present. New pattern of portable Meat safe constructed and brought into use in the Quartermasters Stores. In order to train 12 men of No 2, Special Coy: R.E. a Course of Instruction in First Aid commenced today at this M.D.S.	
-do-	MAY 20th.		Station at BERGUETTE heavily shelled - no military casualties. Small Splinter-proof shelter ready at A.D.S. for use as and shelter during shelling. In case of heavy shelling of GUARBECQUE VILLAGE an alternative A.D.S. is being opened in BUSNES VILLAGE with 3 alternative routes to M.D.S. all, of which were reconnoitred by O.C. Best one marked by arrows via BUSNES CHATEAU and CORNET BRASSARD.	Colu

Army Form C. 2118.

MAP REFERENCE SHEET 36a.

WAR DIARY
or
INTELLIGENCE SUMMARY

(Erase heading not required.)

Instructions regarding War Diaries and Intelligence Summaries are contained in F. S. Regs., Part II. and the Staff Manual respectively. Title Pages will be prepared in manuscript.

Place	Date 1918	Hour	Summary of Events and Information	Remarks and references to Appendices
BERGUETTE. O.16.c.7.8.	MAY 21st.		In connection with an extension of the 184th INFANTRY BRIGADE FRONT the Officer Commanding visited all posts and arranged evacuation routes. 4 extra Stretcher Bearers sent to M.O. of the 2/5th GLOSTERS. Personnel at RELAY POST to be increased. Officer Commanding picked out suitable sites for Ambulance posts in case this M.D.S. and adjacent railway crossings (which have all been registered by the enemy) should at any time become unhealthy. CAPTAIN J.P.O'CONNOR.R.A.M.G.(TC) struck off strength of Unit on transfer to C.C.S., Sick.	Early
-do-	MAY 22nd.		A.D.M.S. 61st DIVISION visited and inspected Hospital. Officer Commanding visited all Ambulance posts. Permanent signs put up on new routes of evacuation. Rearrangement and extension of 184th INFANTRY BRIGADE FRONT and consequent Ambulance personnel alterations carried out this evening.	Early
-do-	MAY 23rd.		Officer Commanding visited all posts and found them much improved. Alterations at BUSNES and at A.D.S., GUARBECQUE continued. Sanitation of BERGUETTE inspected today by CAPTAIN A.P.THOMSON.MC. as ordered by A.D.M.S. Horse Lines of 61st D.A.C. near BERGUETTE STATION shelled this morning. Some casualties collected.	Early
-do-	MAY 24th.		Bad weather interfered with constructional work. More long range shelling of GUARBECQUE and LA PIERRIERE. New system of latrines completed, which admit of immediate incineration by each man of his own excrement. Further sanitary improvements and shelter trenches begun in and around the Camp.	Early
-do-	MAY 25th.		Officer Commanding visited all Ambulance forward posts. Constructional work continued and protective measures at various posts being perfected.	Early
-do-	MAY 26th.		BUSNES POST now ready for occupation. New sanitary system finished and working well. A.D.M.S. 61st DIVISION visited and inspected. New Cookhouse built in the adjacent Railway Engineers Camp which we have taken over from today.	Early
-do-	MAY 27th.		A.D.M.S. 61st DIVISION visited and inspected premises. Officer Commanding visited all forward Ambulance posts.	Early

Army Form C. 2118.

WAR DIARY
or
INTELLIGENCE SUMMARY

MAP REFERENCE.. SHEET 36a.

(Erase heading not required.)

Instructions regarding War Diaries and Intelligence Summaries are contained in F. S. Regs., Part II. and the Staff Manual respectively. Title Pages will be prepared in manuscript.

Place	Date 1918.	Hour	Summary of Events and Information	Remarks and references to Appendices
BERGUETTE. O.16.c.7.8.	MAY 28th.		Officer Commanding visited A.D.S., GUARBECQUE. Some long range shelling of ammunition dumps along the alternative route of evacuation by CORNET BRASSARD.	Fola
-do-	MAY 29th.		Officer Commanding visited forward area. CAPTAIN E.F.O'CONNOR warned to proceed to Headquarters 61st DIVISION on 30th inst, to act as D.A.D.M.S. while CAPTAIN W.VICTOR CORBETT.R.A.M.C. is on leave. An Officer from the 2/2nd FIELD AMBUDANCE, CCAPTAIN A.C.JEPSON.R.A.M.C. attached for temporary duty. CAPTAIN C.T.NEVE.R.A.M.C. with 2 N.C.O's proceeded to No:1,C.C.S. ELNES to attend course of instruction at the First Army R.A.M.C. School. On arrival he was informed that the Course was cancelled and so he returned to these Headquarters.	Fola
-do-	MAY 30th.		Officer Commanding visited forward area. CAPTAIN E.F.O'CONNOR.R.A.M.C. proceeded in accordance with above orders.	Fola
-do-	MAY 31st.		Officer Commanding visited forward area and Headquarters, 61st DIVISION.	

G.Eturacki.
Lieut Colonel:R.A.M.C.T.
Commanding. 2/1st South Midland Field Ambulance.

31st MAY, 1918.

16

MEDICAL.
Vol 26
140/30 %.

June 1918

CONFIDENTIAL.

WAR DIARY
of
2/1st SOUTH MIDLAND FIELD AMBULANCE.
61st DIVISION.
from
1 - 6 - 1918 to 30 - 6 - 1918.

VOLUME 6.

BOOK 4.

-o-o-o-o-o-o-o-o-o-o-o-o-o-o-o-o-o-o-o-o-o-o-o-

COMMITTEE FOR THE
MEDICAL HISTORY OF THE WAR
Date 7 AUG 1918

Army Form C. 2118.

WAR DIARY
or
INTELLIGENCE SUMMARY

(Erase heading not required.)

MAP REFERENCE. SHEET. 36 a.

Instructions regarding War Diaries and Intelligence Summaries are contained in F. S. Regs., Part II. and the Staff Manual respectively. Title Pages will be prepared in manuscript.

Place	Date 1918.	Hour	Summary of Events and Information	Remarks and references to Appendices
BERGUETTE.	JUNE 1st.		Forward posts visited. Construction of Splinter proof shelter at GUARBECQUE continued. Sanitation of camp and area inspected and improved.	
—do—	JUNE 2nd.		Routine work. Cookhouse at BERGUETTE completed. All forward posts visited.	
—do—	JUNE 3rd.		All forward posts inspected by the Officer Commanding.	
—do—	JUNE 4ht.		Routine work.	
—do—	JUNE 5ht.		Routine work. A.D.M.S. 61st Division visited and inspected camp and premises.	
—do—	JUNE 6th.		Routine work at BERGUETTE. All Ambulance posts visited.	
—do—	JUNE 7th.		Officer Commanding gave lecture on Sanitation to the Officers of 2/5th GLOUCESTER REGIMENT at LA PIERRIERE. Steel Shelter collected for erection at GUARBECQUE. It was found that this was just too large for inclosing in a brick building in which it had been proposed to erect it so it was decided to transfer it to BUSNES VILLAGE post and fix it inside the house there where suitably protected it would make an admirable alternative A.D.S. on another route of evacuation.	
—do—	JUNE 8th.		Steel Shelter erected at BUSNES and sandbagging begun. A.A.& Q.M.G. 61st Division visited and inspected premises. Visit of Divisional Educational Officer to explain the scheme for providing men with facilities for special and general education during the ensuing winter months.	
—do—	JUNE 9th.		Wooden splinter proof shelter made of Sleepers commenced at GUARBECQUE in place of the proposed steel shelter.	
—do—	JUNE 10th.		CAPTAIN A.P.THOMSON.MC,R.A.M.C.T. visited lES AMUSOIRES, Headquarters 2/4th OXFORD & BUCKS LIGHT INFANTRY to see a series of cases apparently infectious. Disinfection of Battalion, Headquarters, the billet principally affected, arranged to be carried out before arrival of the 2/5th GLOUCESTER REGIMENT who are to relieve this Battalion. Isolation tents arranged at LA PIERRIERE for contacts.	

Army Form C. 2118.

WAR DIARY
or
INTELLIGENCE SUMMARY
(Erase heading not required.)

MAP REFERENCE.
SHEET 36a.

Place	Date 1918.	Hour	Summary of Events and Information	Remarks and references to Appendices
BERGUETTE.	JUNE	11th.	A.A.& Q.M.G. 61st Division with A.A.& Q.M.G., XIth CORPS visited and inspected M.D.S. and A.D.S. Officer Commanding and CAPTAIN A.P.THOMSON.MC, with CAPTAIN DILL,R.A.M.C(Bacteriologist) visited Headquarters, 2/4th OXFORD & BUCKS LIGHT INFANTRY in order to investigate the nature of disease whereby a large number of all ranks, Officers and men, have suddenly become "sick" while in the line. The symptoms seem to point to infection of an Influenzal type - onset very sudden and infectivity apparently very great. A considerable number of personnel of the Ambulance who have been working in the line also affected.	Evts.
-do-	JUNE	12th.	Officer Commanding visited all forward posts & calling at Headquarters,306 Brigade R.F.A., on return. Rebuilding of Relay Post behind LES AMUSOIRES decided upon and a beginning made to collect material for this purpose.	Evts.
-do-	JUNE	13th.	Officer Commanding went with A.D.M.S. 61st Division to inspect Billets of the 2/4th OXFORD & BUCKS LIGHT INFANTRY at LA PIERRIERE in connection with the prevalent epidemic of Influenzal type of P.U.O. He then visited Officer Commanding, 66 Sanitary Section, HAM en ARTOIS about the same matter.	Evts.
-do-	JUNE	14th.	Forward posts of Ambulance visited and inspected. CAPTAIN C.T.NEVE.R.A.M.C. proceeded to 2/4th OXFORD & BUCKS LIGHT INFANTRY for temporary duty as Medical Officer, the Regimental Medical Officer having contracted the "Three day fever."	Evts.
-do-	JUNE	15th.	Officer Commanding visited A.D.M.S. 61st DIVISION and received instructions that the Unit was to take over the XI CORPS REST STATION and OFFICERS REST STATION from 14 Field Ambulance, 5th DIVISION on the 16th inst. He proceeded to the site of the XIth Corps Rest Station and interviewed Officer Commanding, 14 Field Ambulance reference the taking over.	Evts.
-do-	JUNE	16th.	Advance party proceeded to XIth C.R.S. to take over from 14 Field Ambulance. Officers visited O.C.,XIth Corps Rest Station and made all final arrangements as to the details of the relief. LIEUT & Q.MASTER W.S.RIVERS.R.A.M.C.T. interviewed the Quartermaster,14 Field Ambulance and checked all inventories preparatory to taking over. Observation Balloon at GUARBECQUE fired by enemy aeroplane. Piece of the Burning Balloon set the Walking Wounded Tent on fire. Very slight damage. O.C., 2/3rd S.M.F.AMBULANCE visited Headquarters and made preliminary arrangements about taking over our premises and sector. Forward posts visited & necessary personnel arranged to relieve our forward men by 5.0 pm. CAPTAIN A.P.THOMSON.MC,R.A.M.C.T. evacuated sick (P.U.O) to 39 STATIONARY HOSPITAL,AIRE.	Evts.

2449 Wt. W14957/Mgo 750,000 1/16 J.B.C. & A. Forms/C.2118/12.

Army Form C. 2118.

WAR DIARY
or
INTELLIGENCE SUMMARY

(Erase heading not required.)

MAP REFERENCE.
SHEET 36a.

Instructions regarding War Diaries and Intelligence Summaries are contained in F.S. Regs., Part II. and the Staff Manual respectively. Title Pages will be prepared in manuscript.

Place	Date 1918	Hour	Summary of Events and Information	Remarks and references to Appendices
BERGUETTE & LIGNE.	JUNE 17th.		Remainder of Unit proceeded to XIth CORPS REST STATION. M.D.S., BERGUETTE, A.D.S., GUARBECQUE and all Ambulance posts handed over to the 2/3rd SOUTH MIDLAND FIELD AMBULANCE. General inspection of all patients and premises at XIth CORPS REST STATION. State of Patients taken over.-(Sick...337. State of Officers Rest Station., 7 Officers Sick (Wounded. 16. Officer Commanding and LIEUT W.S. RIVERS.R.A.M.C.T. visited Headquarters, 61st DIVISION and Officer Commanding, 61st Divisional Train, A.S.C. to arrange the future rationing of Unit.	Copies
LIGNE. G.10.b.98.	JUNE 18th.		D.D.M.S., XIth CORPS visited Camp. Suggestions for new Bath house and alterations to Cook house submitted and approved - work begun at once. Site of Ablution House changed - 12 Marquees received to increase accomodation. Sports Field inspected and the following amusements Flower beds at entrance to camp begun. arranged for the patients:- (Margin)	Copies List 1.
-do-	JUNE 19th.		Alterations to Cookhouse and dining hall well in hand - tables and forms being made rapidly. Water supply system for whole of camp reorganised. Reception and storage tanks altered - pipe line commenced - site fixed for new ablution house and tank fixed temporarily. Reorganisation made of system of admission and discharge of patients and bathing routine altered in the endeavour to ensure that all patients in the place are free from lice. Amusement programme arranged for the following week. Ornamental garden begun in front of camp.	Copies
-do-	JUNE 20th.		C.R.E., XIth CORPS TROOPS, A.D.O.S., XIth CORPS and D.A.D.M.S., XIth CORPS called re equipment of patients going out on discharge. Water supply developing - tanks all in position and pipes being laid. Dining Hall in use for the first time. Discharge tents pitched and occupied. Site arranged for the pitching of admission tents. Band performance during afternoon by the band of the 2/4th OXFORD & BUCKS LIGHT INFANTRY. Cinema entertainments begun, No: 2 Cinema having reported here for four days.	Copies
-do-	JUNE 21st.		Reorganisation and rebuilding of cookhouse begun. Ground prepared for new practice cricket pitch. Rebuilding of latrines and alterations of water supply definitely fixed. Band performance during the afternoon and Cinema show in the evening. Rebuilding of dining hall with tables and forms completed. Fitting of a new serving room for meals.	Copies

AMUSEMENTS FOR PATIENTS AT XIth CORPS REST STATION.

DAILY.   CRICKET.
                  QUOITS.
                  BADMINTON?
                  FOOTBALL etc.

THURSDAY AFTERNOON. 20-6-1918.   Band performance.
    "   Evening.   "   Cinema performance.

FRIDAY AFTERNOON. 21-6-1918.   Band performance.
    "   EVENING.   "   Cinema performance.

SATURDAY AFTERNOON. 22-6-1918.   Cinema performance.
    "   EVENING.   "   Cinema performance.

SUNDAY AFTERNOON. 23-6-1918.   Cinema performance.
    "   EVENING.   "   Cinema performance.

MONDAY EVENING.   24-6-1918.   Concert by PRISMATICS.

WEDNESDAY AFTERNOON. 26-6-1918.   Sports.
    "   EVENING.   "   Concert by PRISMATICS.

FRIDAY EVENING.   28-6-1918.   Impromptu concert by patients.

SATURDAY AFTERNOON &
         EVENING.   29-6-1918.   Sports.

Army Form C. 2118.

WAR DIARY
or
INTELLIGENCE SUMMARY

(Erase heading not required.)

MAP REFERENCE.
SHEET 36a.

Place	Date 1918	Hour	Summary of Events and Information	Remarks and references to Appendices
G.10.b.9.8	JUNE 22nd.		Patients had their meals in the new Dining Hall for the first time. New scheme worked well and quickly. Construction of a "Washing Up" pla annexe to the dining hall begun.	Esta
-do-	JUNE 23rd.		Construction work proceeding rapidly. New oven completed. Gardening operations extended. Deputy Chaplain General, XIth CORPS held a service in the dining hall. Cinematograph performance afternoon and evening.	Esta
-do-	JUNE 24th.		First bad weather since arrival. Steam bath boiler found defective and scrapped. Arrangements made to rebuild it on a larger scale. Roof of serving room completed. Concert during evening given by the "PRISMATICS" the Ambulance Pierrot Troupe. Preliminary request sent in for a large new oven to cook for practically the whole of the patients at one time.	Esta
-do-	JUNE 25th.		Further alterations made to Hospital cookhouse to enable larger numbers of patients to be catered for and served. New cricket pitch designed and begun. Gardening operations to improve the entrance to the camp continued.	Esta
-do-	JUNE 26th.		Routine work.	Esta
-do-	JUNE 27th.		Constructional work held up for lack of materials. Notification received from A.D.M.S. 61st Division that CAPTAIN A.P.THOMSON.R.A.M.C.T. had been gazetted Acting Major while in Command of a Section of a Field Ambulance. This to date back to 10.4.1918.	Esta
-do-	JUNE 28th.		Ablution bench moved to a new site in the camp and a Marquee erected over it pending arrival of material to build a proper shed. New type of oven built for cooking for personnel. Alterations to stores and cookhouse at Hospital continued. Impromptu concert given in the Dining Hall by the patients. Arrangements made for sports to be held on Saturday afternoon.	Esta
-do-	JUNE 29th.		Constructional work continued at XIth Corps Rest Station. Sports held for the patients during afternoon and evening. Programme attached. D.D.M.S. and D.A.D.M.S., XIth CORPS, A.D.M.S. 61st DIVISION, A.A.&Q.M.G. 61st DIVISION attended with MAJOR GENERAL DUNCAN.C.M.G. D.S.O., General Officer Commanding, 61st DIVISION who distributed the prizes. CAPTAIN E.F.O'CONNOR.R.A.M.C. proceeded for temporary duty to the 61st Divl. P.U.O. Detention Camp, under instructions received from A.D.M.S. 61st Division.	Esta

Army Form C. 2118.

WAR DIARY
or
INTELLIGENCE SUMMARY.

MAP REFERENCE.
SHEET:- 36a.

(Erase heading not required.)

Instructions regarding War Diaries and Intelligence Summaries are contained in F. S. Regs., Part II. and the Staff Manual respectively. Title pages will be prepared in manuscript.

Place	Date	Hour	Summary of Events and Information	Remarks and references to Appendices
LIGNE G.10.b.9.8.	1918 JUNE 30th.		Routine work. General cleaning up of Hospital and grounds. Un-denominational Church Service held at 11.0 a.m. for personnel and patients. All Small Box Respirators, Iron Rations, Steel Helmets etc inspected. Small Box Respirator Drill carried out by Unit Gas N.C.O's. Medical Inspection of personnel.	Mackie

Mackie.
Lieut Col: R.A.M.C.T.
O.C. 2/1st SOUTH MIDLAND FIELD AMBULANCE.

30/6/1918.

CONFIDENTIAL.

WAR DIARY
of
2/1st SOUTH MIDLAND FIELD AMBULANCE.
from
1st JULY, 1918   to   31st JULY, 1918.

BOOK 4.

VOLUME 7.

Army Form C. 2118.

WAR DIARY
or
INTELLIGENCE SUMMARY.

(*Erase heading not required.*)

MAP REFERENCE: SHEET 36a.

Instructions regarding War Diaries and Intelligence Summaries are contained in F. S. Regs., Part II. and the Staff Manual respectively. Title pages will be prepared in manuscript.

Place	Date	Hour	Summary of Events and Information	Remarks and references to Appendices
G.10.b.8.8.	JULY 1st.		LIEUTENANT GENERAL SIR R.C.B.HAKING, K.C.B., K.C.M.G., COMMANDING X1th CORPS visited and inspected the whole of the Hospital and grounds. Extensions of Cookhouse and alterations Cinema performance for patients in the evening. Extensions of new Quartermasters Stores to fit them for occupation, proceeding.	Copy
-do-	JULY 2nd.		Routine work. Extensions of and alterations to cookhouse so far advanced that the Quartermasters Stores moved up to the camp from the village. D.A.D.M.S. and D.A.C.G., X1th Corps visited camp. Cricket match for patients on sports ground during afternoon and Cinema Show in the evening.	Copy
-do-	JULY 3rd.		Routine work. Constructional work continued. Band performance in the hospital grounds during the afternoon and Cinema performance during evening.	Copy
-do-	JULY 4th.		Routine work. Cinema shows afternoon and evening. Internal fitting of the Quartermasters Stores completed. New meat safe erected.	Copy
-do-	JULY 5th.		Routine work. Cinema performances afternoon and evening.	Copy
-do-	JULY 6th.		Routine work; D.D.M.S., X1th CORPS visited and working.	Copy
-do-	JULY 7th.		Routine work. D.A.Q.M.G., 61st Division visited and inspected camp. Arrangements completed for a visit of "THE FROLICS" - 61st Divisional Concert party - to entertain the patients.	Copy
-do-	JULY 8th.		D.A.D.M.S. 61st Division visited hospital. Another new oven completed in the cookhouse. Concreting of the floor begun. 2 large Marquees pitched at entrance to camp to accomodate all admissions until such time as they are allotted to their proper sections in the camp.	Copy

Army Form C. 2118.

WAR DIARY
or
INTELLIGENCE SUMMARY.

(Erase heading not required.)

MAP REFERENCE: SHEET 36a.

Instructions regarding War Diaries and Intelligence Summaries are contained in F. S. Regs., Part II. and the Staff Manual respectively. Title pages will be prepared in manuscript.

Place	Date 1918.	Hour	Summary of Events and Information	Remarks and references to Appendices
G.10.b.8.8.	JULY 9th.		Water supply system extension begun. Completion of alterations to cookhouse and flooring with concrete. Concert for patients during evening. Warning order of 61st Division received. Officer Commanding visited D.D.M.S., XIth CORPS and ascertained that this Unit was to remain at the XIth CORPS REST STATION for the present.	Early
–do–	JULY 10th.		Washing up house for Dining Hall and Kitchen completed. Construction of Bath house near Brewery proceeding. Water supply of camp reorganised. Sports during afternoon and evening on sports ground. 5th Divisional Band attended.	Early
–do–	JULY 11th.		Routine work. Impromptu concert for patients.	Early
–do–	JULY 12th.		Routine work.	Early
–do–	JULY 13th.		Routine work. Constructional work continued at the Baths near brewery. Sports held in the afternoon attended by Band from 184th Infantry Brigade, 61st Division. Concert in the evening by the PRISMATICS, the Unit Concert Party.	Early
–do–	JULY 14th.		Routine work. D.D.M.S., XIth Corps visited and inspected premises.	Early
–do–	JULY 15th.		Routine work. Impromptu Concert for patients during the evening.	Early
–do–	JULY 16th.		Routine work. Boxing Competition for patients and R.A.M.C. personnel.	Early
–do–	JULY 17th.		Routine work. MAJOR. GEORGE SCOTT-WILLIAMSON. R.A.M.C.T. reported back for duty from the 61st Division Detention P.U.O. Camp.	Early
–do–	JULY 18th.		Routine work. The Officer Commanding visited Headquarters, 61st DIVISION.	Early
–do–	JULY 19th.		Reconnaissance of 31st Division front and system of evacuation of that Division and 5th Div: made by the Officer Commanding with a view to being ready to follow and clear one Brigade of the 61st Division should emergency arise. Officer Commanding reported result of above to A.D.M.S., 61st DIVISION, at Divisional Headquarters.	Early

Army Form C. 2118.

WAR DIARY
or
INTELLIGENCE SUMMARY.

MAP REFERENCE SHEET. 36s.

(Erase heading not required.)

Place	Date 1918	Hour	Summary of Events and Information	Remarks and references to Appendices
G.16.b.8.8.	JULY 20th		Routine work. Sports for patients held during afternoon and evening.	Eufu
do & N.10. b&d.	JULY 21st		Orders received to hand over XIth CORPS REST STATION to 229 Field ambulance, 74th DIVISION. Unit personnel then to proceed to the billets vacated by that unit. D.D.M.S. XIth Corps visited O.C. unit personnel arrived LABRES 4.45.p.m. Usual notifications sent out.	Eufu
" do & B.3.a.3.4.	JULY 22nd		Orders received from A.D.M.S. 61st DIVISION that Unit was to proceed to a camp at PONT ASQUIN, B.3.a.3.4. Unit proceeded by march route arriving at destination at 1.0 p.m. Tents pitched for accomodation of personnel. A.D.M.S. 61st DIVISION visited camp.	Eufu
B.3.a.3.4.	JULY 23rd		Routine work. Cleaning of camp. Overhauling and cleaning of equipment. Officer Commanding visited A.D.M.S. 61 DIV: and then proceeded to forward area to make a reconnaissance of the new front from evacuation point of view.	Eufu
do	JULY 24th		Routine work. - Cleaning of waggons.	Eufu
do	JULY 25th		Routine work. Field training. Second reconnaissance by Officers, N.C.O's and men of the forward area of the AUSTRALIAN and 9th DIVISIONS.	Eufu
do	JULY 26th		Routine work. Field training and anti-gas work carried out by the whole unit working in sections. Congratulatory messages received from CORPS COMMANDER, XIth CORPS, DIVISIONAL COMMANDER, 61st DIVISION through A.D.M.S. 61st DIVISION, congratulating the whole unit on the work done in organising and running the XIth CORPS REST STATION.	Eufu
do	JULY 27th		MAJOR A.P. THOMSON.MC, with a party of other ranks carried out a reconnaissance of the 184 INFANTRY BRIGADE FRONT.	Eufu
do	JULY 28th		Officer Commanding visited Headquarters, 61st DIVISION. Field training - rescuing of wounded under gas precautions. Motor and Horse transport Sections also working in Box respirators.	Eufu
do	JULY 29th		Routine work. Party of Officers and other ranks sent to explore forward area of the XVth CORPS and to familiarise themselves with the evacuation routes. 184th INFANTRY BRIGADE DEFENCE SCHEME gone into in detail on the spot.	Eufu

Army Form C. 2118.

WAR DIARY
or
INTELLIGENCE SUMMARY.

MAP REFERENCE SHEET 36a.

(Erase heading not required.)

Instructions regarding War Diaries and Intelligence Summaries are contained in F. S. Regs., Part II. and the Staff Manual respectively. Title pages will be prepared in manuscript.

Place	Date	Hour	Summary of Events and Information	Remarks and references to Appendices
	1918.			
B3. 2.3.4.	JULY 30th.		Routine work. Orders received from A.D.M.S. 61st Division that reconnaissance of XVth CORPS area was to cease and the unit hold itself in readiness to move back to XIth CORPS area at midnight 31st July / 1st August. Officer Commanding visited A.D.M.S. 61st DIVISION at Divisional Headquarters re the impending move.	Colr.
do	JULY 31st.		Loading of all waggons. Striking of Canvas. Cleaning of Camp etc. Orders received from Headquarters, 184th INFANTRY BRIGADE that unit was to proceed by march route to BOURECQ, passing Starting point at 10.20 p.m.	Colr.

G.E.Mackie

Lieutenant Colonel: R.A.M.C.T.
COMMANDING: 2/1st SOUTH MIDLAND FIELD AMBULANCE.

CONFIDENTIAL.

WAR DIARY

of

2/1st SOUTH MIDLAND FIELD AMBULANCE.

61st DIVISION.

from 1st AUGUST, 1918 to 31st AUGUST, 1918.

VOLUME 4.

BOOK 8.

Army Form C. 2118.

WAR DIARY
or
INTELLIGENCE SUMMARY.

MAP REFERENCE: SHEET 36a.

(Erase heading not required.)

Instructions regarding War Diaries and Intelligence Summaries are contained in F.S. Regs., Part II. and the Staff Manual respectively. Title pages will be prepared in manuscript.

Place	Date 1918.	Hour	Summary of Events and Information	Remarks and references to Appendices
U.1.a.7.8.	AUG: 1st		Unit completed march from B.3.a.3.4. and arrived BOURECQ, U.1.a.7.8. at 3.30 a.m. Usual notifications sent out. Hospital for Brigade sick and Scabies Centre for 61st DIVISION opened. 2 Operating tents, 1 Hospital Marquee and a number of bell tents pitched for the accomodation of patients. Preliminary arrangements made for building a new form of delousing chamber to cope with the whole of the Brigade clothing and equipment.	G.E.Mr.
—do—	AUG: 2nd.		Routine work. Bricks purchased for construction of Bath house at 61st Div : Scabies Centre Officer Commanding visited Headquarters, 61st DIVISION.	Fester. Fester.
—do—	AUG: 3rd.		Routine work. Constructional work suspended on receipt of warning that the Division might be moved.	G.E.Mr.
—do—	AUG: 4th.		Unit received orders to send and advance party to the MAIN DRESSING STATION, 5th DIVISION, preparatory to taking over that M.D.S., on the morning of the 5th inst. MAJOR A.P. THOMSON.MC, R.A.M.C.T. with small party of N.C.O's and men proceeded in accordance with that order. Officer Commanding visited O.C., 13 Field Ambulance, 5th Division and inspected new camp.	Fester.
—do— & 1.17.c.5.1.	AUG: 5th.		Unit arrived at M.D.S. 5th DIVISION at 11.0 a.m. taking over as from 12.0 noon. A.D.M.S., 61st DIVISION, notified that relief was complete at 12.0 noon. A party of 1 N.C.O and 12 men detailed to act as GAS PICQUET on the VIA ROMA in the FOREST of NIEPPE.	Fester.
—do—	AUG: 6th.		A.D.M.S., 61st DIVISION visited and inspected this Main Dressing Station and instructed the Officer Commanding to attend a Conference at Divisional Headquarters at 5.30 p.m. on the 7th inst. Officers and party of N.C.O's and men of this unit carried out a reconnaissance of the forward area so as to be familiar with all evacuation routes in the event of a forward move of the Division. Casualties in Unit personnel (Gas picquet) during night 5/6th:- 435304, PRIVATE W.BECK, KILLED IN ACTION. 435354, PRIVATE L.BEECH., Wounded. Shrapnel wound Thigh (R) and severe Concussion.	Fester.

WAR DIARY
or
INTELLIGENCE SUMMARY.

(Erase heading not required.)

Army Form C. 2118.

MAP REFERENCE: SHEET 36a.

Place	Date 1918.	Hour	Summary of Events and Information	Remarks and references to Appendices
I.17.c.5.1.	AUG: 7th.		PRIVATE BECK, buried in THIENNES MILITARY CEMETERY, (I.23.a.4.8.). Reconstruction of M.D.S., begun. Walking Wounded Collecting Post at TANNAY, I.30.c.7.4. inspected with a view to its being developed into an alternative M.D.S., as it seems probable that if the enemy retires on this front the main road THIENNES- TANNAY-HAVERSKERQUE- LE SART - MERVILLE will become the main evacuation route. MAJOR A.P.THOMSON,MC, R.A.M.C.T. and LIEUT NEARY, M.O.R.C., U.S.A., detailed for duty there with special instructions as to the immediate development and expansion of the place.	G.M.
-do-	AUG: 8th.		Routine work. Many gassed and wounded cases passed through this M.D.S., consequent upon slight advance by 74th and 61st Divisions. D.D.M.S., XIth CORPS visited and Constructional work at M.D.S. and at TANNAY continued. inspected premises.	Foster
-do-	AUG: 9th.		A.D.M.S., 61st DIVISION with Consulting Physician, Fifth Army, visited and inspected this Main Dressing Station. Officer Commanding visited Headquarters, 61st Division. 2 Brigades of this Division attacked the enemy in the region of PLATE BECQUE and crossed forming bridge heads on eastern bank - subsequently being counter attacked by the enemy in force - retired to western bank.	Foster
-do-	AUG: 10th.		A.D.M.S., 61st DIVISION visited and inspected. Steady stream of wounded arrived here throughout night and morning. Evacuation was chiefly by light railway from the FOREST A.D.S., so that TANNAY POST was not utilised to any extent.	Foster
-do-	AUG: 11th.		Routine work - Construction and alterations proceeding. Buffet enlarged and linked up to the Dressing Hut. Paths altered and improved.	Foster
-do-	AUG:12th.		Routine work. D.D.M.S., XIth CORPS, visited and inspected this camp.	Foster
-do-	AUG: 13th.		A.D.M.S., and A.A.&.Q.M.G., 61st DIVISION visited and inspected camp. LIEUT G.W.GROVE, M.O.R.C., U.S.A., reported for duty. 17159, T/S.M. G.JONES,R.A.M.C. having proceeded to ENGLAND for Tour of Duty at Home, 475107, T/S.M. W.F.A.WAY.R.A.M.C.T., took over duties as Sergeant Major of this Unit.	G.M.

Army Form C. 2118.

WAR DIARY
or
INTELLIGENCE SUMMARY.
(Erase heading not required.)

MAP REFERENCE: SHEET 36a.

Instructions regarding War Diaries and Intelligence Summaries are contained in F.S. Regs., Part II. and the Staff Manual respectively. Title pages will be prepared in manuscript.

Place	Date 1918.	Hour	Summary of Events and Information	Remarks and references to Appendices
L.17.c.5.1.	AUGUST 14th.		Routine work. A.D.M.S., 61st DIVISION visited and inspected Camp.	
-do-	AUG: 15th.		Routine work. G.O.C., 61st DIVISION visited and inspected camp. It was suggested to him that a valuable precaution for the winter would be connecting up our new Main Dressing Station at TANNAY with the existing Decauville railway system.	
-do-	AUG: 16th.		Routine work. Reconnaissance of all forward posts carried out by CAPTAIN J. MANUEL, MC and SERGEANT MAJOR WAY, R.A.M.C. A.A. & Q.M.G., 61st DIVISION visited and inspected camp. Officer Commanding visited HEADQUARTERS, 61st DIVISION.	
-do-	AUG: 17th.		Routine work. Constructional work at this M.D.S. and at TANNAY continued. NISSEN HUT drawn for use as a GAS ward in order to keep all GASSED CASES apart from other wounded.	
-do-	AUG: 18th.		Routine work. LIEUT COL: GEORGE MACKIE, D.S.O., R.A.M.C.T. having proceeded on leave of absence to the United Kingdom, MAJOR GEORGE SCOTT-WILLIAMSON, R.A.M.C.T., assumed command of this Unit.	
-do-	AUG: 19th.		Routine work. Preparation of site for new Nissen Hut commenced.	
-do-	AUG: 20th.		Routine work. A.D.M.S., 61st DIVISION visited and inspected Camp. Constructional work at TANNAY continued.	
-do-	AUG: 21st.		Routine work. XIth CORPS Chemical Adviser visited Hospital re Gassed Cases.	
-do-	AUG: 22nd.		Routine work. "Many Gassed" cases and wounded cases treated at this M.D.S. and at TANNAY consequent upon advance made by 61st DIV. Advanced Dressing Stations moved forward. A.D.M.S., 61st DIVISION with D.A.D.M.S., 61st DIVISION visited and inspected Camp.	
-do-	AUG: 23rd.		Routine work. Steady stream of wounded and Gassed cases. Evacuation by Barge and Motor Ambulance Cars from M.D.S. to C.C.S.	

WAR DIARY MAP REFERENCE SHEET 36a.

or

INTELLIGENCE SUMMARY.

(Erase heading not required.)

Army Form C. 2118.

Instructions regarding War Diaries and Intelligence Summaries are contained in F. S. Regs., Part II. and the Staff Manual respectively. Title pages will be prepared in manuscript.

Place	Date 1918.	Hour	Summary of Events and Information	Remarks and references to Appendices
1.17.c.5.1. HAVERSKERQUE.	AUG: 24th.		Routine work. Preliminary arrangements made to move M.D.S. to the Brewery at HAVERSKERQUE. Officer Commanding inspected proposed site.	
do	AUG:25th.		Routine work. A.D.M.S. 61st DIVISION visited and inspected Camp and Hospital. Working party sent to HAVERSKERQUE to commence cleaning operations.	
do	AUG:26th.		Routine work. Notification received that D.M.S., Fifth Army proposed inspecting Field Ambulances of this Division.	
do	AUG:27th.		Routine work. A.D.M.S. 61st DIVISION visited and inspected Hospital.	
do	AUG:28th.		Routine work. D.M.S., Fifth Army accompanied by A.D.M.S., 61st DIVISION visited and inspected this M.D.S. and then proceeded to TANNAY.	
do	AUG:29th.		Routine work. A.D.M.S., 61st DIVISION visited and inspected Camp.	
do	AUG:30th.		Routine work. OFFICER COMMANDING proceeded to forward area.	
do	AUG:31st.		Routine work. MAJOR A.P.THOMSON,MC, R.A.M.C.T. attended conference at office of A.D.M.S. 61st DIVISION re the forward move of Main Dressing and Advanced Dressing Stations.	

31-8-1918.

Geo.S.Williamson

Major:R.A.M.C.T.

A/O.C., 2/1st SOUTH MIDLAND FIELD AMBULANCE:

MEDICAL

Vol 29
14/3239.

Book 4

21
5.10.18
98

CONFIDENTIAL

War Diary
of
2/1 S. Mid. Fd. Ambce

From 1.9.18 to 30.9.18.

Vol 9

WAR DIARY
or
INTELLIGENCE SUMMARY.
(Erase heading not required.)

Army Form C. 2118.

MAP REFERENCE. SHEET 36a & 36.

Place	Date 1918.	Hour	Summary of Events and Information	Remarks and references to Appendices
L.17.c.5.1.	SEPT 1st		Under instructions received, the personnel from TANNAY POST moved forward to MEREDITH Station and opened up M.D.S. there. Personnel from CANAL M.D.S. moved to same place during the afternoon. Bell tents, Marquees etc pitched at MEREDITH for the accomodation of both patients and personnel.	GNS
K.8.c.2.2.	SEPT 2nd.		Routine work and cleaning up of camp surroundings. MAJOR G.SCOTT WILLIAMSON.R.A.M.C.T. carried out reconnaissance of forward area with a view to choosing new site for M.D.S.	GNS
do & L.27.d.central	SEPT 3rd.		Owing to continued advance of the Division, this M.D.S. moved forward from MEREDITH to L.27.d.central - on Canal bank between MERVILLE and LA GORGUE. Tents and Marquees pitched onsite by the Canal for accomodation of patients, the personnel taking over old German billets.	GNS
do	SEPT 4th.		Routine work. Many casualties treated and evacuated to C.C.S. Wooden road from main road to entrance of canvas hospital commenced. This site was considered unsuitable for a M.D.S. for the following reasons:- 1. On account of the traffic routes. 2. Because the river lay between the M.D.S. and the troops engaged. 3. Because the bridges could not be relied upon.	GNS
do	SEPT 5th.		A.D.M.S., 61st DIVISION visited and inspected the camp and hospital. Reconnaissance of forward area carried out by MAJOR A.P.THOMSON.MC.R.A.M.C.T. and a temporary site for M.D.S. selected at G.26.a.2.2.(Sheet 36), presenting Ferro-Concrete shelter for 200 - 300 cases. Route of evacuation :- South of river along excellent roads. A.D.M.S., 61st DIVISION refused to sanction move of M.D.S. to this new site.	GNS
do & L.26.c.8.7.	SEPT 6th.		Camp surroundings heavily shelled during the night. Only one casualty among personnel. M.D.S. moved at 10.a.m. to L.26.c.8.7. CHAPELLE DUVELLE, taking over one large practically undamaged house. Canvas pitched as accomodation for personnel and for temporary use as M.D.S.	GNS
do	SEPT 7th.		Routine work. A.D.M.S., 61st DIVISION visited and inspected new site.	GNS

Army Form C. 2118.

WAR DIARY
or
INTELLIGENCE SUMMARY.

(Erase heading not required.)

MAP REFERENCE: SHEET 36a.

Instructions regarding War Diaries and Intelligence Summaries are contained in F. S. Regs., Part II. and the Staff Manual respectively. Title pages will be prepared in manuscript.

Place	Date 1918.	Hour	Summary of Events and Information	Remarks and references to Appendices
L.26.c.8.7.	SEPT 8th.		Routine work. Hospital Nissen Huts and Armstrong Huts brought from old M.D.S. to be erected here.	
do	SEPT 9th.		Thorough cleaning and searching of house selected for use as M.D.S. commenced. Roof entirely re-tiled. Very heavy rains hampered outdoor construction - also the fact that some 40 men had been sent away on detached duty.	
do	SEPT 10th.		Continuous heavy rains. Skeleton of 1st Nissen Hut erected and floor boards laid. 2 Armstrong Huts erected as accomodation for officers.	
do	SEPT 11th.		Houses in vicinity cleared up and made habitable as billets for the personnel. One Nissen Hut completed and erection of the second commenced. House used as M.D.S. for first time.	
do	SEPT 12th.		A.D.M.S. 61st DIVISION visited and inspected hospital. Wooden road laid between house and main road. Extension to house commenced and platform laid down from door of M.D.S. to the Car Stand to assist in the loading of patients.	
do	SEPT 13th.		Routine work. Rain still continuing. Constructional work continued.	
do	SEPT 14th.		Routine work. Constructional work continued.	
do	SEPT 15th.		Routine work. Extension on one side of house completed and large Red Cross painted on roof.	
do	SEPT 16th.		Routine work.	
do	SEPT 17th.		Routine work. A.D.M.S., 61st DIVISION visited and inspected Hospital.	
do	SEPT 18th.		Routine work. Extension on second side of house completed. D.A.D.M.S., 61st DIVISION visited and inspected camp.	
do	SEPT 19th.		Routine work.	

WAR DIARY
or
INTELLIGENCE SUMMARY.
(Erase heading not required.)

Army Form C. 2118.

Map Reference. Sheet 36 A.

Place	Date 1918	Hour	Summary of Events and Information	Remarks and references to Appendices
L.26.c.8.7	Sept.19th		LT COL G. MACKIE D.S.O, RAMCT returned from leave of absence and resumed command of Unit. MAJOR G.W. SCOTT WILLIAMSON RAMCT proceeded on leave of absence. LT COL G. MACKIE D.S.O, RAMCT took over duties of A.D.M.S. 61ST DIVISION during absence of COL C. HOWKINS D.S.O, A.M.S. on leave to England.	Capt. Capt. Capt.
do.	Sept. 20th		Routine work. Constructional work at Hospital continued.	
do.	Sept. 21st		Routine work. Further alterations and improvements at M.D.S. carried out.	
do.	Sept. 22nd		Routine work. DDMS XI CORPS visited and inspected M.D.S. Bath House for Unit personnel begun.	Capt.
do.	Sept. 23rd		Routine work. Improvisation of shelter &tents begun for personnel. Transport Section ordered out of their billets and moved closer to Unit billeting area.	Capt.

Army Form C. 2118.

WAR DIARY
or
INTELLIGENCE SUMMARY.
(Erase heading not required.)

Map Reference Sheet 36A

Place	Date 1918	Hour	Summary of Events and Information	Remarks and references to Appendices
L26 c 8.7	Sept 24th		Routine work. Construction of winter Horse Standings begun	ECR
do	Sept 25th		Routine work. Officers' mess, which had been brought from Forest D.S., erected. Complete system of acetylene gas lighting installed in hospital premises. Bath house for personnel completed.	ECR
do	Sept 26th		DADMS 61st DIVISION visited MDS. Lecture at the Asylum, St VENANT, by Rt. Hon. G.H. ROBERTS, M.P., on "Reconstruction after the War". MAJOR A.P. THOMSON M.C. and 6 O.R. attended. Meeting held of all available members of the Unit at which the lecture was explained to, and discussed by, all ranks.	ECR
do	Sept 27th		Lecture at the Asylum, St VENANT, by LT. COL. MICKLEM. Subject "Tanks". CAPT. E.F. O'CONNOR R.A.M.C.T. and 1 O.R. attended.	ECR
do	Sept 28th		Routine work	ECR

WAR DIARY or **INTELLIGENCE SUMMARY.**
(Erase heading not required.)

Army Form C. 2118.

Map Reference. Sheet 36 A.

Place	Date 1918	Hour	Summary of Events and Information	Remarks and references to Appendices
L.26.c.8.7	Sept 28th (contd)		Reconnaissance of forward area carried out by MAJOR A.P. THOMSON M.C. R.A.M.C. and CAPT. E.F. O'CONNOR R.A.M.C. Divisional front altered from one Brigade front to a two Brigade front. Orders received from A.D.M.S. that in the event of an advance by the Division the 2/1 S.M.F. AMBULANCE would be responsible for following and collecting wounded from Right Brigade. Necessary dispositions made and orders issued for packing of equipment in preparation for possible move. Officer Commanding visited G.O'sC. 184th and 182 Infantry Brigades.	G.M. G.M.
L.26.c.8.7	Sept 29th		Routine work. Orders received that Right Brigade would again attack a strong point in enemy lines unsuccessfully attacked on Sept 26th, and that this would be taken as the beginning of the possible advance. Bearer parties sent forward to Battalions of Right Brigade and stores moved to A.D.S. for immediate use. MAJOR A.P. THOMSON M.C. R.A.M.C. visited H.Q.RS. 184 INF. BDE. and H.Q.RS. of Battalion which is to carry out attack.	G.M. G.M.

WAR DIARY
or
INTELLIGENCE SUMMARY.

Map Reference Sheet 36.

Army Form C. 2118.

Place	Date 1918	Hour	Summary of Events and Information	Remarks and references to Appendices
L.26.c.8.7	Sept 30th		Routine work.	
			All wounded cleared from 2/5 BATTALION, GLOUCESTER REGT.	Early.
			MAJOR A.P. THOMSON M.C. R.A.M.C.T. visited all R.A.P's and found evacuation	
			of wounded proceeding rapidly.	
			Gilmackie Lt.Col. R.A.M.C. T.F.	
			O.C. 2/1st South Midland Field Ambulance	

MEDICAL

WO 30

CONFIDENTIAL

War Diary

of

2/1 S. Midland Field Ambulance

From 1.10.18
To   31.10.18

Volume 10

COMMITTEE FOR THE
MEDICAL HISTORY OF THE WAR
Date 4 DEC. 1918

Army Form C. 2118.

WAR DIARY
or
INTELLIGENCE SUMMARY.
(Erase heading not required.)

Map reference. Sheet 36A + 36.

Instructions regarding War Diaries and Intelligence Summaries are contained in F. S. Regs., Part II. and the Staff Manual respectively. Title pages will be prepared in manuscript.

Place	Date 1918	Hour	Summary of Events and Information	Remarks and references to Appendices
L26.c.8.7.	Oct 1st		Major O.P. Thomson M.C. visited 18th Brigade Headquarters. 2/4 ROYAL BERKS REGT. ordered to attack strong point on night of Oct 1/2nd and whole Brigade ordered to push forward if possible. Sites for new forward A.D.S. reconnoitred at G.36.a.8.3 in view of possibly of an advance.	Col(W)
L26.c.8.7.	Oct 2nd		Strong Point taken, and general advance of 18th INF. BDE with slight opposition. Additional party of bearers sent forward. A.D.S. established forward in position reconnoitred (G.36.a.8.3). Casualties light. Evacuation easy. Preliminary orders received for relief of 61st DIVISION by 59th DIVISION. Detailed orders received for relief of Ambulance.	Col(W)
L26.c.8.7.	Oct 3rd		Considerable advance. Casualties light. Evacuation very difficult owing to mine craters obstructing motor traffic. Evacuation by relays of bearers. Touch with battalions maintained throughout and no congestion of casualties. Motor Ambs. as far as H.26.d.5.6.	Col(W)

Army Form C. 2118.

WAR DIARY
or
INTELLIGENCE SUMMARY.
(Erase heading not required.)

Map reference. Sheet 36A & LENS II.

Instructions regarding War Diaries and Intelligence Summaries are contained in F. S. Regs., Part II. and the Staff Manual respectively. Title pages will be prepared in manuscript.

Place	Date 1918	Hour	Summary of Events and Information	Remarks and references to Appendices
L26c.8.7 to I22c.9.3.	Oct 4th		Unit brigaded with 184 INF BDE group. Unit proceeded by march route to THIENNES on relief by 2/3 N.M.Fd.Amb. Detailed order received for entraining. CAPTAIN J. MANUEL MC returned from leave.	Copy
I22c.9.3.	Oct 5th		Cleaning and reloading of waggons. CAPTAIN W.S. RIVERS proceeded to BEAUVAL billeting area with motor Transport. Unit with Horse Transport entrained at THIENNES 2217 hours, without incident.	Copy
I22c.9.3.	Oct 6th		Winter time adopted – watches adjusted at 0100 hours (Summertime). Delay at CANDAS owing to Supply waggon attached to the Unit slipping between two trucks. Unit detrained at ROSEL at 0600 hours. Arrived in billets at BEAUVAL 0715 hours.	Copy
BEAUVAL (LENS II)				

A6945 Wt. W14422/M1160 350,000 12/16 D. D. & L. Forms/C./2118/14.

Army Form C. 2118.

WAR DIARY
or
INTELLIGENCE SUMMARY.

(Erase heading not required.)

Map Reference Sheet. LENS 11.

Place	Date	Hour	Summary of Events and Information	Remarks and references to Appendices
	1918.			
BEAUVAL	Oct 7th		Cleaning and refitting of waggons. Orders received for move of Horse Transport to new area. All surplus kit dumped. 18th INF BDE sick evacuated to 21 C.C.S. GEZAINCOURT. Concert party about to 2/5 GLOSTERS. Very successful.	CM
BEAUVAL	Oct 8th		Horse Transport, less one limbered waggon and one water cart proceeded by road to BAILLEULMONT area. Major A.P.THOMSON M.C. reconnoitred XVII CORPS front and inspected site of A.D.S and R.A.P's. Orders received for move of personnel. Evacuation of sick as on 7th. to 2/4 R. BERKS. REGT. Very successful. Concert party about to 2/4 R. BERKS. REGT. Very successful.	CM
BEAUVAL	Oct 9th		Personnel, with limbered waggon and water cart, entrained at DOULLENS in separate trains and moved off at 1526 hours and 1626 hours respectively. Personnel detrained at HAVRINCOURT (at 0530 hours) Horse Transport (limber & water cart) at FREMICOURT (at 2300 hours Oct 9th) Motor Transport proceeded by road to BOURSIES under CAPTAIN W.S. RIVERS. CAPTAIN J. MANUEL M.C. — Divisional entraining M.O.	CM

WAR DIARY
or
INTELLIGENCE SUMMARY.
(Erase heading not required.)

Army Form C. 2118.

Map reference
Sheet 57 C.

Place	Date	Hour	Summary of Events and Information	Remarks and references to Appendices
	1918			
J6.a.	Oct 10th		Personnel proceeded from detraining station by march route to bivouac area (J6a) near BOURSIES. Arrived 0330 hours. Limber & water cart from FREMICOURT arrived 0900 hours. Considerable difficulty experienced in arranging feeding of men owing to the fact that Field Ambulances are not equipped with mobile cookers. Horse Transport, under CAPTAIN E.F. O'CONNOR arrived at 1700 hours. Trek without incident. Evacuation of sick of 184 INF BDE. to XVII C.R.S. at J7.C. Orders received brigading the Ambulance with Advanced Guard Brigade (183 INF BDE). MAJOR A.P THOMSON M.C. saw the Brigade Major 183 INF BDE. and arranged to join Advanced Guard early on Oct 11th	E.D. — E.D. —
J6.a to L3.b.6.	Oct 11th		Ambulance proceeded by march route to CANTAING area to join 163 INF BDE. Arrived 1200 hours. Personnel billeted in tents and bivouacs. Evacuation of sick to XVII C.R.S. Three large cars sent forward at 2000 hours to assist in clearing C.M.D.S. XVII east of CAMBRAI (B7a)	

WAR DIARY
or
INTELLIGENCE SUMMARY.
(Erase heading not required.)

Army Form C. 2118.

Map Reference Sheet 57 C.

Place	Date	Hour	Summary of Events and Information	Remarks and references to Appendices
	1916			
L.36.b.6.	Oct 12th		Three large cars detached returned at 0500 hours. Warning order from 183 INF BDE to move. Squad and Company Drill. Cleaning of Waggons. Repairs to harness and to billets and to room used as Officers' mess. Further reconnaissance of forward area by MAJOR A.P.THOMSON M.C. Officer Commanding returned to Unit after period of duty as A/ADMS. 61 DIVISION	EJh / EJh /
L.36.b.6.	Oct 13th		General Fatigue. Educational system classes begun.	
L.36.b.6.	Oct 14th		Squad and Company Drill. General Fatigue. Further repairs to billets. Secret and Confidential circular G.C. 40/13 - warning against credence being given to Peace talk - read by O.C. on afternoon parade. Discussion in the evening opened by the Officer Commanding and MAJOR A.P. THOMSON M.C. Subject - "The War and the Future." Several members of the Unit took part.	EJh /

WAR DIARY
or
INTELLIGENCE SUMMARY.
(Erase heading not required.)

Army Form C. 2118.

Map Reference Sheet 57C.

Instructions regarding War Diaries and Intelligence Summaries are contained in F. S. Regs., Part II. and the Staff Manual respectively. Title pages will be prepared in manuscript.

Place	Date	Hour	Summary of Events and Information	Remarks and references to Appendices
	1918			
L.3.b.5.6.	Oct 15th		General Fatigue. Repairs to Billets.	Copy
			Officer Commanding visited forward area - Corps M.D.S. & Corps A.D.S.	
			Notification received of award of CROIX DE GUERRE to MAJOR A.P.THOMSON M.C.	
			Educational Class in French conducted by MAJOR A.P. THOMSON M.C.	
L.3.b.5.6.	Oct 16th		New Officers' mess & billets and Orderly Room completed by repair of damaged houses.	Copy
			Class in Shorthand formed under CAPTAIN W.S. RIVERS.	
L.3.b.5.6.	Oct 17th		Physics Class conducted by Officer Commanding. Class in Art. French conducted by MAJOR A.P.THOMSON M.C. Shorthand Class under CAPTAIN W.S. RIVERS.	Copy
			MAJOR A.P. THOMSON M.C. reconnoitred new billeting area.	
			(Orders received for move of 463 INF. BDE. to new area = A.22 & A.23 (Sheet 57B)	

WAR DIARY
or
INTELLIGENCE SUMMARY.
(Erase heading not required.)

Army Form C. 2118.

Map Reference,
Sheets 57B & 57A

Place	Date 1918	Hour	Summary of Events and Information	Remarks and references to Appendices
A22 b0.5	Oct 18th		Ambulance moved off with Transport at 1005 hours and proceeded with	
			183 INF. BDE Group by march route to new area. Arrived in billets at	C&N
			A22 b0.5 at 12.30 hours.	
			Pte B.E. Vick returned to the Unit after undergoing sentence of 60 days'	
			Field Punishment no. 1.	
			Brigade warning orders to move to AVESNES LEZ AUBERT received.	
A22 b0.5	Oct 19th		MAJOR A.P. THOMSON M.C. proceeded as billeting representative to new area in	C&N
			AVESNES LEZ AUBERT. Ambulance complete with Transport moved off with	
			183 INF. BDE Group at 20.33 hours.	
U28 b0.7	Oct 20th		Unit arrived in billets at AVESNES LEZ AUBERT, U28 b0.7 at 00.30 hours.	C&N
			Cleaning of billets which were in an extremely dirty condition.	
			Motor Ambulances under Serjeant R.A. Jones M.M. engaged in evacuating	
			upwards of fifteen civilians from HAUSSY village which was being heavily	
			shelled by the enemy. Wounded sick civilians treated, cared for and	
			transferred to C.M.D.S.	

WAR DIARY or INTELLIGENCE SUMMARY.

Army Form C. 2118.

Map Reference Sheet 51A

Place	Date	Hour	Summary of Events and Information	Remarks and references to Appendices
U.28.b.0.7	Oct 21st		Further evacuation of civilian aged, wounded and sick from HAUSSY village and arrangements made for the feeding of over 250 civilians in the German Soldiers' Home. D.D.M.S. XVII Corps visited the village. A.D.M.S. 61 Div. visited hospital premises. Consent given for the civilian hearse by their convent party to troops of 163 INF. BDE.	Cols.
U.28.b.0.7	Oct 22nd		Further 300 civilians fed. Sick and wounded evacuated. Detailed orders received for move of Division. 2/1 S.M.FLD.AMB. to be responsible for evacuation of wounded from the line. O.C. visited forward area & arranged to take over A.D.S. at HAUSSY (V.11.d.9.2). A.D.M.S. 61 DIVISION visited Headquarters of the Ambulance. O.C. attended conference at Headquarters 163 INF BDE. Concert given in cinema theatre to 9th Bn. NORTHUMBERLAND FUSILIERS and other troops of 163 INF. BDE. Total audience 1140.	Cols.
U.28.b.0.7 to U.18.d.9.9.	Oct 23rd		R.A.M.C. Operation order no 73 received. Further medical instructions for Divisional attack on night of 23/24 October.	Cols.

A6945 Wt. W14422/M1100 350,000 12/16 D. D. & L. Forms/C./2118/14

Army Form C. 2118.

WAR DIARY
or
INTELLIGENCE SUMMARY.
(Erase heading not required.)

Map reference. Sheet 51A

Place	Date	Hour	Summary of Events and Information	Remarks and references to Appendices
	Oct 23rd (contd.)		Unit proceeded by batch route to ST AUBERT. Headquarters established at U.18.d.9.9. (Sheet 51A). O.C. visited O.C. 57 FIELD AMB. and arranged to relieve his bearers in the line by 1600 hours, and his cars in the line by 1800 hours. MAJOR G. SCOTT WILLIAMSON and MAJOR A.P. THOMSON M.C. reconnoitred the line and dispositions of 182 and 183 INF. BDES. for the attack. Meanwhile the 19TH DIVISION had carried out a successful attack known front and were progressing with it. MAJOR G. SCOTT WILLIAMSON proceeded to A.D.S. at HAUSSY, in charge of Lieutenant Scott, taking with him MAJOR A.P. THOMSON M.C., CAPTAIN J. MANUEL M.C. and CAPTAIN W.F.L. LIGGINS A.A.M.C. Have relieved as Arranged, and our staff at work by 1600 hours. Large number of casualties from 19TH DIVISION collected and evacuated during the night. O.C. visited Hd Qrs. 182nd INF. BDE. Bearer parties from 2/1 and 2/3 S.M. FLD. AMBS. with retired attached attached for duty to all Battalions of 182 and 183 INF. BDES. and worked in with them.	

Army Form C. 2118.

Map reference.
Sheet 51A

WAR DIARY
or
INTELLIGENCE SUMMARY.

(Erase heading not required.)

Instructions regarding War Diaries and Intelligence Summaries are contained in F. S. Regs., Part II. and the Staff Manual respectively. Title pages will be prepared in manuscript.

Place	Date	Hour	Summary of Events and Information	Remarks and references to Appendices
U.18.d.9.9.	Oct 24th		MAJOR G. SCOTT WILLIAMSON with CAPTAIN J. MANUEL M.C. visited all R.A.P's concerned at 0300 hours and remained there till 0600 hours when the barrage lifted. Attack carried out with success, but a large number of wounded quickly collected by cars from all forward R.A.P's. Realized and transit rapid. Wounded in motor ambulance owing to insufficiency of Divisional and M.A.C. cars. D.D.M.S. XVII CORPS and A.D.M.S. 61 DIVISION visited A.D.S. By midday all R.A.P's were clear and no cases left at A.D.S. Fred bearers and staff sent to A.D.S. for duty. Germans wounded approximately 20. Rest of day passed quietly. A few cases came down at intervals and our advance was continued. Reconnaissances made forward by O.C., MAJOR G. SCOTT WILLIAMSON and MAJOR A.P. THOMSON M.C. A site was selected for a forward A.D.S. at Q.20.a.17 and arrangements made to move there to meet our advance and to bring up Ambulance Headquarters to HAUSSY	[signature]

Army Form C. 2118.

WAR DIARY
or
INTELLIGENCE SUMMARY.
(Erase heading not required.)

Map reference: Sheet 51A

Place	Date	Hour	Summary of Events and Information	Remarks and references to Appendices
V11 d 9.2.	Oct 25th		Advance of Division resumed towards VALENCIENNES – LE QUESNOY railway. A.D.S. moved to new site and opened for reception of wounded, and rest of Ambulance located at HAUSSY – V.11.d.9.2. Further reconnaissance of forward area by O.C. MAJOR G. SCOTT WILLIAMSON, & CAPT J. MANUEL M.C. and liaison established with all Infantry Battns. of the three Brigades. Car loading posts established at BERMERAIN – Q.22.a.2.1.- and at VENDEGIES – Q.16.a.5.3. after Bridge at Q.20.B.2.9 was opened for traffic. Comparatively few wounded brought in during the day.	
Q.20.a.1.7.	Oct 26th		Division again attacked towards the railway and across it towards the village of MARESCHES. A very considerable amount of hostile shelling of vicinity of A.D.S. & the battery, bridges & cross roads near by, continued most of the day. Unit moved to A.D.S. on 61 DIVISION being ordered to be E. of a certain line before dusk. Owing to the slight advance of our troops it was impossible to establish an A.D.S. further forward than the present one. Roads good – cars well forward rendered evacuation easy. Forward Collecting Post & Store of Medical comforts & appliances established in BERMERAIN at Q.16.C.4.4.	

WAR DIARY
or
INTELLIGENCE SUMMARY.
(Erase heading not required.)

Army Form C. 2118.

Map reference Sheet 51 A

Place	Date	Hour	Summary of Events and Information	Remarks and references to Appendices
Q20 a.1.7	Oct 27th		Infantry attacked again at 0830 hour under a barrage. Some progress reported, but position of line not materially altered. Evacuation routes and Collecting posts remained as yesterday. Wounded brought down easily and quickly and in a steady stream. No congestion. No new Advanced Dressing Station established.	
Q20 a.1.7	Oct 28th		Information received that 183 INF. BDE. had established line in front of the villages of ARTRES and SEPMERIES. ADS moved to BERMERAIN - Q22 a.5.9. Shur car post established at LE TAPAGE - K34 a.0.5. Wounded from 11 SUFFOLKS cleared through this new post this morning. O.C. visited car posts and saw B.G.C. 183 INF. BDE. at LA JUSTICE and arranged other car loading posts as follows:- 1. Working from ADS to LA JUSTICE - Q10 a.5.7 and on to LE TAPAGE at K34 a.0.5. 2. Working from LA RBLIN to Q11 d.8.3. 3. Working to R.A.P. at LA FOLIE - Q23 a - when required. Horse Ambulances - 2 work from BERMERAIN and LA RBLIN to meet walking wounded and sick along any required road.	

WAR DIARY
or
INTELLIGENCE SUMMARY.

Army Form C. 2118.

Map Reference Sheet 51A

Place	Date	Hour	Summary of Events and Information	Remarks and references to Appendices
Q.20.a.1.7	Oct 28th (contd.)		MAJOR A.P. THOMSON M.C. and LIEUT. G.W. GROVE U.S.M.S., M.O.R.C. went up to staff meet A.D.S. CAPTAIN W.E. LIGGINS A.M.C. proceeded to 2/6 R. WARWICKSHIRE REGT. as M.O. vice CAPTAIN W.A.S. McGRATH going home on leave. Transport lines shelled again by H.V. gun, no casualties. Few casualties.	
Q.20.a.1.7	Oct 29th		Heavy bombardment of SOMMAING village with gas shells and H.E. during night. Billets badly damaged. Box respirators destroyed and a large number of men, chiefly 2/6 R. WARWICKSHIRE REGT, severely gassed. Little activity on front. O.C. and MAJOR G. SCOTT WILLIAMSON visited meet A.D.S. MAJOR G. SCOTT WILLIAMSON visited B.G. C'o of 182, 183 & 184 INF. BDES. No operations imminent, no final dispositions made. CAPTAIN J. MANUEL M.C. and two nursing Orderlies severely gassed from dressing cases wounded by H.E. gas shells.	
Q.20.a.1.7	Oct 30th		A.D.S. at BERMERAIN visited and Hd. Qrs. of all three Infantry Brigades. Warning order of an attack to take place tomorrow morning cancelled.	

Army Form C. 2118.

WAR DIARY
or
INTELLIGENCE SUMMARY.
(Erase heading not required.)

Map reference.
Sheet 51 A.

Place	Date	Hour	Summary of Events and Information	Remarks and references to Appendices
Q20 a 1.7	Oct 30th (Contd.)		Attack postponed for 24 hours. Heavy promiscuous shelling of back areas inflicting casualties by wounds & gas in SOMMAING - VENDEGIES - BERMERAIN. Hd. Qrs freely shelled during night. No Unit casualties. Records of several instances of excellent work by our bearers under shell fire received. Ambulance dispositions unchanged.	[initials]
Q20 a 1.7	Oct 31st		Ambulance arrangements confirmed pending postponed attack which is to take place to-morrow morning at 0515 hours. ADMS 61 DIVISION visited Hd Qrs. and approved all the arrangements made. Whole of forward area reconnoitred and directing signs posts on all roads.	[initials]

P.E. Wocke. Lt/Col Renn. STS
O.C. 2/1st S.Mid. Field Amb h. Band.

Confidential.

War Diary

of

2/1st South Midland Field Ambulance
61st Division

from 1-11-1918 to 30-11-1918.

Book II.

Volume 4.

Army Form C. 2118.

WAR DIARY
or
INTELLIGENCE SUMMARY.
(Erase heading not required.)

Map Reference Sheet 51A

Instructions regarding War Diaries and Intelligence Summaries are contained in F. S. Regs., Part II. and the Staff Manual respectively. Title pages will be prepared in manuscript.

Place	Date	Hour	Summary of Events and Information	Remarks and references to Appendices
Q.20.a.1.7.	Aug 1st		61st DIVISION attacked at 0515 hours under a very heavy barrage. Attack very successful – many prisoners taken.	
			Cars pacing through A.D.S. nearly 700 – these figures including over 100 Germans. Evacuation of patients carried out very smoothly & rapidly throughout the day. Cars working right forward to the support line with the utmost disregard of danger.	C.O./
			Further attack at 1930 hours – very few casualties. Considerable amount of gas shelling of track area during night. Orders received for relief of 61 DIV by 19th – 24th DIVS. – relief to commence tomorrow.	
Q.20.a.1.7.	Aug 2nd		Final objectives taken in yesterday's attack had to be in part abandoned to conform our Divisional line with that of division on left. Renewed combined attack early this morning completed the task rapidly & well with small number of casualties. Large number of prisoners taken including many enemy wounded. Evacuation rapid & complete.	C.O./

Army Form C. 2118.

Map Reference. Sheet 51/A.

WAR DIARY
or
INTELLIGENCE SUMMARY.
(Erase heading not required.)

Place	Date	Hour	Summary of Events and Information	Remarks and references to Appendices
Q20 a 1.7.	Nov 2nd (contd)		3 of our men slightly wounded and one or two gassed. A.D.M.S. 61 DIV. visited premises. A.D.M.S. & O.C. Field Ambulances from 19th & 24th DIVS. visited forward area and details of Relief were arranged. A.D.S. in BERMERAIN handed over to 24th DIV. A.D.S. at Q 20 a 1.7 handed over to 57th FLD AMB. as their Hd Qrs to next A.D.S. formed by them at the Chateau, ARTRES. Main body of Hd Quarters marched to AVESNES LES AUBERT leaving MAJOR A.P.THOMSON M.C. rear party with Bearers in the lines, & all the Cars to continue at work with the rest Hd Quarters until all the men of 18th INF. BDE. & all divisional details had left the forward area. Unit arrived at AVESNES LES AUBERT 1800 hours.	Cols
do	Nov 3rd		On completion of divisional relief in the line and when all the troops had left & all our wounded evacuated, the rear party rejoined the unit at AVESNES les AUBERT. Orders received to march to HAUSSY.	Cols

WAR DIARY
or
INTELLIGENCE SUMMARY.
(Erase heading not required.)

Army Form C. 2118.

Reference _Sheet 51a._

Place	Date 1918	Hour	Summary of Events and Information	Remarks and references to Appendices
HAUSSY. V.11.d.8.8	Nov 4th		Unit proceeded to HAUSSY by march route arriving in billets at 12.15 hours. Brigade & local sick opened immediately. German baths found in a fair state of repair — Engine out of order & pump belting broken. Repairs executed by our M.T. Section and cyclers working by 1700 hours. Parties of men bathed there and at own own(?) Unit baths which had been opened.	Col W
do	Nov 5th		Unit remained at HAUSSY. Unit warning orders were received that 182nd Infantry Brigade must be prepared to move forward on 6th inst. Bathing continued for 182nd Infantry Brigade by own men. Clean clothing received from Divisional Baths Officer and an attempt made to get the whole Brigade bathed.	Col W
do	Nov 6th		Routine work. Cleaning and checking of Equipment. O.C. visited Headquarters, 61st Division & 183rd Infantry Brigade to see Brigadier General commanding.	Col W
do	Nov 7th		Orders for move to VENDÉGIES on 8th inst received. Colonel 61st Division visited and inspected personnel. Bathing of whole personnel of Brigade Group completed.	Col W

WAR DIARY
or
INTELLIGENCE SUMMARY.

Army Form C. 2118.

Reference— Sheet 51a.

Place	Date	Hour	Summary of Events and Information	Remarks and references to Appendices
VENDEGIES. Q.20.a.1.7.	Nov 8th		Unit left HAUSSY at 1243 hours and arrived VENDEGIES 1430 hours. Headquarters established at Q.20.a.1.7. the personnel being billeted in the village close by. Small hospital opened to local sick. Parties sent out to Salvage Stretchers, Blankets and other Medical equipment from the area over which the Division had fought.	Col
do	Nov 9th		Routine work. Salvage work continued.	Col
do	Nov 10th		Routine work. Asquid 61st Division visited and inspected premises.	Col
do	Nov 11th		Routine work. Wire received at 0830 hours that hostilities would cease at 0110 hours. Official telegram of suspension of hostilities read to Unit on parade at 0110 hours. All salved material brought to Headquarters for disposal to Salvage Dump - total being:- Blankets 110. Stretchers 34. Shelled Shelters 2 Ground Sheets 62	Col

Army Form C. 2118.

WAR DIARY
or
INTELLIGENCE SUMMARY.
(Erase heading not required.)

Reference. Sheet 51a.
        "   57c.

Instructions regarding War Diaries and Intelligence Summaries are contained in F. S. Regs., Part II. and the Staff Manual respectively. Title pages will be prepared in manuscript.

Place	Date	Hour	Summary of Events and Information	Remarks and references to Appendices
Q.20.a.1.7.	Nov 11th	12h.	Routine work.	Eg/a.
do	Nov 12th	12h.	Orders received that Unit would march to AVESNES les AUBERT on 14th inst. Salvage Officer, 61st Division advised of the location of salved equipment. Major A.P. THOMPSON, M.C. proceeded on 14 days leave to England.	Eg/b.
AVESNES les AUBERT. U.21.d.9.2.	Nov 14th	14h.	Unit arrived AVESNES les AUBERT at 14.30 hours. Usual notifications sent out. Orders received that Unit would march to CAMBRAI on 15th inst.	Eg/a.
CAMBRAI. A.17.b.2.8.	Nov 15th	15h.	Unit arrived CAMBRAI at 14.45 hours and all personnel were billeted in private houses in Fbg de DOUAI. Hospital opened to Brigade & local sick.	Eg/a.
do	Nov 16th		All waggons unpacked and cleaning and checking of equipment commenced.	Eg/a.
do	Nov 17th		Routine work. All surplus material carried on waggons sorted out & dumped. News received that Capt. P.H.GREEN, R.A.M.C. had arrived in England from Germany after 8 months captivity.	Eg/a.

Army Form C. 2118.

Reference
Sheet 57c.
LENS, H (1/100,000).

WAR DIARY
or
INTELLIGENCE SUMMARY.
(Erase heading not required.)

Instructions regarding War Diaries and Intelligence Summaries are contained in F. S. Regs., Part II. and the Staff Manual respectively. Title pages will be prepared in manuscript.

Place	Date 1918	Hour	Summary of Events and Information	Remarks and references to Appendices
CANIBRAM Sq.b.3.8.	Nov 18th		Routine work. O.C. visited Headquarters, 61st Division.	E.O'G
do	Nov 19th		Routine work. Rearrangement of lectures and classes made but work suspended temporarily owing to the large number of men absent from sickness and on leave.	E.O'G
do	Nov 20th		Routine work. Ceremonial Drill during morning & football matches arranged for the afternoon as part of Recreational training.	E.O'G
do	Nov 21st		Orders received that 61st Division would move by train to BERNAVILLE area. Transport to proceed by road, starting on the 23rd inst. probably on 24th inst.	E.O'G
do	Nov 22nd		Captain W.S. RIVERS. R.A.M.C. and 1 N.C.O. proceeded to new area as Billeting and Advance party. Detailed orders for transport received at 2300 hours to move with the rest of the Divisional Transport on a 3 day march, halting at BERTINCOURT, ALBERT and FIENVILLERS.	E.O'G

Army Form C. 2118.

WAR DIARY
or
INTELLIGENCE SUMMARY.
(Erase heading not required.)

Reference.
Sheet 57.
LENS II (V/100,000)

Instructions regarding War Diaries and Intelligence Summaries are contained in F. S. Regs., Part II. and the Staff Manual respectively. Title pages will be prepared in manuscript.

Place	Date 1918	Hour	Summary of Events and Information	Remarks and references to Appendices
A.17.b.3.8.	Nov 23rd		Transport moved off at 0800 hours under Captain O'CONNOR & Capt. MANUEL M.C. arriving BERTINCOURT 1700 hours.	EW
do	Nov 24th		Cleaning of billets & Transport lines. Personnel arrived CAMBRAI Station at 1930 hours. Horse Transport arrived ALBERT 1700 hours. No train available.	EW
do	Nov 25th		Horse Transport arrived HIERMONT at 2000 hours after having marched from ALBERT, a distance of over 30 miles. Personnel remained on CAMBRAI Station till 1300 hours and then entrained, 18 hours after schedule time.	EW
HIERMONT	Nov 26th		Personnel train jumped the rails at AUX-le-CHATEAU. 2 Coaches containing men of the 2/8th Worcesters telescoped — 5 men killed — 11 injured. All casualties attended to by our men. Unit arrived HIERMONT at 1515 hours.	EW
do	Nov 27th		Men rested during morning & Education lecture during afternoon presided over by Major G. SCOTT WILLIAMSON R.A.M.C. Unit baths filled up & bathing commenced.	EW

A6943 Wt. W14422/M1160 350,000 12/16 D. D. & L. Forms/C./2118/4

WAR DIARY
or
INTELLIGENCE SUMMARY.

Army Form C. 2118.

Reference. LENS II. (1/100,000).

(Erase heading not required.)

Instructions regarding War Diaries and Intelligence Summaries are contained in F. S. Regs., Part II. and the Staff Manual respectively. Title pages will be prepared in manuscript.

Place	Date 1918	Hour	Summary of Events and Information	Remarks and references to Appendices
HIERMONT	Nov: 28th		Mock Election arranged in Unit, 1 Coalition & 1 Labour Candidate being nominated by the men. Meeting held at which the two Candidates outlined their policy.	Col.
do	Nov: 29th		Meeting of Committee of the "History of the Unit", presided over by the O.C. Lecture to the Whole Unit by Major G. SCOTT WILLIAMSON, R.A.M.C., on the present Political Situation.	Col.
do	Nov: 30th.		Routine work. Owing to continuous heavy rain, outside work still impossible. Educational training continued.	Col.

30/11/1918.

A. Straker
Lieut.Col. R.A.M.C.
O.C., 3/1st South Mid: Fd: Ambulance

A6945 Wt. W14432/M1160 350,000 12/16 D. D. & L. Forms/C./2118/14.

MEDICAL

1918 4

Confidential

War Diary
of
2/1st South Midland Field Ambulance,
61st Division
from
1-12-1918 to 31-12-1918

Book 1. Volume 12.

JR 33
16/3440

COMMITTEE FOR THE WAR
MEDICAL HISTORY 1919
10 MAR 1919
Date

Army Form C. 2118.

WAR DIARY
or
INTELLIGENCE SUMMARY.

Reference Sheet LENS 11.

(Erase heading not required.)

Instructions regarding War Diaries and Intelligence Summaries are contained in F. S. Regs., Part II. and the Staff Manual respectively. Title pages will be prepared in manuscript.

Place	Date 1918	Hour	Summary of Events and Information	Remarks and references to Appendices
HIERMONT	Dec 1st		Routine work — Improving of billets. Electron-wringe Classes held.	Gr.A.
do	Dec 2nd		Routine work — Waggon Cleaning — Reorganisation of Classes.	Gr.A.
do	Dec 3rd		Routine work — Billet Improvements Continued.	Gr.A.
do	Dec 4th		Routine work — Training for Sports begun.	Gr.A.
do	Dec 5th		Routine work — Lectures & Classes in Club Room.	Gr.A.
do	Dec 6th		Orders received that 91st Cdn.Bgnd. would move with 183rd Infantry Brigade to a new area. Went to billets at BUIGNY e'ABBÉ, 7 kilos due East of ABBEVILLE. Dance given at night by the 91st Cdn.Bgnd. to the members of D.M.A.A. Corps in the Theatre of the 3rd Army School. MUXI-&-CHATEAU. Most successful and enjoyable evening.	Esh.

Army Form C. 2118.

WAR DIARY
or
INTELLIGENCE SUMMARY.
(Erase heading not required.)

Reference Sheet 14, ABBEVILLE.

Instructions regarding War Diaries and Intelligence Summaries are contained in F. S. Regs., Part II. and the Staff Manual respectively. Title pages will be prepared in manuscript.

Place	Date 1918	Hour	Summary of Events and Information	Remarks and references to Appendices
BUIGNY L'ABBÉ	Dec 7th		Unit arrived at BUIGNY L'ABBÉ at 1600 hours. Under orders from ADMS. 61st Division. 1 Sub. Division was sent to 18 C.C.S. DOULLENS for temporary duty.	Eastr
do	Dec 8th		Routine work. Rearrangement of billets. Lecture by Major G. Scott WILLIAMSON on Modern Political Problems.	Eastr
do	Dec 9th		Organisation of billets to provide for Recreation & Education Classes. Improvement to billets started begun. Major G. Scott WILLIAMSON, RAMC, proceeded to ENGLAND under orders from the War Office.	Eastr
do	Dec 10th		Routine work. 61st Division marked village to try to find a site to a local hospital — Quest fruitless. Football pitch level.	Eastr
do	Dec 11th		Major A.P. THOMSON, MC, RAMC returned from leave of absence. Noted in the Times of the 6th inst. that CAPTAIN W.J. HIRST, RAMC, late of this Unit, now a Prisoner of War in Germany, had been awarded M.C. on recommendation submitted by O.C. in April last, immediately after the German Offensive during March.	Eastr

A6945 Wt. W14432/M1160 350,000 12/16 D. D. & L. Forms/C./2118/14.

Army Form C. 2118.

Reference.
Sheet 14 - ABBEVILLE.

WAR DIARY
or
INTELLIGENCE SUMMARY.
(Erase heading not required.)

Instructions regarding War Diaries and Intelligence Summaries are contained in F. S. Regs., Part II. and the Staff Manual respectively. Title pages will be prepared in manuscript.

Place	Date 1918	Hour	Summary of Events and Information	Remarks and references to Appendices
BUIGNY L'ABBÉ	Dec 12th		Notification in Third Army R.O. 891 dated 3.12.18 that №35120 S/Sgt F.G. BURLING and №35309 Corporal G. ZISSMAN, of this Unit had been awarded the D.C.M.	Entd.
do	Dec 13th		Routine work including the following classes - Science, History, French Advanced, French Elementary, Shorthand	Entd.
do	Dec 14th		Cross country run - "A" Section. Intersection Football Match.	Entd.
do	Dec 15th		Cross Country run - "C" Section. Intersection Football Match	Entd.
do	Dec 16th		Routine work. Lecture by O.C., on the History of the causes of the war.	Entd.
do	Dec 17th		Routine work. A.D.M.S. 61st Division visited unexpected premises	Entd.
do	Dec 18th		Routine work. Lecture by Private Briggs on "Democratic Control of Industry"	Entd.
do	Dec 19th		Unit Cross Country run.	Entd.

Army Form C. 2118.

WAR DIARY
or
INTELLIGENCE SUMMARY.
(Erase heading not required.)

Reference.
Sheet 1st - M.B. BEVILLE.

Instructions regarding War Diaries and Intelligence Summaries are contained in F. S. Regs., Part II. and the Staff Manual respectively. Title pages will be prepared in manuscript.

Place	Date 1918	Hour	Summary of Events and Information	Remarks and references to Appendices
BUIGNY L'ABBÉ	Dec 20th		Routine work. Lecture by O.C. on "A Survey of previous European Soldier".	Enclr
do	Dec 21st		Lecture by Private Kaye on "The Demobilised Soldier in Civil Life".	Enclr
do	Dec 22nd		Routine work. Football match in afternoon. Whist Drive in Evening. Erection of Nissen Huts commenced.	Enclr
do	Dec 23rd		Erection of Nissen Huts held up under Brigade Interpreter seen owner of site. Lecture by Major A.P. THOMSON on the American War of Independence.	Enclr
do	Dec 24th		Holiday	Enclr
do	Dec 25th		Fancy Dress Football match in morning. Christmas Dinner 1.0 pm. Impromptu Concert in evening.	Enclr
do	Dec 26th		Holiday. About 61 Officers visited Hospital.	Enclr

WAR DIARY
or
INTELLIGENCE SUMMARY.

Army Form C. 2118.

Reference Sheet 14 - ABBEVILLE.

Place	Date 1918	Hour	Summary of Events and Information	Remarks and references to Appendices
BUIGNY L'ABBÉ	Dec 27th		Routine work. G.O.C, G.S. Thomson visited inspected billets etc	Enclr
do	Dec 28th		Routine work. 3 miners despatched for Demobilization. Lecture by Major A.P. THOMSON on the French Revolution	Enclr
do	Dec 29th		Routine work.	Enclr
do	Dec 30th		Routine work. 3 miners & 2 Pivotal men despatched for Demobilization	Enclr
do	Dec 31st		Routine work.	Enclr

O.C Mackie
Lieut Col R.A.M.C.
O.C. 2/1st Dn Field Ambulance

2/1st. SOUTH MIDLAND FIELD AMBULANCE.

W A R   D A R Y.
ooooooooooooooooooooooooo

for the month of

J A N U A R Y   1 9 1 9.

Army Form C. 2118.

ABBEVILLE 14.

WAR DIARY
or
INTELLIGENCE SUMMARY.

(Erase heading not required.)

Instructions regarding War Diaries and Intelligence Summaries are contained in F. S. Regs., Part II. and the Staff Manual respectively. Title pages will be prepared in manuscript.

Place	Date 1919	Hour	Summary of Events and Information	Remarks and references to Appendices
BUIGNY L'ABBÉ	Jany 1st		Holiday.	A.P.
do	Jany 2nd		Routine work. Tennis & Shorthand Classes.	A.P.
do	Jany 3rd		Routine work. N°5088 Private B. WHITE, of this Unit accidentally killed while attempting to board a moving lorry.	A.P.
do	Jany 4th		Routine work. Lecture by Major A.P. THOMPSON. R.A.M.C. on the "French Revolution".	A.P.
do	Jany 5th		Routine work. Meeting of Unit, presided over by O.C. to discuss prospects of forming a successful club for all past & present members of the Unit in Birmingham. Everybody proved very enthusiastic & it was decided that every endeavour be made to inaugurate such club.	A.P.
do	Jany 6th		Routine work. French & Shorthand Classes.	A.P.

A6945 Wt. W1422/M1160 350,000 12/16 D. D. & L. Forms/C./2118.14.

Army Form C. 2118.

WAR DIARY
or
INTELLIGENCE SUMMARY.

ABBEVILLE. 4.

(Erase heading not required.)

Instructions regarding War Diaries and Intelligence Summaries are contained in F. S. Regs., Part II. and the Staff Manual respectively. Title pages will be prepared in manuscript.

Place	Date 1919	Hour	Summary of Events and Information	Remarks and references to Appendices
BUIGNY L'ABBÉ	Jan'y 4th		Routine work. Second lecture by Major W. THOMSON M.C. RAMC. on "The French Revolution."	Aff
do	Jan'y 5th		Routine work	Aff
do	Jan'y 6th		Routine work.	Aff
do	Jan'y 7th		Routine work. April 61st Division invited & inspected prisoners	Aff
do	Jan'y 8th		Routine work	Aff
do	Jan'y 9th		Routine work	Aff
do	Jan'y 10th		Routine work. French shorthand classes	Aff
do	Jan'y 11th		Routine work	Aff
do	Jan'y 12th		Meeting of Units to elect provisional Committee of management etc for the 3/1 South Midland Field Ambulance Club.	Aff
do	Jan'y 13th		Routine work. April 61st Division invited & inspected hospital	Aff
do	Jan'y 14th		Routine work	Aff

A6945 Wt. W14422/M1160 350,000 12/16 D. D. & L. Forms/C./2118/14.

Army Form C. 2118.

WAR DIARY ABBEVILLE 14.
or
INTELLIGENCE SUMMARY.
(Erase heading not required.)

Instructions regarding War Diaries and Intelligence Summaries are contained in F. S. Regs., Part II. and the Staff Manual respectively. Title pages will be prepared in manuscript.

Place	Date 1919	Hour	Summary of Events and Information	Remarks and references to Appendices
BUIGNY L'ABBÉ	Jany 15th		Routine work	A1?
do	Jany 16th		Routine work	A1?
do	Jany 17th		Routine work. Photographs taken of the Unit, complete with Transport, on parade	A1?
do	Jany 18th		Routine work. Arrival of Shorthand Classes	A1?
do	Jany 19th		Routine work. Lt Col Geo Mackie DSO, on establishment of platoon	A1?
			Maj A P Thomson M.C. Command promoted at the Unit	
do	Jan 20th		Random Work - Lecture on "Profit-sharing - and to the Lower Classes"	A1?
do	Jan 21st		Routine Work "	A1?
do	Jan 22nd		Routine Work - Arrival of Shorthand Classes	A1?

Army Form C. 2118.

WAR DIARY
or
INTELLIGENCE SUMMARY.

ABBEVILLE 14.

(Erase heading not required.)

Instructions regarding War Diaries and Intelligence Summaries are contained in F. S. Regs., Part II. and the Staff Manual respectively. Title pages will be prepared in manuscript.

Place	Date	Hour	Summary of Events and Information	Remarks and references to Appendices
BUIGNY L'ABBÉ	Jan 23rd 1919		Routine work. Conference Liason	AT
"	" 24th		Routine work. Lecture on Stretcher & transport AS Thomson MC	AT
"	" 25th		Routine work. ADMS 1 Division reported signed letter of thanks	AT
"	" 26th		Routine work. Capt E O'Connor reported by	AT
"	" 27th		Routine work. Lecture on English literature Stretchers	AT
"	" 28th		Routine work.	MT
"	" 29th		Routine work. Cap Manuel proceeds to Aust-HR-Chateau to examine German officer Prisoner of War Coy	Officer
				AT

A6945 Wt. W14422/M1160 350,000 12/16 - D. D. & L. Forms/C./2118/14.

Army Form C. 2118.

WAR DIARY
or
INTELLIGENCE SUMMARY.

(Erase heading not required.)

ABBEVILLE

Place	Date	Hour	Summary of Events and Information	Remarks and references to Appendices
Abbeville	1919 Jan 130th	10:1	Parade 30A - Early parade of 1st Sgt. in all properly into review to report to A.D.O.S of base Lines for duty.	Coll 2 Btn
do	Jan 31st		Routine Work - Reported Lt Major O. Tomson M.C. & 2/Lt B. Humphrey	M!!
			for out of station.	M!!

M Thomson
Major for Lt Col R. Carter.
Commanding 2/1/3/30 Lowland Field Amb.

MEDICAL

Confidential.

War Diary
of
2/1st South Midland Field Ambulance.

February 1919.

WAR DIARY
or
INTELLIGENCE SUMMARY.
(Erase heading not required.)

ABBEVILLE. 14.

Army Form C. 2118.

Instructions regarding War Diaries and Intelligence Summaries are contained in F. S. Regs., Part II. and the Staff Manual respectively. Title pages will be prepared in manuscript.

Place	Date	Hour	Summary of Events and Information	Remarks and references to Appendices
BULGNY 1/ABBE.	1919. Feb. 1.		Routine work. - French and Shorthand Classes.	Entd.
do.	Feb. 2nd.		Routine work. - Lecture by Major A.P.THOMSON,M.C. "Demobilization."	Entd.
do.	Feb. 3rd.		Routine work. - English Classes.	Entd.
do.	Feb. 4th.		Routine work. - French Classes. CAPTAIN O'CONNOR, E., R.A.M.C.(T.C.) attached to No. 51 Labour Group, GREVILLIERS as Medical Officer.	Auth.A.D.M.S. 61 D.V. Entd.
do.	Feb. 5th.		Routine work. - A.D.M.S. 61st. Division visited and inspected Hospital and Premises.	Entd.
do.	Feb. 6th.		Routine work. - Capt. RENNIE,J.K. R.A.M.C.(T.C.) taken on strength of Unit on return from leave. Capt. RENNIE,J.K.,R.A.M.C.(T.C.) struck off strength on being posted as M.O. 2/8 WORC.Battn.	Auth.ADMS 61 D.vn. Entd.
do.	Feb. 7th.		Routine work. - French and Shorthand Classes.	Entd.
do.	Feb. 8th.		Routine work.	Entd.
do.	Feb. 9th.		Routine work. - English Classes.	Entd.
do.	Feb. 10th.		Routine work. LT.COL. GEO. MACKIE,D.S.O. relanded in France from leave.	Entd.
do.	Feb. 11th.		Routine work. LT.COL.MACKIE returned to Unit and took over Command of Ambulance from this date.	Entd.
do.	Feb. 12th.		Routine work. French and Shorthand Classes. - Lecture given on "Railway Nationalization".	Entd.
do.	Feb. 13th.		Routine work. - Hon.Capt. & QRMR.W.S.RIVERS,W.S. proceeded on leave of absence Feb. 14 - 28/19.	Auth.ADMS 61 D vn. Entd.
do.	Feb. 14th.		Routine work. - English Classes continued. - "Supper Bar" for men of Unit inaugurated.	Entd.
do.	Feb. 15th.		Routine work. - French and Shorthand Classes. Classes in "Practical Carpentery" commenced.	Entd.
do.	Feb. 16th.		Routine work.	Entd.

Army Form C. 2118.

WAR DIARY
or
INTELLIGENCE SUMMARY.   ABBEVILLE. 14.

(Erase heading not required.)

Instructions regarding War Diaries and Intelligence Summaries are contained in F.S. Regs., Part II. and the Staff Manual respectively. Title pages will be prepared in manuscript.

Place	Date	Hour	Summary of Events and Information	Remarks and references to Appendices
	1919.			
BUGNY L'ABBE.	Feb. 17th.		Routine work. - French and Shorthand Classes. - Capt. MANUEL, J., M.C. proceeded on leave of absence to ENGLAND. Period Feb. 17th. Mar. 3rd.	AUTH. A.E.th. ADMS.
do.	Feb. 18th.		Routine work. - Lecture by LT. COL. MACKIE D.S.O. on "Present Industrial Discontent."	E.th.
do.	Feb. 19th.		Routine work. - Classes in Carpentery continued.	E.th.
do.	Feb. 20th.		Routine work. - A.D.M.S. 61st. Division visited and inspected Hospital Premises.	E.th.
do.	Feb. 21st.		Routine work. - French and Shorthand Classes.	E.th.
do.	Feb. 22nd.		Routine work. - OFFICER COMMANDING assumed duties of A.D.M.S. 61 DIVISION v/ce COL. HOWKINS D.S.O., A.M.S. proceeding on leave of absence.	E.th.
do.	Feb. 23rd.		Routine work. -	E.th.
do.	Feb. 24th.		Routine work. French and Shorthand Classes.	E.th.
do.	Feb. 25th.		Routine work. - Lecture by the Officer Commanding. Subject:- "The Battle of Jutland."	E.th.
do.	Feb. 26th.		Routine work. - Classes in Carpentery.	E.th.
do.	Feb. 27th.		Routine work. - French and Shorthand Classes.	E.th.
do.	Feb. 28th.		Routine work.	E.th.

February 28th. 1919.

G.O.Mackie.
Lieut. Colonel. R.A.M.C.(T).
Commanding. - 2/1st. South Midland Field Ambulance.

MEDICAL
Jul 35
160/3551

17 JUL 1919

WAR DIARY.

2/1st SOUTH MIDLAND FIELD AMBULANCE.

61st DIVISION.

MARCH 1919

Army Form C. 2118.

WAR DIARY
or
INTELLIGENCE SUMMARY.

(Erase heading not required.)

ABBEVILLE. Sheet 14.

Place	Date	Hour	Summary of Events and Information	Remarks and references to Appendices
BUIGNY l'ABBE. (Somme).	Mar.1.		Routine work. – French and Shorthand classes continued.	Esth.
do.	Mar.2.		Routine work. – OFFICER COMMANDING gave second of series of Lectures on "The BATTLE OF JUTLAND".	Esth.
do.	Mar.3.		Routine work. – Class in Practical Carpentry held.	Esth.
do.	Mar.4.		Routine work. – CAPTAIN E.F.O'CONNOR, T.C., R.A.M.C. struck off strength of Unit on proceeding to U.K. to report to the War Office.	Auth. ADMS 61 DIV.
do.	Mar.5.		Routine work. – French and Shorthand classes.	Esth.
do.	Mar.6.		Routine work.	Esth.
do.	Mar.7.		Routine work. – A.D.M.S. 61 DIVISION returned from leave of absence to United Kingdom.	Esth.
do.	Mar.8.		Routine work. – A.D.M.S. 61 DIVISION visited and inspected Hospital and Camp Premises.	Esth.
do.	Mar.9.		Routine work. – OFFICER COMMANDING gave a Lecture, followed by general discussion, on "PRESENT DISCONTENT IN THE LABOUR WORLD."	Esth.
do.	Mar.10.		Routine work. – Concert for Patients and Unit personnel given at the Hospital by "THE PRISMATICS".	Esth.
do.	Mar.11.		Routine work. – Re-adjustment and cleaning of all wagons and Equipment.	Esth.
	to Mar.15th		Lectures, (Medical) and other forms of Educational and Recreational Training, including Billiard Tournaments, Football, and Sports generally. A.D.M.S. left the Division for Demobilization.	Esth.
do	Mar.16th		Information received that Divisional Headquarters were moving, with 184 Brigade to LE TREPORT on March 18th. Officer Commanding visited D.D.M.S. L. of C. and arranged to accompany D.H.Q. with 2/1st and 2/3rd S. Md. Fld. Ambulances.	Esth.

Army Form C. 2118.

WAR DIARY
or
INTELLIGENCE SUMMARY.

ABBEVILLE SHEET 14.

(Erase heading not required.)

Instructions regarding War Diaries and Intelligence Summaries are contained in F.S. Regs., Part II. and the Staff Manual respectively. Title pages will be prepared in manuscript.

Place	Date	Hour	Summary of Events and Information	Remarks and references to Appendices
BUIGNY-L-ABBE (Somme)	Mar. 17th		Capt. Marmiel RANG(T) returned from leave, (extended owing to illness). Officer Commanding, with Capt. Rivers visited LE TREPORT area billeting for the Ambulances.	Col.
	Mar. 18th		Officer Commanding again visited LE TREPORT camp and finally arranged the site of the Hospital and Ambulance Billets.	Col.
	Mar. 19th		Capt. Rivers, visited LE TREPORT to arrange furnishing of the alloted Hutments.	Col.
	Mar. 20th		Preparations begun for move to new Area.	Col.
	Mar. 21st		Major A.P. THOMSON (M.C) appointed to Command 2/3rd S. Md. Fld. Ambulance, vice Major WOOD (M.C) demobilized.	Col.
	Mar. 22nd		Arrangements made to hand over the sick collection in St. RIQUIER, ALLY, ABBEVILLE area to 2/2nd S. Md. Fld. Ambce..	Col.
	Mar. 23rd		Areas, ones handed over.	Col.
	Mar. 24th		Advance Party left for LE TREPORT to open Hospital.	Col.
	Mar. 25th		Unit moved off with Transport complete in conjunction with 2/3rd S. Md. Fld. Ambce, both under Major A.P. THOMSON M.C. Billeted the night at PRESSEVILLE.	Col.
LE TREPORT.	Mar. 26th		Unit arrived at 2-30 p.m. without incident. Excellent accomodation found for all personnel. Horses housed in a French Adrian Hut, after the floors had been removed. Hospital opened in the "Acute" Block, of No. 47. General Hospital, and the necessary Dispositions made.	Col.
	Mar. 27th		Various alterations and adjustments made in accomodation. Sick Parades established and Sanitary Control of area begun.	Col.

Army Form C. 2118.

WAR DIARY
or
INTELLIGENCE SUMMARY.

(Erase heading not required.)

Instructions regarding War Diaries and Intelligence Summaries are contained in F. S. Regs., Part II. and the Staff Manual respectively. Title pages will be prepared in manuscript.

Le TREPORT.   SHEET 14.

Place	Date	Hour	Summary of Events and Information	Remarks and references to Appendices
LE TREPORT.	Mar. 28th.		Library opened for men. Conjoint Cook-House and Dining Hall arranged for the two Field Ambulances.	Ech. Ech.
	Mar. 29th.		Surplus Kit returned to Ordnance to bring Equipment into line with new Medical Store Table.	Ech.
	Mar. 30th.		Billiard Room opened for Patients and Personnel.	Ech.
	Mar. 31st.		Inspection of the whole of the camp premises, by the Officer Commanding. Fire Drill carried out.	Ech.

G.B.Mackie.

Lieut. Col. R.A.M.C.I.
Commdg. 2/1st South Midland Field Ambulance.

116/3550.

17 JUL 1919

2/Lt. L. Nid. F.O.

Army Form C. 2118.

WAR DIARY
or
INTELLIGENCE SUMMARY.

LE TREPORT. SHEET 14.

(Erase heading not required.)

Instructions regarding War Diaries and Intelligence Summaries are contained in F. S. Regs., Part II. and the Staff Manual respectively. Title pages will be prepared in manuscript.

Vol 36

Place	Date	Hour	Summary of Events and Information	Remarks and references to Appendices
LE TREPORT	April 1st.		Officer Commanding visited T & R Tank Depot.	Eostn.
"	2nd.		2/4th Royal Berks Regt arrived in Camp. They had no Medical Officer. Arrangements made for Medical attendance.	Eostn.
"	3rd.		33 men from 2/4th Oxford & Bucks L.I. admitted to Hospital for quarantine for Measles.	Eostn.
"	4th.		Venereal Prevention Rooms instituted.	Eostn.
"	5th.		Sanitation of camp area taken in hand and arrangements made for complete supervision of all departments.	Eostn.
"	6th) 7th) 8th) 9th)		Routine work., Stores and waggons rendered surplus by adoption of the new Mobilisation Stores Table returned to Ordnance.	Eostn.
"	10th.		Officer Commanding visited A.D.M.S. and D.D.M.S. L. of C. Abbeville.	Eostn.
"	12th.		Inspection of all Sanitary arrangements in Camp. Extension of ablution houses and baths recommended.	Eostn.
"	13th.		Inspection of all stables and horse lines in Area. Inspection of Prisoners of War Camp.	Eostn.
"	14th 15th 16th 17th 18th		Routine Medical and Sanitary work. Cases of Mumps and Measles found in Battalions and a good many cases of Scabies and Gonorrhoea evacuated. Special Medical Inspections, ordered for all troops in the Camp.	Eostn.

30 APR 1919
2/1st SOUTH MIDLAND FIELD AMBULANCE
ROYAL ARMY MEDICAL CORPS

Army Form C. 2118.

WAR DIARY
or
INTELLIGENCE SUMMARY.
(Erase heading not required.)

LE TREPORT.   SHEET 14

Place	Date	Hour	Summary of Events and Information	Remarks and references to Appendices
LE TREPORT.	April	19th/21st	Routine work.	Ends.
"	22nd.		Warning noticed received that 2 Battalions might be required for special service. Capt. J. Manuel M.O. detailed as M.O. to 2/4th Oxford & Bucks L.I. to join when necessary.	Ends.
"	23rd.		Regimental Stretcher Bearers of the 2/4th Royal Berks Regt. detailed and sent here for daily special instruction in Ambulance work. Officer Commanding visited A.D.M.S. Abbeville.	Ends.
"	24th.		Routine inspection of all Battalions and other Cookhouses and Sanitary arrangements. Capt. Squires, A.P.M. 61st Division, evacuated to Hospital after severe accidental injuries to Head.	Ends.
"	25th.		Inspection of P.O.W. Camp and all stables and horse lines in the Camp.	Ends.
"	26th.		Capt. Manuel M.O. takes over duties as Medical Officer to 2/4th Oxford & Bucks L.I. on departure of Capt. NEARY MORC.USMS. for demobilization.	Ends.
"	27th.		Routine work.	Ends.
"	28th.			Ends.
"	29th.		Officer Commanding visited A/A.D.M.S. ABBEVILLE.	Ends.

J.E.Mackie
Lieut. Col. R.A.M.C.
Comdg. 2/1st South Midland Field Ambulance.

2/1st S Mid. Leccs Ciul.

WAR DIARY
or
INTELLIGENCE SUMMARY.

(Erase heading not required.)

Army Form C. 2118.

2/1 S M F d Ambce

ABBEVILLE. SHEET 11.

WA 37

Place	Date	Hour	Summary of Events and Information	Remarks and references to Appendices
LE TREPORT.	MAY.		2/1st South Midland Field Ambulance.	
	1 } 9 }		Routine work. and general overhauling, cleaning, and checking of all equipment in readiness for handing in, under the direction of Capt. RIVERS.	w/s
				w/s
	10.		Officer Commanding visited G.H.Q. Routine work.	w/s
	11 } 12 } 13 }		Inspection of all sanitary arrangements in the Camp and the Prisoners of War Camp and billets. Suggested improvements carried out in view of the approaching hot weather, with regard to meat safes etc.	w/s
				w/s
				w/s
	14.		The Officer Commanding. Lieut. Col. Geo. Mackie. D.S.O. relinquished Command of the Ambulance on being posted to No. 2. Stationary Hospital, by reason of reduction in the Cadre Establishment, having been in command of the Unit since 15-10-15. Capt. W. RIVERS. assumed Command of the Ambulance.	w/s
	15 } 18 }		General routine work and hospital duties. Instruction in various Educational subjects being given.	w/s
				w/s
	19.		All the horses of the Transport Section of the Ambulance returned to No. 2. Remount Depot at ABBEVILLE, in accordance with instructions.	w/s
	20 } 22 }		Routine work. and Hospital Duties	w/s
				w/s
	23.		Third anniversary of the landing of the Unit in France.	w/s
	24. 25. 26. 27.		Routine work. Inspection of Camp premises and billets by the Officer Commanding. Inspection of Hospital by O.C.	w/s
				w/s
	29. 31.		Routine work. and cleaning of personal equipment.	w/s
				w/s

W J Rivers Capt. RAMC(T)

Commanding 2/1st Sth.Mid.Fld.Ambce.

110/3785

2/1 Sth. Midl. F.A.

June 1919

WAR DIARY or INTELLIGENCE SUMMARY.

(Erase heading not required.)

Le Treport.

Army Form C. 2118.

Place	Date	Hour	Summary of Events and Information	Remarks and references to Appendices
Le Treport.	June. 1.		Routine work. All harness dismantled, cleaned and oiled and tied together in sections and returned to stores in readiness for packing on G.S. wagons.	WSR
	5.)			WSR
	6.)		Cadre Strength of this Unit reduced by 75%, and personnel sent to dispersal camp for demob'	WSR
	8.)		Major.A.P.Thompson proceeded to No "2 Stationary Hospital Abbeville for duty, and is succeeded by Capt Andrews as Medical Officer Le Treport Area.	WSR
	9.)			WSR
	12.)		General Routine work.	WSR
	13.)		Surplus Medical Equipment to actual requirements returned to No 19 Base Depot Medical Stores Etaples.	WSR
	15.)		Lt Col.G.Mackie.D.S.O. returned from leave and proceeded to Abbeville for duty.	WSR
	16.)		Equipment cleaned labelled and packed under supervision of Capt.W.S.Rivers and loaded on wagons, sheeted and roped ready for embarkation.	WSR
	17.)			WSR
	18.)			WSR
	19.)			WSR
	20.)			WSR
	21.)		Capt.Andrew proceeded to U.K. for demob-lisation, and is succeeded by Lt Col G Mackie D.SO as Medical Officer Le Treport Area.	WSR
	22.)		Routine work. Inspection of Camp premises and billets by the Officer Commanding.	WSR
	26.)			WSR
	27.)		Routine work and cleaning of personal equipment.	WSR
	30.)			WSR

WS Rivers ......Capt.RAMC.T.
Comdg 2/1st Sth Mid Fld Ambce. (Equipment Guard.)

140/36a-

COMMITTEE FOR THE
3 SEP 1919
MEDICAL HISTORY OF THE WAR

WAR DIARY
or
INTELLIGENCE SUMMARY.
(Erase heading not required.)

Place	Date	Hour	Summary of Events and Information	Remarks and references to Appendices
Le Treport.	July	July 1.)	Routine Work, cleaning and Oiling of Wagons.	w/s
		6.)		w/s
		7.)	Wagons un-roped and Equipment examined.	w/s
		10.)	Lt Col G.Mackie.DSO. proceeded to Abbeville for duty, and is succeeded by	w/s
			Capt.L.Meakin. as Medical Officer, Le Treport Area.	w/s
		11.)		w/s
		12.)	General Routine Work.	w/s
		13.)		w/s
		14.)	Officer Commanding Capt.W.S.Rivers proceeded on leave to U.K.	w/s
		15.) 19.)	Wagons stencilled ready for Embarkation. (2/1st S.M.Fld. Amb. Aintree.)	w/s
		20.)	Capt.L.Meakin. proceeded to Abbeville for demobilisation, and is succeeded by	w/s
			Capt.R.Forgan as Medical Officer Le Treport Area.	w/s
		22.)	Capt. W.S.Rivers re-joined Unit from leave to U.K.	w/s
		25.)	Inspection of Camp premises and billets by the Officer Commanding-	w/s
		31.)	General Routine Work.	w/s

W.S.Rivers
Commanding 2/1stSouth Midland Field Ambulance. Capt.RAMC.T. (Equipment Guard.)

www.ingramcontent.com/pod-product-compliance
Lightning Source LLC
Chambersburg PA
CBHW080804010526
44113CB00013B/2321